COMPETITIVENESS AND COHESION
IN EU POLICIES

Competitiveness and Cohesion in EU Policies

Edited by

RONALD HALL
ALASDAIR SMITH
LOUKAS TSOUKALIS

OXFORD
UNIVERSITY PRESS

OXFORD
UNIVERSITY PRESS

Great Clarendon Street, Oxford ox2 6DP

Oxford University Press is a department of the University of Oxford.
It furthers the University's objective of excellence in research, scholarship,
and education by publishing worldwide in

Oxford NewYork

Athens Auckland Bangkok Bogotá Buenos Aires Calcutta
Cape Town Chennai Dar es Salaam Delhi Florence Hong Kong Istanbul
Karachi Kuala Lumpur Madrid Melbourne Mexico City Mumbai
Nairobi Paris São Paulo Shanghai Singapore Taipei Tokyo Toronto Warsaw

and associated companies in Berlin Ibadan

Oxford is a registered trade mark of Oxford University Press
in the UK and certain other countries

Published in the United States
by Oxford University Press Inc., New York

British Library Cataloguing in Publication Data

Data available

Library of Congress Cataloging in Publication Data

Competitiveness and cohesion in EU policies / edited by Ronald Hall, Alasdair Smith,
Loukas Tsoukalis.
p. cm.
Includes bibliographical references and index.
1. European Union countries—Economic conditions—Regional disparities. 2. European
Union countries—Economic policy. 3. European Union countries—Social policy.
4. Competition—European Union countries. I. Hall, Ronald. II. Smith, Alasdair.
III. Tsoukalis, Loukas.
HC241.2.C63448 2000 338.94—dc21 00–046956
ISBN 0–19–829522–7

1 3 5 7 9 10 8 6 4 2

Typeset by Graphicraft Limited, Hong Kong
Printed in Great Britain
on acid-free paper by
T.J. International Ltd.,
Padstow, Cornwall

PREFACE

In preparation of the first report on economic and social cohesion, the European Commission invited the College of Europe in Bruges, the Sussex European Institute in Brighton, and Synthesis, European Studies, Research and Strategy in Athens to study the cohesion effects of EU policies other than structural policies. This book draws heavily on the work undertaken in this context.

A book is, however, very different from an unpublished report with specific terms of reference, which was intended to provide the information and data for an official document. Considerations of space and internal consistency have obliged us to leave out some sections of the original report. Individual chapters have been revised and trimmed down significantly. A book on competitiveness and cohesion could not, of course, leave out the internal market and structural policies. Since those subjects were outside the terms of reference of the original report, new chapters have been commissioned.

We are grateful to the European Commission, and in particular the Directorate-General for Regional Policy, for allowing us to make use of the material contained in our report. It goes without saying that the views expressed in the book engage only the authors.

Several people played a decisive role in the preparation of the original report. George Polenakis at Synthesis was responsible for the overall management of the project which involved many people in different European countries. Eric de Souza helped with coordination and the collection of statistical data. Antonia Carzaniga, Martin Foeth, Beatriz Knaster, Andrea Rossi, Volker Stehmann, and David Young provided valuable research assistance. We are grateful to all of them; and last but not least, to John Chapple, who edited with much care the final text.

February 1999   R. H., A. S., and L. T.

CONTENTS

FIGURES

TABLES

NOTES ON THE CONTRIBUTORS

Maurice A. Baslé is Professor of Economics and Jean Monnet Chair in the Economics of European Integration at CREREG-IREIMAR-CNRS, University of Rennes I. He has worked extensively on evolutionary and institutional economics and economic analysis of regulation (structural economic policies) and is President of the Société Française de l'Evaluation des Politiques Publiques.

Niall Bohan received his B.A. from Trinity College Dublin and his M.A. from the College of Europe, Bruges. He is now an administrator at the European Commission, DG XV, 'Internal Market and Financial Services'.

Michael Dunford is Professor of Economic Geography in the School of European Studies, University of Sussex. He also is editor of *Regional Studies*, Director of the Centre on European Political Economy, and a co-Director of the Rives Manche Economic Observatory.

Ronald Hall is deputy chief adviser to Michel Barnier, Commissioner responsible for regional policy in the European Commission. Former head of Unit in the Agriculture and Rural Development Directorate General.

Robert C. Hine is Senior Lecturer in the School of Economics at the University of Nottingham, and Professor at the College of Europe, Bruges. His research interests are in European economic integration, trade, and agriculture.

Peter M. Holmes is Jean Monnet Reader in the Economics of European Integration, Sussex European Institute, and an Associate Fellow of the Science Policy Research Unit, University of Sussex. He has lectured in Bruges and Rennes, and has written extensively on EU integration and the interaction between trade, competition, and technology policies in the EU.

Achilleas Kemos is a researcher and doctoral candidate at CREREG-IREIMAR-CNRS, University of Rennes I. He is also a lecturer and researcher in the Economics Department of the École Nationale Supérieure des Télécommunications de Bretagne. His work focuses on telecommunications regulation and multimedia technology economics.

Nikos Koutsiaras studied economics at the Economic University of Athens and agricultural economics at Wye College, University of London. He is now completing his Ph.D. thesis on European economic integration and social policy at the University of Athens while teaching in the postgraduate programme on European and international relations.

Olivier Léon is a researcher and doctoral candidate at CREREG-IREIMAR-CNRS, University of Rennes I. He is also a teaching assistant in the Faculty of Economics at the University of Rennes I.

Helen Louri (D.Phil., Oxford) is Associate Professor in Industrial Economics, Department of Economics, Athens University of Economics and Business.

Andrea Mairate, Ph.D. in economics, is principal administrator in the Directorate General for Regional Policy and Cohesion, European Commission.

Francis McGowan is a lecturer in politics at the University of Sussex. He has published widely on EU transport and energy policy and has acted as a consultant to the European Commission, EFTA, and a variety of public and private organizations.

Jean–Yves Muylle received his B.A. from the Université Catholique de Louvain and his M.A. from the College of Europe, Bruges. He now works for the European Commission, DG XV, 'Internal Market and Financial Services'.

Pier Carlo Padoan is Professor of Economics at the University of Rome and Director of Economic Studies at the College of Europe. His main research interests are in the areas of international trade and European integration.

Tiago Santos Pereira is a research student at SPRU, Science and Technology Policy Research, University of Sussex. His research focuses on the importance of collaborative research in the current research systems, with particular emphasis on European RTD policies and the less favoured regions.

Manfred Rosenstock works in the Directoral-General for Regional Policy and Cohesion of the European Commission in Brussels where he is based within the directorate responsible for policy formulation and economic analysis.

Margaret Sharp is a Senior Fellow at SPRU, Science and Technology Policy Research, University of Sussex. She has written extensively on European science, technology, and innovation issues, most recently co-authoring, with John Peterson, a book entitled *Technology Policy in the European Union* (London: Macmillan, 1998).

Alasdair Smith is Vice-Chancellor of the University of Sussex. Until 1998, he was Professor of Economics at the same university and for several years Visiting Professor at the College of Europe in Bruges. He is author of numerous books and articles.

Secondo Tarditi is Professor at the Faculty of Economics of the University of Siena and Director of the Interdepartmental Centre for Agri-food-environmetal Policy (SICAP). He is also chairman of the Network for Agricultural Research and Development promoted by the FAO and Special Adviser to the European Commission on Consumer Policy.

Loukas Tsoukalis is Venizelos Professor at the European Institute of the London School of Economics and Political Science, and Chairman of Synthesis-European Studies, Research and Strategy in Athens. For many years, he was Director of Economic Studies and Visiting Professor at the College of Europe in Bruges. He has written extensively on various aspects of European economic integration.

David Young is a researcher and D.Phil. candidate at the Centre on European Political Economy, Sussex European Institute, and a teaching assistant in the Economics subject group, University of Sussex. Previously he was a teaching assistant in the Economics Department at the College of Europe, Bruges.

George Zanias is Associate Professor at the Department of International and European Economic Studies of the Athens University of Economics and Business and Chairman and Scientific Director of the Centre of Planning and Economic Research. His main research interests are on European agricultural integration and applied econometrics.

ABBREVIATIONS

ACP	African, Caribbean, and Pacific countries
ACT	Agreement on Clothing and Textiles
ASEAN	Association of Southeast Asian Nations
BC-NETs	Business Cooperation Networks
BRE	Bureau de Rapprochement des Enterprises
CAD	Computer-aided design
CAM	Computer-aided manufacturing
CAP	Common Agricultural Policy
CCP	Common Commercial Policy
CCT	Common Customs Tariff
CEC	Commission of the European Community
CEECs	central and eastern European countries
CEN	Centre Européen de Normalisation
CENELEC	Centre Européen de Normalisation Electrotechnique
CEPII	Centre d'Etudes Prospectives et d'Information Internationale, Paris
CEPS	Centre for European Policy Studies
CGE	computable general equilibrium (study, model)
CSF	Community Support Frameworks
CV	coefficient of variation
DAEs	developing Asian economies: Thailand, Malaysia, Singapore, South Korea, Taiwan, Hong Kong, China
EAGGF	European Agricultural Guidance and Guarantee Fund
EBRD (or BERD)	European Bank for Reconstruction and Development
ECOFIN	Council of Economic and Finance Ministers
EDI	Electronic data interchange
EES	European employment strategy
EIB	European Investment Bank
EPC	European Political Cooperation
ERDF	European Regional Development Fund (Structural Funds)
ESF	European Social Fund (Structural Funds)
ETSI	European Telecommunications Standards Institute
FDI	foreign direct investment
FIFG	Financial Instrument for Fisheries Guidance (Structural Funds)
GC	Gini coefficient
GERD	Gross Expenditure on Research and Development
GSP	Generalised System of Preferences
GVA	gross value added
ICT	information and communications technology

IMPs	Integrated Mediterranean Programmes
JIT	Just-in-time
M&As	Merges and Acquistions
MFA	MultiFibre Arrangement
MNCs	Multinational corporations
MNEs	Multinational Enterprises
NACE	Nomenclature des activités économiques dans les Communautés Européennes (a classification system for economic activities)
NGE	Net Grant Equivalent
NIC	newly industrializing country
NUTS	nomenclature of territorial units for statistics
ONP	Open Network Provision
OPA	outward processing arrangements
OPT	outward processing trade
PPS	Purchasing Power Standards
QR	quantitative restrictions
RCA	revealed comparative advantage
RHR	retail trades, hotels, restaurants
RTD	research and technological development
SCAN	Subcontracting Assistance Network
SEA	Single European Act
SEM	single European market
SITC	standard international trade classification
SMEs	small and medium-sized enterprises
SMP	single market programme
TC	textiles and clothing
TEDIS	Trade and electronic data interchange system
TEU	Treaty on European Union
UNICE	Union des Confédérations de l'Industrie et des Employers d'Europe
USOs	universal service obligations
VERs	voluntary export restraints
WAD	weighted absolute deviation
WSD	population-weighted standard deviation

1

Introduction

MICHAEL DUNFORD, RONALD HALL, ALASDAIR SMITH,
AND LOUKAS TSOUKALIS

1.1. The Distributional Dimension in Regional Integration

Traditional economic theory concentrates on questions of efficiency and the maxim-ization of global welfare, while considerations about equity and the distribution of the economic pie are usually left to more 'normative' disciplines; alternatively, they are simply assumed away as problems. But everyday politics is largely about the distribution of gains and losses among participants in any system. Depending on the nature of the latter, the relevant participants can be countries, regions, different social groups, or even individuals.

A relatively equitable distribution of the gains and losses, or at least the perception of such an equitable distribution, can be a determining factor for the continuation of the integration process. Regional integration schemes in other parts of the world have often foundered precisely because of the failure to deal effectively with this problem. It would have been surprising if distributional issues had not figured prominently on the European agenda. Indeed, the distributional impact of integration has been paramount in the minds of national politicians and representatives of various pressure groups; and it has strongly influenced negotiations within the common institutions from a very early stage.

The scale of regional and other disparities as well as the political approach and the specific policy instruments used at the European level to deal with this problem have changed very much over the years. The original six members of the EC constituted a relatively homogeneous economic group, with the exception of the south of Italy; a problem which was, in fact, recognized in the protocol for the Mezzogiorno, attached to the Treaty of Rome. Article 2 of the treaty referred to the objective of a 'harmonious development of economic activities, a continuous and balanced expansion', while in the preamble the contracting parties went even further by calling for a reduction of 'the differences existing between the various regions and the backwardness of the less favoured regions'.

There were, however, only a few provisions made in the treaty for the creation of instruments which could contribute towards this 'harmonious development' and the reduction of regional disparities. The European Investment Bank (EIB) was intended as a source of relatively cheap interest loans and guarantees for the less developed regions of the Community. Provisions for the free movement of labour also had an indirect regional dimension in the sense that labour mobility would help to deal with the problem of high unemployment in a less developed region such as the Mezzogiorno. Last but not least, the setting up of the Common Agricultural Policy (CAP) was expected to help reduce the disparities between countries and regions, since farm incomes were generally much below the national or EC-6 average, while economic backwardness was most often identified with a heavy regional concentration on agriculture.

There was no explicit reference to regional policy, except in the form of derogations from general provisions in the different policy areas dealt with by the treaty. This is true of social, transport, and agricultural policies. The best known derogation which bears upon the regional dimension can be found in Article 92 (now Art. 87) of the original treaty, which has remained almost intact. It indirectly accepts state aid for intracountry regional development purposes, thus making a big exception to the application of the common competition policy. The various derogations, together with the lack of any separate chapter on a common regional policy, suggest that the authors of the Treaty of Rome, while recognizing the regional problem and the need to employ special instruments to deal with it, had decided to leave the main responsibility in the hands of national authorities. The role of the Community would remain marginal in this respect, while the common institutions were asked to show some flexibility in the development of other common policies in order to accommodate the regional policy objectives of national authorities.

Regional disparities were not as yet generally recognized as a major policy concern at the time of the signing of the treaty. On the other hand, large transfers of money across frontiers were considered politically impossible. Since the redistributive mechanisms could only be very modest, the six signatories tried to ensure a more or less equitable distribution of gains and losses among participants. This explains the complicated and perhaps economically 'irrational' nature of some of the treaty provisions. On the other hand, equitable distribution of gains and losses basically referred to the distribution among countries.

Although regional policy had its heyday in most Western European countries during the 1960s and the early 1970s, with large sums of money spent in this direction, very little happened at the EC level. The EIB did, as originally envisaged, orient its lending activities mainly towards the less developed regions of the Six, and the south of Italy in particular. However, the sums of money involved were relatively small and the attraction of EIB loans consisted entirely in the relatively low rates charged on loans, which was made possible because of the high credit rating which the EIB enjoyed in international capital markets and which, therefore, enabled it to borrow at the lowest possible rates. The European Social Fund (ESF) also played a modest redistributive role. As for the EAGGF (European Agricultural Guidance and Guarantee Fund), which accounted for the biggest part of the EC budget, it surely acted as an important redistributive mechanism in favour of European farmers, although its general impact on regional disparities was rather mixed.

Distributional issues in general did not become a serious political problem in the early years of European economic integration. But this was the Golden Age of the Western European economies, characterized by rapid economic growth, high employment rates, and relative monetary stability. The overall size of the cake grew constantly bigger and European integration continued to be perceived as a positive-sum game in which there were gains to be made by all the countries involved. The reduction of intercountry income disparities among the Six during the same period helped to allay earlier fears about the effects of trade liberalization on the weaker economies. On the other hand, national governments pursued active regional and redistributive policies inside their borders, aiming at a reduction of income disparities.

Interest at the Community level grew as a result of the first enlargement of the EC and the rapid deterioration of the international economic environment, both coinciding in the early 1970s. The accession of three new members brought countries with serious regional problems inside the EC. The early plans for economic and monetary union (EMU) also acted as a catalyst. Stabilization and redistribution became intimately linked with monetary union. The European Regional Development Fund (ERDF) was set up in 1975. While constituting an attempt to reduce the net budgetary contribution of the UK, the ERDF also signalled a growing concern with intra-EC disparities. Funds available through the ERDF grew steadily over the years, even though there was little evidence in the beginning that the money spent by the ERDF was in addition to regional aid which would have been given by national governments in its absence. This is the so-called problem of additionality.

A new approach to regional policy was introduced in 1985 with the Integrated Mediterranean Programmes (IMPs), intended for the Mediterranean regions of France and Italy, and the whole of Greece. The main innovation of IMPs was that funding was based on medium-term development programmes, instead of a project by project basis, and that those programmes involved a close coordination of different EC instruments. The IMPs were the precursor of more general reforms that followed in 1988.

The crucial turning point was the signing of the Single European Act (SEA), which inserted a new Title V into the Treaty of Rome, under the heading 'economic and social cohesion'. This was an attempt to link the objective of 'harmonious development' and the reduction of regional disparities, objectives that had been mentioned in a very general manner in the original treaties, with specific policy instruments. According to Article 130a (now Art. 158), 'the Community shall aim at reducing disparities between different regions and the backwardness of the least-favoured regions'. 'The implementation of the common policies and of the internal market' should take this objective into account, and so should member states in the conduct of their economic policies (Article 130b) (now Art. 159). There were, indeed, widespread fears among the weaker countries that the costs and benefits of the internal market programme would be unevenly distributed; hence the emphasis on the link between market liberalization and redistribution. In the same article, reference was also made to specific EC instruments to be used for reducing regional disparities, namely the ERDF, the ESF, and the EAGGF Guidance Section (all three, along with the Financial Instrument for Fisheries Guidance, FIFG, added in 1993, thenceforth referred to as Structural Funds), as well as the European Investment Bank. The ERDF was entrusted with the principal task of redressing intra-EC regional imbalances. The new articles called for the effective coordination and rationalization of the activities of Structural

Funds, and the Commission was invited to submit proposals in this direction. Through the SEA, cohesion thus became a key word of the European vocabulary, while redistribution acquired a new political dimension. Furthermore, a clear intention was expressed to obtain better value for the European taxpayer's money.

The next step was taken with the decision of the European Council in February 1988 to combine a substantial reform of the Structural Funds with the doubling of the resources available for the period until 1993. This was a major political decision which was directly linked to the successful implementation of the internal market programme. Thus, the concept of cohesion, which had been introduced earlier through the SEA, was now being translated into considerable sums of money. The new resources available at the Community level were not supposed, at least officially, to provide some form of compensation for potential losers from further market integration; the emphasis was instead on new policy instruments which should enable economically weaker countries and regions to take better advantage of the new liberalization measures. The doubling of resources went hand in hand with an effort to improve the effectiveness of EC action.

Through the SEA and the subsequent decision of the European Council in 1988, the Structural Funds and redistribution in general have become an integral part of the European construction. A few years later, the Maastricht revision of the treaties and the provision made in it for the establishment of an EMU offered almost a repetition of the same story, thus reinforcing the link between further economic integration on the one hand and cohesion and redistribution on the other. The strengthening of economic and social cohesion was named, together with the establishment of the internal market and EMU, as one of the main economic objectives of the Union in Article B of Title I (Common Provisions) (now Art. 2 of the Consolidated Treaty on European Union). A new addition to the institutional set-up of the Union was the Committee of the Regions. The separate section devoted to economic and social cohesion (Title XIV of the EC Treaty) called for a further reform of the Structural Funds and also provided for the setting up of a Cohesion Fund which would make financial contributions in the fields of environment and trans-European transport networks. The Commission was also invited to submit a report every three years on the progress made towards achieving economic and social cohesion. The first report appeared in the end of 1996, and contained an assessment of the cohesion impact of common policies as well as the main internal policies of member states (European Commission, 1996).

Following on the steps of the 1988 package, a new agreement was reached at the European Council in Edinburgh in December 1992. It included a very substantial further increase in the share of Structural Funds, which, together with the Cohesion Fund, were targeted to reach 35 per cent of total EU expenditure by 1999. This increase in the resources available through the Structural Funds was, in turn, linked to another decision to scale down expenditure on the CAP.

Undoubtedly, the EU has travelled a very long way since the time of the original treaties. The distributional dimension of common policies is now a matter of paramount importance; and there are also important redistributive instruments at the Union level aiming at the reduction of existing disparities. The link between the internal market and

EMU on the one hand and redistribution on the other has become firmly established. With the prospect of further EU enlargement to include countries with significantly lower levels of economic development than the large majority of existing members, cohesion and redistribution have acquired even greater importance. This was very clear in the debate around the *Agenda 2000* leading to the adoption of the financial perspectives, together with the new guidelines for structural policies, for the period between 2000 and 2006 (European Commission, 1997; Tsoukalis, 1998).

1.2. The Meaning of Cohesion

The aim of this volume is to examine the impact of all main EU policies, including structural policies, thus reflecting the identification of cohesion as one of the main economic objectives of the Union. To make judgements about the cohesion effects of policy, a number of elements are necessary. First, we need a working definition of cohesion and a way of applying that definition consistently across different policies. Second, we need to be aware of the background information about what has happened to key measures of cohesion in the Union. Third, we need an understanding of the impact of economic integration processes on location, convergence, and inequality. Finally, we also need a consistent and logical framework for the assessment of policy, policy targets, and policy conflicts.

We can distinguish between inequalities between countries, and particularly between the so-called Cohesion Four (Greece, Ireland, Portugal, Spain) and the rest of the Union; inequalities between regions within the EU; and inequalities between individuals ('social cohesion'). In Articles 130a (now Art. 158) and 130b (now Art. 159), the concept of cohesion is taken to be primarily geographical or territorial in nature. For reasons of data availability, the different chapters in this book will concentrate mostly on the intercountry and interregional dimensions of cohesion although in some cases reference will also be made to the social dimension of cohesion.

As an indicator of cohesion, GDP is measured at Purchasing Power Standards (PPS) to reflect the variations in the purchasing power of money in different parts of the EU. Adjustments for differences in the cost of living are made, however, at member state and not at regional levels, in spite of the fact that there are often quite wide variations in the cost of living within member states. To the extent that costs of living are lower in less developed areas, official statistical series overstate disparities in living standards.

In some states or regions there is a significant gap between production and income because of the role of external investment. The most striking case is the Republic of Ireland, which has attracted large inflows of foreign capital and whose 1995 gross national product (GNP) was almost 16 per cent less than its gross domestic product (GDP). If our interest is in the living standards of the inhabitants of a country or region, there is a case for using GNP measures alongside GDP.

Further, if 'cohesion' is to include a concern for the distribution of income or wealth among individuals and households, attention must be paid to the distributional impact of economic change, including the effects of fiscal redistribution as well as wages, profits, and other factor incomes. Indeed, introduction of the concept of 'social cohesion' in the sense of inequality between individuals or households draws attention to the limitations of a view of cohesion which is focused on the regional distribution of economic activity rather than the distribution of economic outcomes across individuals. We argue below that a regional or territorial definition of 'cohesion' is too narrow.

As already indicated, this book evaluates the cohesion impact of different EU policies. Although the emphasis will be on income inequalities, individual chapters will also address inequalities of employment opportunities between regions, member states, and individuals. The book tries to answer the question whether there is a conflict between competitiveness and cohesion. In addressing competitiveness, we need to introduce an intertemporal element into cohesion, recognizing that policies may have the objective of improving economic opportunities in the future, and that there may be a trade-off between cohesion objectives in the short run and in the long run.

Greater cohesion implies that incomes, employment, and economic opportunities grow faster for groups in weaker areas with low incomes than for groups in richer areas with high incomes. It is not enough, therefore, to argue that certain developments will improve the situation of weaker areas. To promote cohesion, conditions must improve faster in weaker areas than elsewhere and the relative position of disadvantaged groups must improve faster than that of privileged groups. Often, changes that may seem to advantage peripheral areas also benefit more developed areas and, indeed, to a greater degree.

1.3. Measuring Competitiveness and Cohesion

At present there are wide disparities in competitiveness and economic development in the EU. Figure 1.1 indicates the scale of these disparities in 1994 by plotting PPS estimates of regional per capita GDP for nomenclature of territorial units for statistics Level II (NUTS II) regions in fifteen member states, themselves ranked from left to right according to their national GDP per head. In that year output per head in NUTS II regions measured in PPS varied from 196 to 37.7 per cent of the EU average, while in ecus the extreme values were 227 and 31.

The lowest decile, that is the 10 per cent of the population of the Community that lived in the least prosperous areas, had an average GDP per head of 58. The next 10 per cent lived in areas with an average of 71. More than 19 per cent of the population of the EU lived in 'Objective 1' areas with a per capita GDP of less than 75 per cent of the Community average. This included all of Greece, Portugal outside Lisbon, the French overseas *départements*, the former German Democratic Republic, 10 of 18 Spanish NUTS II regions, 5 of the regions of the Italian Mezzogiorno, Burgenland in Austria, and South Yorkshire in the UK. Just outside were the Canaries, Merseyside, Corsica, Molise in Italy, and Flevoland in the Netherlands. In most of these areas the share of income from low-productivity agricultural sectors was large, and unemployment was high. The further 36 per cent lived in areas with a per capita GDP of less than the Community average, which included many rural areas and areas with above-average

GDP per head in 1994 (PPS: EU-15 = 100)

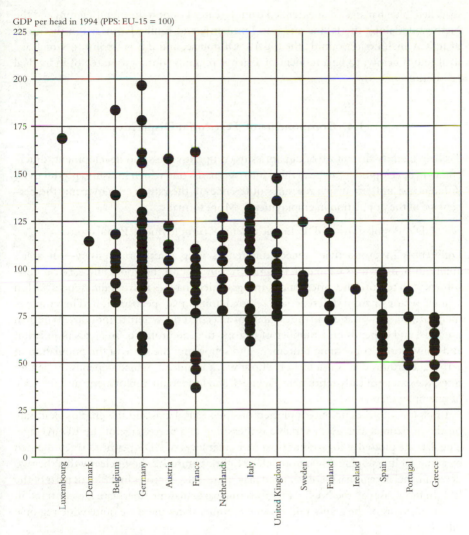

Source: elaborated from REGIO database, 1996.

Fig. 1.1. Gross domestic product per head (in PPS) by NUTS II region in 1994

unemployment rates affected by the decline of jobs in mining, steel, textiles, and shipbuilding.

At the other end of the spectrum, 10 per cent of the population of the Community lived in areas with an average of 153. Included were Hamburg (196), Brussels (183), Darmstadt (178), Luxembourg (169), Ile de France (161), Oberbayern (161), Vienna (158), Bremen (156), Greater London (147), Stuttgart (139), Antwerp (139), Grampian (136) in Scotland, and Lombardy (131). A large share of the regions in this group were West German, and most were metropolitan economies clustered around an axis (the so-called 'blue banana') that extended from Greater London through Belgium and the Netherlands along the Rhine and into Lombardy and Emilia Romagna in the north of Italy, which lie just outside the top 10. Of course, and this is a point to which we shall return below, to be a resident of a richer region is not a guarantee of individual prosperity.

1.4. Components of Territorial Disparities

To help identify the nature of disparities in competitiveness and development, differentials in development can be divided into two parts: one which measures productivity differentials; and one which measures differences in the rate of employment (the percentage of the population in employment). More formally,

GDP/Population = (GDP/Employment) × (Employment/Population).

Differences in productivity reflect differences in physical productivity—an area's ability to transform its natural and human resources into the goods and services consumers wish to purchase, prices and earnings which may result from differences within a single sector or from differences in sectoral/functional specialization. The employment rate reflects variations in the capacity of an economic system to mobilize its human potential and depends on a number of factors: the age profile of an area's population and conventions concerning retirement and schooling; the share of the population in active age groups that is inactive or whose work is hidden, which depends on gender roles, the extent of early retirement, sickness, and hidden unemployment; and the scale of unemployment.

In Figure 1.2, productivity is plotted on the vertical axis and the employment rate on the horizontal axis. Each variable is measured as a percentage of the EU average. The data are plotted as logarithms (so a particular level of GDP per head is represented by a straight line sloping down from left to right). Figure 1.2 shows clearly that the two determinants of regional GDP per head play quite different roles in different parts of the EU. In most cases all the NUTS I regions in a particular member state are clustered in a particular part of the graph, but in some member states there are quite wide regional differences.

Most of the areas with the lowest GDP per head were in Greece and Portugal (data was not available for the French overseas *départements* which also had particularly low levels of GDP per head). However, both Greece (with the exception of Kentriki Ellada in the west) and mainland Portugal had employment rates close to the EU average (92 to 102 per cent). These two cohesion countries thus had employment statistics close to the EU average but levels of productivity (measured in PPS) between 65 and 72 per cent of the EU average.

The situation in Spain and the Republic of Ireland was different. Generally speaking, employment rates were low, varying from 91 per cent in northern Spain (es1 and es2) to 67 per cent in the South (es6). In Ireland the employment rate stood at 84 per cent. Rates of productivity were much closer to the EU average than in Greece and Portugal,

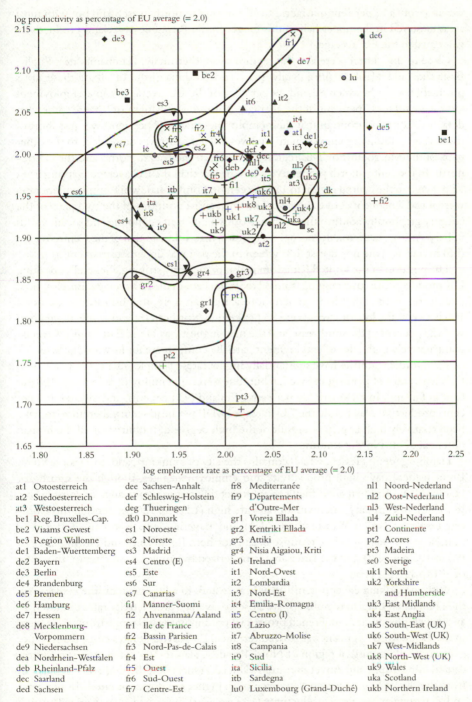

Source: elaborated from data from the REGIO database and DG XVI employment data.

Fig. 1.2. Employment and productivity rates in NUTS I EU regions in 1993

varying from 112 per cent in Madrid to 73 per cent in north-west Spain but with most areas clustered in the upper half of this range. In the Republic of Ireland productivity was equal to the EU average.

Close to this cluster were also the regions of southern Italy: Campania (it8); Puglia, Basilicata, and Calabria (it9); Sicily (ita); and Sardinia (itb). In all of these areas productivity was between 82 and 89 per cent of the EU average, while employment rates were 80 to 87 per cent of the average. Abruzzo and Molise (it7) were somewhat detached from this group in that their employment rate (97 per cent) was just short of the average, although their productivity level (89 per cent) was quite close to the other parts of the Mezzogiorno. This region lay between the Mezzogiorno and the centre-north. In the centre-north productivity was greater than the EU average (varying from 95 per cent in the central region to 115 per cent in Lombardia), while employment rates were 4 to 17 per cent above average. The differential positions of the two parts of the country graphically confirm the existence of two different economic and social worlds in Italy. Austria, interestingly, occupies a position that is close to that of the Centro region (it5) in Italy and the north-east (it3) which in the past was under Austrian control.

The position of the United Kingdom is also particularly striking. Generally speaking UK productivity is low, ranging from 82 to 96 per cent of the EU average. Employment rates were, on the other hand, much more varied and were, in most cases, in excess of 100 per cent: the lowest scores were 95 per cent in Northern Ireland, while the highest was 123 per cent in the south-east, and the next highest was 118 in East Anglia. Overall, comparatively high rates of employment partially compensate for low productivity.

The Nordic countries have substantially higher rates of employment: 125 per cent in Denmark and 121 per cent in Sweden but, due to recent employment loss, just 100 per cent in Finland. In Denmark (90 per cent), Finland (92 per cent), and Sweden (82 per cent) productivity lay below the EU average. GDP per head seems, therefore, to have been relatively high largely as a result of the high degree of mobilization of the human potential of the Nordic countries.

Hamburg (de6), Hessen, which contains the city of Frankfurt, and, to a lesser extent, Bremen (de5) have high productivity and employment rates, though the figures for Hamburg and Bremen are difficult to interpret due to the significance of commuting. In the rest of Germany employment rates are high (125 and 126 per cent) in the south-ern *Länder* of Baden-Württemberg (de1) and Bayern (de2). Rates of productivity in these two *Länder* are close to those in the northern Rhinelands and North Sea coast (98 to 103 per cent), but the latter are characterized by employment rates on the order of 101 to 110 per cent.

With the striking exception of Ile de France and, to a lesser extent, the centre-east, the French and Belgian regions display close-to-average productivity rates but less than average employment rates. French provincial productivity rates range from 96 per cent in the Ouest to 107 per cent in the Mediterranée. Employment rates range from 86 per cent in the old industrial region of Nord-Pas-de-Calais to 105 per cent in the centre-east (Rhône-Alpes and Auvergne) in provincial France. The Ile de France stands out from the rest of France as a consequence of its higher employment rate (118 per cent) and, in particular, its rate of productivity (139 per cent). Belgium is characterized by high rates of productivity and rates of employment that are, on average, low (96 per cent). In Belgium, therefore, the strong positive impact of productivity on relative GDP per head is, in part, offset by the downward pressure exerted by comparatively low rates of employment.

The position of the Netherlands has changed from the top left- to the bottom right-hand quadrant. In 1994 rates of productivity ranged from 87 (Zuid-Nederland) to 99 per cent (Noord-Nederland), while employment rates ranged from 106 to 118.

1.5. Trends in Regional Inequality

Figure 1.3 plots several indicators of inequalities in GDP per inhabitant in the first twelve member states. These data show strong convergence towards territorial equality in the EU until the mid-1970s, but then some divergence until the mid-1980s. From

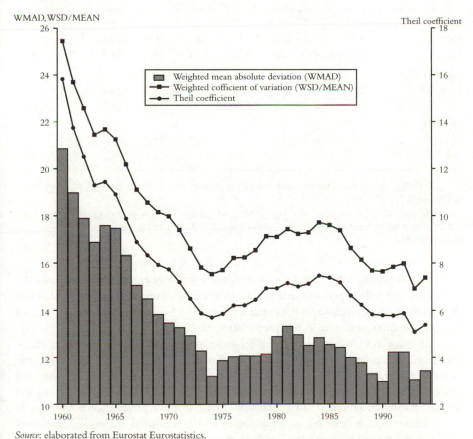

Source: elaborated from Eurostat Eurostatistics.

Fig. 1.3. Trends in inequality between member states

Dunford, Hall, Smith, Tsoukalis

Table 1.1. Trends in regional inequality in the European Union

No. of regions	1977	1978	1979	1980	1981	1982	1983	1984	1985
Member states									
15									
12	12.9	12.9	12.9	13.7	14.2	13.8	13.2	13.5	13.3
NUTS I									
45 to 76[a]	17.5	14.2	15.3	20.2	20.0	19.6	19.4	19.7	20.0
63					20.0	19.6	19.4	19.7	20.0
NUTS II									
82 to 203[b]	18.4	18.3	18.6	22.8	21.9	22.4	22.3	21.3	23.3
166					21.9			21.3	

No. of regions	1986	1987	1988	1989	1990	1991	1992	1993	1994
Member states									
15			11.5	10.9	11.1	10.0	10.1	9.2	9.7
12	12.8	12.4	12.1	11.5	11.6	10.3	10.4	9.4	10.0
NUTS I									
45 to 76[a]	20.4	19.3	18.9	18.5	18.8	20.9	20.4	19.4	19.5
63		19.3		19.0	19.2	19.0	19.0	18.5	19.0
NUTS II									
82 to 203[b]	23.4	21.0	21.0	20.4	20.7	22.2	21.6	20.9	21.0
166		21.0		20.5	20.7	20.5	20.5	20.0	20.5

[a] 45 in 1977, 56 in 1978–9, 62 in 1980 and 1986, 63 in 1981–7, 70 in 1989, 72 in 1990, 77 in 1991–3, and 76 in 1994

[b] 109 in 1977, 82 in 1978, 114 in 1979, 132 in 1980, 166 in 1981, 134 in 1982–3 and 1985, 167 in 1984, 136 in 1986, 170 in 1987, 184 in 1988, 189 in 1989, 191 in 1990, 195 in 1991, 203 in 1992–3, and 199 in 1994

the mid-1980s until 1990 there was convergence in member states' incomes. At the start of the 1990s there was a further upturn in most measures of inequality, with levels close to their 1974 level; so over the period from 1974 to 1992 there was no overall reduction in income disparities between countries.

At a European Union level and even in some member states it is difficult to measure trends in regional inequality due to the absence of data for particular countries in particular years. A far from ideal solution is to drop regions for which values are missing. This course of action is adopted in Tables 1.1 and 1.2, though the complete data series are also recorded. The indicator of regional inequality used is the sum of the absolute deviations of regional per capita GDP (measured at Purchasing Power Standards) expressed as a percentage of the mean. The data in Table 1.1 set out inequalities within the EU at member state NUTS I and NUTS II levels , while Table 1.2 sets

Table 1.2. Trends in regional inequality in member states (NUTS I, II, and III regions)

Member state	No. of regions	1977	1978	1979	1980	1981	1982	1983	1984	1985	1986	1987	1988	1989	1990	1991	1992	1993	1994
NUTS I																			
Austria	3												10.0	9.4	9.4	9.3	9.4	9.5	9.5
Belgium	3	10.8	10.7	10.7	11.5	12.5	12.2	11.4	11.4	12.0	12.3	12.5	12.9	13.1	14.0	13.3	13.0	13.2	13.2
Germany																25.0	22.6	19.8	18.5
West Germany	11 [10 in 1980, 1986, and 1988]		7.6	7.5	8.0	8.1	8.0	8.5	8.7	8.9	8.7	9.5	9.9	9.8	10.4	11.6	11.9	11.5	11.7
Spain	7	15.6			14.0	15.1	14.6	14.6	14.7	16.3	17.0	17.1	16.9	17.9	18.1	18.3	18.4	16.9	17.2
Finland	2													0.3	0.3		0.4	0.4	0.4
France	8 (9 in 1989–93)	15.6	15.8	15.3	15.5	15.9	16.9	17.7	17.2	18.1	17.7	18.5	18.8	19.2	19.5	19.7	19.4	19.3	19.0
France	8	14.5	15.8	15.3	15.5	15.9	16.9	17.7	17.2	18.1	17.7	18.5	18.8	18.8	19.2	19.4	19.0	19.0	19.0
Greece	4	14.5		13.8	8.8	5.6	4.5	6.1	5.4	3.5	4.3	4.5	3.5	4.2	5.0	4.6	6.8	8.5	8.7
Italy	11	22.1	22.6	21.8	22.0	22.3	22.1	20.7	20.8	21.9	22.4	22.3	22.8	23.0	23.0	21.2	21.6	22.1	22.3
Netherlands	4	11.1	10.5	10.7	11.5	13.2	13.4	13.3	13.6	13.5	10.7	8.6	9.0	8.1	7.7	7.6	7.0	7.0	7.1
Portugal	3														2.8	2.7	2.5	2.5	2.6
UK	11	8.8	9.6	10.5	10.7	11.0	9.7	10.2	10.3	10.1	10.9	11.3	11.9	12.3	12.3	11.4	11.3	11.5	11.6
NUTS II																			
Austria	9												18.8	18.7	18.7	19.0	19.2	19.0	19.0
Belgium	11 (9 in 1977–9)	18.2	17.6	17.9	18.7	19.0	19.1	17.6	18.8	19.9	18.7	18.4	18.2	19.1	19.7	19.4	19.2	19.4	19.5
West Germany	31 (5 in 1977–8; 30 in 1980, 1986, and 1988)		20.0	21.1	14.0	13.5	13.7	14.1	14.2	14.4	15.3	14.8	14.7	14.4	14.8	24.6	22.7	20.8	20.0
West Germany	31					13.5	13.7	14.1	14.2	14.4		14.8		14.4	14.8	15.6	15.7	15.5	15.7
Spain	18				14.7	16.1	16.0	15.5	15.3	16.6	17.1	17.1	14.9	14.3	14.9	16.2	15.0	15.7	15.8
Finland	6																		
France	21 (22 in 1982–8 and 1994; 26 in 1989–93)	15.9	16.2	15.8	15.8	15.9	17.0	17.7	17.3	18.1	18.0	18.8	18.9	19.4	20.0	20.0	19.6	19.5	19.1
France	21	15.9	16.2	15.8	15.8	15.9	17.0	17.7	17.3	18.1	18.0	18.8	18.9	18.9	19.4	19.4	19.2	19.1	19.1
Greece	13	16.5		15.9	13.0	8.7	7.5	9.2	8.9	7.3	7.8	8.2	7.5	8.2	8.6	7.7	8.6	9.7	9.7
Italy	20	22.5	23.0	22.0	22.0	22.4	22.1	20.7	20.9	22.0	22.6	22.5	22.9	23.1	23.1	21.3	21.7	22.2	22.4
Netherlands	9 (12 in 1986–94)	12.9	12.3	12.8	13.3	14.9	14.5	14.7	15.3	16.5	12.8	10.8	10.6	9.5	9.3	9.6	9.2	9.3	8.7
Portugal	5 (7 in 1990–4)										25.4	28.9	24.9	24.6	21.3	22.6	20.5	20.5	20.5
Portugal	5		23.0		22.2	23.2	24.0	23.5	23.0	22.5	25.4	28.9	24.9	24.6	21.0	22.4	20.3	20.3	20.3
Sweden	8																8.3	10.5	10.3
UK	35 (34 in 1977–9)	12.6	12.8	13.6		13.8			13.7			14.7	14.7	14.7	14.8	14.4	14.8	15.3	15.4

Table 1.2. (cont'd)

Member state	No. of regions	1977	1978	1979	1980	1981	1982	1983	1984	1985	1986	1987	1988	1989	1990	1991	1992	1993	1994
NUTS III																			
Belgium	43				23.4	23.5	23.6	22.2	23.5	23.4	23.1	23.2	22.9	23.1	23.2	23.4	23.6	23.6	
Portugal	3															15.2	15.2	15.2	
Sweden	24																10.0	9.9	
UK	57 (65 in 1981–93)	13.6		14.6	14.5				14.6			15.5	15.8	15.9	15.9	15.2	14.8	14.7	
Germany	327				30.3	31.0	31.3	31.3	31.6	31.8	32.0	31.8	31.3	30.6	30.5	30.8	31.2	31.6	
Denmark	11 (11 in 1988–93)	2.9	2.9	3.1	3.4	3.5	3.4	3.5	4.3	4.1	5.0	5.1	50.7	50.1	49.8	49.1	48.8	47.4	
Denmark	11	2.9	2.9	3.1	3.4	3.5	3.4	3.5	4.3	4.1	5.0	5.1	6.1	6.1	5.4	6.9	7.0	6.6	
Spain	50				15.8	16.6	16.7	16.3	16.1	17.1	18.0	18.0	18.0	19.0	18.8	18.9	19.3	18.6	
Finland	19												15.8	15.1	15.2	16.6	15.7	15.9	
France	88 (94 in 1986 and 1992–3; 98 in 1987–91)				20.6	20.6	20.9				22.0	22.4	22.4	22.3	22.6	22.6	22.2	22.2	
France	88				20.6	20.6	20.9				23.2	23.2	23.3	23.0	23.3	23.4	23.4	23.4	
Greece	51			17.6	15.2	11.5	11.2	12.7	11.9	10.5	11.4	11.9	11.9	11.0	11.4	12.1	12.4	12.7	
Netherlands	32 (20 in 1983; 40 in 1986–93)						23.0	27.5	24.2	24.7	18.8	16.8	16.6	15.5	15.4	15.8	15.1	15.3	

In the case of those member states where the number of regions, the definition of the regions, or the availability of data has changed, to enable comparisons results are also given just for all regions but also for those regions for which data existed in 1981.

out the results for individual member states. The member state indicators in Table 1.1 identify the same recent tendency for catch-up and for a reduction in intermember state disparities identified in Figure 1.3. Trends in disparities between NUTS I and NUTS II regions, however, suggest that there was very little convergence in 1981–94: for 63 NUTS II regions the weighted absolute deviation (WAD) declined from 20 to 19, while for 166 NUTS III regions it diminished from 21.9 to 20.5.

The reason for the contrast between inter- and intramember state trends is clear from Table 1.2, which shows that disparities in GDP per head increased in virtually all member states. At NUTS II level, disparities increased in all member states except the Netherlands in 1986–94, Greece in 1977–81, Austria where disparities changed little, Portugal in 1991–4, and the new Germany. At NUTS I, disparities increased in the UK from 8.8 per cent in 1977 to 11.6 per cent in 1994, and at NUTS II level from 12.6 to 15.4. In France there was an increase at NUTS II level from 15.9 to 19.1, and in Spain from 14.7 in 1980 to 17.9 in 1994.

1.6. A Disaggregation of Trends in Output Per Head

To what extent are these changes the result of differences in changes in rates of productivity and in employment rates? Are interregional productivity differentials increasing or decreasing? Are variations in the employment rate increasing or decreasing? Are areas that are economically weaker comparatively unsuccessful in their attempts to redeploy people who lose their jobs as a result of structural change or to provide alternative employment possibilities for new generations entering the job market for the first time? Does interregional migration serve to adjust the changing regional supply of and demand for labour?

To answer some of these questions, trends in the rates of productivity and employment were analysed to explore whether disparities in the two constituent elements of differences in GDP per head (rates of productivity and employment) were increasing or decreasing relative to the EU average (which stood at 40.6 per cent in 1980, 41.3 per cent in 1990, and 38.1 per cent in 1993) at the member state level. The results are in Figure 1.4. It shows that different member states are developing along different trajectories with most, at any point in time, either converging on EU rates of productivity while diverging on rates of employment or vice versa. Of the cohesion countries other than Ireland after 1989 there is strong evidence of a trade-off between productivity and employment rate convergence. Spain's overall position also improved but in different ways: until 1986 rates of productivity converged while rates of employment diverged, in 1986–90 the employment rate improved at the expense of divergence in rates of productivity, while in 1990–3 there were a series of switches. In Greece an overall improvement in its rate of employment occurred at the expense of its relative productivity, while in Portugal there was an overall improvement in relative productivity and a small decline in its relative employment rate. Ireland is the striking exception due to the speed of growth in the 1990s, which allowed productivity and employment to converge at one and the same time.

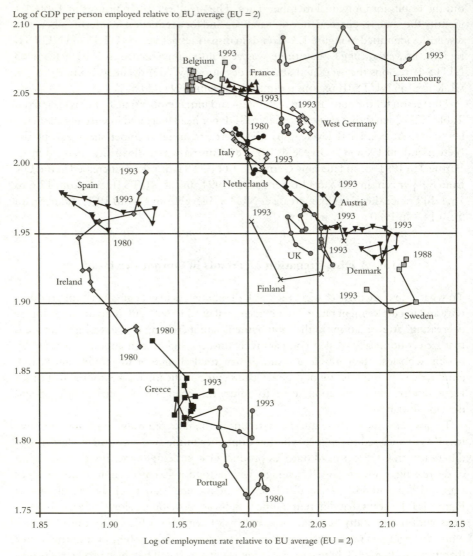

Fig. 1.4. Trends in productivity and employment rates in member states, 1980–93

Of the stronger economies, Belgium and Luxembourg strengthened their positions in terms of productivity and employment; Austria, Italy, and the Netherlands lost ground in terms of productivity.

There are few signs of a virtuous cycle in which relative rates of productivity and employment increase. Instead there is evidence of a trade-off in which gains in relative productivity are achieved at the expense of relative employment and vice versa. The

Table 1.3. Output and employment trends in the EU–15 and OECD

	EU-15				OECD			
	1960–73	1973–9	1979–89	1989–95	1960–73	1973–9	1979–89	1989–95
Real GDP	4.7	2.5	2.2	1.0	4.9	2.8	2.6	1.8
Real GDP per head	4.0	2.1	2.0	1.0	3.7	1.9	1.7	0.9
Civilian employment[b]	0.3	0.2	0.5		1.1	1.2	1.1	0.7[a]
Civilian employment in manufacturing[b]	0.5	−1.0	−0.9	−3.0	1.3	−0.3	−0.3	−2.1[a]
Civilian employment in services[b]	1.8	1.8	2.0	1.1	2.5	2.5	2.3	1.4[a]
Employment as percent of population from 15 to 64[b]	65.3	63.2	60.1	61.3	66.1	65.2	64.8	66.2[a]
Real GDP per person employed	4.4	2.3	1.8	0.0	3.8	1.7	1.5	1.4
Real value added in manufacturing per person employed[b]	6.0	3.7	2.8	2.0	5.0	2.6	2.8	3.0
Real value added in services per person employed[b]	3.3	1.8	0.7	0.0	2.7	1.4	0.7	0.9

[a] 1989–93.
[b] Since 1991 data for Germany refer to the new unified Germany.

Source: elaborated from OECD 1997, 1996, 1995.

per capita rate of growth of employment, measured in terms of jobs, is equal to the difference between the rate of growth of GDP per capita and the rate of growth of GDP divided by employment (or the product of output per average hours of work and average hours of work per person employed). Though productivity growth rates have been low, equalling just 1.8 and 0.7 per cent per year in 1979–89 and 1989–95, growth has also been slow, and employment growth has not been sufficiently fast to allow catch-up to combine simultaneous improvements in relative employment and productivity.

1.7. Trends in Income Inequality

A study of developments in the distribution of disposable income in seventeen OECD countries (OECD 1995) showed that there was a rise in inequality in the 1980s for the majority of countries. Table 1.4 shows that increases in measured inequality were the largest in the Netherlands, Sweden, and, in particular, the United Kingdom and United States.

At the more recent dates for which there was data, relative inequality was smallest in the Scandinavian countries, Benelux, and Luxembourg and greatest in the United States, Ireland, and Switzerland. These figures are a result of a complex set of factors that include changes in the distribution of earnings and workforce participation, ageing of the population, changes in household structures, changes in taxation and income transfers with, in several countries, reductions in taxes in upper incomes and reductions in the level and coverage of benefits and increases·in the return to capital, as well as changes in the ownership of assets, in part as a result of privatization.

Dunford, Hall, Smith, Tsoukalis

Table 1.4. Trends in income inequality in OECD countries

Country	Year	Gini coefficient	Year	Gini coefficient	Change in Gini coefficient
Finland	1990	21.5	1987	20.7	0.8
Sweden	1987	22.0	1981	19.9	2.1
Norway	1986	23.4	1979	22.2	1.2
Belgium	1988	23.5	1985	22.8	0.7
Luxembourg	1985	23.8			
Netherlands	1987	26.8	1983	24.7	2.1
Canada	1987	28.9	1981	28.6	0.3
Australia	1985	29.5	1981	28.7	0.8
France	1984	29.6	1979	29.7	−0.1
United Kingdom	1986	30.4	1979	27.0	3.4
Italy	1986	31.0			
Switzerland	1982	32.3			
Ireland	1987	33.0			
United States	1986	34.1	1979	30.9	3.2

Source: Atkinson *et al.* (1995).

1.8. The Causes of Regional Inequality

Analysis of the location of economic activity is a well-established subject, which has been the subject of the large recent literature on 'the new economic geography' inspired by Krugman (1991). Surveys of the content and significance of that literature are provided by Fujita and Thisse (1996), Ottaviano and Puga (1998), and Martin (1998), while Fujita, Krugman, and Venables (1999) provides much detailed analysis. There are several key themes which emerge from this literature that are of significance in the analysis of cohesion policy.

The location of economic activity can be seen as determined by the interplay of two opposing sets of forces: centrifugal forces that encourage locational dispersion and centripetal forces that encourage agglomeration. The ordinary operation of factor markets is the main source of centrifugal forces: wages and rents are higher in the neighbourhood of existing centres of economic activity and this encourages new activity to locate elsewhere. To explain why agglomeration is a common feature of economic geography we need to have countervailing forces—technological and pecuniary externalities—that encourage activities into proximity.

Technological externalities, when the presence of one producer has the effect of directly reducing the costs of other producers (for example, because of shared infrastructure), tend to be the focus of explanations of local agglomeration, such as the formation of cities. In the explanation of economic geography at the regional level, the literature focuses on pecuniary externalities, where the benefits of agglomeration are mediated through the market. Backward and forward linkages between firms in supply chains, whereby firms gain from proximity to other firms that are their suppliers or their customers, are pecuniary externalities.

The distinction is an important one for policy because technological externalities necessarily imply market failure, so that policy intervention can have an efficiency-enhancing role in providing public infrastructure or discouraging congestion. Pecuniary externalities do not imply market failure, so any case for policy intervention has to be based on considerations of equity rather than efficiency.

The fact that integration has uncertain effects on the balance between centrifugal and centripetal forces is, perhaps, the single most interesting conclusion of the new economic geography literature. With very high transport costs, economic activity will tend to be dispersed because producers have to be near their markets; with very low transport costs, activity will be dispersed because distance is almost irrelevant to cost, so centripetal forces are absent. In many models, however, at intermediate levels of transport costs, centripetal outweigh centrifugal forces and there is agglomeration. The implication is that there is a U-shaped relationship between integration and agglomeration—starting from high trade and transport costs, a reduction in these costs causes agglomeration; but when trade and transport costs are fairly low, further reductions cause dispersion. To put the point another way, reducing the costs of transactions between core and peripheral regions gives peripheral producers better access to markets in the core, but also gives core producers better access to peripheral markets, and the net effect on peripheral producers may be positive or negative. Brülhart and Torstensson (1996) and Brülhart (1998) find some support for the U-shape hypothesis in the patterns of industrial location in the EU: industries with strong scale economies seem to have become more concentrated geographically in the 1980s, but, overall, there has been some reduction in concentration in the core of the EU. The policy implication for the EU is spelled out by Martin (1998): cohesion policy which aims at the reduction of infrastructure costs, as much EU policy has done, will have uncertain effects on regional inequality.

Mobility of labour plays an important role in some models of economic geography and, as Ottaviano and Puga (1998) point out, will reinforce centripetal tendencies for the simple reason that if workers can move from a poorer periphery to a richer core, the core grows and the periphery becomes more peripheral. This has the important implication that inequality in the location of production and inequality in the distribution of income need not move in the same direction: migration from periphery to core surely makes the distribution of production more unequal, but by raising the income of migrants it may reduce the inequality of income distribution. The difference between the European Union and the United States is instructive. The high degree of mobility of labour within the US ensures that intraregional or intrastate income inequalities are less than they are in the EU. Puga (1998) points out that regional equality of income is greater in the USA than in Europe—only two small states in the US are below 75 per cent of the US average of GNP while, as we saw above, almost 20 per cent of the population of the EU lived in regions more than 75 per cent below the EU GNP average in 1994. However, as detailed in Krugman (1991), regional specialization of economic activity is much greater in the US than in the EU. This difference suggests that the policy concerns with respect to the cohesion effects of integration might be different in the short run from the longer run. Suppose that increased integration, including increased mobility of labour, does, indeed, lead to increased concentration of some economic activities, but also to a reduced dispersion of income. In the long run, the reduced income inequality is an improvement in 'cohesion'; but in the short run the changing location of economic activity may create problems of regional adjustment.

Viewing the same issue from another angle, economic integration can deliver equal outcomes for individuals in different locations even if the pattern of economic activity is unequal. This point is nicely made in a simple two-region model of Krugman, where a high-tech sector producing 'chips' is located in one region because of economies of scale while the low-tech 'fish' sector is dispersed between both regions, but if the configuration of factor supplies to both regions is compatible with factor price equalization, real incomes in both regions are the same. The benefits of specialization in the high-tech sector are fully shared, through integrated goods and factor markets, with the region that has no production of the high-tech good. This leads on to the question of what is likely to be the relationship between integration and 'social cohesion', in the sense of inequality among individuals.

1.9. Integration and Personal Inequality

The impact of global economic integration on inequality has been a source of considerable controversy, as is discussed in more detail below in Chapter 3. There has been a dramatic increase in interpersonal inequality in the United States since 1970. The change is reflected in the US Gini coefficients reported in Table 1.4 above and is detailed by Krugman (1994), and by Freeman (1995), who writes, 'an economic disaster has befallen low-skilled Americans, especially young men.' Table 1.4 shows that the European experience has been different, but the dramatic increases in European unemployment in the same period (Alogoskoufis *et al.*, 1995, give data on the differential incidence of unemployment among unskilled workers as well as on the growth of European unemployment rates) can be interpreted as a different manifestation of an underlying common phenomenon: a weakening of the labour market for less skilled workers. The period of these dramatic changes has also seen a very rapid growth of international trade in manufactured goods with developing countries, especially the 'tigers' of south-east Asia. The standard textbook model of international trade provides a link between the two phenomena: growth of trade between developed and developing countries will in developed countries shift production towards skill-intensive products, drive down the relative price of unskilled-intensive goods, raise the real wages of skilled workers, and reduce the real wages of the unskilled. If there is downward rigidity of the real wages of the unskilled in socially regulated labour markets, the process will generate unemployment rather than relative wage changes. Many observers have, therefore, linked the labour market difficulties of the less skilled to global integration.

However, the weight of academic opinion, at least among international economists, is opposed to the view that there is a strong link between the growth of trade and the growth of labour market inequality. Lawrence and Slaughter (1993) argue that the rise in the relative wage of skilled workers is associated with rising employment of skilled labour, which is strongly suggestive of a chain of causation that runs from an exogenous increase in the demand for skilled workers in most sectors driving up the relative wage of such workers, rather than the chain of causation running from trade to inequality. The most plausible source of such an exogenous increase is technological change, particularly the information technology revolution, which may be increasing the demand for well-educated labour and reducing the demand for the less skilled.

Other evidence suggesting that integration is not the driving force behind inequality is that the behaviour of labour markets in sectors producing non-traded goods seems broadly the same as in sectors producing traded goods. If global competition were driving down the demand for and price of unskilled labour, we should expect to see sectors insulated from that competition increasing their employment of unskilled labour, and we do not. It is also notable that the most striking increases in inequality are at the very top of the income distribution both in the UK and the USA, and it is hard to explain such changes as the result of increased global competition.

Whatever the influence of integration at the global level has on the growth of inequality between individuals, it is hard to see that European integration has been a significant influence. There are differences in the skill endowments of different parts of Europe, but they are not nearly as great as north–south differences in the global economy. Furthermore, when we look at the impact of European integration on European inequality, the gainers as well as the losers have to be considered—if increased competition with Portugal tends to depress unskilled wages in Germany, it is because of increased opportunities for unskilled workers in Portugal. Indeed, there is a general expectation that integration between a group of countries will tend to reduce inequality between individuals by providing competition for scarce, high-priced factors and new markets for abundant, low-priced factors. The main counter-forces are the ones we have already discussed in the context of regional inequality: insofar as integration increases the gap between rich and poor regions, its effect on interpersonal equality is likely to be negative.

However, the fact that European integration in itself is more likely to be an equalizing force does not mean that income inequality is off the policy agenda. On the contrary, whether the sources of increased inequality lie in globalization or in technological change, they are likely to be persistent forces. Interpersonal inequality, unemployment, and labour market skills may well deserve a higher policy priority than regional inequalities, which would argue for a fundamental reorientation of the meaning of 'cohesion policy'. Such a reorientation might be accompanied by a shift in the balance between the European Union and the member states: if education and training become the main tools of cohesion policy, it is arguable that policy is better designed and implemented at the level of the member states rather than at that of the Union.

As in the case of regional policy, there may be considerable differences between short-run and long-run policy priorities. In the short run, the position of less skilled workers is best protected by measures that increase their incomes and create suitable jobs; but in the longer run, the emphasis surely should be on raising the skill level in the workforce.

1.10. Integration and Growth

The impact of integration on economic growth is a longstanding area of controversy. Many commentators (see, for example, World Bank 1987) see the international evidence as pointing to a clear association between open markets and economic growth, while others see the evidence as much more ambiguous. The large recent literature on economic growth has not arrived at settled conclusions about the nature of the growth process: the extent to which growth is determined by exogenous forces of factor supply and technological change or by endogenous or policy-influenced factors like saving rates or endogenous technology.

The traditional economic analysis of the sources of economic growth gives little scope for economic policy to affect growth, because long-run growth is explained by exogenous growth in supplies of factors of production and by exogenous technical progress. At best, policy can have transitory effects. For example, a policy which boosts saving will lead to capital accumulation and increased growth, but in the long run, diminishing returns to capital will drive the rate of economic growth back to its exogenous level. However, the recent literature on endogenous growth has broken out of this straitjacket by allowing increasing returns to scale or externalities associated with capital accumulation.

Grossman and Helpman (1991) have provided an analysis of endogenous growth which links growth and trade through the role of research and development. Without spillover effects, R&D would be a private investment activity like any other: investment in R&D is made in order to capture a future stream of profits associated with the new product created by the investment. However, because of the public-good nature of knowledge, R&D has spillover effects: it adds to the stock of 'general knowledge capital' which increases the productivity of all producers. If this public-good effect is strong enough, the returns to R&D do not diminish as the stock of R&D increases, and the rate of growth is endogenous.

The rate of growth, then, depends on saving behaviour and on research productivity, among other things. In an open economy, the relationship between trade and growth is determined by general equilibrium factors. If trade releases resources from manufacturing that are suited to research, growth increases; but if the sectors that expand as a result of trade draw resources out of R&D, growth falls. World patterns of production depend on whether knowledge spillovers are international; if they are not, then 'history matters' a great deal—a national lead in R&D is likely to be self-perpetuating. At this analytical level, there is no presumption that the link between growth and integration, whether regional or international, should be positive.

However, there are more specific linkages between trade and growth: trade can act as a channel for the international diffusion of knowledge; it can reduce duplication of research effort; it enlarges the market, which can encourage innovation because of the potential returns in a larger market; or it can discourage innovation because of the increased number of competitors.

The principal hypotheses emerging from this literature relate to convergence rather than growth *per se*. The traditional neoclassical growth model hypothesizes that countries or regions with below-average income have above-average investment opportunities and so should have above-average growth; while the theory that trade facilitates the international flow of knowledge implies that lagging countries will tend to catch up with the performance of their trade partners.

Coe and Helpman (1995) have provided evidence that trade does provide a conduit for international R&D spillovers: technological progress in countries seems to depend on the technological levels of their trading partners (though Keller 1998 casts doubt on the robustness of Coe and Helpman's statistical methods).

Ben-David has investigated the trade–convergence relationship in a series of papers. Ben-David (1993) shows that the formation and development of the European Community was accompanied by very significant reductions in the inequality of income between the member states. Effectively, he associates the pattern of the reduction of intercountry inequality shown in Figure 1.3 above with the process of European integration. The empirical results of Ben-David (1996) show that groups of countries with strong trade links display convergence in a way that other groups do not. Ben-David and Loewy (1995) provide striking evidence of how the post–war growth experience both in Europe and elsewhere has been much stronger than might have been expected on the basis of historical experience, and suggests that European and global integration is the obvious explanation of the upsurge in growth.

Sala-i-Martin (1996) argues that the speed of convergence of interregional growth in Europe is of the same order as that of interregional growth in the United States and Japan. He argues that the evidence is consistent both with the neoclassical growth model in which diminishing returns to capital produces convergence and with interregional diffusion of knowledge, and he also argues that on current evidence it is impossible to choose between these two hypotheses.

From a policy perspective, the lesson of this literature is that the objectives of policy should be to foster research and development and encourage international knowledge flows. For cohesion policy in Europe, a possible implication is that there should be less emphasis on the location of R&D activity and more emphasis on ensuring that the fruits of that activity flow freely across national boundaries. Martin (1998 and 1999) points out that policy makers may face a tradeoff between aggregate growth at the national level and convergence among regions within a country. Maximizing national growth may require spatial concentration of economic activity. But it needs to be re-emphasized that spatial concentration of activity is not the same as income inequality, and in the two–region model of Martin (1998 and 1999) an improvement in infrastructure in the poorer region decreases spatial concentration, but decreases the growth rate and increases inequality of income between the regions, while a policy that favours innovation can get both growth and equality.

1.11. Policy Targets and Policy Assessment

Given a multiplicity of targets for social and economic policy, a multiplicity of policy measures, and several levels of government with responsibility for policy, the assessment of the effectiveness of a particular policy is a complex matter.

The principle of subsidiarity assigns policy responsibility to the lowest level of government which can effectively carry the responsibility. In this book, we take as given the assignment of policies to the EU level and do not discuss whether that assignment is consistent with the principle of subsidiarity.

The principle of targeting assigns policy targets to those instruments which affect the target most directly. A well-known example of this principle is provided by trade policy, where it is generally agreed (as is argued below in respect of EU trade policy) that protection from import competition is not usually an effective instrument for promoting competitiveness or fairness in income distribution.

In the present context, it is tempting to interpret the principle of targeting as assigning social and economic cohesion to income redistributive measures—tax and social security systems at the national level, Structural Funds at the EU level. Then one could assess other policies purely on efficiency grounds. Such an assignment would, however, be over-simplistic. First, the ability of national governments and of the EU to raise revenue for redistributive policies is severely limited by political and economic constraints on levels of taxation. Where policies that are not themselves directly redistributive have effects on distribution, and the ability of governments to undertake direct redistribution is limited, the redistributive effects and redistributive potential of these policies has to be taken into account.

Further, concerns about social and economic cohesion are not confined to current economic opportunities, but also address the subtle and intertemporal issue of competitiveness. Once it is accepted that market failures create a case for public policy intervention in the creation of future economic opportunities, the targeting of effort to create these opportunities has to be addressed. What is beneficial to the individual enterprise may not be socially desirable. The economic gains from increased competitiveness may not be realized because resources released are not re-employed; the gains from productivity growth may not shared by all members of the community; and there may be underinvestment in 'public goods' like training. As suggested by the evidence of increasing unemployment and non-employment and of greater inequality, simply investing in skills, while important as a determinant of the productivity and quality of work, does not appear to suffice if the aim is the dynamic creation of new jobs to replace those that are lost. However, 'competitiveness' is a concept in need of clearer definition. If EU producers' costs fall relative to competitors because of greater than average improvements in productivity (due to increases in efficiency and in organizational capacities), the change is a positive one according to the criteria discussed above; if, however, increased price competitiveness is achieved through an erosion of wages, job security, or working conditions for the workforce in some enterprises/regions, increased competitiveness would have anti-cohesive effects at least from the producer point of view. It is, thus, impossible wholly to disentangle efficiency and equity and assign different policies to these different objectives. Cohesion objectives will enter into the assessment even of policies whose principle objective is efficiency.

The principle of targeting does not, then, give us a simple set of rules. It does, however, draw attention to the need not to score all EU policies in a mechanical fashion on the single criterion of their cohesion effects. There may well be policies that have a weak impact on cohesion and whose objectives lie elsewhere. If we wish to criticize a policy for taking insufficient account of cohesion objectives, we first have to provide a positive case for the targeting of that policy on these objectives.

1.12. The Key Issues

Against a background of heightened concern about cohesion issues, not just because of the facts demonstrated above about the existing Union, but also because of the prospect of its further enlargement, we can identify a number of key issues that arise in the evaluation of EU policies.

The two key issues which recur throughout this book is whether there are trade-offs between

(1) competitiveness and cohesion, and
(2) liberalization and cohesion.

Has the single market programme led to greater specialization between countries and regions? How has it affected intra-EU trade and investment and what has been the impact on income and employment? And how can we explain the different performance of less developed countries and regions? These are some of the questions to be addressed in the chapter on the single market (Chapter 2).

It is clear that there must be some trade-off between competitiveness and cohesion, to the extent that improvements in productivity require restructuring and re-employment, and those who lose their jobs are, at least temporarily, disadvantaged. The more difficult issue is whether the intensification of international competition and the need for Europe to move up-market if it is to remain competitive mean that the less skilled workers and the less advantaged regions and countries find themselves becoming even more vulnerable. It is in the assessment of research and technological development (RTD) policies that this issue becomes most pressing: but we argue that it would be inappropriate to assess EU RTD policies as if the problem did not exist. On the contrary, given that much of the RTD effort will inevitably be concentrated on the stronger parts of the European economy, it is arguable that it is other policies that have to bear the burden of meeting cohesion objectives.

The possible trade-off between liberalization and cohesion is particularly striking in telecommunications policy, although the same issue arises in transport policy. No simple answer emerges to the question of whether liberalization of infrastructure provision increases or decreases the relative disadvantages of the periphery, and whether a strengthened commitment to universal service provision and cross-subsidization of the weaker by the stronger is needed.

When we turn to social policies, the link between liberalization and cohesion reappears in a new form, a key question being the extent to which harmonization of policy across the EU is needed to cope with an increasingly globalized economic system, or whether excessive harmonization may stifle genuine diversity and harm the competitiveness of the more vulnerable.

Both trade-offs are at the heart of the assessment of agricultural policy and external policy: what are the cohesion effects of policy intervention to protect some sectors from the full rigours of international competition?

Last, but not least, EU structural policies now represent significant transfers of funds across national frontiers and regions. They constitute the most important cohesion (and redistributive) instrument at the European level, concentrating on investment rather than consumption. We need to assess their effectiveness in reducing disparities. We also need to examine whether the cohesion objective is undermined by the decentralized nature of European competition policy and the persistence of large state aids in individual member countries.

APPENDIX. MEASURES OF INEQUALITY

Fig. 1.3 uses three different measures of inequality, the standard deviation, the mean absolute deviation, and the Gini coefficient. As regional units vary significantly in size, all these indicators are weighted by the region's share in the total population. If p_i denotes the population share of the ith region ($i = 1, \ldots, n$) in the total population of all the regions, y_i denotes its per capita GDP, and q_i denotes the region's share of total GDP, the population-weighted standard deviation (WSD) is given by the equation

$$WSD = \sqrt{\sum_{i=1}^{n} (y_i - \bar{y})^2 \, p_i}$$

the weighted absolute deviation (WAD) is given by the equation

$$WAD = \sum_{i=1}^{n} \left| y_i - \bar{y} \right| p_i$$

the Gini coefficient (GC) is given by the equation

$$GC = \left(\sum_{i=1}^{n} \sum_{j=1}^{n} \left| y_i - y_j \right| \right) \bigg/ \left(2n \sum_{i=1}^{n} y_i \right)$$

and the Theil coefficient (TC) is given by the equation

$$TC = \sum_{i=1}^{n} q_i \log \left(\frac{q_i}{p_i} \right)$$

As with the indicators based on the mean, the deviations from which the Gini coefficient was calculated are weighted by the product of the shares of the total population in each pair of regions. To facilitate comparisons, the weighted standard deviation and the weighted absolute deviations are expressed as percentages of the mean to give a coefficient of variation (CV).

References

Alogoskoufis, George, *et al.* (1995). *Unemployment: Choices for Europe*. Monitoring European Integration 5. London: Centre for Economic Policy Research.

Atkinson, A. B., Rainwater, L., and Smeeding, T. M. (1995). *Income Distribution in OECD Countries: Evidence from the Luxembourg Income Study*. Paris: OECD.

Ben-David, Dan (1993). Equalizing exchange: trade liberalization and economic convergence. *Quarterly Journal of Economics* 108: 653–79.

—— (1996). Trade and convergence among countries. *Journal of International Economics* 40: 279–98.

—— and Loewy, Michael B. (1995). *Free trade and long-run growth*. CEPR Discussion Paper 1183, May.

Brülhart, Marius (1998). Trading places: industrial specialization in the European Union. *Journal of Common Market Studies* 36: 319–46.

—— and Torstensson, Johan (1996). *Regional integration, scale economies and industry location in the European Union*. CEPR Discussion Paper 1435, July.

Coe, David T. and Helpman, Elhanan (1995). International R&D spillovers. *European Economic Review* 39: 859–87.

European Commission (1997). *Agenda 2000: For a Stronger and Wider Union*, Suppl. 5/97. Luxembourg: Office for Official Publications of the European Communities.

Freeman, Richard (1995). Are your wages set in Beijing? *Journal of Economic Perspectives* 9: 15–32.

Fujita, Masahisa and Thisse, Jacques-François (1996). Economics of agglomeration. *Journal of the Japanese and International Economies* 19: 339–378.

—— Krugman, Paul, and Venables, Anthony J. (1999). *The Spatial Economy: Cities, Regions and International Trade*. Cambridge, Mass.: MIT Press.

Grossman, Gene M. and Helpman, Elhanan (1991). *Innovation and Growth in the World Economy*. Cambridge, Mass.: MIT Press.

Keller, Wolfgang (1998). Are international R&D spillovers trade-related? Analyzing spillovers among randomly matched trade partners. *European Economic Review* 42: 1469–81.

Krugman, P. (1991). *Geography and Trade*. Cambridge, Mass.: MIT Press.

—— (1994). *Peddling Prosperity: Economic Sense and Nonsense in the Age of Diminished Expectations*. New York: Norton.

—— and Lawrence, Robert (1994). Trade, jobs and wages. *Scientific American* 270: 44–9.

Lawrence, Robert and Slaughter, Matthew (1993). Trade and U.S. wages: great sucking sound or small hiccup? *Brookings Papers on Economic Activity: Microeconomics* 2: 161–226.

Martin, Philippe (1998). Can regional policies affect growth and geography in Europe? *World Economy* 21: 757–74.

—— (1999). Public policies, regional inequalities and growth. CEPR Discussion Paper 1841, March. *Journal of Public Economics*, 73, 1, 85–105.

OECD (1995). *Historical Statistics 1960–1993*. Paris: OECD.

—— (1996). *Historical Statistics 1960–1994*. Paris: OECD.

—— (1997). *Historical Statistics 1960–1995*. Paris: OECD.

Ottaviano, G. I. P. and Puga, D. (1998). Agglomeration in the global economy: a survey of the 'new economic geography'. *World Economy* 21: 707–31.

Puga, D. (1998). Geography lessons. *European Economic Perspectives* 18.

Sala-i-Martin, Xavier X. (1996). Regional cohesion: evidence and theories of regional growth and convergence. *European Economic Review* 40: 1325–52.

Tsoukalis, Loukas (1998). *The European Agenda: Issues of Globalization, Equity and Legitimacy*. Florence: European University Institute.

World Bank (1987). *World Development Report, 1987*. Washington, D.C.: World Bank.

Wood, Adrian (1994). *North-South Trade, Employment and Inequality: Changing Fortunes in a Skill-Driven World*. Oxford: Clarendon Press.

2

The Single Market Programme

NIALL BOHAN AND JEAN-YVES MUYLLE

2.1. Introduction

In the broad church of economics, there is one tenet to which most practitioners subscribe, namely, that liberalizing trade increases efficiency to the benefit of all participating countries. While this consensus has been exposed to new theoretical and political challenges in recent years, it remains intact. The history of multilateral and regional trade liberalization suggests that trade liberalization can be a formidable force for economic growth with the benefits being widely shared. Demonstrating that all participants have benefited substantially or to a comparable extent, however, is a much more challenging proposition. This chapter will assess the extent to which efficiency improvements generated by market integration are shared equitably across the participating regions and countries in the light of the EU's experience in constructing a single market. At the time of its launch, some misgivings were expressed that the advanced degree of factor and product/service market integration envisaged would aggravate pronounced regional imbalances existing in the EU. The most tangible expression of these concerns was the doubling of the budgetary envelope for the Structural Funds and the concentration of these funds on the most disadvantaged regions. This chapter, drawing on a comprehensive analysis of the economic impact of the single market programme, will attempt to establish whether these fears were justified.

2.1.1. A brief history of the single market programme (SMP)

At the outset of the 1980s, a further dose of economic integration was touted as the remedy for the economic ailments afflicting the Community. There was a growing awareness that sluggish macroeconomic growth and spiralling unemployment could be attributed largely to heavy-handed regulation of markets. In the case of the Community,

The authors are administrators of the European Commission. This text reflects their personal interpretation of a broad range of empirical data which has been gathered in the context of the Commission's review of the impact and effectiveness of the single market programme (as presented in Commission Communication 96/520 and the special edition of *European Economy* (no. 4, 1996)). The interpretation presented and any views expressed are those of the authors and do not in any way reflect the official position of the European Commission.

it was claimed that abolition of quantitative restrictions and tariff barriers had not been enough to tap the full range of static and dynamic gains in efficiency which had been expected to flow from trade liberalization. In the early 1980s, business (the Dekker plan) and then the Commission began to rail against the costs imposed by obstacles to cross-border transactions that sprang from differences in national regulations. Different health and safety requirements required products to be adapted before being placed in partner country markets; duplicated prudential controls discouraged financial service operators from moving into partner country markets; restrictions on providing cross-border road, air transport, or audiovisual services barred cross-border competition. The single market plan and Single European Act (SEA) were fruits of a new consensus between policymakers and businessmen that a true 'common market' required a considerable degree of regulatory approximation (Pelkmans 1980).

2.1.2. The nature of SMP benefits

The case for completing the single market remains largely rooted in traditional Ricardian theory, whereby exploitation of comparative advantage results in all parties/countries being better off. This body of theory also maintains that, under strict simplifying assumptions, trade will result in a convergence of income levels between trading partners. This proposition has allowed trade economists to advocate unqualified trade liberalization without harbouring too many qualms about the consequences, in terms of redistribution, such a policy might bring. In the EU, the scope of integration has been extended to the whole gamut of economic activity—goods, services, and factor of production. These latter extensions might be expected to reinforce the validity of the income equalization proposition.

The neo-classical case for completion of a single market was spiced with more intuitive arguments. Market fragmentation was identified as one of the factors contributing to Europe's slide down the international economic pecking order. The inability of European producers of high technology products to exploit economies of scale was touted as one of the causes for loss of market share. Exploitation of economies of scale was expected to generate one-third of the economic benefits predicted to flow from the single market.

The importance of the single market in fostering competition was less prominent in early discussion on the benefits of single market completion. Greater exposure to cross-border competition, however, can trigger increases in allocational, technical, and dynamic efficiency. The centrality of competition as a driving force behind the benefits of the single market justifies the characterization of competition policy as a handmaiden to the SMP: they are two sides of the same coin.

To conclude (in the words of the 1990 Bangemann communication), the single market is an example of a competitiveness policy *par excellence*. Removal of the targeted trade barriers would free ambitious companies from regulatory and administrative costs associated with cross-border business. The resulting spur to cross-border trade would occur largely at the expense of marginal import substituters in partner countries (trade creation), although it cannot be ruled out that partner country imports displace third

Box 1. Hitch-hiker's guide to the SMP

The Commission White Paper of 1985 established a laundry list of 282 Community legislative acts considered necessary to enhance the free circulation of products, services, capital, and persons. The Single European Act in 1987 provided the decision-making machinery needed to carry this agenda through. The White Paper was subsequently completed by the addition of single market initiatives in telecommunications and energy. Without too much immodesty, the Commission can claim that the single market programme represents the single greatest experiment in 'positive integration' ever undertaken.

- **Products:** in the case of product market integration, the SMP can be regarded as adding the finishing touches to an already advanced framework. The principal actions focused on elimination of technical trade barriers (employing a combination of approximation techniques and the mutual recognition principle), abolition of customs and fiscal frontiers, completion of the common commercial policy, and liberalization of public procurement purchasing.

- **Services:** in the case of service markets, the SMP was a pioneering move into uncharted waters. The formula of the 'single passport' developed in the domain of financial services, whereby operators would be authorized to trade throughout the Community on the basis of (partly harmonized) prudential soundness in the home country, represents a bold attempt to facilitate establishment and/or cross-border provision of services. Far-reaching changes were also introduced in air and road transport, where a web of market access and pricing restrictions were torn down. Driven by technological advances, liberalization of telecommunications services has also gathered momentum (although not in the original White Paper). The SMP has also seen first attempts to break down barriers to establishment of cross-border service provision in audiovisual and gas and electricity markets.

- **Capital:** the SMP also heralded the end of capital market controls for investments of all maturities. This was a necessary counterpart to liberalization of financial services.

- **Labour:** in the field of labour markets, the SMP contented itself with consolidating the rules on the free movement of persons. There was no attempt to replicate the sweeping regulatory reform sought in service, capital, and product markets even though rigidities in the labour market probably contributed most to the EU's unhappy unemployment performance. The heated but largely unproductive debate surrounding the 'social charter' clearly demonstrated the determination of member states to resist any encroachment on their prerogatives in the social/labour market field.

- **Flanking policies:** two complementary policies are singled out for special attention. A strengthening of competition policy was considered necessary to curb any private or public measures aimed at blunting the pro-competition effect of the SMP. The most notable development in this field was the adoption of the Merger Control Regulation. Likewise, fears were expressed that completing the single market would aggravate regional imbalances within the EU. To counter this possibility, resources available to the Structural Funds were doubled and the implementation of these instruments was upgraded.

- **Accession effects:** for Spain and Portugal, the integration effects stemming from the SMP will blend in with similar effects arising from EU accession. Although the mechanisms through which integration effects materialize are similar, the magnitude of the SMP shock will be greater for these countries. The combination of accession and SMP represents a more dramatic regime change.[1]

---

[1] This point is conveyed by Vinals (1990) when he coined the term 'EEC cum 92' shock.

country products.[2] The removal of deadweight costs, the promotion of efficiency, and competition were expected to lower costs and prices and stimulate aggregate demand, thereby boosting overall income and employment. More recent theoretical developments suggested that the combination of more intense competition and increased technical efficiency could boost rates of growth through the following channels:

- increased productivity would attract increased investment until the marginal rate of return had been restored to equality with the marginal cost of capital (the 'medium-term growth bonus');
- endogenous growth effects: recent theoretical contributions emphasize investment in human and knowledge capital as the basis for sustained growth. Trade and competition may, by influencing the set of incentives facing the individual investor, influence the rate this capital is accumulated. These theories incorporate external economies and increasing returns—conditions under which it can no longer be assumed that trade will promote regional convergence.

Empirical analysis of the EU growth record over a long-term perspective lends substance to expectations that integration provides a basis for higher levels of growth than would otherwise be attained (Coe and Moghadam 1993, Italianer 1994). In the specific context of the single market programme, the Commission launched a major study to gain a better understanding of the channels through which abolition of non-tariff barriers could bring economic gains and in measuring these gains. The main focus was on short-term effects of allocation and gains in efficiency associated with a fuller exploitation of economies of scale stemming from the size of the EU markets. The dynamic effects on innovation and technological developments expected to come from the impact of increased competition and market size were supposed to arise over the long term and were, therefore, much more uncertain. This body of research predicted increased income of the order of 4.5–7 per cent of GDP over the long term. This increased income was to be accompanied by 1.8 to 5 million new jobs, depending on whether fiscal policy was contractionary or expansionary. These estimates have coloured much of the subsequent discussion amongst students of trade theory and integration.

2.1.3. *Recent assessment of SMP impact*

In 1997, the European Commission published the results of extensive research which attempted to ascertain if the mechanisms expected to underpin these macro-effects had been activated, and/or whether the expected boost to cross-border transactions had been dampened by the persistence of regulatory or administrative barriers. This research

---

[2] Some caution should be exercised before qualifying this change in trade patterns as trade diversion, as the shift in market share does not arise from any discriminatory change in trade arrangements at the expense of third country producers. Rather, it results from the removal of non-tariff barriers on a non-discriminatory basis, which has the effect of enhancing the price competitiveness of partner country output relative to domestic or third country products.

project also attempted to indicate the effects upon income and employment that might be associated with any observed structural changes.

In very broad terms, this analysis confirms that the effects of greater competitiveness in increasing income have begun to be evident. Defensive or even anti-competitive behaviour, however, is often employed to counter changes in market shares. This defensive behaviour weakens the desire to improve competitiveness, which was expected to be the driving force behind the efficiency and welfare improvements of the SMP. At a macroeconomic level, the impact to date falls considerably short of the 'cost of non-Europe' projections. It is estimated that Community income has been increased by up to 1.5 per cent of GDP while 900,000 jobs have been created. Inflation levels have been kept in check by the SMP (price levels 1.5 per cent lower than they would otherwise have been). Keener competition and increased productivity are the mechanisms which underpin these improvements, with each vector accounting for about half of the estimated macroeconomic impacts. These findings are in keeping with results from independent simulations using a variety of models and methodologies (cf. Gasiorek *et al.* 1992).

The shortfall compared to initial predictions can be attributed to several factors. Several unexpected and unforeseeable developments affected the dynamics of the single market. German reunification, the economic transformation in central and eastern Europe, a globalizing world economy, and the revolution in information technology have substantially altered the configuration of the global economy. The SMP is still in a period of gestation. Market structures and behaviour have not adapted fully to the new regulatory framework and the more contestable configuration of Community markets. Much of the single market legislation, especially in some service markets, did not come into force until 1994/5, and some will not be implemented until after the year 2000. Finally, it is also clear, even when they have been adopted and transposed, that not all the legislative instruments provided for in the SMP are fully effective. In several cases, deficiencies in SMP rules or their enforcement seem to have deterred operators from exploiting new commercial opportunities. To correct these deficiencies, the Commission proposed focusing on improving the administration and effective enforcement of single market rules in its *Action Plan for the Single Market* (European Commission 1997) adopted by the Commission in June 1997.

2.1.4. *Redistributional considerations*

As mentioned above, traditional trade theory allows economics to be sanguine about the redistributional consequences of trade liberalization. Exploitation of comparative advantage and appropriate specialization should pave the way for increased wealth in all participating countries, including those which exploit their advantage in low value-added activities (Neven 1990). Neo-classical growth theory reaches the same conclusion, using different theoretical constructs. In the context of the SMP, the inherent tendency towards shared prosperity should be reinforced by the free movement of investment and portfolio capital. Capital-poor countries can relieve their credit problem by attracting capital from member states with greater capital endowment and fewer opportunities for high return on investment. Cross-border capital flows can also form a package embodying technology transfers or managerial know-how. These considerations suggest that internal market integration is one of the most effective means of fostering economic convergence between participating regions.

In reality, redistributional issues are never very far away from the surface of discussion of economic integration in the Community. In recent years, this discussion has focused heavily on the need for policy intervention to accompany SMP completion, culminating in the adoption of the Delors I package and the subsequent increase in the financial allocation under the Delors II package. Market liberalization, and the consequent reconfiguration of the pattern of (revealed) comparative advantage, may not proceed as smoothly as is suggested by the neo-classical paradigm. Once the existence of structural rigidities, imperfect competition, or economies of scale are admitted, the following redistributional issues arise.

• Within regions, resources will need to be reallocated between sectors as the 'exit' of marginal firms from non-competitive import-substituting sectors must be compensated for by increased employment and activity in other sectors. If this reallocation does not take place, integration could result in 'winners and losers' within the region. The inability of regions to shift resources from one activity to another indicates internal structural rigidities and is not a case against liberalization. Nevertheless, the existence of such rigidities can challenge the assumption that the SMP will increase wealth and jobs (Burniaux and Waelbroeck 1993).

• Between regions/countries. If certain regions prove less successful in reallocating resources away from contracting import-substitution sectors to new areas of activity, they may be, overall, worse off as a result of trade liberalization. A related concern is that, through a process of regional specialization based on comparative advantage, certain regions might find themselves sidelined into low value-adding activities. On the basis of analysis of revealed comparative advantage, Buigues *et al.* (1990) concluded that some of the least favoured Community regions were at risk of being trapped in sectors providing limited prospects for sustained growth. Agglomeration effects could reinforce this polarization of economic activity. The removal of trade barriers could enable producers in these areas to serve distant markets better, to the detriment of indigenous suppliers in these regions.

• Between persons as changing patterns of economic activity may favour demand for certain types of human capital formation over others.

According to this viewpoint, integration in itself would not be enough to bring increased real convergence. A range of other policy actions and instruments would be required to counteract the intrinsic tendency towards widening disparities. This position is cogently argued by the Irish National Economic and Social Council (NESC) in its 1989 report on *Ireland in the European Community*, according to which

there is a formidable list of reasons why advanced economic activity will tend to concentrate in certain regions. Among the factors making for concentration are economies of scale, economies of agglomeration and the division of labour, advantageous labour market characteristics, innovation leadership and external economies associated with the generation of knowledge. . . .

After consideration of all the arguments, our general conclusion must be that the long-run benefits of market completion are likely to be unevenly distributed—with the greatest benefits accruing to regions in which industries with economies of scale and highly innovative sectors are *most prevalent.* . . . Consequently, completion of the internal market should not be expected to narrow the income disparities between regions in the EC, let alone bring about convergence. (NESC 1989: 342–3)

Theoretical work does not provide an overriding case for either proposition. It is, therefore, unsurprising that the 'Cost of non-Europe' research was silent on this issue.[3] This chapter will seek to explore, on the basis of empirical evidence gathered for the Commission's single market review, whether the post-SMP outcome conforms more to the neoclassical predictions or whether it provides any support to the concern that closer market integration would merely aggravate regional imbalances.

The chapter will look first at the channels through which the SMP was expected to deliver its benefits. This review will seek to establish whether trade and investment flows have developed in directions which lend prima facie support to predictions of either a widening or a narrowing of differentials. Later sections of the chapter will focus on (a) changes in sectoral fortunes and (b) geographical distribution of the estimated macroeconomic benefits. For the latter, most of the studies conducted within the framework of the Single Market Review focused on cross-country analyses and only very rarely considered interregional redistribution issues. In the same way, issues related to interpersonal redistribution were largely ignored. They will, nevertheless, be highlighted in the following sections where relevant, in particular when assessing the impact of the single market on industrial restructuring and employment creation in the industry and service sectors.

2.2. Specialization through Trade and Investment

At the beginning, the then EEC was composed of member states with similar industrial structures, productivity levels, and capital/labour ratios, and successive enlargements led to a greater diversification of Europe's industrial fabric. New peripheral member states, with low labour costs and high capital costs, were more specialized in labour-intensive industries with low technological content, while the core countries were increasingly specialized in industrial sectors requiring high technology and skill. This section will, therefore, consider whether the single market programme has accentuated this trend towards industry specialization through greater inter-industry trade (on the basis of comparative advantage), and will also look at the role played by foreign direct investments in this respect.

---

[3] It is perhaps worth quoting the 'conclusion' of the European Economy on this point. 'Difficult as it is to estimate the aggregate gains from market integration, this task is relatively manageable compared to that of forecasting its distribution by country or region. While the latter task has not been attempted, it is worth noting that neither economic theory nor relevant economic history can point to any clear-cut pattern of likely distributional advantage or disadvantage.'

2.2.1. Trade and specialization

For all member states (with the exception of imports into Ireland) the importance of the EU as a source of imports and as a destination for exports has increased in the second half of the 1980s and early 1990s. The share of intra-EU imports in manufacturing has increased on average by 6.7 per cent from 61.2 per cent in 1985 to 67.9 per cent in 1995. For services, the share of intra-EU imports has increased on average by 3.1 per cent points from 46.9 per cent in 1985 to 50.0 per cent in 1995. The increasing share of intra-EU imports and exports is most apparent for Spain and Portugal, which continued to increase their share in overall EC trade after joining the EU. This increase was largely predictable, on the basis of the traditional theoretical arguments, for these countries were fundamentally separated by great differences in factor endowments, technological level, and income per capita from other member states. It is estimated (CEPR 1997) that some 80 per cent of the increase in intra-EU trade can be explained by the direct and pro-competitive effect of the single market measures because many of them resulted in non-discriminatory improvement in market access for all suppliers, regardless of their origins. This increase in intra-EC trade has not been achieved at the expense of trade with third countries, as extra-EU import market share increased by 2.5 per cent between 1991 and 1994 in total manufacturing.

According to traditional theory, the dismantling of non-tariff barriers would lead to greater specialization, each country taking advantage of its comparative advantage. The impact on trade would then lead to increases in inter-industry trade, i.e. trade between industries. However, since the removal of all remaining barriers was also aimed at generating substantial economies of scale and the search for greater product differentiation, the single market could also be expected to increase intra-industry trade, i.e. the simultaneous import and export of similar products. Further differentiation could also be made between intra-industry trade in similar products (horizontal differentiation) or in differentiated products (in terms of price and quality). From a theoretical point of view, the single market would be expected to increase intra-industry trade between the more developed member states, and possibly between the less developed ones, and to increase inter-industry trade between the more developed and less developed member states.

While inter-industry trade can lead to efficiency gains, it also has a significant redistribution impact, with a deeper specialization process and significant adjustment costs. In the case of intra-industry trade, adjustment would take place between producers within the same industry rather than among industries and would lead to greater diversification and lower adjustment costs. The type of trade adjustments associated with the completion of the single market has significant implications for economic cohesion. Has completion of the single market been associated with increased specialization of the southern member states in labour-intensive or low-quality products, or has it increased the quality of their tradable products?

The launching of the single market programme occurred at a time when the Community was undergoing a substantial shift in trade patterns, from inter-industry towards intra-industry trade. While the former represented some 45 per cent of total trade in the

Table 2.1. Share of trade types in intra–EU trade

Country	Share in 1994			Variations from 1987 to 1994		
	Intra-industry trade in similar products	Intra-industry trade in differentiated product	Inter-industry trade	Intra-industry trade in similar products	Intra-industry trade in differentiated product	Inter-industry trade
France	24.1	44.3	31.6	2.8	3.6	−6.4
Germany	20.5	46.9	32.6	1.9	3.4	−5.4
Belgium/Luxembourg	23.3	42.0	34.8	1.6	2.2	−3.8
United Kingdom	16.5	47.9	35.6	−1.9	8.9	−7.0
Netherlands	18.9	41.9	39.3	−0.3	5.1	−4.8
Spain	18.9	35.2	45.9	8.7	3.3	−12.0
Italy	16.2	36.9	46.9	5.8	−3.1	−2.8
Ireland	7.9	34.4	57.7	−0.9	−1.3	2.2
Denmark	8.1	31.9	60.0	−1.1	0.0	1.1
Portugal	7.5	23.9	68.6	3.9	4.8	−8.6
Greece	3.7	10.3	86	0.8	−0.6	−0.2
EC-12	19.2	42.3	38.5	2.0	3.1	−5.1

Source: CEPII and CIREM (1997).

beginning of the 1980s, it only represented 38.5 per cent in 1994. The corresponding rise in intra–industry trade has predominantly been in differentiated products, which could partly be explained by different factors endowment (from less than 35 per cent in the first half of the 1980s to more than 42 per cent in 1994), while intra–industry trade in similar products remained constant (20 per cent) (CEPII and CIREM 1997).

A comparison of the performance of member states shows that the decrease in inter–industry trade has been significant in the original six founding member states, all of which are large traders, and dominant in Spain and Portugal. The corresponding increase in the share of intra–industry trade is essentially due to a boost of two–way trade in vertically differentiated products, except for Italy where the drop in inter–industry trade was smoother and there was a corresponding increase in intra–industry trade essentially in similar products. Denmark and Ireland remain characterized by an inter–industry specialization, partly because Denmark specializes in a limited number of products. Ireland in the late 1980s moved from specializing in traditional labour-intensive sectors into capital-intensive, export-oriented sectors (largely driven by direct investment by multinational corporations [MNCs]). Spain and Portugal also underwent remarkable changes in trade patterns, with their trade structures moving closer to those in more developed countries. In Portugal, the share of intra–EU trade as a percentage of total trade increased only in traditional sectors after 1986. In contrast, Greece's trade structure has changed very little over the last 15 years.

As the previous analysis shows, for all countries intra–industry trade is more important for differentiated products than for similar products. This, therefore, raises the question of the market segment within which member states are positioned. Increase in low or high quality products would suggest a specialization across the quality spectrum and differentiation in terms of R&D and training efforts, internal organization of firms, etc. The north/south difference is even more striking here. Germany and Ireland are in

Bohan, Muylle

Table 2.2. Price/quality structures of exports and imports in intra-EC trade
(1985/6 and 1993/4)

Country	Flow	1985/6			1993/4		
		Down	Medium	High	Down	Medium	High
Belgium	X	17.4	57.8	24.9	18.1	50.0	31.9
	M	17.8	54.8	27.3	19.9	54.2	34.9
Denmark	X	16.4	45.6	38.1	19.8	38.4	41.7
	M	16.2	43.9	40.0	20.8	32.9	46.3
Germany	X	11.9	46.4	41.7	14.0	38.6	47.4
	M	14.0	58.7	27.4	14.2	46.4	39.4
Greece	X	32.8	50.8	16.4	31.0	42.3	26.7
	M	21.2	40.9	38.0	21.5	37.0	41.6
Spain	X	29.3	50.8	19.9	28.9	48.0	23.1
	M	24.0	43.4	32.6	23.8	40.4	35.8
France	X	12.2	54.6	33.2	14.9	45.2	39.9
	M	15.7	54.4	30.0	19.2	44.1	36.7
Ireland	X	19.6	31.1	49.3	21.3	24.9	53.8
	M	27.9	42.2	29.9	28.3	30.3	41.4
Italy	X	26.9	47.1	26.0	28.5	39.4	32.2
	M	10.1	52.2	37.7	15.1	43.7	41.2
Netherlands	X	13.2	64.9	21.9	15.4	50.9	33.7
	M	20.5	52.8	26.7	19.6	45.2	35.2
Portugal	X	37.0	42.2	20.8	34.1	39.6	26.3
	M	21.7	36.4	41.9	22.8	41.0	36.2
UK	X	15.5	51.5	33.0	20.5	39.1	40.5
	M	16.1	44.5	39.4	21.8	36.7	41.6
EC-12	X, M	16.1	52.3	31.6	18.7	42.9	38.4

Source: CEPII and CIREM (1997).

the up-market segment, with more than 50 per cent of Irish exports being products
with unit value exceeding the EC average by at least 15 per cent, which is probably a
consequence of the high level of MNC investment in capital intensive industry. On the
other hand, southern countries are mainly exporting products in the medium and low
range of the price/quality spectrum. Up-market export shares, however, are increasing,
which would suggest a process of in-depth specialization by producers in the high range
of the quality spectrum.

The two most striking phenomena in the development of intra-EC trade since the
mid-80s, the large increase in intra-industry trade and the importance of intra-industry
trade in differentiated products, may also have been associated with other features
than the single market: globalization, increasing economic convergence, or monetary
developments. On the basis of the econometric work done by CEPII, some conclusions
can be drawn about the effects of the SMP on trade patterns. The two main channels by

which the single market appears to have boosted intra-industry trade are the reduction of transaction costs stemming from the cancellation of border formalities and the large increase in foreign direct investment (FDI) and mergers and acquisitions associated with expectation of the completion of the single market. On the other hand, the abolition of non-tariff barriers, which were obstacles to a clear-cut specialization among EU countries, seems to have had a more positive effect on inter-industry trade.

These developments in intra-EU trade have important implications from the point of view of economic cohesion. It is, however, difficult to decide if increased regional cohesion has been the force behind this increase in intra-industry trade and convergence of trade structure or if these trade developments have been induced more by (direct or indirect) single market effects, essentially through location effects.

2.2.2. *Foreign direct investment and specialization*

The second half of the 1980s was characterized by an unprecedented surge in FDI flows both worldwide and at European level. While FDI flows grew fivefold between 1984 and 1990, the European Union progressively became the primary target for foreign investments. The share of FDI flowing into the EU increased from 28.2 per cent of total FDI in 1982–7 to 44.4 per cent in 1991–3. This contrasts with the United States, where the share of worldwide FDI fell from 39.9 per cent in 1982–7 to 10.2 per cent in 1991–3. An increasing proportion of these FDI flows has been investment from member states in other member states. In 1984, intra-EU FDI accounted for 41 per cent of total flows, but this share rose to 60 per cent in 1991–3. All these developments suggest that EU multinational firms considered EU countries more attractive than other locations. The impact of the announcement of the single market, although not the only factor responsible, appears to lie at the heart of the increase in FDI activity in the late 1980s.

This raises the question of whether the single market induced a more substantial surge in FDI or in trade, as the two alternatives for supplying foreign markets. Theoretical analysis could lead to the conclusion that the SMP could induce relatively more trade than FDI in sectors more subject to economies of scale, while FDI would increase relative to trade as a result of the SMP in sectors characterized by knowledge-based assets. Although the trade/FDI ratio has declined since the mid-1980s, the CEPS shows that there are very few causal links between FDI and exports, and the links that do exist indicate a positive relationship.

As for the distribution of FDI between high- and medium-income countries, it was anticipated that FDI would concentrate mainly in large technology-intensive sectors and, therefore, in high-income countries. MNCs, however, in particular of non-EU ownership, would also be inclined towards some concentration in medium technology sectors and in low-cost countries. This could then lead to a larger percentage of FDI going to peripheral countries.

As Table 2.3 shows, the proportion of FDI inflows into the high- and medium-income countries has remained constant over the last eight years. Belgium/Luxembourg and France have performed best since the mid-80s in attracting intra-EU foreign investment,

Table 2.3. Share of FDI inflows and significance of FDI inflows as percentage of GDP for member states

	Share of intra-EU FDI to		Share of extra-EU FDI to		Share of total FDI to		Significance of FDI inflow to GDP	
	1986	1990–3	1986	1990–3	1986	1990–3	1986	1990–3
Belgium/Luxembourg	7	17	2	9	5	14	0.75	4.70
Denmark	0	1	2	2	1	2	0.23	0.89
Germany	9	11	3	5	7	8	0.13	0.37
Greece	1	1	3	0	2	1	0.86	0.64
Spain	17	14	15	9	16	12	1.20	1.75
France	14	15	19	16	16	15	0.38	0.89
Ireland	1	7	0	4	0	6	0.25	9.41
Italy	7	5	−6	7	2	6	0.05	0.40
Netherlands	18	12	13	10	16	11	1.54	2.74
Portugal	1	3	1	2	1	2	0.65	2.64
UK	25	14	47	37	34	23	1.04	1.83
EU-12	100	100	100	100	100	100	0.49	1.17

Source: European Commission (1996).

while the UK and the Netherlands experienced quite a significant decrease in FDI inflows, in particular in extra-EU FDI inflows. The share of the four cohesion countries in FDI inflows has not been substantially altered, remaining broadly constant at around 20 per cent of the total for both intra-EU and extra-EU FDI. Among the cohesion countries, Ireland has been the only country experiencing a surge in inward investment, while Spain has experienced a decrease in the absorption of both intra-EU and extra-EU FDI. This does not, however, preclude any substantial effect on the economies of the other cohesion countries. For instance, substantial growth rates in their inward FDI stocks have been experienced in Spain (128.3 per cent average annual increase over the 1985–90 period) and Portugal (141 per cent average annual increase).

This trend is also confirmed when assessing the impact of FDI inflows on the domestic economy. Irish FDI inflows were worth over 9 per cent of GDP in the period 1990–3 (from 0.25 per cent in 1986), Portuguese 2.6 per cent (from 0.65 per cent). In Portugal, the largest increase in FDI was concentrated in the non tradable sectors, such as financial services, tourism, construction, and public works. Taking advantage of domestic market opportunities was one of the main reasons for inward investment, which would cast doubts on Portugal's ability, as a low-wage country, to attract large inflows of export-oriented FDI. Greece, for its part, seems to have suffered strongly from its lack of satisfactory infrastructure in attracting foreign investment. It is also likely that the 'isolation' or distance effect may have significantly influenced this weak performance.

The extent of the single market impact on FDI flows has been difficult to measure. Other variables, such as taxation or structural funds, may have played a more important role than market integration. A recent econometric analysis (CEPS 1996) suggests that the SMP has been responsible for the increase in FDI targeting the EU of about 200 per cent for UK FDI outflows and 100 per cent for French FDI outflows in 1989. On the other hand, the SMP does not seem to have had any effect on the intensity of Japanese and US investment in the EU. The same study also suggests that FDI is highly responsive to the level of income in the recipient country, and that the influence of income on FDI is much greater than the influence of income on exports. This may help explain the relatively insignificant redistribution impact of SMP-induced FDI increase.

The relative recovery in intra-EU trade has been much slower than the increase in the share of intra-EU FDI flows. This could indicate that trade was already highly integrated within the EU and that the integration of FDI flows has been catching up. However, this difference in the behaviour of trade and investment flows within Europe also reflects the growing pan-European nature of business and the desire of companies to react to increased competitive pressures by establishing a firm presence, not only in their own national market, but also in increasingly important partner country markets.

2.3. Changes in Competition and Efficiency at Sectoral and National Level

Much of the beneficial impact of the SMP was expected to derive from the unshackling of competition. More intense competition was expected to generate gains in efficiency, which would be passed through to consumers in the form of price reductions and increased product diversity. On the down side, increased competition was also expected to result in the exit of inefficient players and in widespread restructuring. This section will present some recent findings from research on the effects of the sectoral and geographical distribution of SMP-induced restructuring. An attempt will be made to examine the extent to which the stepping-up of competition has been spread across the member states and whether the resultant benefits in productivity have helped particular countries and regions (where data is available at regional level).

2.3.1. Competition intensity

The increase in trade level and new entries as a result of the single market programme has entailed a substantial intensification of competition. It is clear from various business surveys that market operators have felt the winds of competition more keenly. As illustrated in Table 2.4, companies have been facing more competition, mainly from national and other EU firms, in their market as a result of the SMP.

This was more apparent in the manufacturing sector than in the service sector. In the manufacturing sector, small firms mainly have seen this increase in competition from domestic firms while larger firms mainly have seen it from other European firms. Firms in the transport equipment and food and beverage sectors have been the most subject to this increase in competition from national and other-EU firms. For firms in the electrical machinery and textile sectors, the single market has been associated with a significant increase in competition from non-EU firms. Much of this increased competition emanates from other EU member states. Firms from peripheral countries (particularly, Spain, Greece, and Ireland) seem to be confronted with a stepping-up of competition from home-country and other EU firms. Italian and UK companies, on the other hand, seem relatively impervious to this increase in competition (the simultaneous devaluation

Table 2.4. Change in competition on the domestic market in recent years

Classification	Manufacturing			Services		
	Increase	No change	Decrease	Increase	No change	Decrease
No. of competitors						
Domestic firms	25	64	11	30	63	7
Other EU owned firms	39	59	2	21	77	2
Non-EU owned firms	25	74	2	9	88	2
Price competition						
Domestic firms	44	51	42	37	60	3
Other EU owned firms	41	55	4	16	81	3
Non-EU owned firms	29	67	4	9	87	3
Quality competition						
Domestic firms	33	64	3	27	69	4
Other EU owned firms	29	69	2	14	83	3
Non-EU owned firms	18	79	3	8	89	3

Source: Eurostat (1997).

of their currencies may have blunted increase in competition from the single market). On the whole, there are no discernible differences between 'peripheral' and 'core' countries in terms of perceived increases in intensity of competition. While large proportions of Spanish, Greek, and Irish producers report increased competition, particularly from other EU countries, German, French and Luxembourger enterprises are equally conscious of increased competition.

The increase in competition seems to have been less strongly perceived in the services sector than in the manufacturing sector (cf. Figs. 2.1 and 2.2). This may be explained partly by the fact that the single market is still very much incomplete in some of the key service sectors. One particular feature is that service companies have felt the increase in competition mainly from domestically owned firms, with the exception of the financial intermediation sector, in which competition has mainly come from other EU and non-EU firms. The essentially local nature of the increased competition in services can be explained by the continuing need for establishment in the local market to overcome information asymmetries, even after regulatory obstacles to cross-border service provision have been diluted (Sapir 1993). Cross-border penetration in services has been achieved by establishing a local presence—with the acquisition of local players the preferred strategy. Community service markets remain 'multi-domestic' rather than exhibiting the relatively advanced degrees of integration evident for manufacturing products. The 'nationality' of companies responsible for more aggressive competition is, therefore, more difficult to ascertain. However, the greater national component of increased competition in services reflects the fact that the lowering of regulatory barriers to entry and competition has, at least in a first stage, been most effective in fostering competition between local players.

The accentuation of competition is also reflected in the squeeze upon price–cost margins. Econometric analysis carried out within the framework of the Single Market

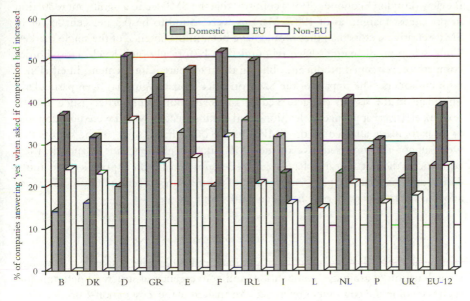

Source: Eurostat (1997).

Fig. 2.1. Perception of increased competition (by origin of new competition): manufacturing

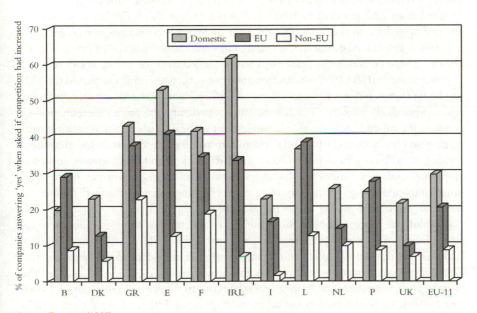

Source: Eurostat (1997).

Fig. 2.2. Perception of increased competition (by origin of new competition): services

Review (London Economics 1997) confirms that the SMP led to a significant reduction in price–cost margins as of 1987. Margins were found to be 0.5 per cent lower in SMP-sensitive sectors than they would have been in the absence of the single market. Thus, while profit margins have rebounded to historically high levels, cross-border competition restrained producers, obliging them to share improvements in efficiency with customers. The impact of the SMP on price–cost margins has been particularly important in the sectors characterized by moderate non-tariff barriers (such as cars, textiles, electrical appliances, televisions) and in those sectors which were not supposed to be particularly affected by the SMP. On the other hand, some of the sectors that were supposedly most sensitive to the SMP (such as pharmaceuticals and electrical equipment) did not appear to have registered a substantial drop in price–cost margins. This is understandable in part because most of the measures affecting these sectors were adopted at a later stage or only had been partly implemented.

2.3.2. Price convergence

In general, the SMP was expected to result in considerable price convergence through a combination of arbitrage, competition, and convergence of structural determinants such as income and consumer preference. An analysis of the 'cost of non-Europe' relied heavily on assumptions of the degree of price convergence in order to arrive at its banner headlines.

In practice, a degree of price convergence has been effected for consumer goods and market services over the period 1985–93. The standard deviation for consumer goods declined from 22.5 per cent in 1985 to 19.6 per cent in 1993. For services, the corresponding reduction was from 33.7 per cent to 28.6 per cent. Price convergence for generally highly traded equipment goods had already attained relatively advanced levels. For energy and construction, price disparities widened over the period under review.

A recent study (DRI 1997) shows that price convergence during the period the SMP was being completed was most pronounced for homogeneous and horizontally differentiated goods. Producers were able to sustain geographical price differentiation on products for which they were able to implement vertical (quality) differentiation strategies, based on investment in R&D and advertising. For producers in less-developed regions, in their capacity as price-takers, the SMP is likely to bring a greater constraint on pricing strategies. Producers of such goods will find themselves under greater pressure to implement single pricing strategies across the single market than will their counterparts at the higher-quality end of the spectrum.

Most of this convergence is the result of a reduction in the difference between price profiles of the new Mediterranean members and the EU-6/9. Although the data analysed does not allow firm conclusions to be reached (only data on the deviation from EU averages were available, and not on absolute price levels), it can be assumed that price levels in the new Mediterranean member countries have been rising from a lower base towards levels observed in the other member states. Higher general rates of inflation in these countries suggest that this interpretation is valid. Such an outcome would, in effect, reduce income for consumers in these countries. Conversely, simulations of the aggregate effect of the SMP find that it has restrained price inflation at levels some 1.5 per cent below those which would have prevailed without the SMP. Less favoured countries have enjoyed these benefits.

However, the analysis also shows that prices, particularly for services, continue to vary. Price levels for services seem to be heavily correlated with GDP. The high level of price differences persisting throughout the Community suggests that a range of structural and behavioural factors remain which offset part of the results expected to ensue from completion of the single market. To this extent, the convergence of prices and other microeconomic conditions across EU member states may prove to a longer process than was expected initially.

2.3.3. The effects of restructuring

Increased competition and the opportunities to make improvements in efficiency have spurred a root-and-branch restructuring of Community industry. The most dramatic changes have been the wave of mergers and acquisitions after the announcement of the SMP. The effects of restructuring have also been reflected in data on firm size (turnover and employment) and in the concentration of market shares.

2.3.3.1. Mergers and acquisitions

In many industries, companies have reacted to the new competitive environment with financial and strategic deals: mergers, acquisitions, and collaborative or cooperative agreements. One of the most striking features of the European business landscape in the late 80s has been the surge in mergers and acquisitions (M&As), both domestic and cross-border. Although not the sole motivation behind efforts by companies to achieve external growth and internal restructuring, the single market has been an important factor behind this dramatic growth in M&As. The increased willingness to engage in merger transactions certainly affects the willingness of companies to restructure early enough to face the new competitive environment created by the SMP. M&As enable companies to adjust promptly to new market conditions. Moreover, M&As were facilitated by the effects of greater capital market liberalization and liquidity, which the SMP ushered in for a number of member states.

Table 2.5. Trends in mergers and acquisitions, 1986–95

	National	Community	International with EU bidder	International with EU target	Total
1986	1,308	162	316	96	1,882
1989	4,344	1,330	698	523	6,895
1992	3,792	968	476	573	5,809
1995	3,492	989	706	693	5,880

Source: London Economics (1996).

Most of the M&As involving European firms (from 20 per cent of the world total in 1985–7 to 43 per cent in 1991–3) took place in domestic markets, suggesting a consolidation of national market structures. Essentially, domestic M&As are a feature of the largest economies in the Union. Domestic M&As in the UK, Germany, and France accounted for some 68 per cent of the total of domestic M&As between 1990 and 1995. Evidence also points to heightened locational advantages for the EU, as the share of M&As accounted for by cross-border acquisitions of EU firms rose from some 14 per cent in 1986 to 28.5 per cent in 1995. French and UK firms have been the most active purchasers of other Community firms, and Germany has become the leading target country for cross-border acquisitions. Looking at the performance in the cohesion countries, Spain has been a target country for some 8 per cent of cross-border M&As while Irish firms have been the most active as purchasers of non-domestic firms.

At the sectoral level, both manufacturing and services have been affected by the wave of mergers and acquisitions. Manufacturing was most active in the run-up to the 1 January 1993 deadline. This may be because the removal of non-tariff barriers could be anticipated for industrial products more easily, but also because most manufacturing sectors were already enjoying the advantages of a large market before the SMP was launched. Sectors such as chemicals, food and drink, and electrical and electronic engineering have undergone the greatest amount of restructuring through M&As in the late 80s and early 90s. The delayed adoption of measures removing barriers in the services sector explains why M&As in this sector only took the lead in 1993–5. Some 70 per cent (against only 63 per cent in manufacturing) of these M&As were domestic, which could be explained in part by a combination of persistent obstacles and structural features restricting competition (such as retail banking, which is characterized by an oligopolistic market structure and high entry costs) as well as by the delay in adopting the measures needed to open these markets to external competition.

2.3.3.2. *Firm size and employment*

Firms in sectors most sensitive to the SMP and having the greatest potential for realizing economies of scale experienced relatively large declines in employment over 1981–91. In most member states, average employment per enterprise declined in both pre- and post-SMP phases. The only exceptions were Spain and Portugal, which witnessed increased average firm size in terms of employment over the period 1986–91. In terms of output per firm, Germany has by far the largest enterprises, followed by the Netherlands, Belgium, France, and the UK. Spain, Greece, and Portugal are at the opposite end of the scale (data problems may be part of the reason). The relative disparity between Germany and its partners in terms of firm size was increased over the period the SMP was implemented (Davies, Lyons, *et al.* 1996).

The above findings are consistent with (unspoken) expectations that the SMP would hasten rationalization or 'downsizing' in sectors which had been partially sheltered from competition by non-tariff barriers. However, that similar trends have been observed across manufacturing industry suggests that there is a latent trend towards reduced staff. At most, the SMP can be regarded as accelerating this process in a number of sectors.

Econometric tests of the relationship between the size of firms as measured by output and the SMP do not find evidence of a significant impact.

2.3.3.3. *Analysis of concentration/market share*

The combination of increased import penetration and restructuring of ownership and production has resulted in an overhaul of market structures, both in terms of increased concentration and in terms of the size of the representative firms in the industry. Analysis of the manufacturing industry (Economists Advisory Group 1997; Davies, Lyons, *et al.* 1996) shows that the impact of the SMP on market structures is heavily influenced by the strategic focus for competition in any given sector.[4]

There are reasons to expect market concentration to decrease as the size of relevant markets increases under the influence of the SMP in sectors characterized by homogeneous goods and technical scale economies. Recent theoretical developments suggest that this relationship between market size and concentration could break down in sectors where large outlays on R&D and advertising are common. In these sectors, concentration could well increase with market size as firms undertake strategic investments to reinforce their market position. Empirical work has confirmed that the SMP has, indeed, been accompanied by such an increase in the degree of market concentration in sectors characterized by this type of strategic behaviour. The clearest effects of the internal market have been in R&D-intensive industries. Furthermore, firm size is positively related to patterns of revealed comparative advantage, so member states with a developed presence in a given sector have tended to see this specialization reinforced.

The effect of cross-border competition on the structure of the services sector has been harder to detect because it has been heavily influenced by the underlying market structure. In situations where competition corresponds roughly to perfect or monopolistic competition (such as road freight transport or distribution), there has been a significant increase in competition as suppliers are willing to jockey for position in partner country markets. This has led to some remarkable gains in productivity. The distribution sector has been characterized by increased vertical integration, with retailers and manufacturers encroaching on functions previously performed by wholesalers. This strategic move to cut unnecessary middlemen out of the loop was often done by manufacturers and retailers acquiring wholesale companies. Along with this increased vertical integration, there is growing concentration at any given stage in the distribution chain. While the SMP should not be regarded as a driver of these changes, it is, nevertheless, thought to be accelerating and facilitating these developments.

In the more regulated sectors, in which national champions were previously dominant (air transport, telecommunications), gains in productivity and efficiency have been less pronounced. Strategic behaviour has probably been more important than the

---

[4] According to Sutton (1991), the critical factor is whether fixed costs are exogenous and decline in relative importance as market size increases or are endogenous, in which case the fixed costs of entry are determined by the strategic behaviour of incumbent firms. In the latter case, a widening of geographical markets need not result in a reduction in concentration levels. Operators may react by increasing strategic investments (R&D or advertising) in order to deter or eliminate new sources of competition. In this case, market expansion might be accompanied by increased concentration.

Table 2.6. Changes in concentration and firm size

	Concentration			Growth in size	
	Four firm concentration ratio at EU level		Mean national change 1986–92	Growth in firm size at national level Firm	Growth in size of industry Industry
	1987	1993	Change		
Conventional Industries	13.2	14.4	1.2	−0.3	10.4	16.0
Adv.-intensive industries	22.3	23.6	1.2	1.3	40.0	24.6
R&D-intensive industries	32.9	38.9	6.0	−1.9	−0.9	13.6
Adv.- & R&D-intensive industries	30.1	32.4	2.3	1.3	18.2	20.4
Unweighted average	20.5	22.8	2.3	−0.1		

The classification used in this table can be explained as follows.

- *'Conventional' industry, in which the competition is production based*: industries mainly associated with processing materials, textile and wood processing industries.
- *Industry in which firms engage in advertising competition*: mainly food, drink, and tobacco sectors. These sectors were characterized by a dramatic decrease in the total number of enterprises and increase in firm size, which easily outstripped the growth in overall national industry size. At EU level, concentration has increased at the same rate as national concentration, suggesting little change in specialization or multinationality. This phenomenon has been most marked in sectors dominated by global and large regional brands (soft drinks, chocolate, and spirits), which leads to the conclusion that the increases in size were mainly achieved to reap economies of scale linked to the creation of strong brand names, new product developments, and heavy up-front advertising investment.
- *Industry in which firms engage in R&D competition*: mainly machinery, instruments telecoms, and transport equipment. This group of industries already had relatively high levels of concentration when the SMP was launched. Average business size tended to decline slightly along with a marginal decline in national concentration. This trend contrasted sharply with the rapid increase in EU concentration as a result of the large number of cross-border mergers and acquisitions that the leading operators have undertaken since the mid-80s to spread their large up-front fixed R&D costs across the Community.
- *Industry in which firms engage in both advertising and R&D competition*: pharmaceuticals, consumer durables (cars, domestic electrical appliances). Concentration in these sectors is a world-wide phenomenon and predates the launching of the SMP. As a result, concentration at national and EU level has drifted up only slightly. There is only limited evidence that the distribution of company sizes has shifted in favour of larger firms. However, average industry size grew substantially.

Source: Economists Advisory Group (1997) and European Commission (1996).

SMP in determining outcome. In sectors such as air transport, incumbent dominant suppliers have not yet engaged in an all-out onslaught on each other's markets. Liberalization of the air transport sector has been accompanied by a limited decrease in route concentration; the share of routes with one or two carriers continues to account for more than 50 per cent of all routes. Companies preferred to concentrate on new products and services (for instance, through an increase in the number of destinations served non-stop) and on their pricing strategy. The overall impact on productivity has been achieved mainly through reduction in the number of staff.

2.3.4. *Productivity*

The overhaul of market structures and the intensification of competition have helped EU operators increase productivity. Real labour productivity has improved most markedly in those sectors which are most sensitive to the single market, suggesting that the SMP has played some causal role. In the post–SMP period, firms in single market sensitive sectors outperformed those in non–sensitive sectors in terms of improvement of labour productivity; 14 per cent increase in average labour productivity for the former as opposed to 8 per cent for the latter (Economists Advisory Group 1997). This marks a reversal of the pre–SMP situation, in which productivity growth in SMP sensitive sectors lagged behind that observed elsewhere. Although it is difficult to draw conclusions from the limited evidence we have on the causal link with the SMP, most of the improvements in productivity seem to be elimination of technical inefficiencies (X–inefficiency) under the pressure of keener competition. Exploitation of economies of scale has not delivered the substantial improvements in efficiency anticipated (equivalent to one–third of the overall welfare improvements). The proposition that the single market was needed to attain minimum levels of technical scale has been shown to be false.

The effects upon productivity of the SMP are not limited to the first–round static improvements in efficiency. In fact, sectoral research suggests that indirect effects, mediated through the SMP–induced changes in upstream or downstream markets, may have been more important in driving gains in efficiency. For example, operating conditions in the telecommunications equipment market have been more profoundly affected by changes in the regulatory environment for telecom services (Analysis 1997). Increased commercial pressures on service operators have forced them to redefine cosy supply relationships with established national suppliers and obliged producers to compete on the basis of price and quality. Similarly, advertising and distribution systems have both been pulled by the desire of producers to gain access in partner country markets.

Examination of country performance over the period 1985–95 shows the less favoured member states at the top of the league table, although core regions such as Germany record a strong performance. When measured in terms of real unit labour costs, the less favoured regions have experienced a larger relative decline over the period than the more prosperous member states. This result is partly explained by exchange rate movements, which have compensated for higher than average nominal–wage growth in some of the less favoured regions (Greece, Spain, Portugal).

There is tentative evidence of convergence of sectoral productivity across the member states (Cambridge Econometrics 1997a). This is evident primarily in a number of traditional, low–value–added sectors relatively sensitive to the SMP (e.g. energy, food and beverages, textiles, and clothing). The convergence seems to be explained primarily by 'catch–up' in the less favoured regions and stagnant productivity performance in the core regions. In a number of engineering industries (electrical goods, transport equipment, agricultural machinery) productivity growth in the richer countries has been markedly higher in the post–SMP phase. While this result is tentative, it could be interpreted as support for the proposition that the less favoured regions are consolidating their comparative advantage in activities with limited growth prospects.

At a more meso/macro–level, breaking GDP growth into its different components (labour accumulation, capital accumulation, or efficiency gains as measured by total

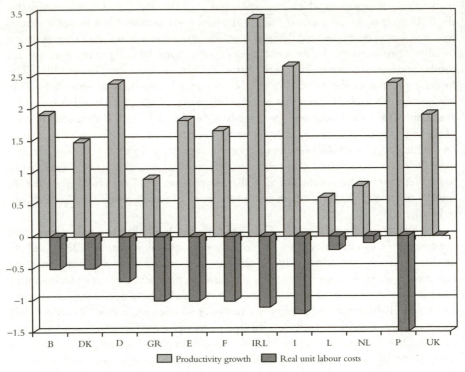

Fig. 2.3. Measures of productivity and competitiveness (annual changes 1985–95)

Table 2.7. Components of real GDP growth in EU-12, 1985–95

	GDP growth	GDP growth due to labour	GDP growth due to capital	GDP growth due to technical progress (TFP)
B	2.19	0.24	0.88	1.08
DK	1.74	−0.02	0.26	1.49
D	2.58	0.45	0.82	1.30
GR	1.54	0.56	0.99	−0.01
E	2.93	0.89	1.36	0.68
F	2.16	0.20	0.90	1.07
IRL	4.75	0.87	0.77	3.11
I	2.05	−0.12	0.76	1.41
L	3.44	1.78	1.46	0.20
NL	2.52	0.80	0.98	0.75
P	3.11	0.21	1.66	1.25
UK	2.27	0.17	0.78	1.31
EU–12	2.35	0.30	0.85	1.19

Source: European Commission 1996.

factor productivity) provides some interesting insights. Spanish and Portuguese growth seems to be more dependent on capital accumulation, which would tally with the large capital inflows recorded over the period. Irish growth seems to be driven by efficiency gains. In Greece, no gains in efficiency whatsoever are evident, which explains Greece's modest growth rates.

2.3.4.1. Competition and efficiency conclusions

Ex ante analysis of the impact of the single market predicted that increased competitive pressures would encourage the restructuring of companies, lead to reallocation, and creative destruction. The sometimes patchy but nevertheless consistent evidence presented above suggests that increased trade and investment contingent on completion of the SMP have, indeed, stimulated restructuring and rationalization. Confronted with the challenges of a larger market and an increase in the number of competitors, companies have been forced to adapt their strategies through internal or external adjustments, the latter implemented primarily through mergers and acquisitions (M&As) both at national and Community level. This restructuring has affected the vast majority of industrial and services sectors sensitive to the single market, with repercussions upstream and downstream in all industrial sectors. The intensity and timing of the restructuring have significantly differed between manufacturing and services sectors. Most industrial sectors were already experiencing the virtues of large market, while services were hampered by well-entrenched national restrictions. Moreover, differences in the timing of the adoption of single market measures have played a role. For instance, measures aiming at liberalizing the services sectors were implemented after 1993.

This restructuring process has finally been accompanied by a shift in patterns of job creation. As expected, increased competition in the manufacturing sector forced many companies to streamline activities and strengthen efficiency, which resulted in some rationalizations and closings and negatively effected overall employment. These changes have been accompanied by impressive improvements in productivity, which do not seem to have been driven by the exploitation of technical scale economies. On the other hand, measures aimed at removing restrictions on the cross-border provision of services and at facilitating establishment in local markets favoured the creation of new markets and new forms of service supply. They also encouraged new entrants and stimulated business and consumer demand, thereby increasing the demand for labour in some of these sectors.

On the basis of the available evidence, the less favoured regions seem to have participated fully in this process. Support for this contention derives primarily from evidence relating to price convergence and the perception of increased competition, particularly emanating from other EU member states, indicating that the SMP has increased cross-border competition considerably. Data on aggregate productivity does not indicate that the less favoured regions are faced with a self-perpetuating productivity gap of the type consistent with effects of strong agglomeration or externality. The conclusions, however, are not solidly enough based to calm fears of productivity patterns consistent with specialization along comparative advantage. A development model relying heavily on comparative advantage would show certain risks for the less favoured regions.

2.4. Macroeconomic Effects

This section will begin by examining developments in employment indicators at sectoral/national level. This will be followed by an analysis of national growth performances in the period following the launch of the SMP. This analysis, although not capturing the specific SMP contribution to growth, is, nevertheless, highly instructive. In section 2.4.3, results of simulations designed to isolate the impact of the SMP on GDP, employment, and other macro-variables are presented.

2.4.1. Employment

This important restructuring of the European economy has been accompanied by diverging patterns in firms and industry size between and within the manufacturing and services sectors. In particular, the single market is considered to have led to a loss of jobs in the manufacturing sector that has been more than compensated for by the creation of new jobs in the services sector. The simulations run by Cambridge Econometrics for the manufacturing industry indicate that the SMP led to an overall decrease in the number of jobs in manufacturing of 0.5 per cent. The study also concludes that the number of jobs in manufacturing has increased in Ireland, Spain, and Portugal while in West Germany, the Netherlands, and Greece the number of jobs in manufacturing has decreased. In general, the impact on employment across all sectors (including services) in the higher-costs countries is more positive than it is for the manufacturing sector alone, suggesting that the SMP has accelerated structural change towards services. Within the manufacturing sector, rationalization by producers of rubber and plastic products, electrical goods, and transport equipment has been offset by the creation of new jobs with producers of ferrous and non-ferrous metal products, textile, clothing, and footwear.

As noted above, this loss has been more than offset by employment creation in the services sectors. *New forms of supplying services*, such as in banking with the development of 'bancassurance', are emerging. *New markets*, such as in the telecom sector (development of mobile services) and the distribution sector (with the growth of logistic companies after the liberalization of road transport regulations and the elimination of border controls), are being created. *New companies are being established and efficiency is being increased* (as in air transport). *Business and consumer demand* are being stimulated, as is evident by the increase of passenger transport (20 per cent), with positive knock-on effects on the tourism sector by the liberalization of air transport.

The SMP contribution to the number of jobs in the service sector has been felt mainly in transport, construction, business, and personal services. Telecommunications and financial services have experienced a slight reduction in the number of jobs because of the SMP, as rapid growth in productivity and rationalization has resulted in the shedding of jobs. It is precisely in these sectors, however, that the SMP is least advanced. That the full effects of integration have not been felt is encouraging, because jobs probably will be created as a consequence of the complete elimination of barriers to entry. But most labour market rigidities are also in these sectors, suggesting that increased flexibility of the labour market would make an overall increase in jobs more likely as a result of further market liberalization.

Table 2.8. Impact of SMP on EU employment by country

	1989		1991		1993	
	Manufacturing	Total	Manufacturing	Total	Manufacturing	Total
Belgium	0.05	0.37	0.25	2.12	0.76	6.02
Denmark	−0.43	−0.07	−1.24	−0.16	−0.77	0.14
Germany	−0.07	0.11	−2.73	−0.07	−2.51	1.16
Spain	0.21	0.04	1.08	0.27	1.52	0.53
France	−0.01	0.00	0.00	−0.01	0.02	−0.25
Ireland	0.38	0.08	2.33	0.44	5.11	0.98
Italy	−0.08	0.02	−0.33	0.18	−1.04	0.30
Luxembourg	−0.22	−0.14	−1.17	−0.71	−2.67	−2.18
Netherlands	−0.26	−0.10	−0.54	−0.23	−1.89	−0.32
Portugal	0.08	0.01	0.31	0.08	1.54	0.87
United Kingdom	−0.02	−0.07	0.08	−0.29	0.76	−0.67
Total	−0.03	0.02	−0.77	0.04	−0.53	0.38

Source: Cambridge Econometrics (1997a).

Table 2.9. Trend growth in employment in selected regions (1987–93)

	1975–87	1987–93
Objective 1	−0.15	0.69
Non–objective 1 regions	0.05	0.65
Objective 2	−0.90	1.46
Non–objective 2	0.11	0.58
Agriculture	0.12	0.54
Manufacturing	0.03	0.94
Services	0.00	0.64
Border	−0.08	0.88
Interior	0.08	0.52
EU–12	0.02	0.66

Source: Cambridge Econometrics (1997b).

Turning attention to the employment performance of the EU's assisted regions, it emerges that Objective 1 regions recorded an upturn. Net annual loss in jobs (−0.2 per cent p.a.) in the pre-1987 period was transformed into annual growth in the number of jobs (0.7 per cent) for the period 1987–93. This contrasts favourably with employment growth of 0.65 per cent in other regions. The increase in the number of jobs in the border regions is even more noteworthy. Objective 2 regions registered a worsening of their output performance per capita along with an increased number of jobs. This apparent paradox can be explained by the diversification of these regions away from concentration in declining industrial activities towards increased sectoral specialization.

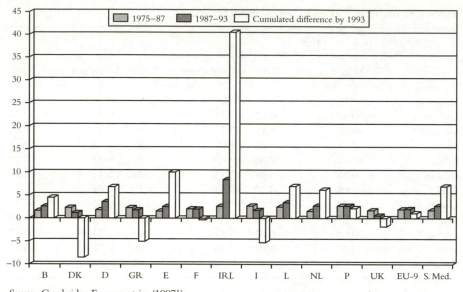

Source: Cambridge Econometrics (1997*b*).

Fig. 2.4. GVA growth rates after 1987 compared with 1975–87 trend

2.4.2. Eyeballing GDP data

When output performance is examined on a country-by-country basis, the four cohesion countries are seen to have recorded the most impressive performance when compared to their pre-SMP experience. Gross value added (GVA) in Spain, Portugal and Greece increased by 7 per cent GDP compared to the levels they would have attained if trends recorded in the pre-87 period had continued. The turn-around for Ireland has been even more remarkable. Ireland achieved a cumulated increase in total GVA of 40 per cent of GDP over the baseline projection based on the continuation of pre-87 trends.

On the basis of the very limited evidence available, it appears that the SMP has not engendered any significant convergence between regions within any member state. Increased convergence on the EU mean reflects convergence of national averages, while the gulf between the richest and poorest regions of the EU remains as pronounced as ever. Data is available on a more desegregated level for Spain and Italy. In the case of Italy, the Mezzogiorno fared even more poorly than northern Italy over the period concerned. While the rate of GVA growth in northern Italy dropped from 2.63 per cent p.a. to 1.75 per cent for the period 1987–93 (amounting to a cumulated loss of 4.73 per cent of GVA compared to the baseline trend), the Mezzogiorno suffered even more, dropping from 2.84 per cent during the pre-SMP period to 1.6 per cent p.a. after 1987. This indicates widening disparities in Italy.

Table 2.10. Trend growth in GVA per capita (1975–93)

	1975–87	1987–93
Objective 1	1.71	2.25
Non–objective 1 regions	1.72	1.50
Objective 2	1.21	1.16
Non–objective 2 regions	1.71	1.68
Agriculture	2.01	1.89
Manufacturing	1.74	1.79
Services	1.62	1.42
Border	1.75	2.04
Interior	1.60	1.36
EU–12	1.66	1.64

The situation in Spain, where the SMP period has been accompanied by stronger GVA growth in both assisted and non-assisted Spanish regions, is in direct contrast. The increase in GVA growth in both cases was on the order of 1.05 per cent p.a. Objective 1 Spanish regions maintained a slightly superior growth performance in the pre-SMP period, which has allowed for a minor reduction in GVA disparities.

Analysis of output trends (measured by GVA per capita) show the less favoured regions performing better (2.3 per cent p.a.) in the post-SMP period than in the pre-1987 period (1.7 per cent). This contrasts with deterioration in the performance of other regions in the period after the launch of the SMP when compared to output trends in the period before the SMP. The combination of enhanced performance in the Objective 1 regions and decline in their richer counterparts has been reflected in marked convergence.

2.4.3. Isolating the effects of the SMP[5]

The mere observation of increased growth and convergence cannot be credited to the SMP solely on the grounds of temporal coincidence (by the same reasoning, the SMP would be held responsible for the worsening economic performance in non-Objective 1 regions). Doomsday predictions that poorer regions would be left further and further behind have not been borne out. More sophisticated analysis has been undertaken in

---

[5] It is important to make one clarification about the results presented in this section. As opposed to previous sections, which charted actual trade and investment flows, this stage of the analysis is based on *estimates* of the effects upon employment and growth. These estimates have been made on the basis of the changes observed in the effects of trade barriers, intensified competition, and intensity that have been occasioned by the SMP. The data sets presented here are, therefore, a relatively unusual beast—simulation results where changes in the structural parameters of the models are based on *ex post* observation (not true for productivity changes).

an attempt to identify what the SMP has contributed to employment creation and welfare over the period since 1985. These simulations compared the results of a model calibrated to developments observed since 1985 (the 'monde') with another model containing features of a fragmented market, such as non-tariff barriers, X-inefficiencies, and market segmentation (the 'anti-monde'). The difference between the two scenarios shows the benefits of completing the single market.

2.4.3.1. *CGE simulations*

The first set of results were obtained from a computable general equilibrium (CGE) model (National Technical University of Athens 1997), according to which aggregate EU GDP was 1.1–1.5 per cent above the level which would have prevailed in the absence of the SMP and some 300,000–600,000 new jobs had been created. This methodology points to large increases in investment and intra-EU trade (over 4–5 per cent higher), which, in turn, substantially influence competition and efficiency and underpin a permanent rise in total factor productivity. The model also allows for endogenous gains in efficiency related to increased product diversity. These effects continue to lend impetus to growth, which reaches 2.4 per cent of GDP by the time a long-run steady state is achieved (estimated 2010).

Whatever the limitations of conducting such simulations at EU-level, they are greater when such simulations are attempted at member state level. While relatively robust results can be obtained for the EU on the basis of aggregate data, national estimates are much more sensitive to slight changes in model specification. Nevertheless, results from CGE simulations at national level show that all countries have increases in private consumption, GDP, investment, trade, and employment as a result of the SMP. The single market has a more pronounced effect upon small open economies than upon their larger brethren. This can be explained by the proportionately greater gains in efficiency possible from taking advantage of unexploited scale economies. The small country effect generally holds true for the peripheral countries. However, the benefits to the peripheral countries are further conditioned by assumptions regarding the degree to which trade flows are restricted by the current account constraint. If this constraint is relaxed, the benefits the SMP brings to the peripheral countries are increased substantially. Even if the current account is held constant, Spain, Portugal, and Ireland are found to enjoy benefits in excess of the EU average. It is important to emphasize that these results are very much model-dependent. Nonetheless, other CGE simulations (Gasiorek *et al.* 1992) also find that small peripheral countries stand to benefit most from the single market (in excess of 2 per cent), compared to long-run welfare changes of approximately 1 per cent in the core member states.

2.4.3.2. *Macroeconometric simulations: EU-wide simulations*

Estimates of the effects of the single market were also obtained by using a macroeconometric model (QUEST II), which is better designed to pick up changes in macrovariables such as income and employment. The downside is that it is more difficult to replicate the initial effects of an essentially microeconomic adjustment in such a model and a certain arbitrariness arises in modelling the effects of the SMP impacts. This simulation indicates that GDP was increased by 1.5 per cent as a result of the SMP while 900,000 jobs were created in comparison with the anti-monde. A breakdown of the geographical distribution of these changes is not available.

2.4.3.3. *Macroeconometric simulations: simulations for the four cohesion countries*

To complement these findings, simulations were carried out for each of the four cohesion countries based on a single macroeconometric model (ESRI 1997). This analysis suggests that the first-round effects of the SMP vary across the member states depending on their sectoral profile. Ireland is the only country which enjoys a favourable balance between SMP sensitive sectors where it has a comparative advantage and those where it is expected to suffer as a result of market integration. The converse is true for Greece and, to a lesser extent, Spain and Portugal. However, the SMP is thought to significantly enhance the attractiveness of the Iberian countries as a location for investment, although it is not clear that the increased FDI inflows into these countries should be attributed to the SMP. A third source of benefit for these countries arises from the greater integration of the peripheral economies into the Community economy, which increases the effects of demand transmission from the core.

In the case of Ireland, the combination of the three effects (all positive) indicates an addition of 9 per cent to GDP by the year 2010. If it is accepted that FDI is driven by the single market, then it can also be expected to have very strong positive effects upon Portugal (11.5 per cent of GDP) and Spain (9 per cent) by the year 2010. If FDI is not regarded as a result of the single market, the contribution to Portuguese GDP is reduced to 7.5 per cent. For Spain, if FDI is considered as independent of the single market, then the SMP has no net impact. Greece registers almost subliminal effects from the SMP, irrespective of whether or not FDI is regarded as a vehicle for transmitting effects of the single market.

These exercises were also used to examine the interplay between Structural Fund expenditure and completion of the single market. Structural Fund assistance will amplify the impact of the SMP through its immediate demand-side effects, but also through a longer term supply-side contribution. Eliminating infrastructural bottlenecks, reducing the costs of peripherality, upgrading human capital, and creating externalities between firms will all help the beneficiary regions harness the potential of the SMP. When both Structural Funds and the SMP are allowed for (assuming that FDI inflows can be ascribed to the SMP), Portugal emerges as the country registering the most impressive gains: on the order of 23 per cent of GDP by 2010. Half of this effect is due to the SMP and half to Structural Fund assistance. Ireland enjoys a GDP increase of 11 per cent and Spanish GDP increases by 12.6 per cent. In these countries, the SMP is held to be responsible for three-quarters of the recorded improvements. Greek GDP gains of 7.5 per cent are explained entirely by Structural Fund assistance. The difference in the relative importance of the Structural Funds can be attributed to differences in the level of per capita assistance, which is assumed to be kept at the same levels in the period up to 2010. The interesting feature of these simulations is that Structural Fund expenditure does not seem to alter significantly the magnitude of the benefits flowing from the SMP. Modelling the impact of Structural Fund assistance in the absence of the SMP results in much smaller effects upon GDP (with the exception of Greece). This suggests that if there is a multiplier effect between Structural Funds and the SMP: it only seems to run from the latter to the former.

2.5. Conclusions

The worst-case scenario of an ever-widening chasm between 'haves' and 'have-nots' has not materialized. The poorer member states have generally tended to fare better than the core regions with the establishment of the single market.

It is difficult to apportion the share of this improved convergence due to the various contributing factors such as Structural Fund expenditure, the single market, and/or technological developments reducing the cost of geographical isolation. The results of different simulations reported above suggest that the SMP has made a substantial and distinct contribution to improving economic performance in at least three of the four cohesion countries.

While it is, perhaps, scientifically appealing to believe that the different factors enumerated above have made distinct contributions to economic performance, and to convergence in particular, it is important to take account of the interaction between the different developments. The combination of Structural Fund assistance, exogenous improvements in communications and logistics, and the SMP have created a potential for development based on firm-led growth in the less favoured regions. The extent of this potential has varied across member states depending on their positioning in the sectors most affected by new trade and investment opportunities.

While the SMP has been an important catalyst for overhauling outmoded systems of service and product market regulation, national policy has had greater influence on economic performance over the period under review. This is particularly true of macroeconomic policy, for which stability-oriented policies in Ireland, Portugal, and Spain have fostered investor confidence. Regulatory reform at national level, however, has played an equally important role. This is particularly so for labour market regulation, which is largely off limits for Community policymakers. National labour market structures are critical in ensuring that resources are quickly redeployed between sectors contracting and expanding under the influence of the SMP. While Spain has traditionally suffered from labour market rules which kept official unemployment at very high rates, belated attention to these rigidities has allowed robust economic growth to be reflected in a dramatic fall in this indicator. In Ireland and Portugal, wage bargaining processes that keep a lid on wage inflation have been key elements in sustaining growth in these countries. The far from earth-shattering conclusion is that while the SMP imposes new constraints upon national policymakers and is an important force for more growth-compatible regulation, it is no substitute for enlightened and effective management at national level.

It would, therefore, be incorrect to view the SMP as holding out the same potential benefits to all the disadvantaged regions. By a combination of fortuitous circumstance and appropriate internal policymaking, some of the poorer regions may reap bigger benefits from the SMP than their counterparts.

References

Analysis (1997). *Telecommunication Equipments. The Single Market Review*, Subseries I, vol. 8.

Buigues, P., Ilzkowitz, F., and Lebrun, J. F. (1990). *The Impact of the Internal Market by Industrial Sector: The Challenge for the Member States. European Economy*, special ed. Luxembourg: European Commission.

Burniaux, J-M. and Waelbroeck, J. (1993). *Effects of Firm Closures on Employment: Is the Single European Market a Shock of the Third Kind?* (mimeo) Université Libre de Bruxelles.

Cambridge Econometrics (1997*a*). *Employment, Trade and Labour Costs in Manufacturing. The Single Market Review*, Subseries VI, vol. 4.

—— (1997*b*). *Regional Growth and Convergence. The Single Market Review*, Subseries VI, vol. 1.

CEPII and CIREM (1997). *Trade Patterns Inside the Single Market. The Single Market Review*, Subseries IV, vol. 2.

CEPR (1997). *Trade Creation and Trade Diversion. The Single Market Review*, Subseries IV, vol, 3.

CEPS (1996). *The Determinants of Foreign Direct Investment Flows in Europe and the Impact of the Single Market*. Paris.

Coe, D. T. and Moghadam, R. (1993). *Capital and Trade as Engines of Growth in France*. IMF Staff Paper, vol. 40, no. 3.

Davies, S., Lyons, B., *et al.* (1996). *Industrial Organization in the European Union: Structure, Strategy and Competitive Mechanism*. Oxford: Clarendon Press.

DRI (1997). *Price Competition and Convergence. The Single Market Review*, Subseries V, vol. 1.

Economists Advisory Group (1997). *Economies of Scale. The Single Market Review*, Subseries V, vol. 4.

ESRI (1997). *The Cases of Greece, Spain, Ireland and Portugal. The Single Market Review*, Subseries VI, vol. 2.

European Commission (1996). *Economic evaluation of the internal market. European Economy* no. 4.

—— (1997). *Action Plan for the Single Market: Communication of the Commission to the European Council*. CSE (97) 1 final, 4 June.

Eurostat (1997). *Results of the Business Survey. The Single Market Review*, Subseries VI, vol. 5.

Gasiorek, M., Smith, A., and Venables, A. (1992). *1992 Trade and Welfare: A General Equilibrium Model*. CEPR Discussion Paper no. 672.

Italianer, A. (1994). Whither the gains from European economic integration? *Revue Économique*, 3: 689–702.

London Economics (1997). *Competition Issues. The Single Market Review*, Subseries V, vol, 3.

National Economic and Social Council (1989). *Ireland in the European Community: Performance, Prospects and Strategy*. Dublin: NESC.

National Technical University of Athens (1997). *Aggregate Results of the Single Market Programme. The Single Market Review*, Subseries VI, vol. 5.

Neven, D. (1990). EEC integration towards 1992: some distributional aspects. *Economic Policy* 10: 13–62.

60   *Bohan, Muylle*

Pelkmans, J. (1980). Economic theories of integration revisited, *Journal of Common Market Studies* 18(4): 333–54.

Sapir, A. (1993). Sectoral Dimension in Services Market and European Integration. *European Economy* no. 3.

Sutton, J. (1991). *Sunk Costs and Market Structure: Price Competition, Advertising and the Evolution of Concentration*. Cambridge, Mass.: MIT Press.

Viñals, J. *et al.* (1990). Spain and the 'EEC cum 1992' shock. In C. Bliss and J. Braga de Macedo (eds.), *Unity with Diversity in the European Economy*. Cambridge: Cambridge University Press/Centre for Policy Research.

3

External Trade Policy

ROBERT C. HINE AND PIER CARLO PADOAN

3.1. Introduction

External trade has a large and expanding influence on European economic activity. Foreign markets absorb almost a tenth of EC goods output. They are major sources of competitive stimulus and technical innovation, and provide crucial supplies of energy and raw materials. Within the European economy, however, the influence of external trade is uneven. For institutional and other reasons, there are marked differences in the extent to which the various sectors of the economy are exposed to import and export competition. Moreover, sectors vary in their ability to respond to externally induced pressures for change and adaptation. Consequently, changes in external trade flows have disparate effects across sectors and social groups and hence on social cohesion. Furthermore, because economic activity in the EC is also spatially diverse, trade developments affect regional as well as social cohesion. These trade influences are subject to modification by governments through trade policy. Instruments such as import quotas and tariffs are used to regulate and manipulate the impact which trade has on the domestic economy. Thus, trade policy is potentially relevant to cohesion, and the aim of this chapter is to explore the nature and extent of this in the case of the EC.

The Treaty of Rome calls for a common trade policy in the EC and, helped recently by the Internal Market programme, uniform trade rules and measures are now in operation in most areas. The Common Commercial Policy (CCP) utilizes a full range of trade policy instruments, including the more controversial aspects such as anti-dumping measures. The EC engages collectively in bilateral and multilateral commercial diplomacy and, as befits the combined economic strength of the member countries, is a major player in world trade institutions. Trade policy is the most developed aspect of EC foreign policy and the CCP has a combination of political and economic objectives, including the strengthening of social and regional cohesion.

Though strengthening cohesion is a broad objective of EC trade policy, trade policy instruments may be very imperfect devices for achieving this. For example, the imposition of a tariff might transfer income to a disadvantaged group of producers which in some circumstances could be seen as improving social cohesion. However, in the process of income redistribution the tariff would also generate production and consumption inefficiencies—a deadweight loss—which might be avoided by other redistributive mechanisms. In general, the most efficient policy will be that which intervenes as closely as possible to the source of the problem which is being tackled. Cohesion problems are outcomes of complex processes, but often are linked to difficulties in responding to market pressures for change. This suggests that in general, non-trade instruments are likely to be more efficient since they can be targeted more accurately at causes rather than symptoms of such problems. Of course, superior instruments may, for some reason, not be available, in which case trade interventions may be regarded as a useful but imperfect substitute. It is important also to recognize that the impact of trade policy on cohesion is often a side-effect when the main objective of the policy lies elsewhere. A free trade agreement designed to cement political ties with a neighbouring country, for example, may also have significant implications for regional and social cohesion within the EC. The aim of this chapter is, therefore, to assess the effects of European trade policies on cohesion, whether deliberate or incidental.

The impact of trade policy on cohesion is a particularly sensitive issue at the present time. One reason for this is the recognition of a growing interdependence of the world's economies through trade and investment linkages. This has generated fears that 'globalization' might bring benefits to certain groups and regions at the expense of others. Another cause for concern is that, for mainly political reasons, the EC is extending and deepening its network of trade preferences, especially in central and eastern Europe, with possibly adverse cohesion consequences within the EC. In discussing these and other issues, this chapter is divided into two separate parts. The first part, by Robert C. Hine, discusses the nature of EC external trade policy, the effects of EC trade and trade policy upon social cohesion, the effects of EC trade policy on regional cohesion, and then the effects upon cohesion of trade liberalization through the Uruguay Round and the extension of trade preferences to the central and eastern European countries. The second part, by Pier Carlo Padoan, analyses the sensitive sectors of textiles and clothing, steel, cars, and electronics and presents a general assessment of the four cohesion countries, Spain, Portugal, Greece, and Ireland.

3.2. Part One: The Effects of Trade Policy on Social and Regional Cohesion in the EU

3.2.1. *The external trade policy of the European Community*

Under the common trade policy, the EC has established a Common Customs Tariff (CCT) and other common trade policy instruments such as anti-dumping measures and safeguards (see Box 1). Trade agreements with foreign governments are negotiated jointly through the offices of the Commission, overseen by a committee of member states. Decision making power rests finally with the Council of Ministers. The articulation of cohesion and other objectives into policy action depends also on the ability of affected interest groups to bring pressure to bear on the Community decision-making process.

The most notable aspects of the trade policy for cohesion can be summarized as follows. First, most EC industries receive little protection from tariffs and quotas—these have been progressively reduced and in some cases eliminated through multilateral

Box 1. Summary of EC trade measures

Tariffs

- generally low (averaging 6 per cent in 1995) on manufactured products.
- but some 'sensitive' products carry tariffs of 10 per cent or more (especially food, clothing, and textiles but also leather and footwear, glassware, certain base metal articles, paper products, certain types of motor vehicles, microprocessors, and radio and television sets).
- high nominal tariffs are often reinforced by an escalation of tariffs with the degree of processing.
- tariffs on agricultural products are high and the protective effect is reinforced by compensatory payments to EC farmers.
- extensive network of tariff preferences.

Quantitative restrictions

- the IM programme resulted in the elimination of a large number of residual, national QRs and the transformation of EC trade arrangements with the Central and East European countries (CEECs) which before 1989 had made heavy use of QRs.
- in the clothing and textile sector under the MFA (MultiFibre Arrangement) quotas have been combined with high tariffs to restrict severely imports from developing countries.

Voluntary export restraints

- have affected imports of some labour-intensive products such as footwear but have mainly been applied on more sophisticated manufactured products such as Japanese motor cars, video tape recorders, fork lift trucks, and ball bearings.
- the share of EC imports affected by VERs has been estimated at 6 per cent in 1984 (Finger and Olechowski 1987) and 10 per cent in the mid-1980s (Kostecki 1987).

Anti-dumping measures

- based on the GATT code, as revised in the Uruguay Round.
- about 150 EC measures in force in recent years, affecting imports valued at 1.8 billion ecus (Schuknecht 1992).
- directed especially at imports of processed materials and chemical elements from China and other low-wage economies, iron and steel products notably from Eastern Europe, textile yarns and fibres from Turkey and Asian countries, and electrical/electronic products from Japan and the Asian NICs.
- the average anti-dumping duty is high (23 per cent, Messerlin 1989); anti-dumping measures have a potentially important influence on trade flows and competitive pressures from third country suppliers. More generally, the mere threat or prospect of anti-dumping actions may be sufficient to introduce systematic market distortions, including strategic export restraint, significant change in the nature of competition and spurious injury (Leidy 1994: 61).
- anti-dumping measures, though in principle a device for maintaining fair trade, have been described as the EC's 'primary way of generating new protection' (Messerlin and Reed 1995).

negotiations. Most traded goods sectors are, therefore, substantially exposed to foreign competition within the EC market as well as externally. Secondly, border protection is concentrated on certain sectors, especially agriculture (through the Common Agricultural Policy), and clothing and textiles (under the WTO's Clothing and Textiles Agreement). Thirdly, the EC responds to perceived unfair trade through the frequent use of anti-dumping measures which give highly selective and substantial protection. Fourthly, EC trade policies are markedly discriminatory—favoured trade partners have freer access to the EC market, and in some cases this is reciprocated. The EC has, thus, built up a hierarchy of preferences, with only a limited number of countries—such as the US and Japan—facing the full CCT.

The trade policy stance of the EC towards further protection or liberalization is important to cohesion. The Rome Treaty committed the member states of the EC to a liberal approach to external trade. Article 110 (now Art. 131) declares that 'by estab-lishing a customs union between themselves the member states intend to contribute, in conformity with the common interest, to the harmonious development of international trade, the progressive abolition of restrictions on international exchange and the lower-ing of customs barriers'. In pursuit of this, the EC has taken part in a series of multi-national negotiations in the framework of the GATT starting in the early 1960s. These have progressively reduced the level of tariffs worldwide, including that of the CCT. However, in the economically troubled years of the 1970s and early 1980s, world trade liberalization suffered a setback. Lacking an effective industrial policy, the EC—along with other industrialized countries—resorted increasingly to non-tariff barriers in-cluding grey area measures such as so-called voluntary export restraints (VERs) with competitive suppliers. Trade in sensitive products like clothing and textiles, steel, agri-cultural commodities, and cars became more managed. These developments had nega-tive effects on EC exports as well as imports. Some observers argue that, on balance, there was no reduction in the level of EC protection against third countries (Henderson 1989). Over the last decade, a more definite liberalizing trend can be identified. First, the EC has largely avoided the dangers of 'Fortress Europe' in establishing the internal market, and in some respects access of third country suppliers improved as a result of the IM programme (Pelkmans, 1993). Secondly, free trade area and customs unions arrange-ments have been negotiated with neighbouring countries to the south and east, which, at least outside agriculture, should stimulate trade. Thirdly, and most importantly in relation to cohesion, the EC has played a central role in the successful completion of negotiations in the Uruguay Round.

3.2.2. EC trade policy and social cohesion

Standard trade theory provides some basis for concern over the impact of expanding international trade on European labour markets. Briefly, opening up trade between a developing (labour-abundant) country and a developed (capital-rich) one will lead the former to export goods requiring a high labour input in exchange for capital-intensive goods. In the developed country, this will lower the price of labour-intensive goods, and depress the demand for, and wages of, labour. If, contrary to standard assumptions, there are rigidities in labour markets, this could lead initially to unemployment. It might take a considerable period of time for production patterns to adjust so as to absorb the displaced workers. The argument can be restated in terms of countries with different relative endowments of skilled and unskilled labour. The opening of trade between them would depress the earnings of unskilled workers in the skilled labour–abundant country, while skilled workers would benefit from the emergence of an export market for the products that use their labour intensively.

The standard theory provides a useful starting point to consider the effects of trade on social cohesion. It suggests that the growth of trade might disadvantage certain producer groups who face import competition. In the European case this seems likely to include unskilled workers, thereby widening income inequalities. At the same time, there would be wider benefits to all social groups from the lower cost of imported products. The theory also suggests that social cohesion might be particularly sensitive to trade with dissimilar countries, hence, for Europe, trade with developing countries. There are also implications for trade policy. Can government intervention modify the incidence of external trade so as to meet policy objectives, including cohesion objectives, more closely? To investigate these issues further, the rest of this section is ordered as follows. First, recent research literature is reviewed to examine what impact trade with low-wage countries has on labour markets. Is there a serious problem that trade and other policies need to address? Next, how important are EC trade relations with developing countries and what arrangements does the EC have for restricting or encouraging this component of its external trade? Finally, the cohesion dimension is explored. How do EC policies affect social cohesion, through both employment and consumption?

3.2.2.1. *Trade and labour markets*

Despite earlier reservations (e.g. Lawrence and Slaughter 1993), recent work confirms that the intensification of trade with developing countries has been associated with a relative decline in the prices of labour-intensive goods, at least in the US (Feenstra and Hanson 1996, Sachs and Shatz 1996). The important empirical issue has, therefore, been to ascertain the magnitude of the impact of such trade on labour markets. Sapir and Schumacher (1985) showed that in trade with developing countries the job intensity of European exports was only around 0.8 of that of the import level in the 1970s. A balanced expansion of trade with these countries in value terms would, therefore, lead to an erosion of jobs. Furthermore, women would be more likely to be affected by rising imports. Sapir and Schumacher show that for Germany, France, and Italy the proportion of women in the labour force is about twice as high in imports than in exports of manufactures traded with developing countries. In the UK and the Netherlands the ratio is also high and only Belgium has approaching a parity share. This implies that an intensification of trade with developing countries that followed the existing pattern of trade would tend both to reduce jobs and to have a more adverse effect on female workers than on men.

More recently, Wood (1991, 1994) has contended that the impact upon jobs would be much more substantial than is suggested by conventional 'factor content' methodologies, which seek to measure the jobs generated by exports and lost to imports.

First, these methods underestimate the amount of labour displaced by 'non-competing' imports from the south (i.e. labour-intensive products no longer produced in the north).[1] Second, imports stimulate defensive productivity improvements so that the same output requires fewer workers (see also Greenaway *et al.* 1997) and, third, northern employment is further reduced by the associated decline in demand for local producer services. Wood concludes that north–south trade may have eliminated 9 million jobs in the north compared with 1 million using the standard methodology, and compared with a jobless total in the OECD countries of 35 million in 1994. Whilst a number of other authors support the view that trade with low-wage countries has had a significant impact on labour markets (e.g. Revenga 1992, Leamer 1993 and 1995, Sachs and Shatz 1994), others are less convinced. They suggest that adverse developments, particularly for unskilled workers, owe much more to skill biased technological change (Bound and Johnson 1992, Katz and Murphy 1992, Lawrence and Slaughter 1993, Berman, Bound, and Griliches 1994, Cooper 1994). Similarly, the applied general equilibrium analysis of Tyers and Yang (1997) finds that the growth of trade with the newly industrializing countries between 1970 and 1992 had very little impact on European labour markets. The main source of job losses was productivity growth, which they assumed to be unrelated to trade expansion.

Much of the concern about the impact of increased trade on labour markets in the north has been focused on the consequences for unskilled workers. In the US and the UK, and to a lesser extent in some other European countries, there has been a widening of the earnings gap between skilled and unskilled workers since about 1980. There is some evidence (Katz and Murphy 1992, Murphy and Welch 1992, Borjas and Ramey 1993) that trade has contributed to this change. In particular, the pattern of increased imports of unskilled labour-intensive products is reflected in the pattern of relative wage changes of skilled and unskilled workers, and also changes in US exports have led to a stronger demand for better educated labour. In the UK, the results of Courakis *et al.* (1995) suggest that trade changes have had a more favourable impact on skilled occupational groups such as managerial, scientific, and technical staff, than on some less skilled groups such as processing or assembly line workers. In France, too, the earnings of skilled labour have been influenced by trade performance: earnings in export industries improved relative to those in import-competing sectors (Messerlin 1995).

As with job losses, few would doubt that trade has played some role in depressing the wages of unskilled workers; again, the important question is, by how much? The relatively small size of imports from low-wage countries in relation to the total size of the economy suggests only a limited impact (Rodrik 1997). The estimate by Cooper (1994) of the wage depressing effects of absorbing trade-displaced workers outside manufacturing argues similarly. For six EC countries, the trade displaced workers from the clothing, textile and leather industries in 1990 represented 2.2 per cent (median value) of employment in the retail trades, hotels, and restaurants (RHR). Using Katz and Murphy's (1992) estimate of the economy-wide elasticity of substitution between

---

[1] Krugman (1995) points out that if the south's exports really are non-competing then this is precisely the circumstance in which the standard trade theory arguments that trade will lead to a convergence of wage rates (factor price equalization) breaks down.

college and high school graduates in the US, Cooper calculated that to absorb these workers in RHR would have depressed wage rates by only 1.3 per cent (median value). This, he commented, represented about 25 per cent of the observed decline in the ratio of high school to college wage rates.

Summing up, there is some evidence that an intensification of trade with low-wage countries may cause a net loss of jobs and, in some countries, put significant downward pressure on the relative wage rates of unskilled and poorly educated workers. But other factors have also played a major role—in particular, skill-biased technological progress (Krugman and Lawrence 1993, Baldwin 1994), relative changes in the supply of skilled and unskilled labour, and changes in taste (Messerlin 1995). Furthermore, the expansion of exports to developing countries has allowed the north to develop the skill-intensive industries in which it has a comparative advantage.

3.2.2.2. EC trade policy and social cohesion

Even if trade expansion has had negative consequences for labour markets, what role have EC trade policies played? To what extent have imports, particularly from low-wage countries, been encouraged and assisted by the EC's trade arrangements? On the one hand, the EC has declared its practical support for Third World development, especially through offering preferential access to the EC market for their exports. On the other hand, EC policy has been sensitive to pressures from EC producers faced with an upsurge in low-cost competition from developing country suppliers.

Trade preferences in favour of Third World countries have been provided under a number of schemes. Under the Lomé Convention the EC allows in most manufactured products from the (largely non-industrialized) African, Caribbean, and Pacific (ACP) countries duty free. Of potentially more significance, the EC's Generalised System of Preferences (GSP) applies to some 145 developing countries and in principle allows virtually all industrial products into the EC at low or zero tariffs. However, as discussed below, in practice the treatment is less generous. Furthermore, the important clothing and textiles sector of the GSP countries is largely excluded from EC preferences and has, instead, been subjected to extensive bilateral quota restrictions under the MultiFibre Arrangement (MFA) and its successor, the Agreement on Clothing and Textiles (ACT). Mediterranean countries are more favourably treated. Their industrial exports to the EC get largely unimpeded entry, including liberal access arrangements for textiles and clothing. In the 1990s, important trade preferences have been extended also to the central and eastern European countries (CEECs) under the Europe Agreements (see section 3.2.4 below).

Despite these special arrangements, the import penetration of low-wage countries in the EC market remains small. Imports from the developing countries and the CEECs combined were equivalent to less than 4 per cent of EC GDP in 1996 (Table 3.1). Moreover, except for the CEECs and the Asian countries, this ratio has been declining —the decline was particularly pronounced for the ACP and the Latin American countries. Developing countries that continue to specialize in agricultural and raw material exports have, in general, fared badly. By contrast, manufactured goods imports from developing countries (including the Asian countries other than Japan) have increased

Table 3.1. EC-15 imports and exports with groups of non-member countries as percentage of EC-15 GDP, 1980, 1990 and 1996

	Imports			Exports		
	1980	1990	1996	1980	1990	1996
Mediterranean	1.01	0.85	0.73	1.26	0.93	1.08
ACP[a]	0.91	0.44	0.35	0.80	0.50	0.44
Latin America	0.73	0.52	0.44	0.58	0.33	0.52
S. and E. Asia	0.87	1.16	1.71	0.69	0.98	1.67
(of which DAEs[b])	0.65	0.91	1.29	0.42	0.71	1.25
Total	3.52	2.97	3.23	3.33	2.74	3.71
CEECs	0.50	0.46	0.74	0.62	0.47	1.05

[a] ACP = African, Caribbean and Pacific countries plus Overseas Territories and Departments.
[b] DAEs = developing Asian economies: Thailand, Malaysia, Singapore, South Korea, Taiwan, Hong Kong, China.

Source: author's calculations based on Eurostat (1997), External Trade Statistics 1970–96 (Luxembourg: Office for Official Publications).

Table 3.2. Share of EC-15 imports of manufactured products by SITC category, by groups of partner countries, 1995

SITC	5	7	8	6	5 to 8
	Chemicals	Machinery & transport equipment	Clothing etc.	Other manufactures	All manufactures
Mediterranean	5.8	3.6	12.6	7.8	6.8
ACP	0.9	0.6	1.0	4.2	1.5
Latin America	2.6	1.4	1.1	6.8	2.6
DAEs[a]	7.1	21.6	28.4	11.1	19.4
CEECs	7.9	6.3	12.9	16.3	10.0

[a] DAEs = developing Asian economies: Thailand, Malaysia, Singapore, South Korea, Taiwan, Hong Kong, China.

Source: author's calculations based on Eurostat (1996), External and intra-European Trade, 6B, November (Luxembourg: Office for Official Publications).

rapidly, almost trebling in volume during the 1980s. The ACP and the Latin American countries, however, remain minor actors, having a combined share of EC manufactured imports of about 4 per cent in 1995 (Table 3.2). The impact of this trade on EC cohesion is, in general, negligible. With the exception of clothing and textiles, the same is true of trade with the Mediterranean countries. Potentially more significant is the EC trade with the Asian developing countries; in total this was equivalent to 1.76 per cent of the EC's GDP in 1996, a ratio which has doubled since 1980. This increase has been driven by manufactured products—the Asian countries' share of EC manufactured imports trebled in the same period from 5.7 per cent in 1980 to 15.1 per cent in 1996. Within the manufactured goods categories, the import share in SITC 8 (dominated by clothing) remained stable; the principal expansion came in chemicals (SITC 5) and especially machinery and transport equipment (SITC 7). In the latter category, the Asian developing countries' share of EC imports rose from 6 per cent in 1980 to 14 per cent in 1990 and 22 per cent in 1996. This growth has been dominated by electronic and electrical goods.

This brief review of recent trade developments indicates two main areas where EC imports from developing countries are substantial: *clothing* from Asia, the Mediterranean, and the CEECs, and *electrical/electronic goods* from Asia. The EC clothing industry has lost jobs on a major scale over many years, reflecting productivity growth in the face of sluggish domestic sales and the EC's comparative disadvantage in labour-intensive industries. Between 1985 and 1994, there was a net loss of 128,000 jobs (15 per cent), many of which were relatively unskilled and low paid. What part did trade and trade policy play in this? Import penetration certainly increased substantially—from 21 per cent in 1985 to 35 per cent in 1994. However, without the MultiFibre Arrangement with its bilateral quota restrictions against Asian and Latin American producers, imports from low-wage countries would undoubtedly have captured a much bigger share of the EC market. In part, the restrictions benefited producers in the Mediterranean and the CEECs who had more liberal access to the EC market. But the impact of Mediterranean suppliers needs to be kept in perspective—the three main suppliers (Turkey, Tunisia, Morocco) account for only about a fifth of EC imports. Moreover, part of this trade is conducted under outward processing arrangements (OPA) that allow EC producers to transfer the more labour-intensive parts of the production process abroad, making the remaining processes in the EC more viable. The main problem for the European industry is how to achieve high enough productivity to offset the wage rate disadvantage in relation to imports. Some parts of the industry have succeeded in this through focusing on fashion and upmarket sectors. Productivity has improved—by 31 per cent from 1985 to 1994—and the share of extra-EC exports in production has increased—from 15 per cent to 18 per cent over the same period. But part of the industry remains vulnerable to very low-wage competition from China and elsewhere, currently held back by quota restrictions. In summary, liberal access to the EC market for *some* suppliers, particularly in the Mediterranean, may have aggravated the difficulties facing some EC producers, particularly those not using OPA. But in general, trade policy has been restrictive. This may have served short-term cohesion objectives of job preservation in vulnerable areas, but long-term problems remain.

European employment in the electrical and electronic engineering industries has also tended to fall in recent years, despite in this case rapid consumption growth. This reflects the impressive growth of labour productivity, which increased by 79 per cent between 1985 and 1994. Import growth from the Asian developing countries has indeed been fast, but in most broad product areas Europe's trade balance has been relatively stable. In telecommunications, for example, the EC has a trade surplus which has grown in the 1990s despite weaknesses in certain products like fax machines. What contribution has trade policy made to these developments? Under the Generalised System of Preferences the Asian countries have benefited from tariff concessions, but their impact has been very limited for a number of reasons:

- many products are classified as sensitive and receive reduced or zero preferences;
- the EC has introduced a graduation mechanism which excludes the more competitive suppliers from GSP treatment;
- rules of origin restrict eligibility.

Already by 1988 the proportion of eligible exports actually receiving GSP treatment was only 23 per cent for Singapore and 17 per cent for Hong Kong.[2] The changes in the GSP made in 1995 will probably diminish these shares further. Trade expansion instead reflected the dynamic growth of the East Asian countries in recent years based on rapid investment expansion and technological improvement. It is notable that Taiwan, which did not benefit from GSP treatment, trebled its share of EC imports of machinery and transport equipment between 1980 and 1996. In some respects, trade policy has actively impeded the growth of imports from Asia, particularly through the proliferation of anti-dumping measures. It should also be recalled that, overall, the EC has approximately balanced trade with the Asian countries excluding Japan, and the region—at least until the financial turbulence in 1997—has been a dynamic outlet for EC exports. It is probably true that, even in the more sophisticated product areas, imports from Asian developing countries are more intensive in assembly-type labour than are European exports. A balanced two-way trade with the Asian developing countries might, therefore, result in a net loss in the number of manufacturing jobs in Europe.[3] Nevertheless, the cohesion implications of this are limited and, indeed, inevitable if European producers wish to share in the market opportunities afforded by the Asian economies.

This analysis has focused on EC trade arrangements with developing countries. The general presumption has been that balanced, largely intra-industrial trade with other developed economies is neutral with respect to the number and nature of jobs, and hence cohesion. However, Rodrik (1997) has argued that this needs to be qualified in relation to job security. The general reduction of trade barriers (including lower transport costs) has made it easier for employers to relocate production internationally. This has increased the elasticity of demand for labour in a given market, thus contributing to a greater sense of job insecurity among workers. It is also the case that the EC does not have bilaterally balanced trade with each of its main developed trading partners. Most notably, the job content of EC exports to Japan is substantially smaller than the job content of imports, despite EC anti-dumping measures and voluntary export restraints. But the trade deficit with Japan is more than offset by trade surpluses with other partners such as the Mediterranean countries and the CEECs. From a cohesion perspective, the EC's overall trade balance dominates particular bilateral imbalances.

---

[2] The proportion of dutiable imports from all GSP countries actually receiving preferential treatment was 38 per cent in 1994 (Sapir 1997).

[3] This depends also on the trend in FDI—in the 1990s, many firms in the East Asian developing countries set up plants in the EC.

Although this section has been primarily concerned with unemployment and relative wages, a further aspect of importance to social cohesion is the impact of trade policy on prices. Protection, whether through tariff or non-tariff barriers, reduces the availability of imports to consumers and drives up the prices of both home products and imports. This results, in the case of EC tariffs, in a transfer of income from EC consumers to EC producers and the European budget (i.e. taxpayers). With non-tariff barriers, consumers are penalized and domestic producers gain, but there is generally no taxpayer benefit. For most products the extent of the income transfer through tariffs is relatively small because of the EC's low average level of tariffs. However, some of the EC's other trade policy instruments are estimated to secure major income transfers from EC consumers to EC producers, and in some cases also third country producers. These transfers are difficult to measure, but a number of estimates have been made of the cost of voluntary export restraints (Greenaway and Hindley 1985, Kalantzopoulos 1985, de Melo and Messerlin 1988, Takacs and Winters 1991). They each point to a very high cost to consumers relative to the number of jobs preserved or created. Anti-dumping duties have also been costly for EC consumers, at least in the short run: Schuknecht (1992) cites an estimate of 1.4 billion ECU in the case of consumer electronics alone. Of course, if anti-dumping measures helped to prevent predatory actions by foreign suppliers, consumers might benefit in the longer term. However, empirical evidence suggests that predatory pricing is uncommon.

What are the implications of these consumer costs of protection for social cohesion? To the extent that VERs and anti-dumping actions have applied to consumer goods they have concentrated on items of interest to more wealthy households. However, tariff and quota barriers on food and low-cost clothing are likely to have a regressive impact since (a) trade barriers (tariffs, import levies, and quotas) are particularly high on these items, and (b) they are relatively more important in the budgets of low-income households (Table 3.3). The MacSharry reforms of the Common Agricultural Policy and the agreement in the Uruguay Round to phase out the MFA will both, therefore, have a positive effect on low-income households, thereby contributing to social cohesion in the Community.

3.2.3. EC trade policy and regional cohesion

How external trade policy affects regional cohesion depends on three main factors: (a) what direction trade policy is moving in—towards more or more severe trade restrictions (protection) or fewer or less severe trade restrictions (liberalization); (b) where industries whose trade exposure is changing are located; and (c) the time perspective under consideration. It is possible that trade policies which in the short term might be favourable to regional cohesion could not be so if they are prolonged. Given this potential temporal inconsistency, it is helpful to leave the discussion of longer-term policy impacts until after the short-term perspective.

Whether, in principle, temporary protection might help regional cohesion clearly depends on where the protected industries are located. Consider, first, a scenario where import competing industries are concentrated in the more prosperous areas while the

Table 3.3. Pattern of household expenditure, by income group and country, 1985
(a) Expenditure pattern of bottom quartile of households (%)

	Germany	France	Netherlands	Italy	Ireland	Spain
Food	20.3	28.4	19.2	42.1	35.2	41.0
Clothing and footwear	6.6	5.7	5.6	5.9	4.7	8.8
Gross rent, fuel, power	31.0	22.7	32.4	26.9	24.5	20.7
Furniture etc.	6.1	7.1	6.2	5.4	4.8	5.7
Medical and health	1.5	7.3	1.1	1.5	1.0	2.4
Transport and communications	9.7	12.3	7.7	7.1	7.9	7.5
Recreation, entertainment, etc.	7.5	5.2	8.3	3.3	6.5	3.5
Miscellaneous	10.1	7.4	8.1	6.4	8.5	7.7
Other expenditure	7.1	3.8	11.4	1.4	7.0	1.0
	100.0	100.0	100.0	100.0	100.0	100.0

(b) difference between expenditure patterns of bottom quartile and top quartile households, in % points[a]

	Germany	France	Netherlands	Italy	Ireland	Spain
Food	5.8	10.4	4.5	18.9	14.9	16.8
Clothing and footwear	−0.8	−1.7	−1.6	−3.2	−3.0	−1.2
Gross rent, fuel, power	10.4	7.6	8.7	10.2	11.6	1.5
Furniture etc.	−1.8	−1.7	0.1	−2.1	−1.1	−1.4
Medical and health	−1.1	2.6	−1.2	−0.5	−0.6	0.2
Transport and communications	−6.1	−9.4	−5.0	−11.2	−6.1	−6.9
Recreation, entertainment, etc.	−0.2	−1.6	−1.3	−4.4	−2.4	−4.1
Miscellaneous	−0.4	−4.4	−2.4	−4.4	−8.3	−3.9
Other expenditure	−5.9	−1.9	−1.8	−2.7	−5.1	−0.5

[a] For each category, % expenditure of bottom quartile minus % expenditure of top quartile.

Source: author's calculations based on Eurostat (1990), Family Budgets, Comparative Tables.

main industries in the less favoured regions are more export oriented. In the short run, protection would be unhelpful to regional cohesion. The industries in the low-income areas, being export oriented, need good access to foreign markets, which is best promoted by liberal trade policies. By contrast, protection preserves jobs and output in the better-off areas, which does not contribute to greater regional cohesion. The more difficult—and more likely—scenario is one where exporting firms are concentrated in the higher income regions and it is industries in the poorer regions that are vulnerable to import competition. In this situation, liberal trade policies might—in the short term—damage regional cohesion. By taking protection away from sensitive industries in disadvantaged regions, jobs and output might be jeopardized. By contrast, the position of the already prosperous regions might improve if their exporters gained better access to foreign markets through the mutual dismantling of trade barriers. In this scenario, regional cohesion might be improved by temporary trade measures to dampen the pressure of foreign competition. Protected firms might be able to maintain a higher level of employment, with positive multiplier effects on the economies of the regions. This might help to combat a build-up of structural unemployment and make hysteresis effects less severe. It might be further argued that temporary protection could give firms a 'breathing space' in which to raise efficiency and thereby secure jobs for the future. However, it must be added that there are serious doubts about the contribution of import protection to regional cohesion. For example, 'breathing spaces' seem rarely to work, as firms generally prove unable or unwilling to make the necessary efficiency improvements. Instead, there is pressure for an extension of trade restrictions. Moreover, there is no guarantee that, even in the short term, protection will succeed in maintaining employment; that depends also on the actions of trade unions who might instead prefer higher wages for their members, and on the response of firms who might opt for lower output with higher prices. These conflicting views lead to the following conclusions: (a) temporary protection will be harmful to regional cohesion if the protected industries are located in the more prosperous regions, and (b) even if the location of the import competing industries is appropriate, there is no guarantee that protection will help, and there is a risk that it could be counterproductive. Given these conclusions, it is clearly important to establish in the EC case how the spatial pattern of industry relates to the distribution of protection.

Evidence for the EC suggests that the potential dilemma over short-term protection is very relevant. In particular, export success is broadly correlated with higher per capita incomes. Thus, whereas Germany and Denmark have trade surpluses in manufactures, the Netherlands, Belgium, and France are broadly in balance while Greece, Portugal, and Spain have persistent deficits. Ireland is an exception to the general pattern: although it is a relatively low-income country it has had a substantial trade surplus over the last decade. There are also differences between the high- and low-income countries in the pattern of specialization and exposure to import competition from low-wage countries outside the EC. Ireland is again an exception. Three of the four peripheral, low-income EC countries (Portugal, Greece, and Spain) have a trade orientation towards labour-intensive products. By contrast, the central EC countries like Germany and the Netherlands have a trade orientation towards more sophisticated manufactures —human capital- and/or technology-intensive products. In summary, therefore, the general position in the EC is that the high-income countries tend to have balanced trade or surpluses and to specialize in technology- and human-capital-intensive industries, while the low-income countries tend to have trade deficits and to specialize in labour-intensive products. The exceptions to this are Ireland (in electronics) among the relatively low-income countries and Italy (in clothing and footwear) among the more prosperous.

How do these trade patterns relate to EC trade measures, and what implication does this have for regional cohesion? First, the pattern of traditional trade measures such as tariffs suggests that they are targeted towards helping weak industries in low-income parts of the EC. There is, for example, a strong concentration of the high-tariff

Table 3.4. Percentage of manufacturing employment in each EC member in high-tariff industries,[a] 1990

	textiles	clothing	footwear[a]	food	total
Portugal	29.3	...[b]	4.8	10.8	44.9
Greece	14.6	8.5	3.7	16.9	43.7
Ireland	7.2	5.1	0.9	18.9	32.0
Spain	6.2	4.8	2.6	13.8	27.4
Belgium	8.9	6.4	0.5	9.7	25.4
Italy	7.7	5.7	3.8	5.1	22.2
UK	4.5	4.7	1.3	10.2	20.6
France	4.6	3.5	1.7	10.6	20.4
Denmark	3.2	1.8	0.4	14.2	19.7
Netherlands	2.9	1.4	0.7	13.9	18.8
Germany	3.5	2.1	0.7	5.2	11.5

[a] Includes employment in leather industry.
[b] For Portugal, clothing is included with textiles.

Sources: author's calculations based on GATT (1993) Trade Policy Review, European Communities vol. 1, Table AV5 (employment by ISIC industry), and WTO (1995), Trade Policy Review, European Union, Table AV3 (tariffs by ISIC industry).

industries in the low-income countries and regions of the Community (Table 3.4). These industries account for almost half of industrial employment in Portugal and Greece, but their share is less than a quarter in Denmark and Germany. Similarly, the MFA/ACT quota restrictions and the voluntary restraints accepted by Mediterranean and other suppliers on textiles affect a sector which is particularly important to the economies of low-income regions. Thus, with regard to traditional measures, EC trade policy could be seen as supportive of regional cohesion interests in the short term. This contrasts, however, with the likely regional impact of measures of 'new protection'; the product coverage of voluntary export restraints (excluding those on clothing and textiles) and anti-dumping measures suggests that they have been mobilized more in favour of producers in high-income countries and regions than those in the more dis-advantaged areas. Messerlin and Reed (1995) find that 72.5 per cent of anti-dumping cases initiated in the EC between 1979 and 1989 involved four industries: chemicals, metals, non-electrical machinery, and electrical machinery. These industries are con-centrated in the high-income EC countries. Furthermore, the measures taken against imports may have weakened the competitive position of low-income EC countries by increasing the cost of imported intermediate products like textile yarns and basic steel products. This concern is heightened by the finding that anti-dumping actions have strengthened the cartelization of these industries (Messerlin 1990). Hence, even if it is accepted that protection may in the short term help regional cohesion, the actual trade measures employed by the EC have often been misdirected. Moreover, they have fre-quently not been temporary—in which case a more negative assessment is justified.

From a long-run perspective, prolonged protection is likely to be damaging to regional cohesion, irrespective of where the protected industries are located. Protection locks resources into low-productivity uses and reduces the pressure on weak industries to adjust. By postponing adjustment in this way, the eventual structural adaptation is made more painful and disruptive (Banks and Tumlir 1986). Furthermore, by supporting weak industries with poor prospects, protection denies resources to those industries which have a potential for expansion. The latter increasingly need access to global markets to achieve commercial success, and this depends on a mutual dismantling of trade barriers. By handicapping strong industries in this way economic growth is jeopardized. This will have negative consequences also for the low-income regions, not least because there will be fewer budgetary resources available for regional development policies. Thus, prolonged protection against import competition is unlikely to foster regional cohesion. As noted in the introductory section, other forms of policy are potentially more efficient.

In section 3.2.1 it was noted that EC trade policy has become more liberal in recent years. Tariffs, once the mainstay of protection, have been progressively reduced in GATT negotiations, though the pace has been relatively slow, and in some product areas—notably agriculture and clothing—little progress was made until the Uruguay Round. Further, the proliferation of non-tariff barriers especially in the 1970s and 1980s was retrograde, and currently the high use of anti-dumping measures gives cause for concern. Nonetheless, the Uruguay Round agreement marked an important step forward towards more open trade, the single market seems on balance to have improved third country access to the EC market, and the EC has played a leading role in recent WTO negotiations on services. Progress has also been made in the case of bilateral trade arrangements, e.g. under the Europe Agreements (see section 3.2.4 below), but discriminatory reductions run the risk of diverting trade from more efficient suppliers. In short, there is now a momentum towards more open markets which should benefit economic growth and regional cohesion in the EC over the longer term. As observed above, however, this has to be tempered by some more immediate concerns. In particular, much traditional protection—though oriented towards problem industries which are important in low-income regions—has been permanent, not temporary. Furthermore, much of the new protection has sheltered firms in high-income regions and could not be justified on regional cohesion grounds.

3.2.4. *The implications of the Uruguay Round and the Europe Agreements for cohesion*

Important changes were initiated in EC external trade policies during the first half of the 1990s which will have a growing impact on the European economy over the next few years. Two developments—the Uruguay Round and the Europe Agreements—are singled out for discussion in this section because of their potential effects on regional cohesion. The multilateral Uruguay Round agreement relaunched the rules-based international trade system which had fallen into serious disrepair during the 1980s. The Europe Agreements have a more restricted application but radically alter the EC's trade relationship with its neighbours to the east. These developments will significantly reshape the CCP over the next decade. This section focuses on their implications for the EC's social and regional cohesion.

3.2.4.1. The Uruguay Round agreement

The successful conclusion of the Uruguay Round of trade negotiations in 1993 resulted in wide-ranging agreements to reduce trade barriers substantially, to redraw the internationally agreed trade rules in areas such as anti-dumping measures, to extend the scope of GATT rules and disciplines to new areas, notably agriculture and services, and to establish a more powerful institutional framework for world trade: the World Trade Organisation. These outcomes will have important implications for cohesion. In particular they will

- open up markets in third countries to export industries, including service industries, bringing direct benefits to the regional economies in which these industries are based;
- progressively reduce protection in import competing parts of industries like the clothing industry (to the extent that EC production is in low-income regions, this may have negative consequences for cohesion); and
- give a stimulus to the European economy by raising EC and global trade and output, generating additional jobs with potentially favourable effects for social cohesion.

Export gains will be stimulated by a one third reduction in tariffs on manufactures in the industrial countries (from 5.4 per cent to 3.5 per cent—IMF 1994) and, in the case of developing countries, by much more comprehensive tariff bindings. The extension of GATT/WTO rules and disciplines to intellectual property rights and services should also help, though the services agreement largely involves securing existing levels of market access. The further integration of EC exporters into world markets is likely to strengthen their competitiveness with favourable implications for employment and social cohesion. As discussed earlier, how regional cohesion is affected depends on the location of the industries which expand. In general, the more prosperous countries and regions have the most successful export industries—in manufacturing and services— and will benefit most from better access to foreign markets. In the services sector, for example, the 'poor four' cohesion countries run trade deficits in financial and business services and communications whereas the UK, Belgium, the Netherlands, and France run surpluses (Eurostat 1992, data for 1989–92). By contrast, the tourism industry—a key sector in the 'poor four'—will be little affected by the outcome of the Uruguay Round.

The counterpart of better access for EC export industries to world markets is a further opening of the EC market to imports, particularly from non-preferred countries. Under the Uruguay Round agreement, the EC will reduce tariffs on non-agricultural products by an average of 37 per cent. This includes the complete elimination of duties in construction, medical equipment, furniture, steel, agricultural equipment, paper, beer and spirits which together account for about 10 per cent of non-agricultural imports. However, any negative effects on cohesion from this loss of protection are likely to be modest since duties will only fall by about two to three percentage points on average, from 5.98 per cent to 3.73 per cent by July 2000 (for manufactured products from 7.4 per cent to 4.5 per cent), and the tariff reductions are to be phased in over five years. Moreover, some industries, such as clothing and textiles, leather and footwear, which are relatively concentrated in the low-income countries, will have below average tariff cuts[4] and will, thus, retain relatively high rates of protection. More significant for these countries is the agreement to end quota restrictions under the MFA, and hence to expose EC producers to more direct competition from low-wage countries. In a computable general equilibrium (CGE) study, Francois, McDonald, and Nordström (1995) estimated that, even under conservative assumptions about returns to scale and competitive structures, the elimination of the MFA and other Uruguay Round measures would result in a substantial fall in output of clothing (−17 per cent) though little change in textiles (−1 per cent). This has important implications for regional cohesion, since the low-income EC countries have relatively large clothing and textiles sectors. The most vulnerable regions—having a concentration of employment in the clothing and footwear sector[5] and per capita incomes below 66 per cent of the EC average—are the Norte and Centro in Portugal, Kentriki Makedonia and Anatoliki Makedonia in Greece, and Castilla–La Mancha in Spain. However, the impact in these regions will be softened by avoiding their main products in the first phase of liberalization and by phasing quotas out over ten years with much of the change delayed until 2005.

Other action taken on non-tariff barriers in the Uruguay Round included banning VERs[6] and converting agricultural levies, etc. to tariffs (see Chapter 6). However, as noted earlier, VERs have not been widely used on items of major production interest to low-income countries and so the cohesion impact of this change will be small. On services, since the Uruguay Round agreement largely endorses current access arrangements, its impact on the low-income regions and countries is likely to be small. Moreover, in telecommunications the EC recognized the adjustment problems of the low-income countries by adopting later deadlines for opening up their markets to competition.[7]

Better access for European export industries to world markets and reductions in EC protection for weak industries may both have negative effects on regional cohesion in the EC in the short run. But how substantial are these effects likely to be? Some idea of the potential order of magnitude may be given by supposing, (a) that the sectoral output effects computed by Francois, McDonald, and Nordström (1995) for the EC as a whole applied uniformly in each region—hence, for example, clothing output fell 17 per cent in each region—and (b) that employment changed in proportion to output.[8] On this basis, no region would experience a net employment loss of more than 1 per cent (Table 3.5). This result reflects, first, that employment in all regions is diversified to some extent, and, second, that no industry, apart from clothing, is projected to experience more than a 3 per cent change in output as a result of the Uruguay Round

---

[4] Cuts, in percentage points, are: clothing 1.8, leather 1.5, and footwear 1.0.

[5] Available regional data do not provide separate estimates for the clothing sector alone.

[6] The EC was permitted to keep its VER on Japanese cars until 1999 and there will be no reduction in the tariff on cars.

[7] The deadline for Ireland is 2000, and for Greece, Spain, and Portugal 2003, compared with 1998 elsewhere.

[8] The analysis identified 19 sectors—6 primary, 12 manufacturing, and 1 service. To assess the regional cohesion implications of these changes the classification was converted to a NACE–CLIO basis for which EC regional employment data is available at the NUTS II level.

Hine, Padoan

Table 3.5. Effects of the Uruguay Round: difference in employment between post-UR and pre-UR over regional employment, by NUTS II regions and GDP per head

NUTS II REGIONS			Total % change	GDP per head (EUR = 100)
	3530	Marche	−0.925	104.88
b230		Rioja	−0.893	87.58
c110		Norte	−0.683	60.13
	7320	Leicestershire, Northamptonshire	−0.603	98.29
	7230	South Yorkshire	−0.566	78.97
	3810	Abruzzi	−0.547	93.88
a110		Anatoliki Makedonia, Thraki	−0.535	56.43
b420		Castilla-La Mancha	−0.534	65.13
	3320	Veneto	−0.532	117.65
b520		Comunidad Valenciana	−0.528	78.08
7b00		Northern Ireland	−0.468	79.40
	3510	Toscana	−0.454	112.01
	1940	Oberfranken	−0.453	108.48
	2510	Pays de la Loire	−0.409	96.02
a120		Kentriki Makedonia	−0.360	59.26
b530		Baleares	−0.322	102.93
	3520	Umbria	−0.319	103.07
	7830	Lancashire	−0.310	91.47
	7820	Greater Manchester	−0.309	90.91
	7310	Derbyshire, Nottinghamshire	−0.302	89.59
c120		Centro (P)	−0.282	48.07
	7120	Cumbria	−0.280	110.05
	5180	Oost-Vlaanderen	−0.277	104.47
	1960	Unterfranken	−0.276	107.46
b240		Aragon	−0.256	84.66
	5190	West-Vlaanderen	−0.240	111.22
	7130	Northumberland, Tyne and Wear	−0.233	85.70
b620		Murcia	−0.231	69.94
	7110	Cleveland, Durham	−0.231	81.75
b510		Cataluna	−0.219	95.32
7a20		Dumfries & Galloway, Strathclyde	−0.216	89.23
	3820	Molise	−0.212	81.86
	7630	Dorset, Somerset	−0.197	89.98
b430		Extremadura	−0.195	51.14
	1730	Rheinhessen-Pfalz	−0.195	110.53
	1920	Niederbayern	−0.187	98.08
	2630	Limousin	−0.186	89.01
	2300	Nord-Pas-de-Calais	−0.186	89.75
a140		Thessalia	−0.183	55.76
	1540	Detrnold	−0.182	108.11
	7810	Cheshire	−0.179	101.96
	3910	Puglia	−0.178	76.95
	7330	Lincolnshire	−0.171	86.95
	7910	Clwyd, Dyfed, Gwynedd, Powys	−0.164	80.39
a230		Dytiki Ellada	−0.164	52.34
a300		Attiki	−0.160	68.57
	2530	Poitou-Charentes	−0.158	89.19
b610		Andalucia	−0.158	59.24
	8000	Ireland[a]	−0.158	76.73
	2240	Centre	−0.156	103.02
	3400	Emilia-Romagna	−0.153	128.65
c130		Lishboa e Vale do Tejo	−0.153	93.54
	7220	North Yorkshire	−0.147	98.09
	3200	Lombardla	−0.145	134.61
	1930	Oberpfalz	−0.144	100.68
a130		Dytiki Makedonia	−0.144	60.39
7a10		Borders-Central-Fife-Lothian-Tayside	−0.135	96.91
	5260	Luxembourg (B)	−0.133	88.19
	1720	Trler	−0.128	89.25

Table 3.5. (*cont'd*)

NUTS II REGIONS			Total % change	GDP per head (EUR = 100)
	5150	Limburg (B)	−0.125	107.66
	2620	Midi-Pyrénées	−0.116	97.00
	3110	Piemonte	−0.112	119.16
	2610	Aquitaine	−0.108	98.94
b300		Madrid	−0.108	97.71
	7720	Shropshire, Staffordshire	−0.106	84.61
	2810	Languedoc-Roussillon	−0.103	88.00
	3700	Campania	−0.103	72.91
13d0		Weser-Ems	−0.102	102.02
	4510	Noord-Brabant	−0.100	101.20
b110		Galicia	−0.098	58.89
	7840	Merseyside	−0.097	73.00
	2220	Picardie	−0.091	95.77
	2520	Bretagne	−0.088	92.94
	7210	Humberside	−0.087	94.89
a210		Ipeiros	−0.080	46.76
	1710	Koblenz	−0.075	95.84
a250		Peloponnisos	−0.075	60.88
	1530	Münster	−0.075	96.21
	2250	Basse-Normandie	−0.074	98.77
	7240	West Yorkshire	−0.074	92.69
	2720	Auvergne	−0.072	90.69
16c0		Kassel	−0.071	112.31
	2420	Alsace	−0.063	113.19
b220		Navarra	−0.060	94.32
b410		Castilla-Leon	−0.060	66.50
	2710	Rhône-Alpes	−0.056	111.04
c140		Alentejo	−0.054	40.85
	7620	Cornwall, Devon	−0.053	82.19
	7400	East Anglia	−0.051	100.32
13c0		Lüneburg	−0.048	87.06
	2410	Lorraine	−0.042	97.36
	3920	Basilicata	−0.041	66.86
	7550	Greater London	−0.040	143.31
	2230	Haute-Normandie	−0.035	107.81
	7920	Gwent, Mid-S-W Giamorgan	−0.034	85.03
a430		Kriti	−0.032	55.01
	1840	Tübingen	−0.032	119.63
	4230	Overijssel	−0.030	90.79
	2210	Champagne-Ardenne	−0.027	114.26
	3930	Calabria	−0.026	62.88
	5270	Namur	−0.026	86.19
	7610	Avon, Gloucestershire, Wiltshire	−0.025	104.13
	4120	Friesland	−0.023	87.51
	9000	Danmark[a]	−0.021	107.24
	2260	Bourgogne	−0.021	99.37
	1970	Schwaben	−0.014	113.60
c200		Acores	−0.014	41.11
	5110	Antwerpen	−0.012	131.38
b630		Ceuta y Melilla	−0.012	61.79
c300		Madeira	−0.011	43.83
	5020	Brabant	−0.008	122.29
	3330	Friuli-Venezia Giulia	−0.008	122.78
b700		Canarias	−0.007	75.21
3a00		Sicilia	−0.007	72.82
a420		Notio Algaio	−0.007	60.11
	4240	Gelderland	−0.005	90.93
c150		Algarve	−0.005	57.83
a410		Voreio Aigaio	−0.004	45.07
a220		Ionia Nisia	−0.002	53.55

Table 3.5. (*cont'd*)

NUTS II REGIONS			Total % change	GDP per head (EUR = 100)
7a40		Grampian	−0.002	134.18
	2100	Ile de France	−0.002	169.70
	3310	Trentino-Alto Adige	−0.002	124.59
	4740	Zeeland	−0.001	100.19
	5300	Bruxelles-Brussel	0.000	174.36
	3600	Lazio	0.002	120.35
	2830	Corse	0.003	79.60
	2820	Provence-Alpes-Côte d'Azur	0.003	101.45
	3120	Valle d'Aosta	0.004	129.78
	4520	Limburg (NI)	0.004	91.92
	4250	Flevoland	0.006	72.71
	4720	Noord-Holland	0.008	115.10
7a30		Highlands, Islands	0.008	87.41
3b00		Sardegna	0.008	79.27
	5230	Hainaut	0.008	81.48
	4710	Utrecht	0.011	112.55
	7570	Kent	0.013	91.41
	1910	Oberbayern	0.014	157.88
	2430	Franche-Comté	0.014	104.05
	7540	Essex	0.018	81.60
	4110	Groningen	0.024	132.84
	7510	Bedfordshire, Hertfordshire	0.025	100.86
16b0		Giessen	0.025	103.81
	4730	Zuid-Holland	0.025	106.17
	7730	West Midlands (County)	0.026	94.43
13b0		Hannover	0.028	120.58
1b00		Berlin	0.031	95.69
b130		Cantabria	0.032	74.42
	7710	Hereford & Worcester, Warwickshire	0.032	87.83
	7520	Berkshire, Buckinghamshire, Oxfordshire	0.034	114.96
	7530	Surrey, East-West Sussex	0.039	94.91
	1100	Schleswig-Hoistein	0.041	104.19
	1830	Freiburg	0.042	115.18
a240		Sterea Ellada	0.043	73.72
	7560	Hampashire, Isle of Wight	0.051	99.50
	4130	Drenthe	0.051	89.75
16a0		Darmstadt	0.052	174.74
	1520	Köln	0.056	116.49
	1950	Mittelfranken	0.058	129.66
	3130	Liguria	0.062	121.37
13a0		Braunschweig	0.063	109.58
	5240	Liège	0.073	100.36
	1400	Bremen	0.077	155.28
	1200	Hamburg	0.085	196.83
	1810	Stuttgart	0.100	146.64
	1510	Düsseldorf	0.101	124.67
	1820	Karlsruhe	0.107	129.80
b120		Asturias	0.108	71.47
b210		Pais Vasco	0.123	90.50
1a00		Saarland	0.162	109.19
	6000	Luxembourg[a]	0.177	156.79
	1550	Arnsberg	0.211	108.54

[a] Data taken from INDE at a national level (Denmark, Luxembourg, and Ireland are considered as one region at the NUTSII level anyway).

The NACE categories 15, 16, 17, 24, 33, 37, 48 and 50 have remained unohanged as far as the effects of the Uruguay Round are concerned.

Figures for Germany exclude the new Laender.

The results have to be interoreted with caution, as for some NACE data was unavailable and this figures as a zero change.

(Table 3.5). The 25 worst affected regions (out of a total of 156) have net employment losses of between 0.25 per cent and 1 per cent. Of these, eight are disadvantaged regions in the sense that per capita GDP is below 80 per cent of the EC average. These include two regions in each of Portugal (Norte and Centro), Greece (Anatoliki Makedonia and Kentriki Makedonia), Spain (Castilla–La Mancha and Communidad Valenciana), and the UK (South Yorkshire and Northern Ireland). Hence there are some grounds for concern but, compared with other sources of adjustment pressure, the regional consequences of the Uruguay Round appear relatively small and are phased in over a lengthy period.

It is important, finally, to bear in mind that the Uruguay Round is likely to have a general, though modest, expansionary effect on world trade and income—estimates range from +0.9 per cent to +1.8 per cent of world GDP (Cline 1995). This should be favourable to social cohesion in the EC if it leads to a sustainably higher level of employment and lower prices.

3.2.4.2. The Europe Agreements with central and eastern European countries (CEECs)
In addition to implementing the multilateral agreements under the Uruguay Round, the EC is also in the process of making important bilateral trade adjustments, most significantly with the CEECs. Before 1989, trade with the CEECs was severely restricted; most of the quantitative restrictions have now been eliminated and preferential access to the EC market has been provided, first, through the Generalised System of Preferences and, then, through Europe Agreements (EAs). The trade provisions of the EAs entered into force on an interim basis in early 1992 for the Visegrad countries and in 1993 for Bulgaria and Romania. In offering preferential access for imports, the EC was very cautious about liberalizing access for certain 'sensitive' products. Thus the agreements largely exclude agricultural products, they permit contingent protection which in the past has been widely used on steel and chemical products, and they delayed trade liberalization for clothing and textiles products until 1998.

How will the Europe Agreements affect EC cohesion? This depends most importantly on the extent to which the CEECs will become rivals to producers in the 'poor four' cohesion countries, both locally in their own markets and elsewhere in the EC. Additionally, cohesion could also be affected by changes induced in the pattern of foreign direct investment (FDI). The outcome is further dependent on which regions and sectors in the EC are most able to exploit the new markets in the CEECs, since the Europe Agreements will eventually lead to mutual free trade. At present—except for Germany—the trade flows are relatively small and consequently do not have a large significance for consumption or employment.[9] But this situation is changing quite rapidly as trade recovers from the previously abnormally low level caused by the postwar division of Europe. Between 1989 and 1996 CEEC exports to the EC grew by 12 per cent a year,[10] and high rates of growth are expected to be sustained over the next

---

[9] Imports from the CEECs were equivalent to 0.46 per cent of EC GDP in 1990 rising to 0.74 per cent in 1996.

[10] For Poland, Hungary, the Czech Republic, and Slovakia, the growth rate was 17 per cent a year.

decade (European Commission, 1994, Table 3.3). Some of this will come from a displacement of imports from other non-EC sources as a result of the improved trade treatment of CEECs. It should be added also that the EC has developed a large bilateral trade surplus with the CEECs. Trade deficits with the CEECs are unlikely to pose problems for the EC as a whole or for the low-income EC countries (Dimelis and Gatsios 1995 for Greece, Gual and Martín 1995 for Spain).

Unease about cohesion effects stems mainly from concern over the competitive strength of the CEECs' export industries or, rather, their future export industries. Here a major problem is to determine where the CEECs' comparative advantage lies and in which direction it will in future evolve. Standard trade theory suggests that the main driver for this is relative resource endowments. Unfortunately, there is a lack of consensus on the empirical evidence. On the one hand, data on education suggest that the CEECs have a relative abundance of human capital (Begg *et al.* 1990, Hamilton and Winters 1992), implying that (a) export growth from the CEECs would come from technologically advanced products and (b) there would be little threat to the more labour-intensive exports of the low-income regions in the EC. On the other hand, Halpern (1995) argues that the data may exaggerate the quality of human capital in the CEECs. The comparative advantage of the CEECs might then lie more in the labour-intensive industries, a view more consistent with the pattern of trade data (Table 3.6). The northern EC countries (including Ireland) have a revealed comparative advantage (RCA) in human capital intensive and R&D-intensive products in their trade with the CEECs, and a disadvantage in labour-intensive products. In the southern countries, this pattern is much less pronounced; indeed in the case of Portugal, and for R&D-intensive products, it is reversed. Portugal also differs in relation to the industries which are intensive in both capital and labour where it has a strongly positive RCA, in contrast to the situation for Greece and Spain.

Hence, an expansion of CEEC exports to the EC might pose problems for the low-income EC countries. At an aggregate level, there is a considerable similarity in the types of industrial product exported to the EC by the CEECs and those exported by Greece and, to a lesser extent, Spain and Portugal. However, at a more detailed level it appears that the degree of overlap at least for Greece and Spain is not marked (see Dimelis and Gatsios 1995 for Greece, and Gual and Martín 1995 for Spain). For Portugal, the position is again somewhat different because of the importance of the clothing and textile sector, which competes more directly with production in the CEECs but has higher costs (Corado 1995). Not only may Portugal lose exports to the CEECs but also to other EC countries.

The Europe Agreements could cause adjustment problems at the regional level where vulnerable EC industries are locally concentrated. This could be a particular problem where the share of employment in the labour-intensive sectors is positively correlated with unemployment and GDP/head, as in the UK and Italy (Neven 1995). However, results from a number of simulation studies suggest that the impact of increased trade with the CEECs on low-income regions in the EC will be generally small (e.g. for France, Cadot and de Melo 1995). Smith *et al.* (1994) conclude that even a quadrupling of trade with the CEECs would have only rather minor impacts on

Table 3.6. European Community (12): revealed comparative advantage[a] in relation to third countries and country groupings, 1988 and 1993

Partners	Years	Groups of sectors				
		1 Technology-intensive	2 Human-capital-intensive	3 Labour-intensive	4 Labour- & capital-intensive	5 Food, etc.
World	1988	−4.1	31.8	7.1	21.6	6.4
	1993	:	:	:	:	:
Extra-EC	1988	−6.6	78.6	16.5	62.9	16.5
	1993	−1.7	85.3	−11.3	48.5	18.2
Intra-EC	1988	−14.9	−0.3	0.8	0.6	−1.7
	1993	:	:	:	:	:
Med. countries	1988	106.8	165.5	−76.0	192.3	1.3
	1993	79.9	171.6	−147.9	210.3	4.2
CEECs	1988	129.2	187.6	−98.7	−58.3	−13.0
	1993	74.5	125.9	−168.9	0.9	−13.6
ACP	1988	161.9	145.4	75.2	78.3	45.1
	1993	156.6	123.4	100.9	91.4	39.7
USA	1988	−206.9	25.7	50.8	201.5	16.7
	1993	−148.3	34.1	34.4	145.1	11.7
Japan	1988	−183.9	−74.8	39.4	38.8	40.1
	1993	−102.8	−69.2	47.8	−17.7	42.2
ASEAN	1988	31.4	77.7	−48.0	70.0	20.5
	1993	−114.4	161.2	−93.3	52.4	15.2
NICs	1988	−120.4	112.2	−187.3	145.6	22.9
	1993	−177.5	117.8	−120.2	81.2	29.9

[a] $RCA = (x/X - m/M) \times 1000$

regional output and income, spread over perhaps 20 years. When trade with the CEECs increases to its 'normal' level by an equiproportional growth in all countries and sectors, no region loses more than 0.1 per cent of output.

As the recent experience of Ireland emphasizes, FDI has an important role to play in the catch-up process for poor countries and regions. Could the CEECs attract FDI which might otherwise have gone to the southern EC countries? For Spain, the FDI diversion effect is likely to be negligible since most FDI has not been motivated by an effort to obtain low-cost labour but rather by a desire to secure access to a large and growing market (Gual and Martín 1995). Similarly, inward investment in Portugal is not focused on low wage or export oriented industries (Fontoura 1995). In the case of Greece, growing integration with the CEECs has had a stimulating effect on Greek FDI in the neighbouring Balkan countries. Thus, there are some indications that investment diversion to the CEECs does not at present pose a major problem for cohesion in the EC.

3.3. Conclusion

High levels of unemployment, particularly when concentrated in certain regions, run the danger of unravelling the social fabric, including undermining the authority of the democratic system, and could result in damaging effects on the international trade system (OECD 1994). The possibility that increased import penetration may have played a role—albeit probably minor—in increasing unemployment especially among unskilled workers deserves, therefore, serious examination. Even if such a role is found, the answer is not, however, a move to protectionist policies. These would have a series of unfortunate consequences such as high costs to consumers, a likely loss of competitiveness, an encouragement to rent-seeking, and job losses in other sectors through retaliatory trade measures. Studies of the effects of measures such as VERs have indicated that the cost per job saved is extremely high (e.g. Greenaway and Hindley 1985). Moreover, the industries in which import penetration is rising (e.g. clothing and textiles) already have very high rates of protection.

The loss of jobs in certain sectors, especially labour-intensive industries, has to be seen in the context of the structural evolution of the European economy towards higher value-added activities. Trade policy has a role to play in supporting the shift towards more skill-intensive and better remunerated employment. This will require a progressive move towards more liberal trade policies, encouraging greater competitiveness rather than propping up inefficient industries which often pay low wages. Such a policy needs to be backed by measures to raise the skill levels of the labour force through education and training. Of course, skill differentials in pay already provide an incentive for private action to increase investment in human capital. But given the likely positive external effects of a more skilled labour force, government action is also warranted. Additionally, measures are needed to help displaced workers with low skills for whom retraining may not be viable because of their age or ill health. Here, there is a case for income support on equity grounds but designed in a way that does not give the wrong signals concerning resource allocation. This may mean, for example, programmes of limited duration tied in to trade liberalization.

3.4. Part Two: Sensitive Sectors, Cohesion Countries

This part considers in detail the situation of the four sensitive sectors in manufacturing which, although in different degrees, are of relevance for the four cohesion countries and for other richer EU members as well. The four sectors considered are textiles and clothing, steel, cars, and electronics. Textiles and clothing, cars, and electronics are affected by the Uruguay Round liberalization, steel is relevant within the Europe Agreements. The Uruguay Round also involves important liberalization in the service sector, but, given the relatively low share of trade in services in the cohesion countries and the relatively low share in employment in market services in the poor regions, this sector is only marginally relevant for cohesion. Available evidence (CER 1995) confirms that, over the decade of 1981–91, the most relevant growth in market services was found in those regions (especially in the richer member states) where manufacturing industry is particularly relevant.

There are two main reasons why an analysis of sectors is relevant for cohesion. First, to some degree all of these sectors have undergone important adjustment and restructuring over the past decade. The results were mixed. Some of these sectors are declining (textile and clothing, steel) and their sectoral value added is below the average of the manufacturing European value added (CER 1995), others are 'mature' (cars), and others are 'booming'. The first two sectors have undergone major employment losses over the past decade in all major EU member countries. The car sector has witnessed employment gains in some member countries and losses in others. Employment in electronics has increased in all major member countries. In addition, since each sector shows distinctive features in the mechanisms of adjustment and restructuring, the possible effects of external policies should be evaluated against this background. Second, one important element of cohesion is the location of foreign direct investment. The role of FDI in supporting regional growth is increasingly recognized as a source of both employment and knowledge diffusion and, more generally, as a factor of change and upgrading the production structure of the host country and region. One established point is that protection may attract FDI as it is implemented as barrier jumping strategies by foreign firms. While there is evidence that the fears of higher barriers to trade following the implementation of the single market have led to an increase of non-EU, especially Japanese, FDI (see e.g. Micossi and Viesti 1992), it is not clear that it has favoured only specific regions; the available evidence suggests that FDI is located in both central and peripheral locations. Nevertheless, cohesion problems may also arise from the consequences of capital mobility, i.e. the relevant competition may be in the markets for locations rather than in the markets for goods. The changing structure of external policies will probably affect the locational strategies of firms. Such strategies, however, through FDI and other forms of internationalization of production, differ according to the sector, and they also produce different consequences on employment. There is evidence (Eurostat 1995) that transnational activities in sectors such as textiles and clothing are very important as factors of relocation of activity and may have negative consequences on EU employment. The same is also true in consumer electronics and electrical components and computers, while it much less so in the motor vehicles sector where effects on employment are ambiguous. These aspects are considered in more detail below.

One way of looking at the relevance of sensitive sectors is to compare the regional share with the EU-12 average. Textiles and clothing (TC) are of some relevance in several member countries, including the larger ones, but with particular weight in the four poor countries and in some regions of Italy and the UK. The twenty regions with the highest share of employment in TC are located in the following member states: Italy (6), Greece (5), Belgium (2), Portugal (2), Spain (2), UK (2), and Germany (1). The case of Italy, however, should be considered with some caution because the footwear industry is included in the regional TC employment figures. Electrical and electronics employment is of substantial relevance only in Ireland as far as the four poor members are concerned, but it is important in several regions of the other richer members.

Transport equipment is relevant in several regions of the large countries, including several regions of the Italian Mezzogiorno, but only in some regions of Spain, with marginal presence in the other poor members. Employment in the metallic products sector is relevant in several regions of the richer members and in some regions of Spain.

To sum up, the regional employment data, while partly distorted because of the unsatisfactory available aggregation, indicate that sensitive sectoral employment is present both in rich and poor EU members. However, as we shall see below, sectoral behaviour and performance may vary across countries.

3.4.1. *Textiles and clothing*

Textiles and clothing industries have undergone major restructuring over the past decade. TC employment has dropped in all member states (see CEC 1995 and Table 3.7), but the textile industry, which is more capital intensive than the clothing industry, has performed somewhat better. The shedding of employment allowed for some increase in productivity in the clothing sector where cost differentials with non-EU competitors are relevant (see Table 3.8).

The consequences of external policies on the behaviour of the sector can be partly inferred from an analysis of the Portuguese case (Corado, Benaceck, and Caban 1995). The textile industry, and to a lesser extent the clothing industry, have reacted to Portuguese EC membership by increasing productivity through a large drop in employment, but productivity gains were also obtained through investment efforts. As another

Table 3.7. Changes in production and employment: textiles and clothing

	Production[a] (total changes %)		Employment[b] (total changes %)	
	Textiles	Clothing	Textiles	Clothing
Belgium	+2.6	+42.3	−26.1	−38.4
Denmark	−24.3	−32.5	−27.9	−32.1
Germany	−20.5	−42.3	−34.2	−48.7
Greece	−19.7	−22.0	−48.4	−8.9
Spain	−1.3	−6.2	−37.3	−7.9
France	−21.3	−37.6	−44.4	−30.0
Ireland	+25.1	−34.8	−23.5	−32.6
Italy	+16.7	−8.1	−16.2	−31.7
Netherlands	−3.0	+13.0	−21.1	−29.9
Portugal	+10.5	+26.8	−6.1	+6.5
United Kingdom	−15.1	−0.4	−20.3	−22.2
EU–12	−5.4	−19.8	−27.2	−26.4

[a] Based on production in Mio ecus (constant 1990 prices) in firms of all sizes.
[b] Based on number of employees in firms of all sizes.

Textiles = NACE 43 + 455
Clothing = NACE 453 + 454

Table 3.8. Unit labour costs in the clothing industry

Country or zone	1990	1991	1993
North America			
Canada	8.76	9.53	9.14
USA	6.56	6.77	8.13
Mexico	0.92	1.17	1.08
European Community			
Germany	7.23	14.81	17.22
Belgium	12.92	12.57	16.2
Denmark	15.93	15.91	17.29
Spain	7.08	7.11	6.41
France	12.52	12.41	14.84
Greece	4.33	4.26	5.85
Ireland	7.5	7.5	7.44
Italy	12.5	13.5	12.31
Netherlands	14.71	14.95	15.41
Portugal	2.3	2.65	3.03
United Kingdom	8.02	7.99	8.42
Western Europe			
Austria	9.96	9.84	14.3
Finland	14.16	13.98	9.25
Norway	16.37	15.92	18.09
Sweden	17.78	18.52	15.84
Switzerland	14.19	14.19	18.08
Eastern Europe			
Bulgaria	1.25	0.25	0.26
Hungary	0.92	1.19	1.62
Poland	0.5	0.42	0.44
Romania	1.73	0.55	0.25
Russian Federation	1.69	0.49	0.57
Slovakia	:	:	1.14
Former Czechoslovakia	2.79	1.59	1.29
Middle East			
Israel	5.17	5.73	5.54
Syrian Arab Republic	0.71	0.81	0.84
Turkey	1.35	2.31	3.29
Africa			
South Africa	1.07	1.12	1.12
Egypt	0.34	0.32	0.43
Ethiopia	0.57	0.57	:
Kenya	0.47	0.44	0.23
Mauritius	:	:	1.04
Morocco	0.92	0.99	1.06
Nigeria	0.2	0.2	0.27

Table 3.8. (cont'd)

Country or zone	1990	1991	1993
Tanzania	:	0.26	0.18
Tunisia	1.46	1.46	1.54
Uganda	0.16	0.18	:
Zambia	:	:	0.24
Zimbabwe	:	0.51	0.35
South America and the Caribbean			
Argentina	1.07	1.81	1.85
Brazil	0.98	0.76	0.73
Colombia	1.23	1.18	1.22
Costa Rica	1.09	0.88	:
Dominican Republic	0.67	0.64	:
Honduras	0.48	0.48	:
Jamaica	0.91	0.83	:
Peru	0.86	0.88	1
Uruguay	1.41	1.59	2.35
Venezuela	1.11	1.38	1.48
Asia—Pacific			
Australia	8.79	9.58	8.67
Bangladesh	:	:	0.16
China	0.26	0.24	0.25
Korea	2.46	2.75	2.71
Hong Kong	3.05	3.39	3.85
India	0.33	0.25	0.27
Indonesia	0.16	0.18	0.28
Japan	6.34	7.44	10.64
Malaysia	0.56	0.62	0.77
Pakistan	0.24	0.24	0.27
Philippines	0.46	0.46	0.53
Singapore	2.43	2.72	3.06
Sri Lanka	0.24	0.39	0.35
Taiwan, China	3.41	3.74	4.61
Thailand	0.63	0.59	0.71
Vietnam	:	:	0.26

Source: Werner International Inc. (New York, 1994).

study shows (CEC 1995), the large restructuring wave in the clothing sector has been the consequence of the large surge in imports and the fall in demand for domestic products.

The organization and structure of TC strongly favours processes of relocalization of parts of the production process. While one should distinguish between the textile sector and the clothing sector, important internationalization patterns can be observed in both segments.

The most visible consequence is the relevant increase of outward processing trade (OPT) from CEECs (especially Poland and Hungary) that has developed especially in the clothing sector, but growth in the textiles sector has also been substantial. Growth of OPT in both sectors has been higher than growth of total imports. This development is due to several factors: (a) OPT are not affected by tariffs as heavily as 'direct imports', (b) they can exploit the low cost and relatively high quality of TC labour in CEECs in processing high quality textiles produced in rich EU regions, (c) the industrial structure in CEECs is quite similar to that of TC industries in most EU countries, (d) geographical proximity plays a relevant role. OPT is competing with low-quality, low-value-added segments of TC production, so it is not affecting high-value-added segments located in rich EU areas. OPT has so far been granted on a national basis. Rich countries, Germany in the first place, have greatly encouraged this form of trade, and very recently Italian firms have begun to follow the same strategy. OPT was encouraged with respect to Portugal and, less so, Spain before their entry into the EC. Introduction of the Europe Agreements has produced a rapid relocation into CEECs because of labour cost advantages. Clear indications are emerging that OPT will be relocated in Turkey, following the recent trade agreements, and North African countries.

As of 1 January 1995 the concession of OPT quotas has become much stricter and will be eventually phased out for CEECs. Full membership of CEECs in the EU probably will lead to an increased relocation in these countries through FDI and joint ventures, as barriers to 'direct imports' are eliminated. Once this process is begun, production relocation through FDI also may affect rich EU countries and regions.

From this point of view further liberalization may hurt low-quality TC production located in EU countries as labour costs pressures become stronger. Elimination of the MultiFibre Arrangement may increase this pressure but, possibly, to the disadvantage of CEECs as OPT is directed to non-European low labour cost areas.

More generally, the impact of the Uruguay Round will be of some importance in adding pressures to TC industries. According to a recent study (CEC 1995), however, Uruguay Round liberalization will cover only 30 per cent of EU imports in TC (to become 43 per cent once China joins the WTO) and, if one considers imports in restricted categories with a quota utilization above 80 per cent, Uruguay Round liberalization is relevant for 13 per cent (16 per cent with China).

The effects on EU imports that should derive from the customs union with Turkey, the Europe Agreements, and closer trade links with CIS countries should amount to about four per cent of total imports of restricted categories (with a quota utilization of more than 80 per cent).

3.4.2. Steel

The EU is the world's largest producer and exporter of steel. Over the recent past the sector has been facing severe restructuring problems and suffering from significant amounts of excess capacity. This feature also explains the irrelevance of FDI in the sector.

Between 1980 and 1990 sectoral employment has declined in all major EU countries (ranging from a decline of over 13 per cent in Germany, 28.6 per cent in France,

30.1 per cent in Italy, 39.53 per cent in Spain, to 50.1 per cent in the UK; see CER 1995). The decline in domestic consumption has been worsened by the introduction of new materials as a consequence of technological innovations. As in the case of TC, the steel sector is facing internal structural problems and urgently needs restructuring, problems which may be worsened by the liberalization process. The consequences for cohesion, however, might be different given the distribution of employment. With the exception of Spain, where some regions show higher than average employment shares, the highest shares of employment in this sector are not located in the four poor countries.

It is also important to note that most of the support for the sector is granted through state aids. To understand the implications of liberalization, however, a basic distinction must be made between high-quality (flat) steel products and low-quality (long) products (Winters 1994). The four large EU countries are also the four largest producers of steel products, all specializing in flat products. Spain, as mentioned, is also an important producer but is more specialized in long products, and hence more sensitive to competition from CEECs.

Effects on EU output and employment has been assessed through CGE simulations (Winters 1995). Rationalization of production may lead to limited output losses because of generalized excess capacity in both the EU and CEECs, but most of the effect will come as a consequence of deeper specialization following liberalization, as CEECs will specialize in lower-quality products and should increase imports of higher-quality products. This should favour rich countries, which have already completed most of their restructuring, and hurt poor EU members (Spain and other EU southern members). The pattern of regional specialization discussed above shows that Spain is the only poor country with a relevant employment concentration in this sector. However, low-quality production will also be displaced in some rich EU countries, particularly in Germany. While the overall effects could be modest, this would worsen cohesion problems in the EU.

3.4.3. *Cars*

As in the case of the steel industry, the car industry is concentrated in the four major rich countries and in some regions of the large southern member (Spain). Part of the Italian car industry is also located in the poor southern regions (Mezzogiorno).

The structure of industry is oligopolistic and competition through mergers and acquisitions is a standard feature (Smith and Venables 1990). This trend probably will increase industry concentration over the medium term. Another relevant feature is the consistent multinational activity of both EU and non-EU firms. The European car industry is protected through quantitative restrictions and VERs set on a national basis and with country-specific characteristics, while substantial support has been granted through state subsidies.

Before the implementation of the European single market, national quotas defined market access. Southern EU members presented the highest restrictions, a measure of which are the shares of Japanese cars in national markets. In 1992 the three large southern producers (France, Italy, and Spain) had shares largely below 5 per cent (while

Germany had almost 14 per cent, above the EU average of 11.8 per cent) (Turrini 1995). While the implementation of the SEM implies the substitution of national quotas by a EU quota, the 1991 agreement between the EU and Japan calls for the gradual phasing out of all restrictions by 1999. Simulation exercises (Turrini 1995) show that, at the end of the transition period, Japanese market shares should rise above five per cent in the three large southern producers. (The quota in Portugal, which is not a producer, should rise from 7 to almost 8.5 per cent.)

What is of relevance for cohesion, therefore, is the reaction of the Spanish industry (and from the point of view of regional cohesion, of the Italian car industry in the Mezzogiorno) to the phasing out of quantitative restrictions. VERs usually produce a quality upgrade of the imported cars as well as profit increases for foreign car producers. They also encourage FDI, which are attracted towards 'central locations' where agglomeration economies can be exploited. From this point of view, VERs are beneficial to richer countries and regions rather than peripheral and poor ones to the extent that only the former offer profitable locations for foreign firms. Data on FDI (see Tables 3.11 and 3.13) indicate that foreign investment, both of EC and non-EC origin, in the transport equipment sector has been substantial in Spain and negligible in Portugal.

Another important component of external policies for the car industry is the rule of origin and local content of foreign production. Its relevance for cohesion stems from the fact that it can alter location opportunities. There has always been fear that production of foreign (especially Japanese) transplants might reach a very low local share with modest local employment benefits and large domestic market penetration. The UK experience, where Japanese FDI has been particularly active, shows that, after an adjustment period, Japanese transplants had reached, by the beginning of the present decade, the limit of 80 per cent of local content, considered to be the acceptable target from the EU perspective (Smith and Venables 1990). The UK experience suggests that external policies aimed at increasing FDI location provide substantial benefits to the receiving country or region. The Spanish experience with FDI shows that the entry of foreign firms has led to dramatic changes in the production and export specialization of Spain over the past ten years, thereby confirming the point (Outes Ruso 1995, Martín 1995).

3.4.4. Electronics

The European electronics industry has been lagging behind US and especially Japanese producers over the last fifteen years both in terms of export and production performance (Vickery 1992, Guerrieri 1994). While the gap has not narrowed, EU firms have undergone important restructuring programs. The global growth of the sector has boosted the EU industry as well. Between 1980 and 1990 employment in the computer industry has increased in all major EU countries, with Italy and Spain showing the highest increases (47 and 40 per cent respectively, CER 1995) .

EU firms operating in the sector (there are only three large European producers in semiconductors) have started redirecting their strategies away from the domestic (European) market and towards the global market. This has led to agreements and joint ventures with non-EU firms. US, Japanese, and Korean firms have followed a strategy of plant location in Europe so as to jump quantitative restriction on imports that have been growing steadily over the past decade, especially in consumer electronics. The location of foreign production facilities accounts for a large share of the export base of electronics products in Europe. This share is remarkably high in large countries such as France and the UK and reaches almost one hundred per cent in Ireland, which shows the lowest share of imports from the rest of the European Union and one of the highest shares of exports towards EU countries (Vickery 1992). This country also accounts for the largest share in employment in the sector among the four poor EU members.

Foreign direct investment in electronics has been increasing also in Spain and Portugal, surpassing in some cases FDI in other crucial sectors such as transport equipment. Available data, however, indicate a relevant employment share only in the Madrid region, where also a substantial FDI location is present.

While the sector is usually classified as human-capital-intensive, some of the labour-intensive activities are usually relocated in low labour cost regions. This has also been the case for FDI location in peripheral EU countries. This issue is also central to the policy debate between the EU and foreign producers which deals mainly with the rule of origin issue. This is particularly relevant in the case of semiconductor production and utilization (Flamm 1990). As of 1989 the EU requires that the rule of origin be granted to production actually 'fabricated' and not just 'assembled' in the Union. This policy is hitting especially Japanese, but also US producers, and concerns location in three of the four poor EU countries . In 1990 Ireland had four locations, two Japanese and two US, three of which were classified as assembly and one as fabrication locations; Spain had one (US) fabrication and Portugal one (US) assembly location (Flamm 1990).

The reaction to the rule of origin clause may spur relocation in other areas, especially in CEECs, where the availability of human capital represents an important attraction. One should not overestimate the effects of external (protection) policies in terms of employment effects in the electronics sector. Specific locations, such as Ireland, are chosen not so much because of external policies but because of attraction factors. In sum, in the case of electronics, external policies do not seem to produce cohesion benefits.

3.4.5. *The four cohesion countries*

In this section we take a broad look at the four cohesion countries, not only to provide an overall evaluation of external polices concerning these economies, but also to assess their adjustment potential to a changing external environment by looking at the evolution of both their trade specialization and their international investment flows over the period 1988–93. We will also briefly consider the intertemporal dimension of cohesion discussed in the previous sections.

We will look at three aspects of the economies of the cohesion countries: the overall employment structure by regional disaggregation, revealed comparative advantages, and FDI flows.

Before looking at each cohesion country separately let us consider the overall picture of the trade adjustment process which has affected the EU over the same period. One quick way of doing this is to consider the changes in the signs of the RCA for EU and

Table 3.9. Number of changes in RCA

	Positive	Negative
By Country		
EU–12	1	3
Germany	1	1
France	4	4
Italy	1	3
UK	1	3
Spain	—	5
Portugal	3	5
Greece	3	2
Ireland	3	6
By sector		
1. Technology intensive	3	6
2. Human capital intensive	3	6
3. Labour intensive	5	10
4. Labour and capital intensive	7	11
5. Food	5	2
By partner		
Mediterranean	1	—
CEEC	8	5
ACP	2	3
US	2	4
Japan	2	5
ASEAN	1	11
NIC Asia	2	2

Positive change = RCA changes from negative to positive
Negative change = RCA changes from positive to negative

for a group of eight EU member states, the four cohesion countries and the four largest EU economies (Germany, France, Italy, and the United Kingdom), so as to compare adjustment in the 'core' and in the 'periphery' of the Union.[11]

Table 4.1 reports the number of changes in the RCA indicators presented for the eight countries considered as well as for the EU–12. A positive change implies that there has been a shift from a comparative disadvantage to a comparative advantage (a positive adjustment), a negative change implies the opposite (a negative adjustment); changes are reported respectively by country, by sector, and by trading partner. By looking at the intensity and concentration of changes the following points may be singled out. (1) The cohesion countries show the highest number of changes, both positive and negative, indicating a rather intense process of restructuring in trade specialization. (2) Sectors

---

[11] RCA tables for the four core countries are not reported. A more detailed analysis is in Padoan (1997).

where most changes have taken place are the labour-intensive and the labour- and capital-intensive ones (i.e. those sectors where at least three out of four cohesion countries show positive RCA). (3) Changes are particularly frequent (and positive) in trade with the CEECs. In sum, it is safe to say that an important process of geographical and sectoral trade restructuring has taken place over the period considered, and that the cohesion countries seem to have reacted positively to the changing environment. This confirms what has been mentioned in the previous sections and suggests that the intertemporal dimension of cohesion may be strengthened by progressive liberalization processes, especially if one notes that peripheral rather than core countries seem to have experienced the most intense restructuring.

As far as the role of FDI flows is concerned, some general aspects should be mentioned. The relationship between transnational business activities and regional integration and liberalization presents (at least) two aspects, themselves related to the two dimensions of regional integration, both relevant for the understanding of cohesion: deepening and widening.

The first aspect, the 'deepening effect', can be described as follows. When a process of regional deepening is started—or simply announced—i.e. when a new regional agreement is formed or when an existing one proceeds towards further integration, firms, whether or not they are operating on a transnational or global scale, will react both by increasing their concentration (for example, to increase the minimum efficient scale) and, if they are firms operating outside the region, by establishing new plants within the region to exploit the benefits of a larger market and avoid possible discriminating measures which the integrating region might establish. In both cases, deepening will lead to an increase of multinational activities within the existing region.[12] The second aspect, the 'widening effect', can be described as follows: an enlargement (or the announcement thereof) of the regional agreement opens the possibility of establishing production activities in the peripheral areas of the region, which might offer locational advantages, in terms of e.g. labour costs, with respect to the central areas of the region.

The deepening effect will lead to a spatial and economic concentration of firms. The widening effect will lead to a diffusion of firms' locations. Which effect will prevail will ultimately determine whether transnational activities favours or hinders cohesion.

The available literature does not offer a definitive answer on this issue.[13] Let us just recall what may be considered as the two opposite views on the topic. According to the traditional 'product cycle approach', FDIs are responsible for relocating the production of mature goods in the periphery where cost differentials are important. In this process, FDIs act as a vehicle of technology diffusion from the core to the periphery, but they do not contribute to the 'upgrading' of the productive specialization of the periphery as long as technological innovation takes place in the core locations.[14] Nonetheless, so long as relevant cost differentials persist, peripheral regions may benefit from capital inflows which can partially alleviate the asymmetric distribution of net benefits from integration.

---

[12] For a discussion of this point with respect to the single European market, see Baldwin, Forslid, and Haaland (1995). See also Padoan (1997).

[13] For a review of the theory supporting these effects see Barry (1996).   [14] See Ozawa (1992).

A different conclusion can be reached according to the new trade theory (Krugman and Venables 1993), which maintains that the decision to locate industrial activities depends on elements other than (labor) costs. In particular, these decisions depend on the possibility of exploiting or acquiring technological advantage and benefits from innovation and, as a consequence, they will privilege locations where technological innovation activities are relevant. This implies that FDIs will be closely associated with the trade specialization of core locations (and countries), themselves characterized by knowledge-intensive productions (Markusen 1995, Markusen and Venables 1995). In other words, FDI flows will originate from and direct themselves towards knowledge intensive locations.[15] An important implication is that, because of the cumulative nature of the innovation process, the diffusion of new technology, at least insofar as it is generated through forms other than trade, is limited.[16] In such a case, intraregional differences are likely to increase.

The consequences of increased transnational activity for regional cohesion are diverse, both in the sense that they are related to the different intensity of the widening and deepening effects and in that they are 'sector dependent', as the direction of FDI flows within an integrated area depends on the sectoral characteristics and on the role that knowledge accumulation plays in each specific sector. FDIs will contribute to a polarization of the specialization patterns (and hence they will not increase cohesion) to the extent that knowledge-intensive productions will concentrate in central locations.

FDIs will contribute to the diffusion of technology and production locations in the case of the less knowledge-intensive productions (or the less knowledge-intensive segments of the production process where labour costs play a more relevant role), the more so in the perspective of regional enlargement. We will refer to this case as the 'diffusion pattern'.[17] In this case, however, another problem may arise for the cohesion of regional agreements as peripheral locations will compete among themselves to attract labour-cost driven FDIs.

One issue relevant for cohesion is the relationship between increased capital mobility and changes in the specialization structure. In the previous section we discussed the characteristics of transnational activities in different sensitive sectors. While the relationship between the structure of trade and the sectoral structure of FDI is still to be clarified both in theory and in empirical investigation, recent evidence (Guerrieri and Manzocchi 1995, Padoan 1997) indicates that in sectors such as electronics and chemicals where the degree of industry concentration as well as technology intensity is high, comparative advantages in trade are correlated to strong FDI outflows; i.e. exports and FDI are complements rather than substitutes. This evidence, however, can be observed for large countries, i.e. where the home firm is located. In the case of smaller countries (such as the cohesion countries), however, this relationship may be different as large FDI inflows can be associated with strengthening comparative advantages in trade. In addition, intense FDI flows may lead to changes in the patterns of RCA to the extent that they activate important intrafirm trade flows.

[15] This at least partially explains why the largest part of world FDI takes place among OECD countries. See OECD (1995) and Reinicke (1996). [16] See Guerrieri and Manzocchi (1995) on this point.
[17] Guerrieri and Manzocchi (1995) offer a first empirical analysis of this distinction.

Table 3.10. Revealed comparative advantages, Spain

Partners	Years	Groups of sectors				
		1 Technology-intensive	2 Human-capital-intensive	3 Labour-intensive	4 Labour- & capital-intensive	5 Food, etc.
World	1988	−82.3	−53.5	56.2	114.4	21.4
	1993	:	:	:	:	:
Extra-EC	1988	−67.7	3.4	102.8	176.8	48.8
	1993	−6.7	18.1	105.3	144.3	39.3
Intra-EC	1988	−90.4	−93.6	22.2	71.9	3.1
	1993	:	:	:	:	:
Med. countries	1988	113.0	133.4	40.7	288.8	14.4
	1993	85.0	94.2	49.7	305.5	34.4
CEECs	1988	3.8	54.7	63.9	−69.7	−57.4
	1993	−21.0	57.9	−7.0	−88.7	−62.2
ACP	1988	105.2	58.5	259.9	96.6	114.0
	1993	63.9	−0.8	476.1	149.6	72.9
USA	1988	−313.5	−56.2	141.3	236.1	92.5
	1993	−255.7	−52.7	122.3	224.1	54.0
Japan	1988	−347.7	−149.8	57.6	190.7	33.4
	1993	−98.7	−102.7	98.3	−104.4	50.8
ASEAN	1988	67.5	22.4	112.8	187.2	−34.4
	1993	80.4	110.2	−42.9	99.9	−9.0
NICs	1988	−269.6	−22.9	56.3	322.0	3.9
	1993	−89.9	−70.2	54.7	129.5	11.2

3.4.6. Spain

Spain shows a diversified structure with higher than EU average shares in sensitive sectors such as transport equipment, textiles and clothing, and metallic products (including steel). Also, seven out of nineteen regions show a share in manufacturing employment that is higher than the EU average. The employment diversification is evident both in terms of sectors and in terms of regions. There is no single region (perhaps with the exception of Aragon) where one can find important concentration of employment in more than one sensitive sector. This diversification suggests that, in the case of Spain, cohesion problems that may arise from trade liberalization do not have an important regional dimension, but rather a national one.

Spain (see Table 3.10) shows comparative advantages[18] with respect to extra-EU trade in all sectors except the technology-intensive goods (group 1). However, this structure changes significantly if one considers specific partner countries. Over the period considered, Spain maintains comparative advantages in all sectors *vis-à-vis* the Mediterranean

[18] Revealed comparative advantages are defined as

$$\star\star \text{ RCA} = (x/X - m/M) \times 1000$$

x = sectoral exports, X = aggregate exports, m = sectoral imports, M = aggregate imports.

countries but, in trade with the CEECs, advantages persist only in sector 2 (human-capital-intensive goods). Trade with Japan and Asian NICs shows advantages in sectors 3 (labour-intensive) and 4 (labour- and capital-intensive), but only with respect to Asian NICs and 5 (food industries).

A somewhat less reassuring picture emerges if one look at changes in RCA. As shown in Table 3.10, Spain is the only cohesion country where no positive changes in RCA occur (with five negative changes). Two of the negative changes occur in the labour-intensive industries and are related to trade with CEECs and ASEAN countries. This suggests that while the Spanish economy has undergone a significant restructuring process in the period considered, this has highlighted weak points in her specialization structure but has not indicated new strong points.

These indications suggest that liberalization in favour of the CEEC countries as well as liberalization following the Uruguay Round would hurt labour-intensive sectors (including clothing but not textiles) and labour- and capital-intensive sectors (including steel) to the advantage of specific partner countries. They also indicate, however, that Spanish producers might exploit their comparative advantages in these sectors with respect to other markets, and they support the view (CEC 1995) that increased market access in other areas could, partly, compensate for market losses determined by liberalization in favour of CEECs. Also, competitiveness in labour-intensive sectors may be enhanced by quality upgrading, which seems to be taking place in the Spanish industry (Martín 1995).

The interpretation of the negative change in labour- and capital-intensive trade with Japan is rather different, for it can be explained as a consequence of the increase in intrafirm trade following the large Japanese FDI inflow in the transport equipment sector over the second half of the past decade (Micossi and Viesti 1992). In this respect, this evolution would signal only a temporary worsening of the trade potential in this sector, i.e. a prevalence of a diffusion pattern associated with transnational activities.

In the recent past Spain has followed a very active policy of attracting foreign investment (Martín 1995, Outes Rouso 1995). This has strengthened the FDI attraction effect (i.e. the widening effect) generated by the simultaneous entry into the EC and the launching of the single market (Baldwin *et al.* 1995). Spain (see Table 3.11) presents a high share of FDI with respect to total trade (which can be taken as a measure of the internationalization of the economy), more than twice as large as the EU average. Sectors most interested by FDI inflows, such as food industries and transport equipment, show trade comparative advantages, hence FDI inflows seem to strengthen the trade specialization structure of the country. FDI in chemical industries (included in the technology-intensive group 1) are also relevant, although they are not matched by positive (or positive changes in) RCA. In this respect the Spanish case is in line the EU-12 one, where important FDI flows in the sector reflect merger and acquisition policies in the Union. In general, FDIs have contributed to the strengthening of the international position of the country even if this is yet to be fully translated into gains in the structure of RCA, and confirms that attraction policies should be considered as an important instrument of cohesion.

Table 3.11. Spain FDI/imports: sectoral breakdown

	88		89		90		91		92		93	
	intra-EC (%)	extra-EC (%)	intra-EC (%)	extra-EC (%)	intra-EC (%)	extra-EC (%)	intra-EC (%)	extra-EC (%)	intra-EC (%)	extra-EC (%)	intra-EC (%)	extra-EC (%)
Total	13.90	8.55	14.38	7.79	18.62	10.85	14.11	7.33	9.49	7.05	:	7.31
Building and construction	:	:	:	:	:	:	:	:	:	:	:	:
Energy	3.52	1.40	0.34	0.00	36.61	0.17	29.49	3.41	5.92	0.17	:	:
Agriculture and food	:	:	9.97	5.87	6.84	4.21	6.86	3.55	5.98	4.37	:	3.34
Metallics	:	:	4.17	2.71	2.16	3.31	:	:	:	:	:	:
Machinery	:	:	1.01	1.40	0.54	2.33	0.48	4.49	1.30	2.91	:	1.67
Transport Equipment	:	:	4.25	2.50	4.47	5.69	2.31	3.43	1.29	2.53	:	:
Electrical and electronics	:	:	1.99	2.16	3.12	3.86	:	:	:	:	:	:
Chemical industries	:	:	6.81	14.91	6.74	9.64	3.38	11.49	6.63	11.43	:	8.40
Other industries	:	:	10.90	13.77	14.82	24.36	3.83	7.52	3.79	6.94	:	3.47
Total industries	4.22	5.68	5.32	5.96	5.59	7.90	3.38	5.34	5.62	5.14	:	5.40
Trade, hotel, and catering	85.64	67.21	87.78	126.67	84.98	155.82	135.74	92.02	99.55	145.92	:	84.71

Source: Eurostat.

Table 3.12. Revealed comparative advantages, Portugal

Partners	Years	Groups of sectors				
		1 Technology– intensive	2 Human–capital– intensive	3 Labour-intensive	4 Labour– & capital– intensive	5 Food, etc.
World	1988	−78.7	−84.0	275.3	−58.8	−0.9
	1993	:	:	:	:	:
Extra-EC	1988	−39.5	−22.8	331.7	70.0	12.3
	1993	−59.2	−17.0	293.1	57.4	9.5
Intra-EC	1988	−98.5	−110.8	257.3	−125.8	−5.0
	1993	:	:	:	:	:
Med. countries	1988	155.1	84.4	55.6	290.3	33.8
	1993	76.6	91.5	72.8	245.9	2.4
CEECs	1988	−193.2	−100.0	−46.3	501.0	1.2
	1993	−26.4	−39.9	98.7	228.7	1.1
ACP	1988	122.5	118.7	134.1	285.4	53.6
	1993	98.3	92.9	281.7	211.9	65.1
USA	1988	−165.0	15.8	257.8	227.8	−113.4
	1993	−163.8	1.5	220.2	291.5	−87.0
Japan	1988	−141.5	2.7	−10.5	−238.0	155.7
	1993	−87.5	−99.5	93.2	−351.0	61.8
ASEAN	1988	207.6	4.3	132.2	222.9	63.5
	1993	−35.6	47.9	−90.8	−12.9	−14.9
NICs	1988	−112.7	−73.5	6.3	100.6	35.2
	1993	−147.9	27.5	46.7	75.8	3.7

3.4.7. *Portugal*

The structure of Portugal's RCA (see Table 3.12) resembles that of Spain, although with some important differences. Extra-EU trade shows persistent advantages in labour intensive, labour and capital intensive and food sectors. The food industry presents the highest employment share (concentrated especially in the Alentejo region). Trade with Mediterranean countries, and with ACP countries, shows comparative advantages in all sectors. While trade with Japan shows persistent advantages only in food sectors, trade with Asian NICs shows a more favourable position. A more articulated picture emerges by looking at changes in RCA. Contrary to Spain, Portugal presents a number of positive as well as negative changes. Interestingly, two positive changes are in the labour intensive sectors in trade with the CEEC's and with Japan, showing capacity to adjust in this highly sensitive group of sectors. This may be partly the result of the intensive restructuring that has taken place in the textile and clothing industry over the past decade (Corado, Benaceck, Caban 1995). Note, however, that three of the five negative changes in RCA take place in trade with the ASEAN countries, signaling problems in competition with low wage countries. From this point of view, while liberalization with respect to CEECs is likely to put some pressure on Portugal, the consequences of the Uruguay Round may be more relevant in affecting regional cohesion in this country.

Table 3.13. Portugal FDI/imports: sectoral breakdown

	88 intra-EC (%)	88 extra-EC (%)	89 intra-EC (%)	89 extra-EC (%)	90 intra-EC (%)	90 extra-EC (%)	91 intra-EC (%)	91 extra-EC (%)	92 intra-EC (%)	92 extra-EC (%)	93 intra-EC (%)	93 extra-EC (%)
Total	5.26	4.25	8.97	6.59	10.10	9.55	9.19	8.70	6.46	6.05	..	4.90
Building and construction	..	..	..	..	..	..	..	..	..	..	..	..
Energy	5.41	0.10	4.31	0.28	1.48	0.12	1.54	0.20	-5.88	1.06	..	..
Agriculture and food	2.16	1.45	3.25	0.71	2.81	0.94	3.70	1.92	2.26	0.77	..	-0.07
Metallics	0.00	0.00	0.09	0.35	0.35	1.14	0.08	3.73	0.15	1.96	..	1.73
Machinery	..	..	..	..	..	..	..	..	0.05	0.00	..	0.00
Transport Equipment	..	..	..	..	..	..	..	..	0.19	0.71	..	0.00
Electrical and electronics	..	..	..	..	..	..	..	..	1.62	2.69	..	..
Chemical industries	1.95	2.86	1.64	5.90	1.93	7.76	3.92	15.17	0.00	0.24	..	..
Other industries	..	..	..	..	..	..	..	..	1.03	9.92	..	..
Total industries	1.47	1.18	1.81	1.62	1.63	2.67	2.32	-0.25	0.95	1.96	..	2.39
Trade, hotel, and catering	190.19	238.46	339.47	1,189.23	165.78	92.70	408.12	320.71	-17.16	-143.45	..	99.40

Source: EC.

While not as intense as in the case of Spain, the flow of international capital into Portugal from sources both inside the EU and outside the EU is significant. The sectoral evolution of FDI (see Table 3.13) shows the relative importance of the food industry sector as a recipient of FDI inflows, an element which may be associated with the relatively strong trade position in the same sector. More recently there also have been some inflows into the electrical and electronics sector. These may also explain, as in the case of the transport equipment sector in Spain, the sharp deterioration of RCA in the human–capital–intensive sector in trade with Japan, signalling an increase in intrafirm trade which should be interpreted as a relative strengthening of the sector (although its size and employment share is modest).

3.4.8. Greece

The sectoral employment distribution in Greece highlights the role of the food industry, heavily present in all regions, and of the textiles and clothing sector, also present in several regions. These sectors account for most of the manufacturing employment in an economy where the manufacturing sector is smaller than the EU average.

The structure of manufacturing employment is also clearly reflected in the structure of RCA. Greece presents positive RCA in labour-intensive, labour- and capital-intensive, and food processing industries (see Table 3.14). Advantages in groups 2 and 5 are present in trade with the Mediterranean countries and also with the CEECs. However, in the labour-intensive group of sectors (group 2) the country shows disadvantages in trade with Asian NICs. The number of changes in the sign of RCA (Table 3.9) shows limited restructuring. Negative changes appear in extra-EC trade in the labour-intensive sector. Positive changes appear in extra-EU trade in labour- and capital-intensive sectors, which include textiles, but this change seems to be accounted for only by trade with ACP countries. These data suggest (see Dimelis and Gatsios 1995) that the country should benefit from trade liberalization with the Mediterranean countries, but much less so with the CEECs, with the exception of trade in food products. Over the recent past, however, trade integration with the CEECs has increased. Previous developments could be somewhat misleading, underestimating Greece's crucial geographical advantage for trade with the former planned economies, the Balkan countries, and Turkey.

A less reassuring picture emerges from the evolution of FDI. The extent of the economy's internationalization stands well below the EU average.[19] In absolute terms, the amount of FDI in the recent past has been barely one-third of the FDI in Portugal. No sectoral breakdown is available but, given the trade and manufacturing specialization, the country does not seem to offer substantial prospects for an increase of inward FDI. An exception is the food industry, which is characterized by a high degree of FDI activities. The overall picture might change, however, as integration within the Balkan region and with Turkey, following the Custom Union treaty, as well

---

[19] One reason for this performance may be the relative high and persistent macroeconomic and financial instability.

Table 3.14. Revealed comparative advantages, Greece

Partners	Years	Groups of sectors				
		1 Technology-intensive	2 Human-capital-intensive	3 Labour-intensive	4 Labour- & capital-intensive	5 Food, etc.
World	1988	−113.4	−88.2	148.6	−54.0	57.8
	1993	:	:	:	:	:
Extra-EC	1988	−47.8	−47.2	30.4	−7.7	94.5
	1993	−75.4	−7.5	−61.0	12.0	81.5
Intra-EC	1988	−151.4	−111.6	217.7	−101.4	35.6
	1993	:	:	:	:	:
Med. countries	1988	−13.3	60.2	−9.8	174.9	92.2
	1993	−23.3	71.3	−73.8	173.8	75.2
CEECs	1988	−7.5	−91.5	−106.0	−123.9	71.5
	1993	−93.2	15.4	−55.6	−236.0	55.8
ACP	1988	128.6	63.3	−1.4	−108.1	16.3
	1993	124.8	89.0	−414.5	57.6	100.8
USA	1988	−170.9	−112.3	129.1	86.9	195.9
	1993	−315.5	−120.8	109.3	141.0	106.0
Japan	1988	−92.0	−119.4	−324.5	158.4	91.1
	1993	−50.7	−68.9	−435.7	−165.1	206.5
ASEAN	1988	−156.7	−185.2	−6.2	174.7	−25.6
	1993	−162.8	−123.8	−117.3	2.5	22.9
NICs	1988	−51.8	−47.2	−452.9	178.7	19.7
	1993	−119.2	−34.5	−452.3	322.0	21.3

as with the Mediterranean countries, gathers momentum. The geographical location of the country might represent an important factor of attraction for foreign capital.

3.4.9. Ireland

This country stands out as unique in the group of the four poor EU members. While the share in manufacturing employment stands slightly below the EU average, it is concentrated in the electrical and electronics sector (where it is almost twice the EU average) and in food industries. This is reflected in the structure of RCA (see Table 3.15), which is markedly different from that of the other three countries showing comparative advantages in technology intensive sectors (and in food processing industries). Advantages in group 1 are present in trade with almost all partners, including Japan, but excluding ACP and Asian NICs. Trade with CEECs shows advantages also in human capital intensive sectors.

Ireland presents the same number of positive changes in RCA as Portugal and Greece, but also the highest number of negative changes (see Table 3.14). Two positive changes are present in trade in technology-intensive goods with extra-EU partners and the US. A negative change, however, is present in the same sector in trade with ASEAN countries. These developments seem to be closely related to the performance of the largely multinational-based manufacturing sector of the Irish economy, which accounts

Table 3.15. Revealed comparative advantages, Ireland

Partners	Years	Groups of sectors				
		1 Technology-intensive	2 Human-capital-intensive	3 Labour-intensive	4 Labour- & capital-intensive	5 Food, etc.
World	1988	118.4	−49.0	−51.0	−21.3	101.2
	1993	:	:	:	:	:
Extra-EC	1988	−8.5	−13.0	−10.6	2.4	142.2
	1993	98.9	−36.5	−29.4	−35.6	110.7
Intra-EC	1988	171.6	−61.7	−67.9	−67.4	88.1
	1993	:	:	:	:	:
Med. countries	1988	−147.0	79.6	−178.7	154.0	68.0
	1993	−192.6	23.5	−110.1	119.9	45.9
CEECs	1988	174.1	155.7	−101.1	84.8	124.0
	1993	479.7	102.6	−63.2	−105.7	26.5
ACP	1988	247.6	92.0	−10.6	41.4	330.4
	1993	119.0	22.5	−17.4	131.9	366.2
USA	1988	−185.1	14.3	25.0	42.9	115.2
	1993	25.7	−40.7	3.7	−13.1	80.3
Japan	1988	190.1	−42.9	−6.6	−241.4	33.2
	1993	296.5	−35.9	0.0	−201.5	20.9
ASEAN	1988	174.8	17.7	−119.4	−253.1	355.2
	1993	−279.6	33.6	−52.9	−8.5	315.1
NICs	1988	−49.7	90.2	−127.3	4.1	151.3
	1993	−166.3	9.1	−49.2	−20.3	182.4

for almost the full amount of employment in technology-intensive sectors.[20] The changing pattern of trade in this sector suggests increased exports of finished products to extra-EC markets and increased imports of parts and intermediate products from low-wage ASEAN countries within intrafirm trade networks. Further liberalization is bound to deepen this kind of process without significantly altering the employment base in Ireland. Other negative changes in RCA pertain largely to trade in sector 4 (labour- and capital-intensive goods), where the share of domestic firms is more relevant and where trade with non-EC partners is likely to be enhanced by liberalization.

The evidence above suggests that the process of liberalization, especially towards the CEECs and the Mediterranean, should greatly benefit Ireland as it would offer further export outlets in countries needing technology-intensive products.

Some authors (Barry 1996) suggest that the location of technology-intensive industries seems to be explained largely by the localization in the country of the labour intensive segments of the production process. The possibility of exploiting Ireland's specialization pattern requires that the presence of foreign firms in the country be maintained at a substantial level. There is a risk that further liberalization, especially towards the CEECs, might divert some foreign direct investment towards areas where low labour costs and relative abundant skilled labour endowments represent an important factor of attraction, once FDI flows to these countries resume after the recent slowdown.[21]

---

[20] See Barry (1996).   [21] See Hoekman and Djankov (1996).

References

Baldwin, R. E. (1994). The effects of trade and foreign direct investment on employment and relative wages. *OECD Economic Studies*, 23: 7–53.

—— Forslid, R., and Haaland, J. (1995). Investment creation and investment diversion: simulation analysis of the single market programme. CEPR Working Paper no. 1308.

Banks, G. and Tumlir, J. (1986). *Economic Policy and the Adjustment Problem.* Thames Essay no. 45, Trade Policy Research Centre. London: Gower.

Barry, F. (1996). Peripherality in economic geography and modern growth theory: evidence from Ireland's adjustment to free trade. *World Economy* 19: 345–65.

Begg, D. *et al.* (1990). *Monitoring European Integration: The Impact of Eastern Europe.* London: CEPR.

Berman, E., Bound, J. and Griliches, Z. (1994). Changes in the demand for skilled labour within US manufacturing: evidence from the annual survey of manufactures. *Quarterly Journal of Economics* 109: 367–97.

Borjas, G. and Ramey, V. (1993). Time series evidence on the sources of trends in wages inequality. *American Economic Review* 84: 10–16.

Bound, J. and Johnson, G. (1992). Changes in the structure of wages in the 1980s: an evaluation of alternative explanations. *American Economic Review* 82: 371–92.

Cadot, O. and de Melo, J. (1995). France and the CEECs: adjusting to another enlargement. In Faini and Portes (1995).

Caves, R. and Krepps, M. (1993). Fat: the displacement of nonproduction workers from US manufacturing industries. *Brookings Papers in Economic Activity: Microeconomics* 2: 227–73.

CEC. (1995). The impact of international developments on the Community's textile and clothing sector. Communication from the Commission COM (95) 447.

Centro Europa Ricerche (CER). (1995). *Convergenze e Divergenze*, Report no. 5.

CEPII. (1995). *The Development of Intra versus Inter Industry Trade Flows Inside the EU Due to the Internal Market Programme.* Report for the EC Commission.

Cline, W. R. (1995). Evaluating the Uruguay Round. *World Economy* 18: 1–25.

Cooper, R. (1994). Foreign trade, wages, and unemployment. Harvard Institute of Economic Research Discussion Paper no. 1701.

Corado, C. (1995). The textiles and clothing trade with Central and Eastern Europe: impact on members of the EC. In Faini and Portes (1995).

—— Benaceck, V. and Caban, W. (1995). Adjustment and performance of the textile and clothing industry in the Czech Republic, Poland and Portugal. CEPR Working Paper no. 1260.

Courakis, A., Maskus, K. E. and Webster, A. (1995). Occupational employment and wage changes in the UK: trade and technology effects. In J. Borkakoti and C. Milner, eds., *International Trade and Labour Markets*, 169–202. London: Macmillan.

de Melo, J. and Messerlin, P. (1988). Price, quality and welfare effects of European VERs on Japanese autos. *European Economic Review* 32: 1527–46.

Dimelis, S. and Gatsios, K. (1995). Trade with Central and Eastern Europe: the case of Greece. In Faini and Portes (1995).

European Commission. (1994). The economic interdependence between the EU and Eastern Europe. *European Economy* no. 6.

European Commission. *Panorama of EU Industry (1995/96).* Luxembourg: Office for Official Publications of the EC.

Faini, R. and Portes, R. (eds.) (1995). *European Union Trade with Eastern Europe*. London: CEPR.

Faini, R. and Heimler, A. (1991). The quality and production of textiles and clothing and the completion of the internal market. In L. A. Winters and A. Venables (eds.), *European Integration Trade and Industry*. Cambridge: Cambridge University Press.

Feenstra, R. C. and Hanson, G. H. (1996). Foreign investment, outsourcing and relative wages. *American Economic Review* 86: 240–5.

Finger, M. J. and Olechowski, A. (1987). Trade barriers: who does what to whom? In H. Giersch (ed.), *Free Trade in the World Economy*. Tubingen: Mohr.

Flamm, G. (1990). Semiconductors. In G. Hufbauer (ed.), *Europe 1992*. Washington, D.C.: Brookings Institution.

Fontoura, M. P. (1995). O effeito do IDE na composição das exportações da indústria transformadora Portuguesa (mimeo).

Forti, A. (1995). Il traffico di perfezionamento passivo nelle nuove strategie delle imprese italiane del tessile-abbigliamento. In *Istituto Per Il Commercio Estero Annual Report 1995*. Rome.

Francois, J. F., McDonald, B., and Nordström, H. (1995). Assessing the Uruguay Round (mimeo).

Gregory, M. and Greenhalgh, C. (1995). International trade, de-industrialisation and labour demand: an input-output study for the UK 1979–90. In J. Borkakoti and C. Milner, (eds.), *International Trade and Labour Markets*, 169–202. London: Macmillan.

Greenaway, D. and Hindley, B. (1985). *What Britain Pays for Voluntary Export Restraints*. London: Trade Policy Research Centre.

—— Hine, R. C., and Wright, P. W. (1997). Trade and wages. CREDIT Discussion Paper, University of Nottingham.

Gual, J. and Martín, C. (1995). Trade and foreign direct investment with Central and Eastern Europe: its impact on Spain. In Faini and Portes (1995).

Guerrieri, P. (1994). International competitiveness, trade integration and technological interdependence. In C. Bradford (ed.), *The New Paradigm of Systemic Competitiveness: Toward More Integrated Policies in Latin America*. Paris: OECD.

—— and Manzocchi, S. (1995). Patterns of trade and foreign direct investment in European manufacturing: convergence or polarization? Paper presented at the 21st EIBA Annual Conference, Urbino, 10–12 December, and published in *Rivista Italiana degli Economisti* 1 (1996): 213–31.

Halpern, L. (1995). Comparative advantage and likely trade pattern of the CEECs. In Faini and Portes (1995).

Hamilton, C. and Winters, L. A. (1992). Opening up international trade with eastern Europe. *Economic Policy* 14: 78–104.

Henderson, D. (1989). *External Dimension of '1992'*. New York: Group of Thirty.

Hoekman, B. and Djankov, A. (1996). Intra-industry trade, FDI, and the reorientation of East European export. CEPR Working Paper no. 1377.

IMF. (1994). *International Trade Policies*, vol. I. *The Uruguay Round and Beyond: Principal Sources*. Washington, D.C.: IMF.

Katz, L. F. and Murphy, K. M. (1992). Changes in relative wages, 1963–87: supply and demand factors. *Quarterly Journal of Economics* 107: 35–78.

Kalantzopoulos, O. (1985). *The Costs of Voluntary Export Restraints*. Washington, D.C.

Kostecki, M. (1987). Export-restraint agreements and trade liberalisation. *World Economy* 10: 425–53.

Krugman, P. (1995). Growing world trade: causes and consequences. *Brookings Papers on Economic Activity* 1: 327–77.

—— and Lawrence, R. (1993). Trade, jobs and wages. *Scientific American* 270: 44–9.

—— and Venables, A. (1993). Integration, specialization, and adjustment. NBER Working Paper no. 4559.

Laussel, D., Montet, C. and Peguin-Feissolle, A. (1988). Optimal trade policy under oligopoly: a calibrated model of the Europe–Japan rivalry in the EEC car market. *European Economic Review* 32: 1547–65.

Lawrence, R. Z. and Slaughter, M. J. (1993). International trade and American wages in the 1980s: giant sucking sound or small hiccup? *Brookings Papers on Economic Activity: Microeconomics* 2: 161–226.

Leamer, E. E. (1993). Wage effects of a US–Mexican free trade agreement. In P. M. Garber (ed.), *The Mexico–US Free Trade Agreement*. Cambridge, Mass: MIT.

—— (1994). Trade, wages and revolving door ideas. National Bureau of Economic Research Working Paper no. 4716.

—— (1995). The Heckscher-Ohlin Model in Theory and Practice. Princeton Studies in International Finance 77.

Leidy, M. P. (1994). Quid pro quo restraint and spurious injury: subsidies and the prospects of CVDs. In A. Deardorff and R. Stern (eds.), *Analytical and Negotiating Issues in the Global Trading System*. Ann Arbor: University of Michigan Press.

Markusen, J. (1995). The boundaries of multinational enterprises and the theory of international trade. *Journal of Economic Perspectives* 9: 169–89.

—— and Venables, A. (1995). Multinational firms and the new trade theory. National Bureau of Economic Research Working Paper no. 5036.

Martín, C. (1995). Spain in the EU: adjustment in trade and direct investment and their implication for real convergence. In *CEPII 1995*: 35–69.

Martin, J. P. and Evans, J. M. (1981). Notes on measuring the employment displacement effects of trade by the accounting procedure. *Oxford Economic Papers* 33: 154–64.

Messerlin, P. A. (1989). The EC antidumping regulations: a first economic appraisal, 1980–85. *Weltwirtschaftliches Archiv* 117: 563–87.

—— (1990). Anti-dumping regulations or pro-cartel law? *World Economy* 13: 465–92.

—— (1995). The impact of trade and capital movements on labour: evidence of the French case. *OECD Economic Studies* 24: 89–124.

—— and Reed, G. (1995). Antidumping policies in the United States and the European Community. *Economic Journal* 105: 1565–75.

Micossi, S. and Viesti, G. (1992). Japanese direct manufacturing investment in Europe. In Winters and Venables (1992).

Murphy, K. M. and Welch, F. (1992). The structure of wages. *Quarterly Journal of Economics* 107: 285–326.

Neven, D. (1995). Trade liberalisation with the eastern nations: how sensitive? In Faini and Portes (1995).

OECD (1992). *Structural Change and Industrial Performance: A Seven Country Growth Decomposition*. Paris: OECD.

—— (1994). *The Jobs Study*. Paris: OECD.

—— (1995). *Financial Market Trends* 51, June, Paris.

Outes Rouso, X. et al. (1995). *Foreign direct investment in spain*. University of Vigo (mimeo).

Ozawa, T. (1992). Foreign Direct Investment and Economic Development. *Transnational Corporations*, 1: 27–54.

Padoan, P. C. (1997). Globalisation and European regional integration. *Economia Internazionale* 50: 1–38.

Pelkmans, J. (1993). Regionalism in world trade: vice or virtue? In L. Bekemans and L. Tsoukalis (eds.), *Europe and Global Interdependence*. Bruges: College of Europe.

Reinicke, W. (1996). *Deepening the Atlantic*. Gutersloh: Bertelsmann.

Revenga, A. (1992). Exporting jobs? The impact of import competition on employment and wages in US manufacturing. *Quarterly Journal of Economics* 107/1: 255–84.

Rodrik, D. (1997). *Has Gobalization Gone Too Far?* Washington, D.C.: Institute for International Economics.

Sachs, J. D. and Shatz, H. J. (1994). Trade and jobs in US manufacturing. *Brookings Papers on Economic Activity* 1: 1–84.

—— —— (1996). US trade with developing countries and wage inequality. *American Economic Review* 86: 234–39.

Sapir, A. (1997). The political economy of EC regionalism. CEPR Discussion Paper no. 1739.

—— and Schumacher, D. (1985). The employment impact of shifts in the composition of commodity and services trade. In OECD, *Employment Growth and Structural Change*. Paris: OECD.

Schuknecht, L. (1992). *Trade Protection in the European Community*. Chur, Switzerland: Harwood Academic Publishers.

Smith, A. *et al.* (1994). Modelling the effect of Central and East European trade on the European Community. *European Economy* No. 6: 521–38.

—— and Venables, A. (1990). Automobiles. In G. Hufbauer (ed.), *Europe 1992*. Washington, D.C.: Brookings Institution.

Takacs, W. and Winters, L. A. (1991). Labour adjustment costs and British footwear protection. *Oxford Economic Papers* 43: 479–501.

Turrini, A. (1995). La graduale liberalizzazione delle importazioni di automobili dal Giappone: alcune simulazione di politica commerciale. In *Istituto per il Commercio Estero Annual Report*. Rome.

Tyers, R. and Yang, Y. (1997). Trade with Asia and skill upgrading: effects on factor markets in older industrial countries. *Weltwirtschaftliches Archiv* 133/3: 383–417.

UNIDO. (1992). Handbook of Industrial Statistics. Vienna: UNIDO.

Vickery, G. (1992). The European experience in advanced electronics. *STI Review* 7: 171–95.

Winters, L. A. (1994). *The liberalization of European steel trade*. CEPR Working Paper no. 1002.

—— and Venables, A. (eds.). (1992). *European Integration: Trade and Industry*. Cambridge: Cambridge University Press.

Wood, A. (1991). The factor content of north-south trade in manufactures reconsidered. *Weltwirtschaftliches Archiv* 127: 719–43.

—— (1994). *North-south trade, employment and inequality: changing fortunes in a skill-driven world*. Oxford: Clarendon Press.

WTO. (1995). Trade Policy Review of the European Community. Geneva: World Trade Organisation.

4

Competition, Competitiveness, and Enterprise Policies

MICHAEL DUNFORD, HELEN LOURI, AND MANFRED ROSENSTOCK

4.1. Introduction

In this chapter our aim is to examine the effects on cohesion of European Union competition and competitiveness policies. More specifically, attention will be paid to three sets of measures: the rules of competition policy (Articles 85–94 of the EU Treaty—now Articles 81–89); industrial competitiveness policies (Articles 3 and 130—now Articles 3 and 157); and enterprise policies (Article 130—now Article 157). What these measures share is a concern to create a competitive environment and increase the competitiveness of European enterprises. To evaluate them, it is necessary to define competitiveness and explore its relation to cohesion.

4.2. Competitiveness and Cohesion

The use of concepts of competitiveness in relation to the performance of regional, national, and supranational economies has been a subject of significant controversy. This controversy has centred on the validity of analogies between microeconomic definitions of competitiveness of enterprises and definitions of the competitiveness of national economies, and it has led to a certain degree of convergence between measures of competitiveness and the measurement of cohesion.

At a microeconomic level, enterprises that are competitive are those that achieve a greater than average improvement in the quality of goods and services and/or a reduction in their relative costs that enable them to increase their profits (revenues–costs) and/or market share. The more a firm reduces its costs relative to its competitors—whether through increases in efficiency and in its organizational capacities or through reductions in wages, job security, social protection, or working conditions for the workforce—for a given level of product quality, or the more it increases its product quality (and the prices it can command) relative to its competitors for a given cost of production, the more competitive it is.

This microeconomic concept of competitiveness can be applied both to the short term and the long term, and it may well be the case that competitiveness in the long term requires rather different strategies from short-term competitiveness, as an ability to compete in the long term depends not just on a capacity at one moment in time to produce at costs and levels of quality which enable products to be sold profitably, but also on an ability to keep abreast of, or shape, the evolution of markets. Normally, therefore, the word competitiveness is used to refer to the longer run.

Also, of course, competitiveness in the sense of profitability depends on the degree of concentration in a sector or the monopoly power of an enterprise, as nothing generates more value added per worker than monopoly. Accordingly, the concept of competitiveness is usually defined in relation to competitive markets.

At the level of a national economy it is not possible to sustain simple analogies with this definition of the competitiveness of companies and to argue, for example, that national competitiveness is reflected in the gap between exports and imports, in part because of the implication that trade is a zero-sum game in which the existence of winners implies the existence of losers. If a European company reduces its relative prices and increases its market share at the expense of a Japanese rival, it is not automatically the case that Japanese citizens lose, as the increase in some European incomes will increase the demand for Japanese goods, and the fall in prices will benefit Japanese consumers (see Krugman 1994).

While this trade theory argument is widely accepted, Krugman's wider claim that there is no theoretical rationale for the view that the growth of national and regional economies is determined by their performance in international product markets, and that international economic performance reflects differences in competitiveness, is more controversial. At the root of this claim and of most mainstream work centred on 'Solow–type' growth models is the view that growth is determined by largely domestic supply-side factors (such as the rate of growth of the population or the labour force, factor prices, the savings rate, and, in more recent 'new growth' models, the generation of technological knowledge). This account of growth has, however, been contested. In the Keynesian tradition, for example, it has been argued that exports (Kaldor 1966, 1970) and trade performance (Thirlwall 1979), in particular, and demand-side factors, in general, are the main determinants of growth, while 'evolutionary' growth models identify technical change as the main determinant of growth but reserve an important role for demand-side factors in the shape of exports and imports (see Dalum, Laursen, and Verspagen 1999).

Despite these disagreements about the impact of trade on growth, attempts to make sense of the notion of national competitiveness have led to a certain degree of agreement about the meaning of national or regional competitiveness. As the First Report on the Competitiveness of European Industry indicated (CEC 1996a), competitiveness is a means to an end and not an end in itself. The end is a country's capacity to deliver high levels and rates of growth of welfare and high and increasing living standards for its citizens. The means are measures which enable it to generate more wealth per head than its competitors in world markets. To preclude monopolistic behaviour, most definitions add the qualification that competition should take place in the context of free and fair market conditions (see D'Andrea Tyson *et al.* 1984).[1] This qualification itself

---

[1] 'Competitiveness has different meanings for the firm and for the national economy. A nation's competitiveness is the degree to which it can, under free and fair market conditions, produce goods and services that meet the test of international markets while simultaneously expanding the real incomes of its citizens. Competitiveness at the national level is based on superior productivity performance and the economy's ability to shift output to high productivity activities which in turn can generate high levels of real wages. Competitiveness is associated with rising living standards, expanding employment opportunities, and the ability of a nation to maintain its international obligations. It is not just a measure of the nation's ability to sell abroad, and to maintain a trade equilibrium.' (D'Andrea Tyson *et al.* 1984: 1).

requires qualification. In particular, it assumes that free markets lead to full employment and that the resources released as a result of structural change will be re-employed. Second, it does not acknowledge that 'how such competitiveness is achieved can also be a matter of concern. Devaluation of currencies to compensate for costs which have been allowed to get out of line, cutting real wages to compensate for insufficient efficiency or a relaxation of environmental standards may provide superficial relief for underlying problems' (D'Andrea Tyson *et al.* 1984: 1).

If these qualifications are set on one side, and if competitiveness is defined as the capacity of a country to ensure relatively high and sustained incomes for the owners of its economic assets and for its population, a good first indicator of competitiveness is GDP per head measured at PPS.

As indicated in the introduction, the cohesion objective is expressed in the treaties in terms of the equilibrated development of the Community as a whole and a reduction in disparities in the levels of development of its different regions, and is measured by indicators of the degree of inequality in Gross Domestic Product (GDP) per head between member states (national cohesion) and regions (regional cohesion).[2] To these indicators should be added an indicator of the distribution of wealth between individuals and households (social cohesion).

Cohesion is, therefore, measured using the same indicator as is used to measure competitiveness. In the case of competitiveness, what matters is whether measures increase the level and rate of growth of GDP per head and whether they result in a *potential Pareto improvement*. In the case of cohesion, what matters is whether measures lead to a more equal distribution of GDP per head and contribute to processes of catch-up in which less developed countries and regions and lower income groups enjoy faster rates of income growth than more developed or richer groups.

4.3. Competition Policy and Cohesion

The 'institution of a system ensuring that competition in the common market is not distorted' was one of the central founding objectives of the Community and was laid down in Article 3g of the Treaty of Rome. The rules of competition policy (Articles 85–94 of the EU Treaty (now Articles 81–89)) were, thus, introduced into the founding Treaty of the Community in 1958 and have subsequently remained virtually unchanged. These rules, in principle, disallow cartels, abuses of dominant positions, public monopolies, and state aids whenever they distort competition and affect intra-Community trade, and give the Commission direct competences to investigate these distortions and abolish them or grant derogations. With respect to the rules applying to enterprises, Commission control ensures that negative effects on competition that go beyond single member states, and might, thus, not be taken into account by national competition authorities, will be investigated. With respect to public monopolies and state aids, Commission control is necessary to prevent member states themselves from causing distortions of competition by favouring companies located in their own countries.

---

[2] These indicators require some modification to allow for differences in the cost of living within member states, the gap between GDP and GNP, and the availability of non-commodified resources.

Although the fundamental aims of Community competition policy are to prevent the abuse of monopoly power and improve the efficiency of the European economy, it does have an impact on cohesion, first, as a result of the impact of anti-trust measures and, second, as a result of Community control over state aids, on which this section will concentrate.

4.3.1. Antitrust measures and cohesion

Antitrust measures can have an effect on geographical cohesion, in particular through their effect on mergers, if the resultant restructuring efforts and possible job losses have an uneven regional distribution. With the establishment of the internal market, the number of mergers in the Community increased significantly. The share of transnational but intra-Community mergers in the total grew as well (Amin, Charles and Howells 1992). In order to be able to examine the competition effects of such mergers, a Community merger control regulation came into force in 1990.

Apart from the competition issues, it can be asked whether increased mergers and acquisitions have a systematic effect on cohesion. Under the assumption that companies in assisted areas are more frequently the subject of a takeover by external companies than they are the acquirer themselves, there are worries that restructuring efforts after the merger may have negative consequences for the companies in less developed areas. These possible consequences include: a run-down of the scale of production operations or a lower rate of growth; a reduction of the 'sophistication' of operations in less developed areas through the loss of key control and other functions, such as R&D or marketing; the consequent outmigration of qualified management and staff; and, finally, the removal or simplification of products and product lines. These effects would also have secondary consequences on the performance of the regional economy as a whole (Love 1989).

Empirical studies undertaken in the UK do not deliver clear conclusions, except for the loss of management functions and of regional service linkages (such as auditing, banking, and insurance) where functions are centralized after a takeover. The studies also suffer partly from methodological problems (see Love 1989). Other studies looking for possible systematic links between the characteristics of the acquirer and the performance of the acquired company (Ashcroft and Love 1992) have not specifically looked at the regional implications. It would thus be useful to carry out studies that show whether mergers and acquisitions have systematic cohesion-related effects by leading to a concentration of high qualification activities in central regions and/or to job losses that fall predominantly on the less qualified. Such studies would help establish whether Community actions in structural policy fields were warranted in such circumstances.

4.3.2. Control of state aids and cohesion

A more direct effect of competition policy on cohesion exists through the control of state aids exercised by the Commission (Art. 92/93 EC (now Art. 87/88)).

Article 92[3] disallows in principle all forms of state aid which distort competition by favouring certain undertakings or products, and which affect trade between member states. However, this article also identifies a series of exceptions from this general prohibition. The first group of exceptions concern social aids to individual consumers without discrimination related to the origin of the products, aids in cases of natural disasters, and aids for certain areas of Germany to compensate for disadvantages caused by the division of Germany. These types of aid are automatically considered compatible with the Treaty. The second group of exceptions (Art. 92.3) can be considered compatible, but a considerable degree of discretion is left to the Commission as to whether to approve the proposed aids. Foremost among these exceptions is aid for regional development. A distinction is made between aid for the development of regions with a very low standard of living or serious underemployment (Art. 92(3)a) and aid for the development of other problem areas (Art. 92(3)c). The latter are usually areas with industrial or agricultural conversion problems, and the aid for them is less generous than for the very poor areas of the Community. Under Article 92(3) aid can also be allowed for important projects of common European interest, and for the remediation of serious disturbances in the economy of a (whole) member state. Further exceptions can be granted for aid for the development of certain economic activities, i.e. aid for specific sectors, as long as trading conditions are not adversely affected so as to be contrary to the common interest. This last condition also applies to aid for the promotion of culture. While decisions on these exceptions remain the exclusive domain of the Commission, the Council can, upon a Commission proposal, declare further types of aid compatible with the Treaty. This provision has been used to approve aid for shipbuilding.

In Article 93 (now Art. 88), the EC Treaty also lays down procedural rules which oblige the member states to notify the Commission of all proposals to grant state aid before they are put into force. It is only after approval by the Commission that aid schemes or projects can be executed. If the Commission has doubts about the compatibility of an aid project, it has to initiate a procedure, in the course of which third parties can also present their comments, to allow the Commission to get a fuller picture of the proposed aid and its effects before taking a final decision on the project (Schina 1987).

Two main phases can be identified in the development of the Commission's state aid policy (Warnecke 1978). During the first phase, from 1958 until the introduction of the first directive on shipbuilding aid in 1969, the Commission developed its interpretation of the scope of the Treaty rules and its approach to the treatment of cases. Decisions were taken on an *ad hoc* basis. During the second phase, which covers the period after 1969, the Commission developed systematic rules for the control of different types of aid as well as for the procedures to be followed. This second period can subdivided into two sub-phases, the first of which ran from 1969 until the mid/late 1980s, and the second from the end of this sub-phase to the present. In the first sub-phase, which was characterized by cyclical and sectoral crises, the Commission faced increasingly interventionist attitudes by member states and a series of measures to delay structural change, in particular in the crisis sectors of shipbuilding, steel, and textiles. The frameworks

---

[3] Article 92 is now Article 87.

for state aid control developed by the Commission for these sectors during this period reflect far-reaching concessions to national industrial policies. During the second sub-phase the Commission intensified its control. It was helped by the challenges of the single market project and by a reorientation of government policies towards more horizontal objectives. While the sectoral aid codes became stricter, the Commission also introduced or significantly extended guidelines and frameworks for the control of horizontal aid, such as aid for R&D, environmental protection, SMEs, etc. (Rosenstock 1995). While a set of rules for the control of regional aids was first introduced in 1971 and modified on several occasions up to 1979, a new Communication in 1988 codified a greatly refined approach, which, *inter alia*, provided clear criteria for eligibility under both Article 92(3)a and (3)c. In March 1998, the Commission published new guidelines which bring together all those provisions from the previous communications that are still in force and also introduce a reduction in aid intensities (cf. below). These guide-lines will apply from 2000 onwards, i.e. from the date when the new Structural Fund regulations come into force.

These measures that, in principle, forbid state aid distorting competition and affect-ing trade also allow the Commission to grant derogations. They have a clear impact on cohesion, as different types of state aid may benefit companies in poorer regions dispro-portionately more or less than companies in other regions. In granting derogations from the general prohibition of state aid, the Commission takes these effects into account. During 1992–4, the latest period for which data are available for all member states, 53 per cent of all aid by member states was of a regional type, enabling long-term structural disadvantages as well as short- and medium-term problems of regions caused by crises in certain industries to be addressed by state aid (CEC 1997a). On the basis of the dero-gations foreseen in the EC Treaty, the Commission has, however, also approved aid for horizontal objectives, such as R&D, environmental protection, and support of small and medium-sized enterprises (SMEs) as well as sectoral aid for specific crisis sectors, such as steel and shipbuilding. In 1992–4, 29 per cent of all aid was of a horizontal type, and the remaining 17 per cent was sectoral aid. The Community, therefore, has also supported these horizontal objectives, though the Commission has to ensure that mem-ber states do not contravene regional policy objectives by using such aid schemes for 'hidden' investment aid outside of assisted areas. Even if horizontal aids are applied 'properly', the question of their regional distribution arises, as we shall indicate below (cf. below, sect. 4.3.2.3).

4.3.2.1. *Member state regional policies*

In defining their regional policy, member states can make use of three main variables: the choice of assisted areas; the aid intensities granted to investments in those areas; and the size of the budget allocated to regional policy in total.[4] As member states' regional

---

[4] The regional development policies of member states usually involve not just incentives to support invest-ment in assisted areas but also include funds for infrastructure expenditure, improved public services, etc. Insofar as they are not company specific, these measures do not fall under the Commission's competences of state aid control and will be neglected in this chapter. They play, however, an important role in the locational choice of companies (see Netherlands Economic Institute 1993).

Table 4.1. Population covered by regional aid under Article 92 EC (now Art. 87)
(as percentage of national population)

Member state	Article 92(3)a		Article 92(3)c		Article 92(3)a and 92(3)c	
	Current situation	Former situation[a]	Current situation	Former situation[a]	Current situation	Former situation[a]
Austria	3.5	—	31.7	—	35.2	—
Belgium	0.0	0.0	35.0	33.1	35.0	33.1
Germany	20.8	20.8	16.8	24.0	37.6	44.8
Denmark	0.0	0.0	19.9	20.7	19.9	20.7
Spain	59.6	46.5	16.3	18.5	75.9	65.0
France	2.5	2.5	39.9	41.8	42.4	44.3
Finland	0.0	—	41.6	—	41.6	—
Greece	100.0	100.0	0.0	0.0	100.0	100.0
Italy	34.2	36.6	14.7	5.6	48.9	42.2
Ireland	100.0	—	0.0	0.0	100.0	—
Luxembourg	0.0	0.0	42.7	79.7	42.7	79.7
Netherlands	0.0	0.0	17.3	19.3	17.3	19.3
Portugal	100.0	100.0	0.0	0.0	100.0	100.0
Spain	0.0	—	18.5	—	18.5	—
United Kingdom	2.9	2.9	35.2	35.3	38.1	38.2
EU-12	24.9	23.9	22.8	23.6	47.7	47.5
EU-15	23.6	—	23.1	—	46.7	—

[a] Situation in 1993, except DK (situation in 1991), I (situation in 1992), IRL (previous situation too old and irrelevant for comparison).

Note: The calculations are based on population data for 1992. The decisions on the eligible regions were taken between 1993 and 1996.

Source: Directorate General of Competition Policy.

aid schemes have to be notified to the Commission for approval, it can influence these variables with a view to supporting cohesion objectives.

A. The definition of eligible areas. As mentioned above, Article 92(3) EC distinguishes between two types of regions that are eligible for regional aid: the least developed areas (92(3)a regions) and areas facing other problems (92(3)c regions). Table 4.1 shows the share of population covered by these two types of assisted areas broken down by member state.

The Commission's objective has been to ensure that regional aid is concentrated on those areas most in need while at the same time preventing distortions of competition through investment aid in regions which do not face structural handicaps (see CEC 1997*b*). In spite of pressures from member states to widen the coverage of eligible areas, in particular in the more central areas of the Community (usually covered by the derogation of Article 92(3)c), recent revisions of the maps of assisted areas have shown a slight reduction in the share of population covered by this provision, from 23.6 per cent to 22.8 per cent of EU-12.[5] At the same time other peripheral areas, particularly in Spain, were added to the list of eligible regions under Article 92(3)a, taking the whole coverage from 23.9 per cent to 24.9 per cent of the Community population (EU-12). Since only Austria of the new member states has a small area designated as a lagging area (Burgenland), coverage under Article 92(3)a for the Community of 15 is slightly lower at 23.6 per cent, while the share of population covered by Article 92(3)c areas has risen marginally, to 23.1 per cent.

As a result of the Commission's policy, a framework has been set so that regional aid can now be relatively more concentrated in the most disadvantaged regions of the Community. This greater concentration is also apparent from the shares of population covered by regional aids broken down by member state. While the four cohesion countries have the status of assisted areas either in their entirety (Portugal, Greece, and Ireland) or to a very large degree (Spain with 75.9 per cent), coverage in most other member states is between 35 per cent and 49 per cent, while in those countries with high levels of income per head and low internal divergences (Denmark and the Netherlands), coverage is even lower (below 20 per cent).

B. Aid ceilings. Control of the areal coverage of incentive schemes is reinforced by the aid intensity ceilings approved by the Commission, which in general are significantly higher in the Article 92.3.a areas. This differential is to give those regions with the biggest structural handicaps and enterprises usually lacking competitiveness sufficient scope to increase their attractiveness to potential investors.

The weighted average approved intensity of aid in all assisted areas of the Community is 32.3 per cent, with 18.1 per cent for Article 92(3)c areas and 46.2 per cent for Article 92(3)a areas (see Table 4.2, where all figures are for EU-15 and in Net Grant Equivalent (NGE).[6] Therefore, intensities in the latter areas are, on average, 2.6 times greater than in the former, reflecting the greater development needs of the Article 92(3)a areas. This positive result in terms of cohesion has, however, to be qualified. As these intensities are approved intensities, they only create the framework conditions for a policy conducive to cohesion. The effective intensities granted by member states are often significantly below these levels. Effective intensities fall short of the ceiling, particularly in Spain and Ireland, which contain some of the poorest regions benefiting from the highest approved intensities but where aid on average only reaches 40 per cent of those intensities. By contrast, in countries such as Belgium and Germany, aid reaches around 60–70 per cent of their ceilings (Marques 1994). Thus, the advantage granted to the poorest countries through their high ceiling is eroded, as these ceilings are not effectively used. For the other regions, 92(3)a as well as 92(3)c, utilization rates of the

[5] The main changes in this area were a significant reduction of assisted areas in the western part of Germany (where coverage was reduced from 24 per cent to 16.8 per cent) and a significant increase in assisted areas in Italy (from 5.6 per cent to 14.7 per cent), while at the same time areas falling under Article 92(3)a in Italy were reduced slightly (see CEC 1996f: 68).

[6] The maximum approved intensities are for large enterprises and include aid from all sources (including Community Structural Funds). The differentiation of ceilings reflects the different intensities of regional problems inside and between member states. In general, SMEs can benefit from higher aid intensities up to the limits of 75 per cent and 30 per cent NGE respectively (see below).

Table 4.2. Weighted average approved aid intensities[a]

		Current situation		Previous situation	
	Type of region	Population covered	Weighted average of approved aid intensity (NGE)	Population covered	Weighted average of approved aid intensity (NGE)
EU–12	92(3)a	24.9	46.3	24.7	54.2
	92(3)c	22.8	17.9	22.7	19.5
	Average	47.7	32.7	47.4	37.6
EU–15	92(3)a	23.6	46.2	—	—
	92(3)c	23.1	18.1		
	Average	46.7	32.3		

[a] The current situation refer to the situation in 1996. The previous situation refers to 1993, except for Denmark, Ireland, and Italy. Aid intensities are those which are applicable to all companies, independent of their size, and include all possible cumulations of aid calculated on the same basis as regional aid. In some regions, SMEs can benefit from higher aid intensities than those shown in the table.

Source: Directorate General of Competition Policy.

ceilings are around 50 per cent. As a result the absolute supplementary incentive that investors can receive in Article 92(3)a regions as compared to Article 92(3)c regions is, in fact, halved. The remaining difference in aid may be insufficient to cover the extra handicaps of locating in the poorest regions and may consequently be insufficient to attract the large amounts of inward investment necessary to improve their economic structures.

In order to tackle this problem, the Commission's general policy recently has been to insist on a reduction of regional ceilings in all assisted areas. In the past, it had approved intensities of up to 75 per cent NGE in Article 92(3)a areas and up to 30 per cent NGE in Article 92(3)c areas. With the new guidelines on regional aid, these ceilings will be reduced significantly.[7] As the maximum intensities in Article 92(3)a areas were almost never reached, while in Article 92(3)c areas the maxima constituted effective intensities for some projects, this parallel reduction can, in fact, increase the effective advantage of Article 92(3)a areas and thus contribute to cohesion.

The effects of this new approach can already be seen in the recent evolution of approved aid ceilings, which have fallen in both Article 92(3)a and 92(3)c areas, although slightly faster in 92(3)a areas. As ceilings were seldom reached in weaker areas, this change is unlikely to have a significant negative effect on the effective support levels in the least developed regions of the Community. Furthermore, the slower reduction of intensities in Article 92(3)c regions is because ceilings in some of these regions, which are at the same time eligible for Structural Funds support under Objective 1, have been increased. From a Structural Funds point of view, this alignment also has contributed to cohesion.

[7] As from the year 2000 onwards, the maximum aid intensity will fall to 50 per cent NGE for Article 92(3)a regions and 20 per cent for 92(3)c regions. Steps in the direction of this new approach have already been taken in Portugal, Spain and Italy, where the new ceilings for Article 92(3)a regions do not exceed 60 per cent NGE.

Table 4.3. Indicators of regional state aid

	1981–6	1986–8	1988–90	1990–2	1992–4
Aid to manufacturing industry as percentage of value added in manufacturing	4.8	4.0	3.8	3.8	4.0
Regional aid as percentage of total aid to manufacturing industry	37	39	38	50	53
Regional aid as percentage of value-added of manufacturing industry	1.78	1.56	1.44	1.85	2.12
Regional aid as percentage of total public expenditure	n.a.	0.75	0.65	0.78	n.a.

C. Budgets: the quantitative weight of regional aid. By influencing the choice of assisted areas and by limiting the aid intensity that can be granted in any area to the amounts needed to compensate investors for the regional handicaps, supplemented by additional incentives to choose these regions, the Commission can prevent investment aid being given to projects outside areas in difficulty. This creates a framework supporting cohesion and, at the same time, limits distortions of competition through the granting of excessive aid to specific projects.

The furthering of cohesion will, however, be limited if member states support their 92(3)c regions with huge budgets, enabling them to attract many mobile projects, while other member states lack the financial resources to support a significant number of projects in their 92(3)a regions.[8] So far, the Commission has not been in a position to influence national aid budgets. The problem can be solved by support from the Structural Funds for the Community's poorest regions.

As Table 4.3 shows, while state aid to manufacturing industry as a percentage of its value added has not shown a sustained tendency to fall since 1986–8, the share of regional aid in this total has significantly increased since 1990, as has the ratio of regional aid to value added in manufacturing industry. The average annual amount of state aid for regional purposes during this period was 23.1 billion ecus (see Table 4.4).[9] Compared to this figure, the contribution from the Structural Funds that could be characterized as equivalent to state aid[10] has been relatively small (an annual average of 1.6 billion ecus).

[8] In a member state in which all regions have a per capita GDP below the EU average, national regional aid cannot contribute to intra-Community cohesion, as funds are transferred 'from the poor to the poor'. In such countries, cohesion can only be furthered by Community support.

[9] This figure includes around 370 million ecus of general investment aid, which in the cohesion countries in particular is partly co-financed by the Community and in effect is close to regional aid. In those member states where only a part of the population lives in assisted areas, the total expenditure for general investment aid has been multiplied by the share of the population living in assisted areas, on the assumption that this kind of aid is distributed evenly.

[10] These figures are based on estimates limited to the following fields of intervention: industry, services and crafts; increasing business competitiveness; and rural development SME (see CEC 1995d).

Table 4.4. Regional aid measures by member states and the Structural Funds in 1992–4 (annual averages in million ecus)

	Regional aid	Of which in Art. 92(3)a and 92(2)c areas[c]	General investment in assisted areas[a]	Total national aid	Aid per capita in assisted areas (ecu)	National aid per capita (Germany = 100)	ERDF	Total	Total per capita in assisted areas (ecu)[b]	Total aid per capita (Germany = 100)
Germany	13,643.52	13,191.4	0.0	13,643.5	379.4	100.0	304.4	13,947.9	387.9	100.0
Italy	5,988.49	5,742.2	115.8	6,104.3	250.9	66.1	181.1	6,285.4	258.3	66.6
Ireland	342.91	342.91	0.0	342.9	97.9	25.8	120.6	463.5	132.3	34.1
Luxembourg	33.06	0.0	0.0	33.1	108.9	28.7	3.9	37.0	121.7	31.4
Belgium	196.57	0.0	11.1	207.6	62.9	16.6	30.0	237.6	72.0	18.6
Portugal	151.56	151.56	66.9	218.5	22.1	5.8	279.3	497.8	50.4	13.0
France	1,061.22	546.7	49.0	1,110.2	44.2	11.6	145.6	1,255.8	50.0	12.9
Netherlands	119.9	0.0	6.9	126.8	44.0	11.6	12.9	139.7	48.4	12.5
Greece	216.58	216.58	42.4	258.9	25.4	6.7	131.9	390.8	38.3	9.9
United Kingdom	704.37	460.8	18.9	723.3	33.0	8.7	113.9	837.2	38.2	9.8
Spain	251.12	55.7	56.3	307.4	12.1	3.2	273.7	581.1	22.9	5.9
Denmark	13.7	0.0	0.0	13.7	13.4	3.5	6.5	20.2	19.7	5.1
Total	22,723	20,707.8	367.2	23,090.2	180.7		1,603.8	24,694.0	193.2	

[a] In those member states which are assisted areas in their entirety under state aid rules, total general investment aid has been apportioned on a pro-rata basis according to population.
[b] The nominal amounts are divided by the population of the assisted areas according to regional state aid schemes. As some Community aid goes to regions which are not eligible under state aid rules, the figures given here slightly overestimate real aid intensity per capita. Given that national aid far exceeds Community aid, this overestimation is of minor significance.

Source: European Commission 1997.

Almost 85 per cent of regional aids from national sources go to areas eligible under Article 92(3)a, i.e. to the poorest areas of the Community. A further 7 per cent of total regional aid went to (West) Berlin and the former Zonal Border Area, which during the period 1992–4 were still eligible under Article 92(2)c. The size of this aid has, however, fallen significantly.

Table 4.4 shows that more than 85 per cent of regional aid is granted in just two member states, Germany and Italy, which are characterized by the dual nature of their economies and which have by far the widest internal regional disparities. For these two countries, the big transfers from their richer to their poorer regions will help internal convergence by attracting investment. The underdeveloped regions in Germany and Italy compete, however, with similar regions in the Cohesion Countries, where the regional aid budgets are much lower, so that these countries can only support a few investments or can only aid projects at lower intensities, which may not be sufficient to attract investors. The Structural Funds compensate in part for this disadvantage, but as Table 4.4 shows, even after including ERDF spending,[11] total aid per capita in assisted areas in the Cohesion Countries is only between 5 and 34 per cent of German levels. Compared with the ranking on the basis of national aid alone, Spain and Ireland advance by one position, while Portugal climbs four positions. With the increases in the Structural Funds budgets foreseen for the period up to 1999, this large difference in per capita aid is likely to decline.

4.3.2.2. *State aid control and the activities of the Structural Funds*
Since Structural Fund interventions and control of regional state aid both help develop the disadvantaged regions of the Community, the efficiency of these policies depends to a great extent on their coherence. This coherence, in turn, depends upon the extent to which the eligible areas, the programming periods, and the decision-making processes correspond.

A. Eligible Areas. Insofar as the choice of eligible areas is concerned, there is a high degree of consistency between the two instruments. As Table 4.5 shows, however, there are some differences which will continue to exist until 1999, the end of the current programming period. While virtually all Objective 1 areas have also been accepted as assisted areas under Article 92(3)a or c,[12] some areas covered by Objectives 2 or 5b of the Structural Funds are not eligible for state aid (representing 6.6 per cent of Community population). In these areas, Community assistance is confined to other forms of investment aid, e.g. aid for SMEs at lower rates, the environment, R&D, infrastructure, and training support. Conversely, areas containing 2.7 per cent of the Community

---

[11] Some of the expenditures of the EAGGF Guidance section in Objective 5b regions also will have the character of regional aid. There is, however, no breakdown of this category of expenditure, which would allow elements of state aid to be isolated. The figures in the table are, therefore, limited to aid to the manufacturing sector.

[12] The one small exception is in Scotland, where the Objective I area is the Highlands and Islands Development Board area. Since the decision on assisted areas under state aids rules was based on NUTS classifications, the UK authorities did not propose certain areas (parts of the NUTS III regions of Strathclyde, Highlands, Islands, and Grampian) as eligible for state aid.

Table 4.5. Correspondence between areas eligible for member states' regional aid and Structural Funds (as percentages of Community population)

	Eligible regions under Structural Funds	Regions not eligible under Structural Funds	Total
Regions eligible for regional aid under Article 92(3)	44	2.7	46.7
Regions not eligible for regional aid	6.6	46.7	53.3
Total	50.6	49.4	100

population that are eligible for state aid under Article 92(3)c are not eligible for assistance under any of the Structural Funds objectives. Not only are there areas in which the two sets of definitions do not overlap; the size of the coverage also differs, with 50.6 per cent of the Community population living in areas eligible for Structural Funds support, compared with 46.7 per cent of the population living in areas eligible for national assistance.

There are two reasons for these discrepancies. First, there are differences in the criteria for eligibility and their interpretation. More specifically, the eligibility criteria under both Objective 1 and Article 92(3)a EC are the same, namely, that regional GDP per capita falls below 75 per cent of Community average. Under the Structural Funds regulations, this criterion has, however, been interpreted less strictly to allow the inclusion of regions in which the income level is close to this threshold or where special reasons apply. As a result, some Objective 1 regions (containing 1.5 per cent of the Community population) are not included under Article 92(3)a, but only under Article 92(3)c. (Examples are Highlands and Islands, Corsica, Abruzzo, and Hainaut.) In the case of the areas covered by Objectives 2, 5b, and 6 and Article 92(3)c, conversely, the criteria of eligibility differ. Under current competition rules, the regions in question must cross thresholds related to the national averages for unemployment and GDP per capita and defined separately for each member state, taking into account its situation relative to the Community averages. The criteria for Objectives 2 and 5b give more emphasis to unemployment and the evolution and level of industrial employment (Objective 2) or to the importance of agricultural employment, low agricultural income, and outmigration (Objective 5b). Both sets of rules employ secondary criteria that allow the specific problems of regions to be taken into account. For the northern regions of Sweden and Finland suffering from remoteness and very low population densities, the basic criterion is identical under both sets of rules (low population density), but the thresholds differ (8 inhabitants per km² under Structural Funds rules and 12.5 inhabitants per km² under Article 92(3)c).[13]

---

[13] The higher threshold under state aid rules identifies regions eligible for national government transport aid.

The second reason for these differences lies in the decisions member states make when they submit proposals for assisted areas to the Commission. Two situations arise. First, member states may decide not to grant nationally funded regional aid to areas receiving assistance from Structural Funds. Although it is conceivable that, in a reference scenario in which the Structural Funds did not exist, the member state in question might still have confined its support for these areas to measures funding infrastructures or aiding SMEs, it is also reasonable to ask whether, in these circumstances, a member state is partially substituting Structural Fund support for its own effort. The opposite situation, which arises in areas receiving national but not Structural Fund assistance, is less difficult, as the Structural Funds address problems on a Community level, whereas national aid can also tackle issues which are of national significance but are less acute from a Community point of view. Ideally, therefore, the population coverage of the Structural Funds should be below the coverage of member state aid for regional purposes, while all areas eligible for Structural Fund support should also be covered by state aid. In this way, consistency could be ensured, while at the same time member states would have some leeway to set national priorities for regional development.

B. Programming periods and the decision-making process. At present the programming periods largely correspond, as decisions on member states' regional aid normally relate to the same period as the Delors II package. In some member states, however, national programming periods have not been brought into line with those of the ERDF, particularly in those cases for which national aid for the areas concerned is much greater than Community funding. Further progress on this issue is expected for the new programming period starting in 2000.

Insofar as making decisions about demands for co-financing is concerned, there are sometimes delays when national aid schemes have not been approved because member states have provided the Commission with incomplete information and also because of the abovementioned inconsistencies in regional coverage.

4.3.2.3. *Impact of other state aid*

The state aid control instruments of competition policy apply not just to the regional aid packages of member states but also to horizontal and sectoral aid. Although sectoral aid now accounts for just 17 per cent of all aid to manufacturing industry, due in particular to the decline in the magnitude of aid for the steel industry, horizontal forms of aid, which include aid for R&D, SMEs, environmental protection, and energy conservation, represent 29 per cent of the total. It is often argued that these types of aid, and in particular R&D aid, tend to benefit the richer regions of the Community, where the major company research centres are concentrated. Studies of the regional distribution of *Community* R&D aid during the period 1983–90 (Seidel 1994) indicate that this aid was, indeed, concentrated in the economically strongest regions of the EU-12, so that Community support for R&D does tend to counteract the pro-regional cohesion effects of regional aid. Similar studies of the regional distribution of state aid for R&D have been undertaken for several large member states. These studies indicate that national aid for R&D has tended to reinforce the concentration of privately funded

R&D in the most prosperous regions. At the same time, government funded R&D has also been significantly higher in relation to GDP in the richer member states (see CEC 1996*f*). In the specific frameworks and guidelines it establishes for these types of aid, the Commission does give incentives for the location of R&D in assisted areas by allowing higher aid intensities for projects in such regions. Clearly, however, these measures are not sufficiently strong to counter the forces leading to a concentration of R&D aids in stronger regions and member states, though it must be remembered that such aid is granted mainly to increase the overall competitiveness of Community industry and overall levels of per-capita income.

4.3.3. Conclusion

Through its influence over the choice of assisted areas and ceilings for aid intensities, Community state aid control has created conditions that allow a concentration of member state regional assistance in those areas most in need. However, the poorer member states lack the financial resources to take full advantage of these opportunities and are, therefore, unable to match the support Italy and Germany, the 'dual economies' with huge national budgets, provide for their underdeveloped regions. No precise statements can be made on the regional distribution of non-regional state aid and, thus, the question as to whether this aid supports or counteracts cohesion remains open.

4.4. Industrial Competitiveness

Industrial competitiveness measures fall under Articles 3 and 130 (now Articles 3 and 157) of the Treaty of European Union, which require the Community and the member states to adopt policies and actions capable of 'strengthening the competitiveness of Community industry' and ensuring 'that the conditions necessary for the competitiveness of the Community's industry exist'.

More specifically, the aim of EU industrial policy is create an environment that stimulates the constant 'structural adjustment' of European industry (redeployment of resources into sectors where demand and profits are greatest) to enable it to compete successfully in European and global markets (CEC 1990; see Table 4.6).[14] At the centre of this approach lay the free trade view that open and competitive markets lead to an optimal allocation of resources, that the way industry reacts to the market is through constant 'structural adjustment', and that competitive adjustment depends first and foremost on the initiatives of the industrial sector (and not on the actions of public authorities whose role is not to take action in favour of a particular enterprise or industry). To enable these industrial initiatives to occur, certain conditions were viewed as essential: that EU industry remain at the forefront of industrial and technological

---

[14] The 1990 Communication (see Table 4.6) outlined a new approach to industrial policy that (1) rejected sectoral strategies and protectionism as instruments of industrial policy, (2) emphasized the leading role of industrialists, and (3) identified the role of public authorities with the creation of a dynamic environment favourable to industrial development.

Table 4.6. A framework for industrial policy in an open and competitive environment

Structural adjustment	Catalysers	Accelerators
Meeting the preconditions:		
• Guarantee a competitive environment		• Research, development, technology, and innovation
• Maintain a stable economic context	• Internal market (standards, public markets, abolition of national quotas, coherent legal framework, trans-European networks)	• Improve training and use of human resources
• Ensure high educational attainment		• Policies for small and medium-sized firms
• Promote economic and social cohesion[a]	• Trade policy	• Producer services
• Protect the environment		

[a] In the cohesion section of *Industrial policy in an open and competitive environment*, it is suggested that flexible, innovative and knowledge-intensive industry presupposes the existence of cohesive societies. The sharing of information, consultation and participation create trust and encourage structural adjustment. Social protection provides security and facilitates adaptation and co-operative industrial relations. An improved allocation of time between work and non-work permit agreement over flexible hours which enable a more efficient use of equipment. There are therefore ways in which measures that add to social costs offer certain advantages to industry though, the communication adds, such measures require greater productivity.

Source: CEC (1990).

innovation; that innovations diffuse; that rates of profit remain sufficiently high and wages and taxes sufficiently low to provide the resources for financing investment; and that skills be constantly upgraded. In this context the aim of public policy is to create a common environment (a level playing field) conducive to an acceleration of industry led structural adjustment through a coherent use of all EU policies (competition, trade, internal market, R&D, education and training, environmental protection, transport and communications, small and medium-sized enterprise, and structural policy) that influence the industrial sector (CEC 1990). As these policies are the responsibility of a number of directorates general, agencies, and national organizations, each with their own objectives and spheres of action, this approach entails action designed to shape a wide range of different policies which are the responsibilities of, and are implemented by, other actors.

How these principles were to be put into action was mapped out in the chapter entitled 'Towards global competitiveness' of the white paper on *Growth, Competitiveness and Employment* (COM (93) 700 final; Table 4.7) in which the Commission identified a number of instruments and four objectives: to help European firms adapt to the global competitive situation; to exploit the shift to a knowledge-based (information) economy; to support sustainable development of industry; and to aid the reabsorption of the human resources released as a result of productivity growth.

Table 4.7. Towards global competitiveness

1. Help European firms adapt to the new globalized and interdependent competitive situation	• capitalize on the Community's industrial strengths • develop an active policy of industrial cooperation with transition economies and the Pacific rim • establish a concerted approach to strategic alliances • ensure competitive functioning of markets opening up markets that are closed
2. Exploit the competitive advantages associated with a gradual shift to a knowledge-based (information) economy and the increasing relative importance for competitiveness of (1) non-physical, knowledge-based investment and activities such as research and training, and accounting, marketing and other services and of (2) organizational capacities	• shift taxes from employment disincentives to incentives for efficient and less polluting use of resources • restructure financial instruments and use of public funds to reduce incentive to increase capital intensity and increase incentive to raise immaterial investment in research and training in order to increase incorporaton of innovation in new products and processes • streamline and rationalize regulatory framework and launch a policy aimed at quality avoiding fragmentation of the internal market and stimulating the move away from 'Taylorism'
3. Promote a sustainable development of industry	• increase and coordinate R&D into clean technologies • develop economic incentives to prevent pollution and to support diffusion of R&D into products and processes
4. To counteract the failure to reabsorb the human resources released as a result of productivity growth, and reduce the time lags between the pace of change of supply and the corresponding adjustments in demand. Time lags are due to cumbersome rigidities in income distribution, in modes of consumption, in the relatively low level of receptiveness to innovation within the Community, in the geographical structure of growth, and in the unsatisfactory functioning of markets.	• on the demand side adopt initiatives aimed at speeding up a concerted recovery of demand and examine measures likely to promote the emergence of new markets for goods and services and, in particular, for environmental protection, biotechnologies, and information services including multimedia • on the supply side encourage structural adjustment and support development of small and medium-sized enterprises • in relation to the coordination of demand and supply, facilitate partnership between large firms and subcontractors, establish interfaces between producers and users, and stimulate collaborative local networks and clusters that exploit the potential of the geographical diversity of the EU

The 1994 Communication on an Industrial Competitiveness Policy for the EU (COM (94) 319 final) sought to identify and propose a programme of action. This Communication was centred on earlier principles, though more emphasis was placed on job generation, which was itself seen to depend on the efficiency and innovativeness of European industry and the attractiveness of the EU as a site for industrial investment (in the context of a more labour-intensive model of development). The communication started with an evaluation of a number of factors on which competitiveness depends (knowledge and human resource development, development of interoperable trans-European networks, improved productive organization, increased economic and social cohesion, and a closer articulation of strengthened scientific and technological development with the market sector) and of the potential of EU industries to enter growth markets (knowledge and culture, health care and biotechnologies, and environmental protection). In the light of this analysis, and of the importance attached to new growth sectors and the generation of employment, the communication identified four industrial policy priorities:

- to promote intangible investment in areas such as training, R&D, and methods of work organization (in line with the move to an information society);
- to develop industrial cooperation and networking inside and outside the European Union and to stimulate collaboration to increase the presence of European companies in high growth markets;
- to strengthen competition by completing the internal market, establishing open standards (technical regulations, standards and certification), eliminating factors which distort competition, and securing access to non-EU markets;
- to modernize the organizational structures and support procedures of public authorities,[15] to limit taxes and social security contributions and make them more responsive, to improve the industrial environment, and to use public purchasing and investment activities to stimulate development.

Each of these priorities was translated into a wide range of related objectives and horizontal policy actions, designed to coordinate and shape actions under a number of common policies, particularly with respect to research, cohesion, vocational training, networks, and trade, and to improve coordination and consultation between member states.

In March 1995 a draft proposal for an Action Programme (CEC 1995a) was published. Four industrial competitiveness policy objectives were highlighted: the development of the internal market which includes making it operational through the 'new approach' and harmonization of national legislative frameworks; greater consideration

---

[15] Of the measures adopted to modernise public authorities, the most important is the Integration of Administrative Data (IDA) programme adopted by Council decision 95/468/CE of 6 November 1995. The major aim of the IDA programme is 'to improve the interchange of data between administrations and to provide companies and the public with easier access to information' which is essential 'to ensure the smooth operation of the internal market'. The idea is to develop the exchange of electronic data between public authorities and administrations at local, regional and national level, Community institutions, the European Parliament, the Council, and the European agencies; and to improve Community decision-making processes and the implementation of common policies, offering possibilities of greater cohesion through a greater and more equal uptake of the opportunities of integration.

of industry's needs in research policy; the establishment of the information society; and the promotion of industrial cooperation. To meet these objectives actions on immaterial investment, industrial cooperation, competition, and modernization of the public authorities were identified. Their financial impact was principally on the budgets for the Community Support Frameworks, Cohesion Fund, and research and development Framework Programme.

A very large number of Community polices, therefore, contribute to industrial competitiveness. In section 4.3 attention was focused on the impact of actions to ensure fair competition through the regulation of state aids. In this section attention will be focused on the impact of the 'new approach' to standards and the harmonization of national legislative frameworks and the promotion of industrial cooperation. Attempts to give greater consideration to industry's needs in research policy will be considered in the chapter on research and development polices (Chapter 5).

4.4.1. *Harmonizing technical rules and standards*

Setting standards and introducing technical regulations are key elements of the single market programme and are important components of competition, market integration, and industrial policy. The case for competitive markets rests substantially on a comparison of situations of perfect competition, which is optimal for consumers, and monopoly situations, in which there is a transfer of consumer surplus to producers and a reduction of that surplus. To act to limit monopoly situations and preserve competition (while creating scope for the realization of scale economies), Community industrial policy seeks to limit the segmentation of markets through the harmonization of standards and assurance of the compatibility of products. Harmonization can provide consumers with a number of advantages: compatibility is needed to enable consumers to purchase complementary goods; compatibility enables demand to be satisfied in a number of ways with possibilities of switching from one make to another without substantial switching costs; compatibility increases network externalities defined as situations in which the utility of a good for a user depends on the number of users; and compatibility increases the substitutability of goods and, accordingly, the cross–elasticities of demand, making consumers less captive to particular firms. At the same time, standards raise the quality and safety of products and facilitate comparisons between different products, while scale advantages reduce costs. Of course, some of these gains presuppose that the resources released as a result of a loss of protection are re-employed.

The question of the impact on cohesion involves two main sets of issues. First, the establishment of restrictive technical regulations may fragment the internal market and may protect industries in more advanced areas from industries in less developed parts of the EU. Second, the establishment of standards may damage cohesion insofar as large groups in core areas represented in the standard setting agencies secure decisions that give them a market advantage. In some cases there is evidence that changes in the economic environment can have effects on cohesion that are so adverse or sensitive that derogations are required to give weaker areas and member states more time in which to adapt.

4.4.1.1. Cohesion and the setting of European standards

Setting standards is a critical instrument of EU market integration. At present, setting standards conforms to the new approach introduced in May 1983. Under the old approach, the Commission developed detailed directives for individual products which national governments were required to adopt. The new approach directives (which have the status of law) were limited to essential requirements of safety and environmental protection, and the setting of European standards was mandated to three agencies: Centre Européen de Normalisation (CEN); Centre Européen de Normalisation Electrotechnique (CENELEC); and European Telecommunication Standards Institute (ETSI). In 1992 a White Paper on Standard Setting envisaged that standards would be used in all European policies.

CEN has eighteen members: the fifteen EU states and Iceland, Norway, and Switzerland. There are three methods used by CEN to set a European standard. First, a standard is elaborated by a technical committee in which participation is confined to European actors (national delegations, Commission representatives, associated bodies, and observers representing European federations). Second, an existing international standard is adopted. Third, the setting of standards is subcontracted to the ISO. In this case, European members of the ISO will vote twice; first, in the ISO where each country has one vote and, second, in the CEN where the Council's system of weighted votes is practised. This third procedure was created in accordance with the 1991 Vienna Agreement.

In May 1995 CEN produced its 2,000th standard, of which 700 were Community mandates (see Table 4.8). The new approach directives comprise the main area where European standardization is needed to support Community policies. Another area where standards are necessary is public procurement, as reference to standards is obligatory in all public tenders. With two exceptions, at the point when directives come into effect there is a sufficient number of supporting standards available to industry. The exceptions are machinery, where industry was slow to react, and construction, where there is no consensus on European standards.

In June 1992 a new category of associate members joined the CEN to represent industrial bodies (European Chemical Industry Council (CEFIC), European Construction Industry Federation (FIEC), European Confederation of Medical Devices Association (EUCOMED)), trade unions (European Trade Union Technical Bureau for Health and Safety (TUTB), itself part of the European Trade Union Confederation (CES)), and consumer groups (European Association for the Co-operation of Consumer Representation in standardization (ANEC)). A more recent development is establishment on the initiative of DG XXIII of a new organization, the European Office of Crafts, Trades, and Small and Medium-Sized Enterprises for Standardization (NORMAPME) to represent the interests of SMEs in the light of a Euromanagement study which identified a number of shortcomings in the areas of standards compliance, certification, and quality assurance. SMEs can, however, be divided into two groups differently affected by the standardization process: a number of active SMEs (often in high technology sectors) follow and sometimes shape (European) standards and find standardization helpful; and the vast majority who are either indifferent or hostile towards standardization, perceiving standards as obstacles driving up their costs. Associates participate in discussions but do not have voting rights. Apart from their direct involvement at EU level, interest groups are also represented within national standard-ization bodies, giving them some indirect influence in approving European standards. In addition, programming committees and technical sector boards have been created better to coordinate CEN activities with interested parties.

The concession of associate membership status to new interest groups indicates recognition of a problem which has a cohesion dimension. As far as SMEs are con-cerned, the organizations setting standards argued that the relatively high cost of com-pliance is a consequence of the lack of visibility of the standard-setting procedure, the lack of participation, and a lack of information. As SME participation is new, it is too early to assess their success in influencing the procedures for setting standards. The SME–large firm divide also has a territorial dimension: if the interests of SMEs are not sufficiently taken into account, the process of setting European standards may work against the catching-up of Mediterranean cohesion countries, where the enterprise population is more dominated by smaller enterprises. At the same time, there are grounds for thinking that the winners from technical harmonization at EU level are companies in those countries which already have a strong standard-setting culture (such as Germany). Even amongst countries with strong standard-setting traditions there are marked differences. Companies in France, for example, are used to coping with national standards which are often less demanding than the equivalent standards in Germany. On the other hand, the conformity of products with standards is verified much more frequently in France than in Germany, with testing taking place, on aver-age, once a year in France and every five years in Germany.

As consumer awareness rises, however, so does the need for standardization. A SME in a cohesion region which is less used to complying with standards than a competitor from the core countries can use the European standard as a marketing argument and, since compliance with only one standard opens up the whole Community market, costs should be limited. By the same token, however, competitive rivalry intensifies in its home market. At this stage there is little evidence as to whether the existence of new opportunities in a wider European market offset the increased threat faced in the home market. What is lacking is analysis of the way in which standards are used in practice and what effects they have on economic performance, market share or, cohesion. More sys-tematic feedback is clearly needed, and CEN is considering how to set up a reporting system on the impact of standards.

Case study evidence indicates that, in the past, the interests of smaller producers were given insufficient attention. A case in point, which arose under the old standard-setting procedures when detailed specifications were the order of the day, was the setting of standards for lifts. The European lift industry consists of four big multinational suppliers and a very large number of small producers. These two groups operate in somewhat different markets. The MNCs concentrate on large projects with standardized lift cages and the small producers offer lifts for buildings with non-standardized cages. The Commission planned to propose a directive on the technical specifications lifts should respect throughout the Community. As a result of the active lobbying by the MNCs, the proposed technical specifications closely reflected their interests. Adoption of this

Table 4.8. Progress of mandated programme for 'new approach directives'

Directives	Standards		
	Ratified	Under approval	Under development
Simple pressure vessels	30	11	42
C93/319 (Projet de directive)	1	26	106
Safety of toys 88/378	8	1	9
Construction products 89/105	156	304	763
Safety of machinery (static, lifting, and mobility aspects) 89/392, 91/368, 93/44	41	234	540
Personal protective equipment 89/686	105	71	250
Non-automatic weighing instruments 90/384	1	0	1
Active implantable medical devices 90/385	14	17	41
Medical devices 93/42	4	49	108
Gas appliances 90/396	17	45	77
Explosives for civil uses 93/15	0	0	54
Recreational craft 94/25	9	10	37
Efficiency of boilers 92/42			8
Total	386	768	2,036

Source: Da111

legislation would have threatened the survival of SMEs in that sector and, eventually, the project was abandoned.

In the 1980s the EU manufacturers of lawnmowers were very competitive on world markets. Then Denmark adopted a national regulation on the noise emission from lawnmowers. The Danish rule was much stricter than every other rule in the Community and obliged the European producers to design a model specifically for the Danish market. As there is a trade-off between noise emission and the efficiency of lawn mowers, the Danish model was not competitive on other markets. After the Danish initiative, another member state adopted legislation which was more demanding than that of the rest of the EU but less strict than the Danish legislation. As a result, producers had to adapt their product range to that new regulation. A proposal was then made to the Commission to set a standard at a European level that would require the noise emission to be reduced throughout the Union. This standard was seen by industry as a threat to their competitiveness on world markets. The view of the Commission is that uniform environmental rules for products and processes are not very helpful. From a competitiveness point of view, differentiated standards or voluntary commitments (like Eco-Auditing and Eco-Labelling) are regarded as superior approaches.

Through their effects on costs, quality, safety, and compatibility, standards offer substantial potential welfare advantages. The Commission is aware, however, of the possibilities of negative distributional effects. In the past, some moves to establish standards were stopped out of concern that large and powerful producers would lobby for standards that would enable them to increase their market share at the expense of smaller competitors. More recently, steps have been taken to make the setting of standards more responsive to the concerns of SMEs and national differences in standard-setting cultures.

4.4.1.2. Community policy to enhance implementation of regulations and standards
Giving European standards an operational meaning involves a series of actions. First, for a Community standard to be effective there have to exist adequate testing facilities throughout the EU. At present, a map of decentralized testing (and also research) institutions throughout the EU is being established. This list of institutions will help avoid the unnecessary creation of new ones. A comparison with the map of industrial sites will show where the main gaps are and will underpin a strategy to enhance the endowment of European regions with these institutions. As the main gaps exist in some of the less developed southern parts of the EU, completion of this map will involve a series of investments that are pro-cohesive in character.

Second, once proper testing of products is ensured, either by independent institutions or by enterprises themselves, there also have to be bodies which then certify the test results and control the conformity of tested and certified products with the standards. A region's endowment with such a technical infrastructure for testing, certification, and control is an essential prerequisite for endogenous regional development and is also a requirement of inward investors. The Commission is initiating action by member states and regions in the field of quality policy, providing co-financing for the setting up of new institutions (DG XVI, DG XXIII, and PEDIP I), supporting related training programmes (DG V) encouraging a networking of existing institutions, and taking a more active approach to raising the public profile of these institutions. These activities contribute to economic and social cohesion, though their impact varies from the positive results under PEDIP I in Portugal[16] to the less positive outcomes in the field of quality policy in Greece. (Organizing the partnership between the Commission, national governments, and regional players for these programmes is difficult.)

4.4.1.3. Technical regulations, the single market, and cohesion
A range of technical rules regulate the placing of categories of products on the internal market (safety rules for chemicals and pharmaceuticals and for protective equipment in construction, environmental protection, and interoperability rules in telecommunications). For example, 30–40 per cent of products are subject to safety regulations. The Commission has a coordinating role. What happens in one sector should be consistent

---

[16] PEDIP I was a programme that implemented a protocol attached to the Act of Accession of Portugal to the Community. The programme involved the supply of technical and financial support to help 'modernize the [Portuguese] production sector and to adapt it to European and international economic realities'. Assistance was given to firms accounting for 42 per cent of Portuguese industrial employment, but with an overrepresentation of firms with over 100 employees and of firms in modern (metals and electrical goods) industries, and an under-representation of firms with fewer than 50 employees and in traditional industries (textiles and forestry). The firms involved in PEDIP I were those that were more dynamic but that were also more vulnerable due to their higher rates of investment.

with what happens in another (e.g. vehicle emissions), and where regulatory principles exist they should be complied with.

The Treaty of European Union requires that member states should not take measures that undermine the internal market. The aim is to suppress measures inhibiting the free movement of goods as far as possible or to ensure, either through mutual recognition of equivalence or through the approximation of laws, that the internal market is not affected.

The principal measure through which the Commission seeks to monitor developments in member state regulation and preserve the internal market is through the information procedure of Directive 83/189, under which member states must notify the Commission and through it other member states of intended technical rules while they are at a draft stage. The Commission can ask for a three-month waiting period during which it can react, and if the proposal is of concern it can issue a detailed opinion which can extend the waiting period.

The information procedure reveals a large volume of detailed and complex national technical regulations concerning products, their specifications, their conditions of use, the tests they must undergo, and the certificates of approval they require. In any one year the number of regulatory measures adopted by the fifteen member states regularly exceeds the whole Community *acquis* (415 Community directives and regulations established in 35 years). Of some 1,136 draft technical regulations proposed in 1992–4, the Commission requested changes in about 526 and detailed opinions in 357. At the root of these requests is the view that divergent technical regulations fragment the internal market, and that onerous and complex regulation may for reasons that are real or imagined discourage the investment required to exploit wider European markets.

As well as fragmenting the internal market, national technical regulations could be viewed as anti-cohesive if restrictive regulations close markets to producers in weaker countries. In textiles, for example, German rules concerning the labelling of garments made from reprocessed textiles prevent the sale in Germany of products whose production involves the use of specific chemical processes (involving, for example, the use of arsenic compounds) widely used in other member states. The trade-off in these cases is complicated. Ecological and quality factors are determinants of the quality of life and increased quality standards across the EU would make EU industries less exposed to competition from low-wage countries. At the same time such measures erode the wage-cost dependent competitive advantage of enterprises in less developed areas.

Of the draft technical regulations notified to the Commission by the EU-12 over the three years 1992–4, most came from three countries. Germany submitted 21 per cent, the United Kingdom 21 per cent, and France 17 per cent while, in relation to their size, the Netherlands (9 per cent) and Denmark (7 per cent) provided more than their share (see Table 4.9). (These member states are the ones that have expressed most concern about the negative impact on industry of excessive EU regulation.)

Eighty-five per cent of the notifications came from five sectors: telecommunications equipment (29 per cent), agriculture and food products (17 per cent), construction (13 per cent), mechanical engineering (13 per cent), and transport (12 per cent). In the case of telecommunications, liberalization creates a need to replace the internal requirements of former national monopolies by public specifications, as does the need for

Table 4.9. Technical regulations notified by member state 1992–4

	1992	1993	1994	Total	Share
Germany	65	80	98	243	21.4
United Kingdom	67	106	62	235	20.7
France	73	65	60	198	17.4
Italy	40	36	34	110	9.7
Netherlands	38	24	40	102	9.0
Denmark	28	18	34	80	7.0
Spain	12	15	25	52	4.6
Belgium	11	18	16	45	4.0
Greece	11	12	12	35	3.1
Portugal	12	7	7	26	2.3
Ireland	2	3	1	6	0.5
Luxembourg	3	1	0	4	0.4
Total EU	362	385	389	1,136	100.0

Source: Da111

equipment to operate in a mixed environment in which new digital technology has to interoperate with differently specified national analogue systems. The risk is that a *de facto* differentiation of national digital networks may result. In construction there is a proliferation of different national rules (with 73 notifications from Germany and 29 from the UK) due to the difficulties of implementing the Construction Products Directive and agreeing harmonized European standards. What is more, difficulties in adopting European standards and the creation of national technical regulations are obstacles to implementing public procurement (public works and utilities) directives, impeding their purpose of opening up the market for works contracts and the construction products used in them.

In the expectation that the public procurement directives would have a negative impact on the construction sectors in cohesion countries and less developed areas, temporary derogations were allowed to facilitate adaptation. In these areas construction is a critically important sector, accounting for a very high percentage of the number of enterprises and employment. In some respects national technical regulation offers a degree of further protection for this sector though, as the data show, the main source of notifications is Germany and the UK rather than the cohesion countries.

4.4.2. *Industrial policy and cohesion: Policies to develop industrial cooperation*

The creation of a Commission unit in charge of industrial cooperation followed the G24 study on ways to promote investment in countries in transition and a 1992 Council resolution that invited the Commission to develop industrial cooperation with third countries (JO, C178 of 15 July 1992). In the 1994 Communication on an Industrial

Competitiveness Policy for the EU (CEC 1994*b*), industrial cooperation within the EU and with third countries was identified as a priority action. As many member state governments are disinclined to grant the Commission a significant degree of competence with respect to enhancing cooperation within the EU, for the most part industrial cooperation policies relate to collaboration with countries that are not member states.

4.4.2.1. *Actions with respect to industrial cooperation in the EU*

The Commission seeks to facilitate cooperation between European firms, especially where SMEs are involved. Within the limits set by the laws of competition and acceptance of the view that the initiative must lie with industrialists, a number of initiatives have been taken in consumer electronics, information technology, cars, and textiles and clothing.

A communication on subcontracting in the textile and clothing industries envisaged a set of actions and supporting measures in which the Commission with the help of a European forum of industrialists would endeavour to help subcontractors increase their competitiveness. An important element of this strategy was an increase in cooperation between subcontractors, distributors, and manufacturers. After the first forum in Madrid in 1992, a study on subcontracting in clothing in 1994, and another forum in Brussels, a series of pilot projects were implemented and round tables were organized in five member states (Belgium, France, Italy, Greece, Portugal) of which two are cohesion countries.

Further steps to improve industrial cooperation between customers and subcontractors include the development of regular statistical information on trends in subcontract activities; the production of a guide on the legal aspects of subcontracting whose aim is to improve contractual relations; and the development, in conjunction with the Union des Confédérations de l'Industrie et des Employeurs d'Europe (UNICE) and employers' organizations, of a professional code of practice and associated certification. A multilingual guide to sectoral terminology has been produced and is being further developed. In 1994 the Commission set up the Subcontracting Assistance Network (SCAN). The aim is to improve access to information about subcontract markets and its regularity and quality by interconnecting and making interoperable subcontract databanks in Europe. In 1992 the Commission published a directory of organizations representing subcontractors in Europe. This directory was updated in 1994. All of these actions are designed to improve the efficiency of subcontract industries and ensure that they function on a European scale. Measures of this kind create opportunities but also competitive challenges for subcontractors in less developed areas, while improving the terms of their contracts.

Of particular importance is the Trade and Electronic Data Interchange System (TEDIS) programme. This programme has launched over 150 projects aimed at deepening knowledge of EDI, stimulating its development and encouraging its implementation in Europe in ways ensuring that there are no sectoral or geographical barriers to trade and that the single market is not fragmented. Action has also been taken at an international level in close collaboration with international bodies, particularly the United Nations, to ensure that European companies can reach any partner anywhere in the world using standard messaging. Further actions were designed to ensure the geographical and sectoral integration of EDI trading markets, and to promote awareness of EDI throughout Europe by creating a decentralized network of awareness centres with an emphasis on regional management and the involvement of SMEs.

While the initiatives that the Commission has so far taken to increase interfirm cooperation in the EU are relatively few, it is right to recognize the importance of such cooperation, especially for firms in less developed areas. An aspect of new technologies is their communicational character and the associated development of new intra- and interorganizational relationships. An important characteristic of the new principles of productivity associated with these technologies is that they are not simply additive. A global optimum is not necessarily the sum of a set of local optima. It is for this reason that organizations seek to integrate activities from the design of goods and services to their distribution into an interdependent system. These efforts to coordinate and integrate activities lead to the development of networks and management models whose characteristics include the fact that their domain extends beyond the firm, upstream to suppliers and downstream to customers. This development tends to stabilize the networks of upstream and downstream relations of firms and leads to the creation of partnerships with a reduced number of suppliers and subcontractors. A characteristic of these networks is that they are technical and not just commercial in character. In upstream just-in-time (JIT) sytems, for example, medium-term cost control requires that stocks are not simply pushed back on to suppliers. To reduce costs, suppliers must themselves use similar methods of stock control. Moreover, quality and product specification considerations require tighter control over the suppliers' process of manufacture with, in some cases, direct control over manufacturing in the shape of distributed CAD and integrated CAD/CAM between a firm and a supplier. The clear implication is that in the years to come the survival and development of firms in less developed areas will, in some cases, depend upon their ability to meet the more rigorous requirements of their customers and establish relations of long-term cooperation with them.

4.4.3. Conclusion

Traditional industrial policies defined specific targets for industrial performance and capacity and used institutional, financial, material, and human instruments to attain these targets. Implementation involved joint action by public authorities and their industrial partners. The aim was to control from above the coherence of the national economy within the world economy, in particular through a quest for an equilibrium judged desirable between different activities (sectors and *filières*). Current approaches to industrial policy differ. Decisions are left firmly in the hands of industrialists and policy action focuses on the creation of a competitive and supportive environment.

The liberalization of markets and the intensification of competition has led to a dramatic restructuring of European industry. Increases in productivity have not, however, been matched by correspondingly fast rates of output growth, with the result that industrial employment has declined and the economies of the EU have so far failed to reabsorb the human resources released as a result of productivity and structural change.

Industrial competitiveness policies have played a part in this process of liberalization. They also have helped put in place the support structures that were more weakly developed or absent in the less developed parts of the EU, thereby helping these enterprises to adapt to the internal market.

4.5. SME Policies and Cohesion

Enterprise policies (Article 130 of the Maastricht Treaty—now Art. 157) are designed to improve the economic environment and promote the development of enterprises, particularly small and medium-sized enterprises. These measures, set out in the Commission report on the 'Coordination of activities in favour of SMEs and the craft sector' (CEC (1995*c*)) as well as the more recent 'Integrated programme for SMEs and the craft sector' (CEC (1996*c*)) and the 'Third multi-annual programme for SMEs' (CEC (1996*e*)), relate to a number of areas of Community responsibility set out in the Treaty of Rome but only institutionalized at a Community level from 1983 onwards.

SMEs have a flexible and more adaptable structure, enabling them to survive in turbulent economic environments more easily than larger firms (Cortes, Berry, and Ishaq 1987). They are a major source of employment in EU economies (CEC (1995*b*)) and leading employment creators due to their relatively high labour intensity. As Eurostat (1994, Table 2, p. 7) shows, in EU-12 in 1988–90, large enterprises increased their share of turnover by 6.9 per cent, yet reduced their share of employment by 1.2 per cent. On the contrary, micro-units (0–9 people) increased their employment share by 4 per cent. It should be stressed that SMEs (micro-units included) are particularly active in distribution and services. In 1990 in these two sectors SMEs accounted for 88.7 per cent and 77.6 per cent of employment and for 86.2 per cent and 85.0 per cent of turnover, respectively. Industry, conversely, is dominated by large firms, which accounted for 40.5 per cent of employment and 52.4 per cent of turnover.

SMEs face special difficulties (European Observatory for SMEs 1995). Of these difficulties the most important are the lack of start-up capital and of suitably skilled workers. The existence of a complex legal and administrative environment is also a serious obstacle to their development, as is a lack of information about important matters such as relevant R&D results, possible suppliers or customers, and joint interest in research, production, and distribution. The isolation of SMEs and their inability to search for partners because of scarce resources are further constraints.

Measures designed to help SMEs deal with these difficulties can be divided into horizontal and support measures. Horizontal measures include improving the legal and administrative environment in which SMEs have to grow. Simplifying matters and abandoning complex procedures are given priority, and higher aid thresholds are adopted. Support measures include: (1) financial instruments such as subsidized European Investment Bank (EIB) global loans, the SME facility introduced by the 1993 Copenhagen Council for loan subsidies, and loan guarantees from the EIB; (2) programmes and networks encouraging and supporting transnational cooperation between SMEs, namely the Business Cooperation Networks (BC-NETs), the Bureau de Rapprochement des

Entreprises (BRE), EUROPARTENARIAT, and INTERPRISE, as well as measures to enhance the dissemination of information about markets, customers, and the scope for cooperation through the Euro-Information Centres (EICs); and (3) pilot actions such as the Seed Capital Funds and Euromanagement RDT.

SMEs and especially micro-units are important from a cohesion perspective because they play a more dynamic role in employment creation than large enterprises (European Observatory for SMEs 1995, ch. 4). At the same time, SMEs account for particularly large shares of employment, especially in Objective 1 regions, while, insofar as industrial employment is concerned, SMEs are either more dynamic job creators or reduce employment more slowly than large enterprises in the majority of Objective 1, 2, and 5b areas.

The actual as opposed to the potential impact of SME policies on cohesion depends on the geography of the take-up of SME assistance and the consequent effects on the growth of SMEs. One complication is that the development of SMEs cannot be attributed to specific SME policies alone. Other policies, such as Structural Funds, or other programmes, such as LEONARDO, which supports vocational training, may also assist SMEs. The trends observed should be interpreted with this reservation in mind.

4.5.1. The impact of financial instruments

Table 4.10 sets out an index of the per capita use of individual loans and the allocations from ongoing global loans to SMEs in 1990–4 by member state. Belgium, Italy, and Denmark have the highest per capita indices, while UK, Greece, Spain, and Germany have the lowest. (SMEs may benefit from categories of EIB loans other than those specifically addressed to them, such as loans for regional development, but their effects cannot be measured.) The countries with the highest index of EIB loans, namely Belgium and Denmark, have the largest shares of employment in services (more than 68 per cent) in EU-12, while Greece, Spain and Germany account for some of the lowest shares of employment in services (less than 60 per cent). The UK, with 70 per cent of its employment in services, is an exception.

The SME facility, which provides an extra 1 billion ecus in subsidized (interest subsidy of 2 per cent) EIB loans, was established at the invitation of the 1993 Copenhagen European Council meeting. As Table 4.10 shows, the percentage of utilization up to 31 July 1995 was low in the cohesion countries, with Greece and Portugal, the poorest in terms of per capita disposable income, having the lowest take-up rates.

4.5.2. The impact of pilot actions

DG XXIII's Seed Capital pilot scheme designed to support private investment in new innovative enterprises, regional development, and job creation has backed the creation of twenty-three independent investment funds. These funds provide venture capital. In 1989–96 they supported the creation of 306 new innovative enterprises, creating 2,332 jobs. The distribution of funds, investment, and jobs by member state is shown

Table 4.10. SME policies in EU countries

Country	(1) EIB	(2) SME facility	(3) No. of SMEs	(4) % of proposals	(5) Funds	(6) Inv.	(7) Jobs
			Euromanagement		Seed capital		
Belgium	72	97	60	10.9	2	20	96
Germany	16	100	137	24.2	4	49	473
Denmark	57	99	5	0	0	—	—
Spain	16	82	100	10.3	3	47	292
France	32	100	159	9.7	5	72	719
Greece	16	17	65	9.1	0	—	—
Ireland	20	80	40	0.6	1	24	136
Italy	64	100	103	12.7	3	29	125
Netherlands	20	100	26	1.8	2	24	136
Portugal	36	21	40	3.6	0	—	—
United Kingdom	4	100	112	5.5	3	41	355
Austria			20	1.2			
Finland			20	4.8			
Sweden			40	5.5			
EU			927	100.0	23	306	2,332

(1) Index of per capita value of EIB loans to SMEs in 1990–4. *Source*: 1994 EIB Annual Report.
(2) Percentage of utilization of SME facility until 31 July 1995. *Source*: DG XXIII.
(3–4) In 1995. *Source*: DG XXIII.
(5) Number of funds (1996).
(6) Number of investments (1996).
(7) Number of jobs created (1996). *Source*: Seed Capital Advance Report 1996, DG XXIII and DG XVI.

in Table 4.10. Denmark and Portugal did not apply at the time of the initial call for tenders, while Greece dropped out of the scheme. On a per capita basis, Belgium and Netherlands seem to fare better than the rest. Of the four cohesion countries, only Spain, with three funds, is an active participant. Ireland has only one.

The Euromanagement programme, which was successfully introduced in 1992, was given a second launch in 1995. DG XXIII selected, trained, and funded on a 50 per cent basis forty-seven consultancies specializing in research, technological development, and innovation for SMEs. Their mission was to select 927 SMEs and implement a programme of strategic planning, analysis of needs, partner search, and assistance to design RTD projects for these SMEs during 1995. Almost 60 per cent of the assisted SMEs had fewer than 50 employees, while 58 per cent had significant RTD activities committing at least 3 employees per year to RTD. The four cohesion countries contained 26 per cent of the SMEs participating in the programme and generated 24 per cent of the proposals (Table 4.10). Both percentages are higher than the cohesion countries' share of the EU population (17 per cent).

Table 4.11. SME policies in EU countries: support for transnational cooperation

Country	BC–NET[a]	Public	Private	Semi–public	BRE[b]	EIC[c]
Belgium	19	3	12	4	28	14
Germany	40	9	26	5	27	32
Denmark	6	1	4	1	4	8
Spain	35	17	17	1	54	25
France	41	15	17	9	67	32
Greece	18	6	10	2	23	11
Ireland	5	1	3	1	6	6
Italy	60	13	40	7	103	27
Netherlands	10	1	8	1	10	7
Portugal	13	4	8	1	19	12
United Kingdom	30	12	15	3	55	23
Sweden	6	2	2	2	6	9
Finland	6	1	2	3	2	7
Austria	7	0	6	1	4	7
EU	296	85	170	41	408	220

[a] Structure of the BC–NET, number of members, Dec. 1996.
[b] Number of correspondents, Dec. 1996.
[c] EURO–Info Centres, Dec. 1996.
Source: DG XXIII.

4.5.3. *Transnational cooperation*

BRE and BC–NET were established mainly to help enterprises find new contacts in other European or third countries. These measures have been complemented by the INTERPRISE and EUROPARTENARIAT programmes as well as other by activities to encourage sub-contracting. In December 1996 BC–NET had 330 members, of whom 296 were in the EU–15. Seventy-one (24 per cent) were located in the four cohesion countries (see Table 4.11). Overall, 29 per cent of these enterprises were public, 57 per cent were private, and 14 per cent were semi-public. In the four cohesion countries, however, just 39 per cent of the members were private. As for BRE, Table 4.11 shows that in 1996 there were 408 correspondents, of whom 102 (25 per cent) were in the cohesion countries. The European Information Centres (EICs) network includes 220 members in EU countries. Almost 70 per cent of the network is located in eligible, peripheral areas, allowing links to be created among them as well as between them and central regions. The four cohesion countries (see Table 4.11) have fifty-four EICs (25 per cent), although Greece lost two and Spain lost one in 1996 due to rationalization. The EICs, which are recognized as 'first-stop shops', play a crucial role in easing SME participation in the internal market by providing updated information to local SMEs, acting as technical advisers and facilitating SME participation in EU programmes.

4.5.4. Development of SMEs 1990–1

Eurostat's third report on Enterprises in Europe (Eurostat 1994), which offers detailed evidence of the development of SMEs by member state in terms of number of enterprises, employment, value added, and turnover, shows that the member states that fared better in all the SME schemes had an *ex ante* healthier development of their enterprise sector. The opposite applied to the least active participants.

Belgium and Denmark were strongly involved in the relevant schemes and improved in all the performance ratios of their enterprises.

In Belgium, enterprise productivity was 16 per cent higher than the EU-12 average in 1990. Turnover per person increased by 4 per cent between 1990 and 1991 (and by 15 per cent between 1988 and 1991). Distribution showed by far the highest turnover per person. The number of VAT units increased by 2.3 per cent in the same period. Of the 1994 labour force, 68.2 per cent was employed in services.

In Denmark, in 1990–1, the number of enterprises (with an annual turnover of more than 15,000 ecus) increased by 0.5 per cent (2.1 per cent in services), turnover per person increased by 5.8 per cent, and value added per person by 7.7 per cent. In 1991 service enterprises accounted for 71 per cent of Danish firms, 53 per cent of employment, and 62 per cent of turnover. Of the entire labour force, 68.4 per cent is employed in services. SMEs accounted for more than 80 per cent of employment, turnover, and value added in the sector.

In Portugal, which also participated actively in the relevant schemes, the number of enterprises increased by 50,000 or 8 per cent in 1990–1 (33 per cent in 1988–91). Employment increased by 13 per cent, and turnover by 8 per cent. As a result, turnover per person decreased. It declined by 2 per cent in manufacturing and 10 per cent in construction, but increased by 10 per cent in services. The rest of services, NACE 7–9, showed the strongest variation in 1988–91. The number of units increased by 68 per cent, employment by 17 per cent, and turnover by 59 per cent.

In Ireland, the data refers only to industrial enterprises (NACE 1–4) employing more than three persons and construction firms (NACE 5) employing more than twenty persons. In 1989–90 the number of units, employment, and net output increased slightly. Net output per person increased in 1987–89 by 22 per cent but decreased in 1989–90 by 5 per cent, although small establishments showed an increase.

In contrast to the four preceding countries, Greece, which seems to be the least active participant in the SME support schemes, shows a general decline. The information for Greece is not directly comparable to that for other countries, since it refers only to industrial (NACE 1–4) and repair industry (NACE 67) firms employing more than 10 persons. The service sector is not included. In 1988–91 turnover and value added per person declined by 15 per cent and 19 per cent respectively. Turnover per unit and value added per unit decreased by 20 per cent and 23 per cent respectively. The number of establishments was reduced by 2 per cent and employment by 7 per cent.

4.5.5. Development of SMEs and uptake of SME programmes

The evidence presented in this section suggests that there is a reciprocal relationship between the dynamism of the SME sector and involvement in SME programmes. Declining figures for Greece on all the performance variables examined may underlie a reduced interest or even potential to participate in schemes that support young, dynamic, and preferably technologically advanced enterprises. That services are not included in the statistics makes the comparisons awkward, but the fact that the service sector employs only 55.6 per cent of the Greek labour force (the lowest share in EU–12 in 1994) shows that services have lacked the dynamism required to counterbalance the negative trends in the industrial sector.

Conversely, Belgium, which is probably the most active participant in all SME schemes, shows a positive development trend with increases in productivity, employment and in the number of establishments (see also section 4.2). The young and dynamic enterprises created in Belgium seem to be able to exploit the SME support schemes. The same holds for Denmark. An extra advantage the two countries have is the relative importance of their service sectors.

Portugal, which also participated very actively in the SME schemes, exhibited a positive development trend as well. There was a dramatic increase in the number of new enterprises, and employment and turnover followed suit. Although services accounted, in 1994, for just 55.8 per cent of the labour force, the service sector participated dynamically in enterprise creation and increased its relative importance.

4.5.6. Conclusions

There are persistent differences in the extent to which member states take advantage of SME policies. These differences stem at least in part from three factors: (1) differences in the economic structure of the member states with large shares of employment in services generally playing a positive role; (2) differences in national development trends with the countries that are most dynamic in new firm creation being best placed to participate in SME support schemes; (3) the general performance, in terms of productivity and competitiveness, of the enterprise sector.

As far as the impact of SME policies on cohesion is concerned, it seems as if peripheral countries in which there is a strong dynamic to enterprise creation benefit from such policies with positive effects on cohesion. Other peripheral countries where economic activity is slowing down do not and possibly cannot benefit from such aid to the same extent and may secure fewer benefits than more developed member states.

The majority of regions to be assisted are in Portugal, Spain, Italy, Greece, and Ireland. They all seem to do well with the frequent exception of Greece. It does seem, however, that the general improvement of an economy should come first, and that once the potential for new enterprises to grow is strong there will be a strong uptake of Community policies. If SME policies do not make an equal contribution to income convergence in all member states, it is probably more due to differences in their economies than to policy inefficiencies.

4.6. Conclusion

Assessing the impact of competition, competitiveness, and enterprise policies is difficult because it is not easy to establish what would have happened in the absence of EU action. What one can observe is how well manufacturing in cohesion countries performed relative to other member states.

In 1992 manufacturing industry accounted for 22.3 per cent of EU value added, services 65 per cent, construction 6 per cent, energy 4.2 per cent, and agriculture 2.5 per cent. The share of manufacturing was in decline, falling from 31 per cent in 1970 to 27 per cent in 1980 and 22.3 per cent in 1992. Germany was the country in which manufacturing accounted for the highest share of output (29.4 per cent). Portugal (29.8 per cent in 1990), Austria (25.9 per cent), and Ireland (27.7 per cent in 1991) were above the EU average. The lowest shares were for Greece (15.4 per cent), Spain (17.4 per cent), the Netherlands (17.9 per cent), and Denmark (18.8 per cent). The cohesion countries, therefore, fell at the two ends of the spectrum, with either relatively large shares of industry in output (Portugal and Ireland) or very low shares (Greece and Spain).

At present EU manufacturing is dominated by four large countries: Germany, France, Italy, and the UK accounted for almost four-fifths (78.9 per cent) of EU manufacturing output. Germany alone accounted for almost one-third. In 1980–92 the cohesion countries (excluding Ireland) dropped from 7.3 to 7 per cent, while the four leading economies saw their share increase from 78.4 per cent in 1980 to 78.9 per cent in 1992. Within this leading group there were, however, significant changes as the French and UK shares fell and the German and Italian shares increased. As far as output growth was concerned, Germany and Italy were the main winners.

Manufacturing employment was in decline, standing at 36.5 million in 1980, 31.8 million in 1985, 32.2 million in 1990 and 28.5 million in 1995. As in the case of output, the four large member states dominate employment, with more than one-quarter of all manufacturing jobs in Germany alone. In 1980–95 a small decline of 1.3 per cent in the share of the four largest countries was accompanied by small increases in the small, older members (especially Denmark and the Netherlands) and three of the cohesion countries, whose share rose from 11.5 per cent in 1980 to 12.2 per cent in 1995, though Spain's share declined from 1992–5.

Although the trade balance of the member states is not a good indicator of comparative national economic performance, it is of value in identifying the trajectories of different member states. In the 1990s the trade balance of the EU increased five-fold, approaching 4 per cent of Community GDP in 1995 (238.8 billion ecus). In 1995 all member states exported more than they imported except the UK (−1.3 per cent of the Community trade balance or −0.4 per cent of UK GDP), Greece (−3.2 and −8.9 per cent respectively), and Portugal (−3.5 and −10.4 per cent). In 1995 West Germany accounted for 59.3 per cent of the EU surplus, lying well ahead of Italy (12.1 per cent) and France (10.1 per cent).

What this data suggest is that Germany, Italy, and France were the principal beneficiaries of increased international competition in the 1980s and 1990s. The increase in their exports outstripped increases in import penetration more than in any other member states. The cohesion countries, conversely, saw their deficits rise sharply in the second half of the 1980s. A sustained deficit implies a transfer of output and employment to surplus countries. Indeed, in the 1980s and early 1990s the value of output did increase faster than average in some of the larger and richer member states, though their share of EU manufacturing employment declined due to shifts in specialization towards activities with a greater value added per person employed.

A further factor which shaped the geography of output and employment was the map of international investment. In the 1980s there was a large increase in inter-firm agreements, mergers, and alliances, and a sharp increase in direct foreign investment in EU countries. In 1990 direct overseas investment in EU countries reached $98.4 billion, compared with $14.8 billion in the early 1980s, increasing some three times more than gross domestic fixed capital formation, though in most of the large EU economies outflows exceeded inflows. In 1990 in the UK, inward investment accounted for 17.3 per cent of investment.

Most of the inward investment was directed from and towards the United Kingdom and France. The Netherlands, Benelux, and Spain received large volumes of inward investment. For its size Germany attracted relatively little inward investment, due perhaps to a desire to ensure domestic control of German industry and the competitive strength of German producers, though it was, with the Netherlands and Benelux, an important capital exporter.

If, however, inward and outward investments are measured relative to GDP, a somewhat different picture emerges. Since 1980 the most important recipients of inward investment were Belgium, the UK, and the Netherlands, followed by Portugal, Spain, and Greece. Next came France, Sweden, and Ireland. Three cohesion countries were, therefore, relatively important recipients of inward investment. Finland had the lowest inward investment relative to its GDP, followed by Germany, Italy, and Austria.

With the exception of Spain, capital export was insignificant from the cohesion countries, implying a limited degree of internationalization of indigenous industries. (Portuguese overseas investment did increase as a percentage of GDP in the early 1990s.) The Netherlands, the UK, Sweden, and Belgium topped this list. A second group was made up of Finland, France, and Germany, which were followed by Denmark and then by Italy and Austria.

In the period from 1980–92, therefore, the absolute volume of direct inward investment in the cohesion countries was comparatively small. In relation to GDP, however, the cohesion countries received quite a large share. Direct overseas investment by cohesion country enterprises was, however, relatively weak, though there were significant differences among the stronger countries with key industrial countries such as Germany and Italy attracting and undertaking much less overseas investment than countries such as the United Kingdom and the Netherlands.

The four large member states—Germany, France, Italy, and the UK—accounted for more than 70.5 per cent of extra-EU goods exports (compared with 65.8 per cent of all exports), and Germany alone accounted for 28.3 per cent. The cohesion countries accounted for just 1.5 per cent. Amongst the large states, the share of the UK was in decline. The share of Greece and Ireland and of the cohesion countries as a whole increased a little over the period from 1970, though Greece of the cohesion countries together with Austria and the Nordic countries are, perhaps, also well placed to develop future links with Eastern and Central Europe and the CIS.

The evidence on trends in GDP per head indicates that in the 1980s and 1990s three of the cohesion countries converged, and in this sense their competitiveness increased. In manufacturing, however, the position was mixed with a fall in their share of output but a small increase in their share of employment. Three of the four cohesion countries were relatively important recipients of inward investment, though their export sectors remain weakly oriented towards non-EU markets, reflecting their specialization in industries oriented towards the internal market.

It is far from easy to identify the impact of EU competition, competitiveness, and enterprise policies on these changes in relative economic performance. What this chapter has highlighted, however, is that, in a context of market integration, the EU has put in place measures (whose take-up is variable) that seek to support and facilitate the adaptation of weaker regional and national economies to the internal market. The EU has sought, in particular through the regulation of state aid, to ensure that a European perspective acts as a counterweight to national perspectives on cohesion.

References

Amin, A., Charles, D. R. and Howells, J. (1992). Corporate restructuring and cohesion in the new Europe. *Regional Studies* 26: 319–31.

Ashcroft, B. and Love, J. H. (1992). External takeovers and the performance of regional companies: a predictive model. *Regional Studies* 26: 543–53.

CEC (1990). Communication on Industrial policy in an open and competitive environment, COM (90).

—— (1993). White paper on Growth, Competitiveness and Employment, COM (93) 700 final.

—— (1994a). Fourth Commission activity report on enterprise policy: Year 1993, COM (94) 221.

—— (1994b). Communication on an Industrial Competitiveness Policy for the EU, COM (94) 319 final.

—— (1995a). Draft proposal for an action programme and timetable for implementation of the action announced in the communication on an industrial competitiveness policy for the European Union, COM (95) 87/2 final.

—— (1995b). The craft industry and small enterprises: keys to growth and employment in Europe, COM (95) 502.

—— (1995c). Report on the coordination of activities in favour of SMEs and the craft sector, COM (95) 362.

—— (1995d). Second report relative to the implementation of the decision regarding the provision of Community interest subsidies, COM (95) 485.

—— (1995*e*). Fourth progress report on the Community pilot scheme-Seed Capital, DG XXIII.

—— (1996*a*). Competitiveness of European industry, 1996 Report. Brussels: CEC.

—— (1996*b*). Report on Community measures affecting tourism, COM (96) 29 of 05.01.1996.

—— (1996*c*). Integrated programme for SMEs and the craft sector, COM (96) 329 of 10.07.96.

—— (1996*d*). Evaluation of the second multiannual programme for SMEs (1993–1996), COM (96) 99 of 20.03.1996.

—— (1996*e*). Maximizing European SMEs' full potential for employment, growth and competition, COM (96) 98 of 20.03.1996.

—— (1996*f*). First Report on economic and social cohesion.

—— (1997*a*). Fifth survey on State aid in the European Union in the manufacturing and certain other sectors.

—— (1997*b*). European Community competition policy, 26. Report on competition policy.

Cortes, M., Berry, A., and Ishaq, A. (1987). *Success in Small and Medium-Scale Enterprises*. A World Bank Research Publication. Oxford: Oxford University Press.

Dalum, B., Laursen, K. and Verspagen, B. (1999). Does specialization matter for growth? *Industrial and Corporate Change* 8: 267–88.

D'Andrea Tyson, L., Cohen, S. S., Teece, D. and Zysman, J. (1984). *Competitiveness: The Report of the President's Commission on Competitiveness*, vol. iii. Washington, D.C.: Government Printing Office.

DG XXIII and DG XVI (1996). Seed capital advance report.

EC (1995). SMEs: a dynamic source of employment, growth and competitiveness in the EU. Report presented by the EC for the Madrid European Council, CSE (95) 2087, December 1995.

EIB (1993). Annual Report.

—— (1994). Annual Report.

European Observatory for SMEs (1995). Third Annual Report. Brussels: European Network for SME Research.

Eurostat (1994). Enterprises in Europe: third report, vols. i and ii. Luxembourg.

Kaldor, N. (1966). *Causes of the Slow Rate of Growth of the United Kingdom*. Cambridge: Cambridge University Press.

—— (1970). The case for regional policies. *Scottish Journal of Political Economy* 17: 337–48.

Krugman, P. (1994). Competitiveness: a dangerous obsession. *Foreign Affairs* 73: 28–44.

Love, J. H. (1989). External takeover and regional economic development: a survey and critique. *Regional Studies* 23: 417–29.

Marques, A. (1994). Regionabeihilfen und Kohäsion: Tragweite und Grenzen gemeinschaftlicher Maßnahmen. *Raumforschung und Raumordnung* 52: 127–37.

Netherlands Economic Institute and Ernst & Young (1993). New location factors for mobile investment in Europe. *Regional Development Studies* no. 6, Study financed by DG XVI of the European Commission.

Observatoire Européen des PME (1995). Troisième rapport annuel. European Network for SME research.

OECD (1995). Historical statistics 1960–93. Paris, OECD.

—— (1996). Historical statistics 1960–94. Paris, OECD.

—— (1997). Historical statistics 1960–95. Paris, OECD.

Rosenstock, M. (1995). *Die Kontrolle und Harmonisierung nationaler Beihilfen durch die Kommission der Europäischen Gemeinschaften*, Frankfurt: Peter Lang.

Schina, D. (1987). *State Aids under the EEC Treaty Articles 92 to 94*. Oxford: ESC Publishing.

Seidel, B. (1994). The regional impact of Community policies, in J. Mortensen, ed., *Improving Economic and Social Cohesion in the European Community*. Basingstoke: Macmillan.

Thirlwall, A. P. (1979). The balance of payments constraint as an explanation of international growth rate differences. *Banca Nazionale del Lavoro* 32: 45–53.

Warnecke, S. J. (1978). *The European Community and National Subsidy Policies*. London: Macmillan.

5

Research and Technological Development

MARGARET SHARP AND TIAGO SANTOS PEREIRA

5.1. Introduction

Policies to promote research and technological development (RTD) within the EU are of relatively recent origin. No reference was made to the subject in the Treaty of Rome[1] and although there were a number of initiatives seeking to promote joint action (Guzzetti 1995; Peterson and Sharp 1998: ch. 2), it was not until the early 1980s that a series of strong Community initiatives emerged. These were prompted by the perception at that time of a major technological gap between the performance of Community enterprises and their US and Japanese counterparts, especially in the important area of electronics. The different initiatives were rapidly drawn into an overall Framework Programme which has developed into one of the more important areas of policy, commanding an annual budget of over 3 billion euros and subject to co-decision procedures between Council and Parliament (see Box 1). Nevertheless, it is important to realize that 3 billion euros is less than 5 per cent of the EU's total annual budget and less than 4 per cent of the total expenditures on R&D by all the national governments of the EU-15 (Peterson and Sharp 1998: ch. 1). In other words, while EU initiatives have acquired a relatively high profile, they rely for their impact on the 'marginal' nature of their activities. Their clout lies in their providing extra resources on top of normal national expenditures.

The purpose of this chapter is to consider how far EU RTD policies have helped, and are helping, to promote cohesion within the EU. As in other chapters, the term cohesion is taken to mean a diminishing of disparities between the more and the less advanced, and here it is considered only in relation to countries and regions. The central question considered is, therefore, how far the raft of RTD policies that has emerged since the early 1980s is helping the less advanced countries and regions catch up with the more advanced.

On the face of it, given the well-established relationship between economic performance and technological activities (Fagerberg 1994), this might seem a non-issue. Promoting RTD helps to promote growth from which the whole community will benefit. It turns out to be anything but a trivial question; partly because EU legislation itself is obscure as to whether cohesion or competitiveness is the overriding objective;

---

[1] Both the ECSC Treaty of Paris (1951) and the Euratom Treaty of 1957 gave research action in these areas a clear legal basis. In the 1950s nuclear power was regarded as by far the most important area of new technology and it was logical for RTD to focus on this activity. See Guzzetti (1995).

partly because in any case skewing the distribution of inputs does not necessarily skew outputs. Account has to be taken of the ability of the least advanced countries and regions to 'absorb' RTD resources and convert them into useful outputs, which shifts the focus to the issue of what constitutes 'absorptive capacity' and whose responsibility (Framework Programme? Structural Funds? National government?) is it to upgrade this capacity.

The chapter is organized as follows. The next section (5.2), considers the issues of cohesion and competitiveness in more detail; section 5.3 analyses the current RTD situation in the EU and identifies the existence of a technology gap between the more and less advanced countries and regions; section 5.4 considers the impact of EU RTD policies; and section 5.5 draws the argument together to present some broad conclusions.

Box 1. The Community's research and technological development programmes

It was not until the early 1980s when Commissioner Davignon, building on the widespread pessimism at that time about Europe's technology gap, established the high profile ESPRIT Programme that Community activities in RTD came into prominence.

ESPRIT established a new type of Community programme—*shared cost* (between industry and the Community), *collaborative* (between countries and between industry and academic research), *bottom up*, with priorities established by industry as much as the Commission, and *competitive*, with open competition for successive rounds of cash and contracts awarded on the basis of 'excellence' as judged by peers. The aim was to mobilize Europe's academic/industrial competence in the information technology field, and to apply this to upgrading the industry's competitiveness. It had the added advantage of encouraging Europe's national champions to come out of their national bunkers and face up to global competition.

ESPRIT provided the model for a whole new style of Community programme. It was rapidly followed by RACE (telecommunications), BRITE (industrial technology), BAP (biotechnology), and a host of other programmes (Guzzetti 1995: ch. 3; Sharp 1993). At the same time the Community adopted the practice of pulling together all its R&D activities into a single budget head—the Framework Programme. The First Framework Programme spanned the years 1984–7 and covered seven areas (agriculture, industry, raw materials, energy, development, health and safety, and the science and technology base, reflecting the diverse activities of the Commission) with energy (i.e. nuclear power) taking 47 per cent of the budget and industry, including ESPRIT, 36 per cent. Since that time there have been a succession of 5-year Framework Programmes the latest of which, the Fifth Framework Programme, came into effect in 1999. Expenditures and priorities of these programmes are summarised in the table.

The Framework Programmes have also included activities to foster the training and the transnational mobility of European researchers, e.g. the Stimulation programme in FP I, Science in FP II, Human Capital and Mobility (HCM) in FP III, and Training and Mobility of Researchers (TMR) in the present FP IV. These actions are of particular relevance for cohesion because they contribute to building up the future European resources for research. The corresponding funds are included in the item 'Other' of the following table. They were substantially increased in FP III within the HCM programme (560 MECU) and in FP IV (nearly 800 MECU).

Box 1. (*cont'd*)

RTD Priorities and the Framework Programmes

Programme Years	FP I 1984–7	FP II 1987–91	FP III 1990–4	FP IV 1994–8
Total MECUs	3,750	5,396	6,600	13,100[d]
Priorities	%	%	%	%
ICT[a]	25	42	38	28
Industrial Technologies[b]	11	16	15	16
Environment	7	6	9	9
Life Sciences	5	7	10	13
Energy	50	22	16	18
Other[c]	2	7	12	16
Total	100	100	100	100

[a] ICT—Information and Communications Technologies.
[b] Includes industrial processes and new materials.
[c] Includes human capital and mobility, development, diffusion and exploitation and social economic research.
[d] Figure adjusted to take account of 1995 entry Austria, Finland and Sweden with the EU originally 12,300 MECUs.

Source: The European Report on Science and Technology Indicators, 1994: Appendix, Table IV.2.

Although the Single Act and the Maastricht Treaty have given legal base to these activities, it should be emphasized that the style and procedures established in the 1980s remain—monies are distributed by a selection procedure of open, competitive bids and peer review. While cohesion takes its place as one of the Maastricht objectives, research excellence remains the dominant criterion in selection.

5.2. Competitiveness and Cohesion

5.2.1. The legal basis

As already noted, no reference was made to RTD in the Treaty of Rome. The Single European Act of 1987 for the first time gave the Community competence in this field and established its broad modalities—the multi-annual Framework Programmes (FPs) and the specific programmes (or lines of action) which implement the activities outlined in the Framework Programme (Guzzetti 1995; Peterson and Sharp 1998).

The objectives of the Community's RTD policy were reiterated in Title XV—Articles 130(f)–130(p) of the Maastricht Treaty (now Articles 163–173). It is worth quoting the first clause of this Title—130(f)1(now Art. 163.1)—in full:

The Community shall have the objective of strengthening the scientific and technological base of Community industry and encouraging it to become more competitive at the international level, while promoting all the research activities deemed necessary by virtue of other chapters in this Treaty.

This makes it clear that the twin objectives of Community policy were to strengthen science and technology (S&T) capabilities of Community industry and to promote competitiveness. Activity 130(h) went further and gave the Commission powers (for the first time) to coordinate policy between and the Community in order to promote these objectives.

The position on cohesion is less clear. Article 130(a) (now Art. 158) of Title XIV of the Maastricht Treaty (which *precedes* Title XV dealing with RTD) states:

the Community shall aim at reducing disparities between the levels of development of the various regions, and the backwardness of the least favoured regions, including rural areas.

Taken in conjunction with the final sentence of Article 130(f)1 (now Art. 163.1) (to promote 'all the research activities deemed necessary by virtue of other chapters in this Treaty'), it may be inferred that the Union is committed to promote, simultaneously, *both* competitiveness and cohesion. One does not take precedence over the other.

5.2.2. Competitiveness

It is worth getting definitions clear. Let us start with competitiveness. Krugman (1994) famously attacked the use of the term in relation to countries, arguing that it is firms, not countries, that compete with each other:

[T]he major industrial countries, while they sell products that compete with each other, are also each other's main export markets and each other's main suppliers of useful imports. If the European economy does well, it need not be at US expense; indeed, if anything a successful European economy is likely to help the US economy by providing it with larger markets. (Krugman 1994: 27)

While Krugman was right to attack the 'zero-sum-game' mentality of some of the debate over competitiveness, the Porter (1990) concept of 'holding market share in the face of competition' has its uses. In particular, and importantly for the present discussion, it was this concept which was taken up in the EC's White Paper on Growth, Competitiveness and Employment (CEC 1993):

The globalisation of economies and markets, which involves the intensification of international competition through the emergence of a potentially unique world-wide market for an expanding range of goods, services and factors, brings out the full importance of that responsibility on the part of national and Community authorities as regards competitiveness. We must increasingly think in terms of competitive rather than comparative advantages. Comparative advantages traditionally relate to endowment in factors such as natural resources and are therefore fairly rigid. *Competitive advantages are based on more qualitative factors and can thus be influenced, to a large degree, by corporate strategies and public policies.* (CEC 1993: 57, italics added)

Jacquemin, one of Delors's advisers on economic policy, goes further. 'In global terms', he writes, 'competitiveness in the European Union is seen as an instrument to create an attractive Europe in terms of activities and jobs, leading ultimately to sustainable development.' As if to illustrate the (italicized) final sentence in the quotation from the white paper, he then goes on to identify potential improvements which the public sector could make to the efficiency of the domestic (European) economy, identifying such factors as 'tangible and intangible infrastructures, the quality of research, training and education' (Jacquemin 1995: 2).

In short, competitiveness in terms of relative 'competitive advantage' for European enterprises across different sectors is meaningful. It is not an end in itself but a means to achieving prosperity, jobs, and sustainable development and, as such, part of a positive sum game. What is more, while there are great limitations on the degree of influence any government can have in the modern globalized economy, there are some policies, including promoting RTD and providing RTD infrastructures, which can help the corporate sector gain competitiveness.

5.2.3. Cohesion—and differential growth

Cohesion is likewise not a simple concept. As stated, the interpretation in this book is that cohesion entails the less privileged doing relatively better—catching up with the more privileged. The key issue is growth—of productivity and GDP per capita. Much of the contemporary discussion of these issues concentrates on the macroeconomic: convergence in income and productivity is seen to depend upon convergence in macroeconomic indicators such as inflation, the public sector deficit, and external account. Yet, as Fagerberg and Verspagen point out (1996), there is little evidence to support this view. Indeed, as they suggest, regional growth differences can be better understood by looking at microeconomic factors.

'New growth theories' focus on innovation as the driving force behind capitalist development (Romer 1986, 1990; Grossman and Helpman 1990; Aghion and Howitt 1992). They highlight the 'endogenous' nature of technological development and the externalities (spillovers) that derive from the process. At the level of the individual firm, investment, whether to defend market share or to exploit new opportunities, and whether in R&D or in physical plant, leads to a simultaneous upgrading of technological capabilities within the firm—hence the endogenous element in growth.

It is worth noting a number of features. First, the influence of these ideas on the Delors White Paper. In effect the White Paper was about endogenous growth: investment will embody new technology and will help to promote competitiveness. Secondly, the externality issue, which is an important constituent in new growth theory, is caught up with the creation of knowledge and the degree to which it inevitably becomes a public good. Romer and his colleagues follow the neoclassicals in assuming that knowledge generated through (basic) research and published in scientific journals is a public good—non-rival, non-excludable, and non-appropriable. The externalities in themselves justify public involvement.

Neo-Schumpeterians think the new growth theorists put too much emphasis on the public-good element in knowledge generation and underplay the person-embodied element. Rosenberg (1990), for example, argued that the advocates of the information-based view tend to regard scientific knowledge 'as being "on the shelf" and costlessly available to all comers once it has been produced. But this model is seriously flawed because it frequently requires a substantial research capability to understand, interpret and to appraise the knowledge that has been placed on the shelf—whether basic or applied' (Rosenberg 1990: 171). In similar vein, Cohen and Levinthal (1989) argued that firm-based R&D serves two functions. One is the obvious one of generating new knowledge from within (which is the function on which the new growth theorists concentrate); the other, and in their view much the more important function, is to allow a firm to 'absorb' new knowledge generated outside the firm.

This ability to 'absorb' knowledge is a key issue in the debate over RTD and cohesion. Following the logic of Rosenberg and Cohen and Levinthal, spillovers or no, individuals, firms and organizations need substantial skills, and have to expend considerable resources on maintaining and upgrading those skills, *just to be able to understand the technological knowledge that is in the public domain.* Without these skills and capabilities, organizations are unable to interpret and derive value from the growing body of codified (i.e. written and published) knowledge available to them. Faulkner and Senker (1995) go further and suggest that codified knowledge itself is capable of transmitting only partial information, and that a full understanding requires personal interaction. This passing on of tacit skills and knowledge may be particularly important for relatively backward economies which have been cut off from mainstream RTD activities. Being involved in international partnerships provides valuable opportunities for acquiring such tacit skills and knowledge.

Abramovitz (1986) captures a similar theme in his famous study 'Catching-up, forging ahead and falling behind'. In this he argues that convergence (i.e. catching up with the leaders) is limited by 'social capability'. Only by developing complementary capabilities, alongside new investment, can the potential of that investment be realized.

We may conclude, therefore, that in the context of cohesion, catching up requires investment, including investment in both the tangible RTD structures (laboratories, equipment, etc.) and the intangible ones (training scientists and technicians). The issue is, however, a systemic one. There is little gained, for example, in pouring large sums of money into RTD in a country which has few research scientists capable of undertaking work of the standard required. It lacks the necessary 'absorptive capacity'—better to spend some of the money on training people to the required standard. In other words, building 'a system of innovation', as Lundvall (1992) put it, requires a whole series of complementary investments—in building up the science base and infrastructures; in training people to the requisite levels of knowledge and skills; and in developing an industrial R&D capability.

5.3. The Current RTD Situation in the EU

5.3.1. *Variations between countries*

Between 1980 and 1990 the EU's total outlays on R&D as a proportion of GDP increased from 1.6 to over 2 per cent (Table 5.1). Between 1990 and 1995 it dropped back to 1.84 per cent of GDP, with the four big countries—Germany, France, Italy, and the UK—all registering falls, although many of the smaller countries, and especially Denmark, Ireland, Finland, and Sweden, showing continued gains. The 1995 figures are depressed by the long recession which hit Europe in the early 1990s and there were some signs of recovery by 1996/7. The German figures (which weigh heavily in the total) were also affected by the inclusion after 1990 of the East German Länder (so that the series is not continuous), but even with these new inclusions it continued to be one of the highest spenders in Europe. France considerably improved its standing over the fifteen years. The UK is the only country to show a sizeable fall, partly associated with the cut in defence R&D. Some of the middle-ranking countries—Denmark and Finland notably—have shown considerable growth, but the outstanding gains, albeit often from a low base, have come from the four 'cohesion' countries—Greece, Spain, Portugal, and Ireland. Even so, Greece and Portugal still spend only 0.48 and 0.60 per cent of GDP on R&D respectively while Sweden, the top spending EU country, is up to 3.45 per cent.

Table 5.1. Gross expenditure on research and development (GERD) as percentage of GDP

	1980	1985	1990	1995	Growth 1980–95 (1980 = 100)
EU-12	1.60	1.90	2.03	1.84	115
Belgium	1.45	1.67	1.65	1.61	111
Denmark	1.05	1.25	1.63	1.82	173
Germany	2.50[a]	2.75	2.75[b]	2.28[b]	91[b]
Greece	0.20	0.28	0.36	0.48	240
France	1.82	2.25	2.41	2.34	129
Ireland	0.80[a]	0.82	0.85	1.50	188
Italy	0.75	1.13	1.30	1.04	139
Netherlands	1.76	2.06	2.15	2.04	116
Austria	1.17[a]	1.27	1.43	1.58	135
Portugal	0.29	—	0.57	0.59	203
Finland	1.19[a]	1.58	1.91	2.36	198
Sweden	2.22[a]	2.88	2.85	3.45	128
UK	2.50[a]	2.23	2.18	2.05	82

[a] 1981.
[b] After 1990 includes former East Germany—series not therefore comparable.

Source: Second European Report on S&T Indicators, 1997, Tables A.2.1 and B.1.1.

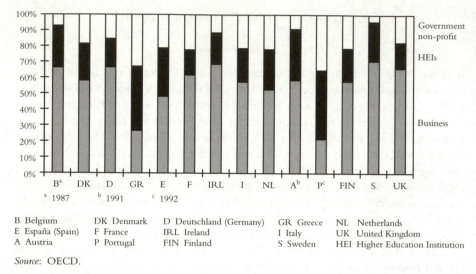

Fig. 5.1. Shares of GERD by research performers, 1993

Figure 5.1 shows how this spending is divided between the various research performers and illustrates how little R&D in Greece and Portugal comes from the business
sector, with, in each case, roughly 75 per cent of R&D coming from the government
and higher education sectors. By contrast, in Germany and Sweden over 70 per cent of
total R&D is performed by the business sector. Ireland is the exception among the
cohesion countries—over 68 per cent of it its R&D expenditures come from industry,
mainly from overseas multinationals.

Table 5.2 gives figures for business expenditures on R&D both in absolute terms and
per worker. Once again the stronger performance of Sweden, France, and Germany is
notable, and the very low relative levels of spending in Greece, Portugal, and Spain.
Spain, nevertheless, has seen impressive growth and, as with GERD, the fastest growth
rates have come from the cohesion countries.

Table 5.3 has the figures on R&D personnel normalized by both population and
workforce. Again Germany and Sweden top the rankings, but it is worth noting the
strong performance of Denmark and Finland compared, for example, with France and
the UK. Of the four cohesion countries, Ireland tops the league, with Spain and Greece
not far below but Portugal well down the rankings. Note also that Italy performs less
well than either Ireland or Spain in terms of R&D personnel per 1,000 of the workforce.

Three sets of 'output' indicators are presented in Table 5.4 and Figure 5.2. Of the
43.4 per cent of patents registered at the European Patent Office (EPO) coming from
the EU–15 in 1995, 17 per cent came from Germany, with the remainder coming
primarily from France (6.8 per cent), the UK (6.6 per cent), and Italy (3.1 per cent). A
similar pattern (but understandably lower shares) is revealed by US Patent Office data.
As regards publications, the EU–15 contributed 39.5 per cent of the world's scientific
publications as recorded in the Science Citation Index in 1995 (considerably more than

Table 5.2. Business expenditures on research and development (BERD) per worker

	1985		1995		
	BERD (MECU)	BERD per worker (ECU)	BERD (MECU)	BERD per worker (ECU)	Growth index 1985/95 1985 = 100
EU	53,200	399	64,000	431	108
Belgium	1,558	444	1,760	464	105
Denmark	506	199	954	366	183
Germany[a]	18,563	709	19,499	545	77[a]
Greece	—	—	115	30	—
Spain	1,040	98	1,671	138	140
France	10,424	489	13,893	629	129
Ireland	125	116	486	385	332
Italy	4,764	231	5,076	255	110
Netherlands	2,197	429	2,680	395	92
Austria	703	217	1,053[b]	286[b]	131
Portugal	53	10	110	25	250
Finland	589	239	1,079	535	224
Sweden	2,366	550	3,683	890	162
UK	10,204	420	11,916	459	109

[a] Figures for Germany post-1990 include the former East Germany. The two sets of figures are not, therefore, really comparable.
[b] 1993 not 1995.

Source: Second European Report on S&T Indicators, 1997, Tables A.2.2 and B.5.1.

Table 5.3. R&D personnel per thousands labour force and population (1995)

	Total R&D personnel (head count)	R&D personnel per thousand population	Employed labour force (thousands)	R&D personnel per thousand labour force
Belgium	38,450	3.80	3,793	10.1
Denmark	29,350	5.64	2,601	11.3
Germany	475,016[a]	5.86	35,782	13.3
Greece	14,549[a]	1.41	3,821	3.8
Spain	80,400[b]	2.06	12,027	6.7
France	315,159[b]	5.44	22,057	14.3
Ireland	10,833[b]	3.00	1,262	8.6
Italy	143,823[b]	2.51	19,943	7.2
Netherlands	78,980[b]	5.61	6,782	11.6
Austria	24,458[a]	3.06	3,675	6.7
Portugal	15,540	1.57	4,417	3.5
Finland	33,635	6.60	2,016	16.7
Sweden	62,840	7.14	4,134	15.2
UK	277,500	4.78	25,936	10.7

[a] Data from 1993.
[b] Data from 1994.

Source: Second European Report on S&T Indicators, 1997, Tables A.3.1, B.4.1 and B5.1.

Table 5.4. World shares of patents and publications
(%)

	Patents (EPO)		Patents (USPTO)		Publications (SCI)	
	1985	1995	1985	1995	1980	1995
Belgium	1.0	1.2	0.4	0.4	0.9	1.2
Denmark	0.6	1.0	0.3	0.2	0.9	1.0
Germany	22.2	17.0	9.4	6.5	6.2	7.9
Greece	0.0	0.1	—	0.0	0.2	0.5
Spain	0.3	0.5	0.1	0.2	0.6	2.4
France	8.6	6.8	3.4	2.8	5.4	6.3
Ireland	0.1	0.2	0.0	0.1	0.2	0.3
Italy	2.9	3.1	1.3	1.1	2.1	3.9
Netherlands	2.8	2.1	1.1	0.8	1.6	2.6
Austria	1.2	1.0	0.4	0.3	0.6	0.8
Portugal	0.0	0.1	0.0	0.0	0.1	0.2
Finland	0.4	1.2	0.3	0.4	0.6	0.9
Sweden	2.2	2.5	1.2	0.8	1.6	2.0
UK	7.7	6.6	3.5	2.4	8.8	9.5
EU-15	50.0	42.4	21.4	16.0	29.8	39.5

Source: Second European Report on S&T Indicators, 1997, Tables A.5.1, A.6.2, A.6.6.

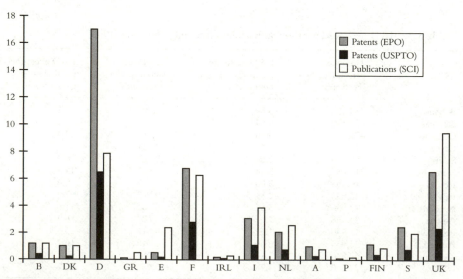

Source: OST data: European Patent Office, US Patent Office, Science Citation Index. See Fig. 5.1 for letter codes.

Fig. 5.2. World shares of patents and publication, 1995

the 16.0 per cent of patents recorded by the EU-15 with the US patent authorities, upholding the view that Europe is better at knowledge production than application). The UK here stands out as the leading contributor, with 9.5 per cent of the total, followed by Germany, 7.9 per cent; France, 6.3 per cent; and Italy, 3.9 per cent. Of the cohesion countries only Spain, 2.4 per cent, makes a sizeable contribution.

The picture that emerges from this set of indicators reinforces the view of a substantial technology gap between the more and less advantaged countries of the EU. Germany, France, Finland, and Sweden stand out for their commitment to investing in science and technology, while the UK joins the 'central' group of Belgium, Denmark, the Netherlands. Italy's performance is below average and the cohesion countries—Spain, Portugal, Ireland, and Greece—are well below average. Over the last decade, however, Spain, and particularly Ireland, have managed to pull themselves well clear of the bottom position and now occupy an intermediate position between Greece and Portugal at the bottom and the 'central' group, while Finland has been forging ahead to join the top performers. It is noteworthy that the disparities in terms of personnel are nowhere near as great as those in respect of other indicators. Wages and salaries in the cohesion countries are, of course, much lower than elsewhere and labour can (and is) used more lavishly. It does, however, suggest that there may be a problem in terms of quality of personnel, their productivity being well below what might be expected given the numbers.

5.3.2. *Variations between regions*

There are relatively few science and technology indicators broken down by NUTS regions for the EU. From the little that is available, the picture of 'technology rich: technology poor' that emerges from the country-based data is repeated *within countries*. Table 5.5 presents a set of concentration ratios to illustrate the degree to which R&D capabilities are concentrated in specific regions within countries. For example, in Greece, the strongest region (around Athens) conducts 53 per cent of GERD and 62 per cent of BERD and contains 50 per cent of Greece's R&D personnel (but only 30 per cent of the population). In all the countries in Table 5.5, however, research activities and capabilities are more highly concentrated than GDP or population—in France, for example, the strongest region (Ile de France), with almost 19 per cent of the population, conducts 53 per cent of business R&D; in the UK, London and the South-East contains 30 per cent of the population and does 56 per cent of business R&D.

These figures confirm the view from earlier studies which have described the RTD situation in the EU as 'Archipelago Europe'.[2] These studies found that the laboratories and enterprises involved in RTD are highly concentrated into comparatively few 'islands of innovation', each of which comprises a fairly dense network of enterprises and research laboratories. Within Europe, the study found that a limited number of

---

[2] This term was coined by Ulrich Hilpert to describe his investigation into the geographical pattern of RTD activities in Europe. See FAST 1992.

Table 5.5. Regional concentration: concentration ratios by various indicators for top four regions in various EU countries

		R1	R2	R3	R4
D	Population	21.8	36.2	48.5	55.8
	GDP	23.8	41.0	56.1	66.2
	R&D personnel (FTE)	22.3	44.5	64.9	75.5
	GERD				
	BERD	26.7	50.0	68.7	79.3
GR	Population	34.3	51.2	58.4	65.2
	GDP	38.3	54.3	61.1	67.6
	R&D personnel (FTE)	50.0	71.3	79.5	86.4
	GERD	52.5	71.2	79.7	85.5
	BERD	62.2	78.4	86.5	90.1
E	Population	26.9	47.6	61.6	74.2
	GDP	31.0	47.5	63.1	75.3
	R&D personnel (FTE)	34.5	57.9	69.8	81.4
	GERD	38.6	64.7	77.0	86.3
	BERD	42.4	71.3	87.0	91.8
F	Population	18.8	37.0	50.1	61.9
	GDP	28.2	44.7	56.0	67.0
	R&D personnel (FTE)	39.0	48.2	55.1	61.9
	GERD	43.7	52.8	60.7	67.6
	BERD	53.2	64.1	73.3	82.3
I[a]	Population	15.5	27.4	38.6	49.4
	GDP	20.3	33.2	45.6	56.1
	R&D personnel (FTE)	35.1	62.8	72.9	80.0
	GERD				
	BERD	32.9	65.6	76.6	82.0
P	Population	35.0	68.6	86.1	91.6
	GDP	48.0	80.6	93.5	96.9
	R&D personnel (FTE)	61.0	82.0	94.7	97.4
	GERD	58.7	80.7	95.0	98.0
	BERD	51.0	76.0	93.0	100.0
UK	Population	30.4	41.5	50.6	59.5
	GDP	36.1	46.3	54.8	63.1
	R&D personnel (FTE)	45.0	53.3	61.4	68.2
	GERD	51.9	60.1	67.1	74.1
	BERD	56.2	66.1	74.8	82.7

[a] Data on R&D personnel in Italy based on personnel on the business enterprise sector.

Note: The concentration ratios given here, R1, R2, R3, R4, represent the cumulative per cent of each indicator for the top region (R1) and second, third, and fourth, respectively and relate to the period 1990–3. The figures, therefore, illustrate how far resources in any country are concentrated in one or two particular regions. Regional data for Germany, Spain, France, Italy, and the UK are aggregated at the NUTS I level while data for Portugal and Greece are aggregated at the NUTS II level in order to have a similar number of regions (varying from 7 in Spain and Portugal to 16 in Germany).

Source: European Commission Services (Framework Programmes Funding Data); Eurostat (other indicators). See Fig. 5.1 for letter codes.

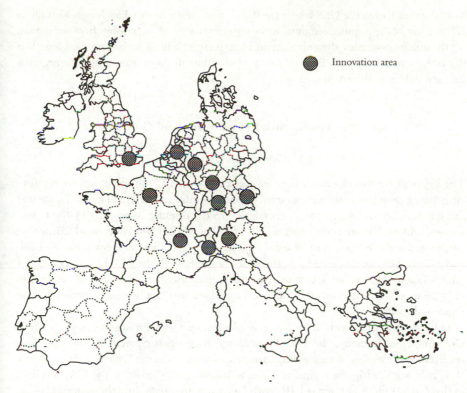

Innovation area

Source: FAST 1992.

Fig. 5.3. Archipelago Europe

'super-islands' stand out—Greater London; Amsterdam/Rotterdam; Ile de France; the Ruhr; Frankfurt; Stuttgart; Munich; Lyon/Grenoble; Milan and Turin (see Fig. 5.3).

Hilpert's Archipelago Europe Study based on 1980s data (FAST 1992) found that three quarters of all public research contracts were concentrated in these regions and that the institutions involved actively collaborated with each other, thus reinforcing the concentration. By contrast Hilpert found that laboratories and enterprises located in peripheral regions recorded only a 5–8 per cent participation rate in collaborative networks, except (significantly) EU networks where the figure was as high as 35 per cent. The data presented in Table 5.5 makes it clear that these 'islands of innovation' carry over to the Union's weakest technological partners. In Greece and Portugal, technological activities are disproportionately located around the capital city area, and given the concentration of public and private R&D facilities in these areas, it is difficult for the Community programmes not to reinforce these trends.

Nevertheless, the intraregional picture should be put in perspective. In a country such as Portugal, with a total population of 10 million (about the size of Greater London) and where over one-third of the population lives in the Greater Lisbon area, the issue of the dispersion of technological activities is of a different order of magnitude from the problem in the UK, where the dominance of the South-East leaves 35 million (70 per cent of the population) outside the dynamic thrust of the region. In other words, for the smaller countries, the cohesion problem is essentially an *intercountry* problem. For the larger countries of the EU, including Spain, the cohesion issue is an interregional one as much as an intercountry one.

5.4. The Framework Programmes and Cohesion

5.4.1. Country-based comparisons

The key issue for this chapter is how far the EU's own RTD programmes are reinforcing these trends towards concentration at both country and regional level. To answer this question we had access to figures relating to the funding of projects by the Commission under the shared cost programmes of Framework II and Framework III, which constituted some 80 per cent of total expenditures.[3] At that time Sweden, Finland, and Austria were not members and the data deals only with the EU-12. For reasons of confidentiality the actual levels of expenditures cannot be released and relativities only are used. The intercountry dispersion is tackled first. Section 5.4.2 deals with the regional dispersion.

In terms of absolute sums received, as might be expected, the largest countries of the Community—Germany, the UK, France, and Italy—participated in, and therefore received, considerably more funding than other countries in the Union. In Framework II, France was the highest recipient of funds, followed by Germany, the UK, and Italy in that order. Under Framework III, with Germany now including the eastern Länder, the German share of the total was slightly higher than that of the French, with the UK a good third, but Italy well behind in fourth position. This is reflected in the numbers of research groups participating in the two Framework programmes. France, the most active participant, had twice as many participations in each programme as did Italy, with the UK the next most active participant and Germany behind the UK. The cohesion countries, as might be expected, were better represented in the general science programmes administered by DG XII, which include also BRITE-EURAM, than in the ESPRIT/ICT programmes of DG III, or the telecoms programmes administered by DG XIII. The high proportion of big firm representation in the latter programmes vitiates against cohesion country participation, which would mainly come from small and medium-sized firms (SMEs), although there has been a substantial improvement in recent years as more emphasis has been placed on cohesion issues. Had Framework IV figures been available this trend would have been even more marked.

Absolute values or shares in total expenditures have little relevance if no allowance is made for differences in size of population. Obviously one would expect Germany, with its population of 80 million, to receive more funding than Ireland, with its population of 3.5 million. Normalizing on a per capita basis gives a very different distribution. This

---

[3] The data cover only the programmes run by DGs III, XII (without fusion), and XIII (without SPRINT and the innovation programmes). They do not cover DG XVI, XIV, or XVII. Nor do they cover the fellowships granted under the science programme (FP II) and the Human Capital and Mobility Programme (FP III).

is illustrated in the first two columns of Diagram 4. On a per capita basis, especially in Framework III, France, Germany, and the UK are close to the EU average. The clear gainers are the small, northern EU countries—Denmark, Belgium, the Netherlands, and, the only cohesion country among them, Ireland. Greece and Portugal are slightly below the average in Framework II, but Greece moves up to a position slightly above the average in Framework III. In both Framework Programmes, Italy and Spain share bottom place in terms of per capita distribution.

A very similar distribution is recorded when figures are normalised on a per employee basis, shown in the second and third columns of Figure 5.4. Again, the gainers are the small, northern European countries.

The interesting distribution, however, is recorded in the last two columns which show receipts for the two Framework Programmes normalized by the number of R&D personnel in each country. As Table 5.3 makes clear, Germany, France, and the UK all have at least twice, and in Germany's case three times, the number of R&D personnel per 1,000 inhabitants as countries such as Portugal and Greece. Adjusting receipts according to numbers of R&D personnel shows Greece and Ireland well above (indeed more than three times) the average, with Portugal, together with Denmark, Belgium, and the Netherlands, at about twice the average, Germany clearly below average, and the remaining countries grouped around the average. In other words, in relation to their R&D capabilities measured by numbers of people involved in R&D activities, three of the cohesion countries—Greece, Portugal, and Ireland—have received a

Table 5.6. 'Equity' indices for Framework Programme funding (shared cost actions only)

	FP II period 1987–90	FP III period 1991–4
Belgium	215	217
Denmark	194	175
Germany	63	56
Greece	876	884
Spain	173	181
France	101	86
Ireland	566	466
Italy	85	109
Netherlands	163	187
Portugal	653	525
UK	99	107
EU–12	100	100

Note: The index is derived from a similar index used by the Commission in an earlier study (CEC 1991) and seeks a measure of how far distributions of Framework Programme money match domestic R&D efforts (measured by GERD). Matching distributions are measured by a figure of 100; a figure of 200 indicates funding at twice the level expected given that country's internal R&D effort and a figure of 50 indicates half the level of funding that might be expected if the distribution matched GERD efforts. For details of methodology, see CEC (1991).

Sources: Index for FP II period based on 1989 GERD figures; for FP III on 1993 GERD figures. Funding figures—shared cost actions only—supplied by the Commission.

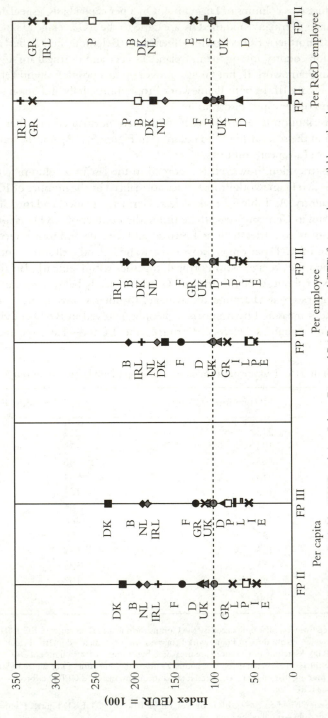

Framework Programme II Funding divided by 1990 Population, Labour Force and R&D personnel (FTE) figures or latest available to that date.
Framework Programme III Funding divided by 1993 Population, Labour Force and R&D personnel (FTE) figures or latest available to that date.
Statistics for Germany used for the Framework Programme III include the new Länder.

Source: European Commission Services (Funding Data): Eurostat (Population, Labour Force and R&D Personnel (FTE) Data). See Fig. 5.1 for letter codes.

Fig. 5.4. Distribution of funding in the Framework Programmes per capita, employee, and R&D employee (shared cost actions only)

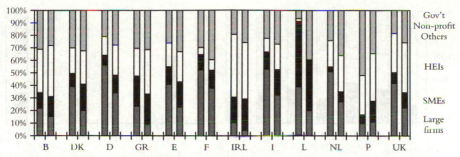

For each country the left-hand column represents FP II; the right-hand column FP III.

Source: European Commission Services. See Fig. 5.1 for letter codes.

Fig. 5.5. Distribution of Framework Programmes funding (shared cost actions only) by research performers in Framework Programmes II and III

disproportionate share of funding. As with the per capita distributions, the two countries which seem to do least well in relation to resources are Italy and Spain, both of which have substantial areas designated as Objective I status.

The number of RTD employees provides a good measure of the size of the RTD sector in any country and can be taken as a broad measure of its absorptive capacity in relation to R&D. An earlier Commission study (CEC 1991) developed an 'equity' indicator based on matching the distribution of funds in relation to domestic-based RTD expenditures—the higher the relative level of expenditure (GERD as proportion GDP), the higher the expected capabilities and therefore the higher the absorptive capacity. A similar index was calculated using the more recent Framework Programme data. This is presented in Table 5.6. A figure of 100 indicates matching distributions (i.e. the Framework distributions exactly match domestic RTD 'effort'), a figure of 200 indicates twice the expected level, and 50 half the expected level. The results show a similar pattern to the index based on R&D employees. Greece, Ireland and Portugal top the league table, with Greece, in particular, doing well by the distribution. By this measure, however, Spain does considerably better than Italy, and the UK considerably better than France or Germany.

5.4.2. *Variations between countries by type of participant*

An additional area of interest concerns the distribution of research funding between countries by type of participant. Figure 5.5 shows the overall breakdown between the FP II period and the FP III period. Three aspects relate to the cohesion issue. First, the proportionate participation of large firms fell markedly between FP II and FP III; and the beneficiaries of this drop have not uniquely been small firms, but rather research and higher education establishments. Secondly, as might be expected, small firm participation is higher from the smaller, poorer countries, if for no other reason than because large firms are seldom based in these countries. Given the difficulties encountered by

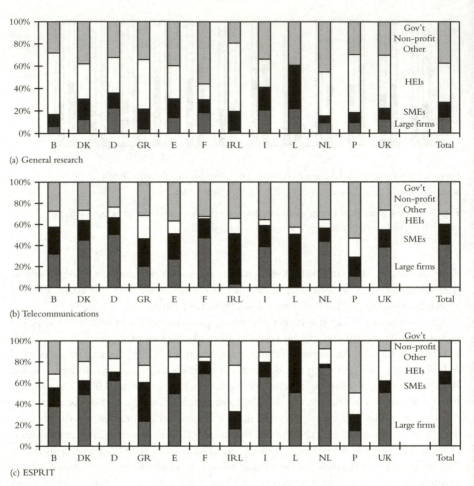

(a) General research

(b) Telecommunications

(c) ESPRIT

Source: European Commission Services. See Fig. 5.1 for letter codes.

Fig. 5.6. Distribution of Framework Programmes funding for (shared cost actions only) by research performers

small firms in participating in these programmes (the cost of finding time to learn about the programmes and get involved in collaborations) the representation is impressive and has been growing over time. Thirdly, it is important to flag the substantial involvement of the higher education sector from the cohesion countries, with 30 per cent or more of the participations tending to come from this source. Given the importance of improving the absorptive capabilities of these countries, which means, amongst other things, increasing the *number* of qualified scientists and engineers capable of leading research teams in the future, such participations provide an important means of training research leaders for the future.

Figure 5.6a, b, and c breaks this data down between the three categories of research programme—general research, ESPRIT, and telecommunications—and shows for

Framework Programmes II and III combined the distribution of funding between the different types of research performer by country. It shows clearly that large firms were much more active in the ESPRIT and telecommunications programmes than in the general research programmes, and, again, shows the poor representation by large firms from the cohesion countries, but the surprisingly good representation from small firms from Greece (especially in ESPRIT) and Ireland (predominantly in telecoms). Putting the higher education (HEI) sector together with the government/non-profit sector, indicates also how strong these two sectors are in the general research programmes with over 75 per cent of the funding coming from this source, whereas their share of ESPRIT funding was only 30 per cent. Only in Ireland and Portugal were ESPRIT funds disproportionately skewed to the HEI/government sector. This reinforces the earlier observation about the importance of the public sector to research capabilities in the cohesion countries.

5.4.3. Patterns of collaboration between countries

Table 5.7 gives a detailed analysis of the intercountry collaborations for the general research programmes for the period 1987–94. As might be expected, Germany, France, and the UK dominate the linkages, each having on average an 18–20 per cent stake in projects led by others. For example, taking the column headed I for Italy, it is possible to see that a project led by an Italian contractor would tend to have British, French, and German partners each with a 15–20 per cent share, and then other minor partners.

From a cohesion point of view, the key question concerns the extent of participation of the poorer countries and in particular how far emphasis on cohesion since 1987/8 has resulted in increased involvement of players from these countries? Figure 5.7—showing country by country share of partnerships with the four cohesion countries—provides some answers. With the exception of Portugal and Spain (which have old links but have

Table 5.7. Collaborative linkages in general research programmes (1987–94)

OF WITH	D	F	I	NL	B	UK	IRL	DK	GR	E	P	L
D	**20.2**	16.4	15.2	21.8	17.1	17.9	16.7	18.0	18.0	15.0	13.0	22.4
B	17.9	**22.0**	19.2	18.1	20.0	18.0	15.2	14.2	20.5	19.4	17.9	24.0
I	10.4	12.1	**19.0**	10.5	9.0	10.4	10.3	8.5	15.6	12.4	10.7	8.0
NL	8.2	6.2	5.8	n/a	7.9	8.2	7.4	9.2	n/a	6.6	7.0	2.4
B	5.5	6.0	4.3	6.8	**10.2**	4.9	5.7	5.2	6.2	4.9	5.3	18.4
UK	18.7	17.4	16.0	23.2	15.9	**19.1**	21.1	20.0	21.0	16.8	17.9	12.0
IRL	1.9	1.6	1.7	2.5	1.9	2.3	**5.4**	2.1	1.9	1.7	2.2	4.0
DK	4.0	2.9	2.8	5.4	3.5	4.2	4.3	**10.0**	4.5	2.8	3.1	2.4
GR	3.9	4.1	5.0	n/a	4.2	4.4	3.3	4.5	n/a	3.8	5.1	0.8
B	6.8	8.1	8.2	8.0	6.9	7.3	6.8	5.7	7.8	**12.5**	10.1	4.0
P	2.4	3.1	2.9	3.5	3.0	3.2	3.7	2.5	4.3	4.1	**7.7**	1.6
L	0.1	0.1	0.1	0.0	0.3	0.1	0.1	0.0	0.0	0.0	0.0	**0.0**
Total	100.0	100.0	100.0	100.0	100.0	100.0	100.0	100.0	100.0	100.0	100.0	100.0

Source: European Commission Services. See Fig. 5.1 for letter codes.

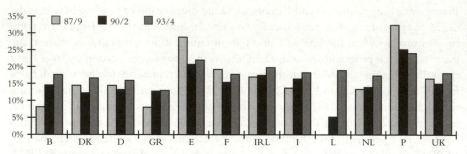

Source: European Commission Services. See Fig. 5.1 for letter codes.

Fig. 5.7. Share of partnerships with Greece, Ireland, Portugal, and Spain in general research programmes (shared cost actions only)

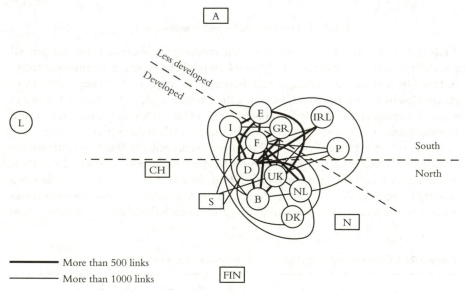

Note: FP III data only until the end of 1993.

Source: European Reports on S&T Indicators 1994: Diagram 8b.1. See Fig. 5.1 for letter codes.

Fig. 5.8. Structure of transnational cooperation—Framework Programmes II and III (shared cost actions)

experienced falling levels of mutual collaboration as other new collaborations have developed) there is a clear trend towards increased collaboration for most member states.

These relationships are well illustrated by Figure 5.8 taken from the Commission's own report on Science and Technology Indicators (CEC 1994), which shows an analysis of the intensity of cooperation based on multidimensional scaling (MDS). At the core of the diagram are three countries, France, Germany, and the UK, which cooperate most intensively. A further five—the Netherlands, Belgium, Italy, Spain, and Greece—belong to a second order with Denmark, Portugal, and Ireland somewhat less

Table 5.8. Distribution of science (1988–92) and HCM (1992–4) bursaries

	Nationality of science	Grantee HCM	Country of host science	Laboratory HCM
B	19	70	16	105
DK	4	36	9	35
D	63	319	20	179
GR	18	158	0	18
E	20	280	7	86
F	45	257	91	487
IRL	11	69	2	13
I	37	226	15	88
NL	21	107	12	125
P	24	36	2	7
UK	21	142	100	540
Others	20	78	19	65
Total	293	1,748	293	1,748

Source: European Report on Science and Technology Indicators 1994. See Fig. 5.1 for letter codes.

tightly bound, and Luxembourg very much at the periphery. Linkages have both a north/south and a less developed/more developed country dimension.

Table 5.8 shows the distribution of Science and Human Capital and Mobility (HCM) bursaries by grantee and host laboratory. This presents a different aspect of participation, namely the exchange of personnel and experienced staff between laboratories in different EU member countries. The HCM bursaries include the social science bursaries formerly granted under the SPES programme (127 contracts), but even so the programme brought a major expansion of exchange between member states. The table shows clearly the flow of students from the technologically weaker to, in particular, France and the UK, both of whom have received approximately 500 students under the programme (not all of them, of course, from less favoured regions). Such programmes play a valuable role in helping upgrade capabilities.

Collaboration between establishments across national boundaries has, of course, been a requirement of successive Framework programmes. There is now substantial evidence to show that collaboration in such public networks has encouraged subsequent involvement in other public and private collaborations (see Table 5.9). The effect appears to be higher for universities and research institutes than for industry, and higher for the technological leaders (Germany, France, the UK) than for the poorer countries. This could reflect the fact that partners in the poorer countries are more often subcontractors, rather than full partners, to projects and therefore play a lesser role in formulating and implementing the project ideas. Studies of the process of collaboration over time have increasingly emphasized the importance of building up trust. The Community programmes have been valuable in establishing 'bridgeheads' of trust which have subsequently ben built upon.

Table 5.9. Continuation of cooperation after EU project completion: responses to impact study questionnaires

Country	Percentage reporting cooperation after the EU project completion[a]			
	Universities	Research Institutes	Industry	Average
B	n/a	n/a	n/a	60
DK	90	95	85	91
D	60	69	53	60
GR	77	79	72	74
E	49	49	46	48
F[b]	←————75————→		61	68
IRL	←————49————→		44	48
I	n/a	n/a	n/a	52
NL	n/a	n/a	68	n/a
P	61	24	31	37
UK[c]	86	86	55	n/a

[a] Percentage of respondents declaring that they often or always continue to cooperate with some of their partners after completion of the EU project.
[b] Provisional figures.
[c] Minimum percentage.
Source: European Report on Science and Technology Indicators 1994, Table 8c.1. See Fig. 5.1 for letter codes.

5.4.4. The framework programmes and regional cohesion

The regional analysis allows a sharper geographical focus on the areas benefiting most from funding under the RTD programmes. The Archipelago Europe study (FAST 1992) suggested that 75 per cent of public R&D expenditures were concentrated in ten prosperous regions. Calculations based on the Commission data reveal that these regions contain only 28 per cent of the EU-12's population but received 51 per cent of funding under Framework Programme II and 47 per cent under Framework Programme III. Interestingly, the numbers in relation to R&D personnel match more or less exactly—47 per cent of funding for 47 per cent of R&D personnel. Funding from EU programmes is, therefore, nowhere near as concentrated as Hilpert suggests it might be, but it is, nevertheless, quite highly concentrated. Moreover, there was a significant drop in concentration between the earlier and later periods. When the full figures for FP IV are available, these are likely to show a further drop in concentration.

Figure 5.9 uses the data from Table 5.5 to look at how far distributions under the Framework Programmes were more or less concentrated than domestic indicators. As noted in Table 5.5, regional RTD statistics are not available for all countries. For the seven countries in Figure 5.9, where reasonably comparable regional data are available, indicators are shown in blocks of six, the top indicator of each block showing the distribution of FP funds in the top four regions. The key question is whether the FP indicator is more concentrated than other indicators. For Greece, Spain, and France,

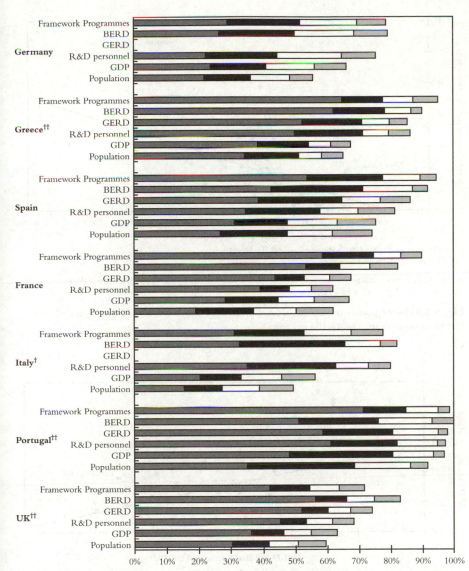

* Framework Programmes funding includes only shared cost actions; all other data is from most recent year available.
† Data on R&D Personnel in Italy based on personnel on the business enterprise sector.
†† Framework Programme Funding data for Greece excludes ESPRIT data, for Portugal includes only General Research data, and for the UK excludes Telecommunications Programmes.
Note: The concentration ratios given here, R1, R2, R3, R4, represent the cumulative total of each indicator for the top region (R1) and second, third, and fourth, respectively. The figures therefore illustrate how far spending in any country is concentrated in one or two particular regions. Regional data for Germany, Spain, France, Italy, and the UK are aggregated at the NUTS I level while data for Portugal and Greece is aggregated at the NUTS II level in order to have a similar number of regions (varying from 7 in Spain and Portugal to 16 in Germany).

Source: European Commission Services (Framework Programmes funding data); Eurostat (other indicators).

Fig. 5.9. Regional concentration of Framework Programme funding (shared cost actions only) in comparison with various indicators*

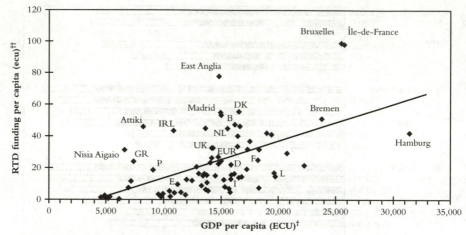

† GDP per capita data for 1991, at National and NUTS I level.
†† RTD funding figures for Framework Programmes II and III.

Source: European Commission Services (Framework Programmes Funding data); Eurostat (Population and GDP data). See Fig. 5.1 for letter codes.

Fig. 5.10(a). Regional distribution of funding in the Framework Programmes (shared cost actions only) per capita vs. GDP per capita

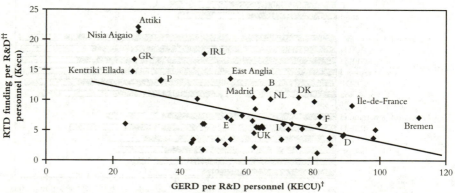

† Data from the most recent year available, at National and NUTS I level.
†† Funding figures for Framework Programmes II and III.

Source: European Commission Services (Framework Programmes Funding data); Eurostat R&D Personnel (FTE) and GERD data. See Fig. 5.1 for letter codes.

Fig. 5.10(b). Regional distribution of Framework Programmes funding (shared cost actions only) per R&D personnel vs. GERD per R&D personnel

the distribution is more concentrated, and in each case the share going to the top region is also greater. For Germany, Italy, and Portugal, the FP distribution is slightly less concentrated than BERD/GERD distributions (although the Lisbon region in Portugal receives a much higher share). For the UK the FP distribution is considerably less concentrated than the BERD distribution (less so the GERD distribution), reflecting (probably) the strength of the university sector outside the south-east.

Finally, it is worth pondering Figures 5.10(a) and 5.10(b), which illustrate different aspects of FP distributions. The first shows FP funding per capita alongside GDP per capita and, as might be expected, the richer regions in general receive considerably more than the poor, although there are a sufficient number of 'outliers' above the trend line (e.g., East Anglia, Madrid, Attiki and Nisia Aigaio) to make for an interesting distribution. Diagram 10b reverses the trend line, for in this diagram Community funding per R&D worker is shown against home country R&D funding per R&D worker. Here, the poorer, less well endowed regions in Greece, Portugal and Ireland are well above the trend line, as indeed are East Anglia and Madrid (while the UK and Spain *country* averages are close to the trend line). As with the country distributions, when measured against their own R&D efforts/capabilities, the cohesion regions do very well.

More generally, the basic capabilities of many of the lagging regions in relation to RTD are often very low and, for this reason, their abilities to benefit from participation in the Framework Programmes are limited. Over time it is a question of building up capabilities—of training people and providing the infrastructures in terms of universities and research institutes which, in turn, can participate in the Framework initiatives and learn from the process of research and collaboration.

Prime responsibility for building up the infrastructures and improving scientific education and training does not lie with the Framework Programme but with national governments in conjunction with the Community Structural Funds. Already, considerable allocations from the Structural Funds have gone towards RTD (see Box 2). The Framework Programme can perform a complementary role, for example, by encouraging research institutes from the weakest regions to gain the experience of working alongside elite institutes from France, Germany, or the UK.

5.4.5. *Cohesion and RTD capabilities—what do the evaluations tell us?*

Impact evaluations were undertaken for all countries for the second Framework Programme (1987–91). Those for the cohesion countries throw light on some of the benefits gained by these countries (Juega 1994, Deloitte and Touche International 1993, CISEP 1992, Tsipouri and Xanthakis 1993):

(1) participation has been disproportionately through research institutes and/or universities;
(2) industrial participation was largely by SMEs, mainly because these countries *do not have* many large firms;
(3) ESPRIT and BRITE-EURAM were the programmes with the highest levels of involvement from cohesion countries and regions;

Box 2. RTD and the European Structural Funds

With the reform of the Structural Funds in 1988, RTD became one of the main instruments of the funds, it being recognized that in the long run the reduction of disparities between regions would be dependent upon the ability of the regional economies to foster innovation and promote new economic activity.

  The main aims of RTD support under the Structural Funds are:

• to develop the physical RTD infrastructures—e.g. research institutes, RTD establishments, etc.;
• to promote technology transfer and the acquisition of know-how by encouraging the setting up and use of consultancy services, support mechanisms for SMEs, etc.;
• to promote the training of researchers, engineers and technicians in research centres, higher education institutes, and enterprises;
• to encourage cooperation between the various sectors and participation in the Community RTD programmes.

The design and management of RTD-related actions lies with national and regional governments, with the role of the Commission being limited to establishing broad guidelines. What can be achieved therefore depends crucially on the degree to which national and regional authorities seize the opportunities available. The table below sets out the sums that have been spent.

RTD initiatives within the EU's Structural Funds

	1989–93 RTD expenditures		1994–9 commitments on RTD	
	Total expenditures million ecu	As % all Obj. 1 + 2 expenditures	EU support million ecu	As % all Obj. 1 + 2 outlays
Belgium	29	13.3	97	9.1
Denmark	3	12.8	—	—
Germany	82	2.3	613	4.0
Greece	143	1.9	663	4.7
Spain	349	3.4	1,007	3.5
France	142	14.4	80	1.3
Ireland	178	3.9	362	6.5
Italy	498	5.7	970	6.0
Luxembourg	—	—	—	—
Netherlands	13	7.6	23	2.8
Portugal	465	5.5	576	4.1
UK	124	4.4	138	2.0
EU–12	2,023	4.1	4,529	4.1

Note: Objective 1 regions can have up to 75 per cent of the costs funded by the Community, whereas for Objective 2 regions the maximum is 50 per cent. This helps to explain the varying national proportions.
Source: Commission (1994) and (1996b).

Box 2. (*cont'd*)

When added to the funds obtained from Community RTD actions under the Framework Programme, the sums are now considerable for countries such as Ireland, Greece, and Portugal and make a sizeable contribution to capabilities. The Thematic Evaluation of the RTD actions in three Objective 1 countries completed in 1993 by Circa Consultants (CIRCA 1993) indicated the range of activities carried out in these countries under the Structural Funds:

- in Ireland the funding was concentrated on direct support for industry to carry out product and process development and aid for universities, together with industry and research institutes, to develop new technologies;
- in Portugal the CSF funds helped create 50 new RTD facilities and strengthen a further 100 existing units; the Ciencia Programme established 2,212 scholarships for researchers training to Masters and Ph.D. levels, while the PEDIP programme supported 754 training projects in industry. It is estimated that these two programmes between them by 1994 had increased trained R&D personnel by 60 per cent over 1988 levels;
- in Greece, the main focus of the programme was to stimulate product and process development, promote training, improve infrastructure, and strengthen links between academic research and industry. The evaluation found, however, that in contrast to Portugal, there had been 'no significant growth in the Greek RTD system since 1989'.

The varying use made (and value obtained from) these funds in these different countries illustrates the importance of complementarity between regional/national actions and Community objectives. Where the two reinforce each other, as in the Ciencia programme in Portugal, considerable achievements can be recorded.

(4) the main benefits gained from involvement were the acquisition of scientific knowledge, skills and training. In spite of the pre-competitive bias, a majority of the enterprises from these countries identified their main gain as being new products and processes launched within three years of completion;
(5) continuation rates were high. For example, amongst Greek participants, 18 per cent said they now had permanent links with EU partners, and 54 per cent said they had frequent linkage.

Both the Portuguese and Greek evaluation studies (CISEP 1992, Tsipouri and Xanthakis 1993) identified some tendencies for the elite institutions in these countries to club together with their northern counterparts to the detriment of their home countries. The selection procedures of EU programmes, being based on scientific excellence, inevitably tended to attract and pick the elite institutions of these countries, often staffed at their highest levels by scientists who have had considerable experience abroad, frequently in the US. These scientists and their research groups have had little difficulty relating to their peers from the UK, France, or Germany and hence are readily accepted into research consortia. The problem is that while this process may help establish and maintain state-of-the-art research capabilities amongst these teams, the actual research questions they investigate may have little relevance to the needs of the poorer countries. In other words, while not denying the benefits gained in terms of developing scientific knowledge, skills, and managerial capabilities, the EU programmes, by putting emphasis on research excellence, may have done little to promote technologies which have more direct application to the less technologically advanced countries.

The other side of this coin is that Community programmes, by reinforcing the more academic side of RTD, are failing to encourage what is most sorely needed in these countries, namely applied research, which promotes the diffusion of new technologies. In this respect it is interesting that the Ledoux evaluation of BRITE-EURAM, which generally found that gains were positive, although the larger firms gained more than the smaller, found the textile programme within this initiative to have been a great success. 'Following interviews in this sector, it should be stressed that probably the greatest success of the BRITE programme was to have been able, through process automation, either to maintain established textile firms in Europe, or, even better, to repatriate some of the production which had been deported to other geographical areas of the world with low wages' (Ledoux *et al.* 1993: 48). This suggests that programmes aimed at diffusing new process technologies into relatively low-tech industries may have considerable pay-off. This has been recognized in a number of the programmes set up under the CRAFT and VALUE programmes to help SMEs apply for and gain benefit from the EU's collaborative research programmes. To date, however, the main dissemination efforts have concentrated on diffusing new products and processes developed within EU programmes. The urgent need is to help the SME sector develop and use up-to-date technologies across the board. There may be more to gain from local collaboration, with other SMEs and/or with the academic sector in the local geographic area, rather than in seeking to engage such firms in international programmes (see Peterson and Sharp 1998 ch. 10).

Another detailed investigation into the workings of BRITE-EURAM (Gambardella and Garcia 1995) suggested that, while there may have been an increase in collaborations from 'southern' institutions, too often these participations were with other southern partners and there was too great a tendency for 'elite' firms and institutions from northern countries to club together, accepting southern partners as subcontractors rather than main players in collaborations. Generally, the study found that BRITE-EURAM was effective in encouraging the formation of networks which generated innovations and new technologies, but it was less effective in encouraging diffusion of these technologies especially across the north-south divide, with little joint participation among partners from north and south regions in the same networks.

5.5. Conclusions

The purpose of this chapter has been to examine how far the European Union's RTD programmes, administered through the multi-annual Framework Programmes, have helped to promote cohesion within the EU. As in other parts of this book, the criterion applied is that, for cohesion to improve, we have to show that the disadvantaged have in relative terms improved their position faster than the more privileged. The chapter has dealt only with the issue of spatial cohesion. The focus has been on how far the poorer countries and regions have benefited from the EU's Framework Programmes and used them to improve their position in relation to the richer, more advanced regions.

The analysis presented in this chapter can be summarized as follows:

1. The data presented in section 5.3 indicate that a sizeable technology gap exists between the most and least advanced regions of the European Union. The considerable concentration of activities *within* each country means that the gap is more extreme between regions than between countries. This tends to endorse Hilpert's Archipelago Europe hypothesis, which sees technological activities concentrated in relatively few advanced regions. Nevertheless, growth rates of business and general R&D, in terms of numbers of R&D personnel, are notably faster in the cohesion countries, which indicates that, at least in relation to countries, the gap is shrinking.

2. The data presented in section 5.4 analyse the distribution of funding from Framework Programmes II and III. As might be expected, in absolute terms, the largest countries receive most funding. In per capita terms, however, it is the small, northern countries, in particular Denmark, the Netherlands, and Belgium, that do well, while when measured in terms of R&D capabilities—R&D personnel per 1,000 population, or GERD as a percentage of GDP—the cohesion countries and their stronger regions do particularly well. These two measures of R&D capabilities are also probably the best measure of absorptive capacities and these figures therefore suggest that, in relation to absorptive capacity, the cohesion countries are well served by the Framework Programmes. Framework Programme disbursements also prove to be considerably less concentrated than the public sector funding found in the Hilpert Archipelago Europe study, indicating that EU funding is helping to disperse capabilities more widely than hitherto.

3. The data in section 5.4 also reveal an increasing trend towards participation on the part of the cohesion countries and regions, but little evidence of an increasing presence from the business sector, large or small, in these regions. Rather, the increased participation has come largely from government laboratories and/or the higher education sector. Given that the main benefit derived from participation in EU collaborative programmes is perceived to be 'learning' new techniques and skills, participation from public sector laboratories and universities can be seen as a form of technology transfer— an important part of the learning process. Nevertheless, the relatively small presence from SMEs and the known difficulties they find in participation in EU programmes is a cause for concern, especially given the importance of this sector in expanding industrial capabilities in these countries.

4. Although it is clear that the Framework Programmes have, at a country level, worked with the grain of cohesion and helped the process of catch-up, it is less clear that this is happening at regional level. The concentration of regional R&D capabilities and especially public research facilities within one or two regions in the cohesion countries means that Framework Programme funds are also highly concentrated. The same is true of Italy and Spain, where the cohesion regions have been relatively less successful

overall than their counterparts elsewhere, partly because of the concentration of RTD capabilities in the non-cohesion regions of these two countries. Again, judged in terms of absorptive capacity—how far are these regions in a position to participate in the Framework Programmes?—the distribution looks less unreasonable, but it emphasizes the need for domestic policy and the Structural Funds to be used to build such capabilities.

There are four main conclusions to be drawn from this analysis. The first conclusion is that, in spite of criticism, the Framework Programmes have helped promote cohesion. The evidence is overwhelming. They have involved scientists and engineers from both public an private sectors from the cohesion countries and regions in a plethora of collaborations and exchanges which, whatever their specific outcomes, have widened horizons, raised aspirations, and improved knowledge, techniques, and skills.

The second conclusion is that for these countries and regions the Framework Programmes cannot be considered in isolation, but have to be considered in conjunction with complementary programmes being implemented by national governments and the EU Structural Funds. The Framework Programme cannot—and is not expected to—provide funds for the development of the RTD infrastructures in cohesion countries and regions. It is this infrastructure, both in terms of physical capital (laboratories) and in human capital (graduates and PhDs), which provides their 'absorptive capacity'— their ability to participate usefully in collaborations and partnerships. Ireland provides an excellent example of how, when domestic and EU policies are set to complement each other, substantial benefits can be reaped. (See CIRCA 1995 referred to in Box 2 above.) Indeed, in Ireland's case the policy has been so successful that it will shortly no longer be considered a cohesion country.

The third conclusion relates to SMEs and the difficulties such firms encounter (not just in cohesion countries) in participation in Framework Programme initiatives. In this chapter we focused on the BRITE-EURAM programme because, with its emphasis on improving industrial technologies, it has been the programme with the greatest application to cohesion countries and regions. A major theme within the EU since the Green Paper on Innovation (CEC 1995) has been the need to upgrade and improve the general capabilities of SMEs. Yet the difficulties of getting SMEs to participate in BRITE-EURAM, even with help programmes such as CRAFT, suggests that perhaps *international* collaborative programmes are not necessarily the way forward. For many of these companies, local collaborations, bringing together firms within one sector with a university/public laboratory, might prove a more viable way forward. In this respect the Framework Programme may need to take some lessons from the Structural Funds on how best to work with local or regional authorities.

Finally, it is worth remarking on the tendency which seemingly emerged in the BRITE-EURAM case study (Gambardella and Garcia 1996) for collaborations to split on a north-north, south-south axis. This was not in fact borne out in the wider data on collaborations on Framework Programmes II and III presented earlier, although those who have urged a 'variable geometry' approach for the Fifth Framework Programme come close to advocating such a split. If followed through it would directly undermine the cohesion principle and in the long run there is little doubt that the EU as a whole would be the loser. As Lundvall says in his conclusion to his book on national systems of innovation, 'The most important aspect of the [European] integration process is that it opens up new avenues for institutional learning and institutional innovation' (Lundvall 1992: 316). It is precisely these 'avenues for institutional learning' that the Framework Programme provides for the cohesion process.

References

Abramovitz, M. (1986). Catching up, forging ahead and falling behind. *Journal of Economic History* 46: 385–406.

Aghion, P. and Howitt, P. (1992). A model of growth through creative destruction. *Econometrica* 60: 323–52.

CEC (1991). *Evaluation of the Effects of the EC Framework Programme for Research and Technological Development on Economic and Social Cohesion in the Community*. Research Report no. 48, EUR 13994 EN, Brussels.

—— (1993). White paper on *Growth, Competitiveness, Employment*. (Delors Report). Brussels.

—— (1994). *The European Report on Science and Technology Indicators*. Luxembourg: Office for Official Publications of European Communities.

—— (1995). Green Paper on Innovation. Luxembourg: Office of Official Publications of European Communities.

—— (1997). *Second European Report on Science and Technology Indicators* (EU 17639). Luxembourg: Office for Official Publications of European Communities.

CIRCA (1993). *Thematic Evaluation of the Impact of the CSFs for Research and Technology in Greece, Ireland and Portugal*. Report to the European Commission.

CISEP (1992). *Study of the Impact of Community RTD Programmes on the Portuguese S&T Potential*. Final Report to the EC, July.

Cohen, W. and Levinthal, D. (1989). Innovation and learning: the two faces of R&D. *Economic Journal* 99: 569–96.

Deloitte and Touche International (1993). *Impact of EC Science and Technology Policy on Irish Science and Technology Policy*. Report for the EC, August.

Fagerberg, J. (1994). Technology and International Differences in Growth Rates. *Journal of Economic Literature* 32: 1147–75.

—— and Verspagen, B. (1996). Heading for divergence? Regional growth in Europe reconsidered. *Journal of Common Market Studies* 34: 431–48.

FAST (1992). *Archipelago Europe: Islands of Innovation*. Prospective Dossier no. 1 of Science, Technology and Social and Economic Cohesion in the Community, May.

Faulkner, W. and Senker, J. (1995). *Knowledge Frontiers*. Oxford: Oxford University Press.

Gambardella, A. and Garcia, W. (1995). Regional linkages through European research funding. *Economics of Innovation and Technologies* 14: 123–38.

Grossman, G. and Helpman, E. (1990). *Innovation and Growth in the Global Economy*. Boston, Mass.: MIT Press.

Guzzetti, L. (1995). *A Brief History of European Union Research Policy*. Luxembourg: Office for Official Publications of European Communities.

Jacquemin, A. (1995). European competitiveness: challenges ahead (mimeo). French version published in *La Revue du Marché Commun*, November 1995.

Juega, A. B. (1994). *Impact of the EC R&D Policy in the Spanish System of Science and Technology*. Study funded by the Commission of the EC.

Krugman, P. (1994). Competitiveness: a dangerous obsession. *Foreign Affairs* 73:

Ledoux, M.-J. *et al.* (1993). *Economic Evaluation of the Effects of the BRITE-EURAM Programmes on the European Industry*. Final report for DG XII–4 Evaluation Unit, January.

Lundvall, B.-A. (1992). *National Systems of Innovation: Towards a Theory of Innovation and Interactive Learning*. London: Pinter.

Peterson, J. and Sharp, M. (1998). *Technology Policy in the European Union*. London: Macmillan.

Porter, M. (1990). *The Competitive Advantage of Nations*. New York: The Free Press.

Romer, P. M. (1986). Increasing returns and long run growth. *Journal of Political Economy* 94: 1002–37.

—— (1990). Endogenous technology change. *Journal of Political Economy* 98: 71–102.

Rosenberg, N. (1990). Why do firms do basic research (with their own money)? *Research Policy* 19: 165.

Sharp, M. (1993). The Community and new technologies. pp. 200–23 in J. Lodge (ed.), *The European Community and the Challenge of the Future*. London: Pinter.

Tsipouri, L. J. and Xanthakis, M. (1993). *Impact of the EC Science and Technology Policy on the Greek S&T Policy*. Final report to the EC, Athens.

6

Common Agricultural Policy

SECONDO TARDITI AND GEORGE ZANIAS

6.1. Introduction

6.1.1. The CAP in EU economic policy

The Common Agricultural Policy (CAP) has been, and still is, the sectoral policy of the EU generating the largest redistribution of income among European citizens. The Guarantee Section of EAGGF (the European Agricultural Guarantee and Guidance Fund) absorbed 46 per cent of the total EU budget in 1997, while a substantial share of the Structural Funds, which account for an extra 36 per cent of the EU budget, are designated for rural areas and agricultural firms. Moreover, the price support policy transfers a similar amount of household income to farmers by creating a price wedge between domestic and world market prices.[1]

The Producer Subsidy Equivalent (PSE) (OECD 1997a), deriving mainly from the CAP, was nearly fifty per cent in 1996, which means that effectively almost half of the value of agricultural production is accounted for by monetary transfers to producers from taxpayers and consumers of agricultural products. The impact of the CAP on European cohesion is substantial also because agriculture extends across the entire EU territory and directly affects the standard of living in all rural areas.

Assistance for improving farm structures, with the purpose of creating a more competitive and viable agriculture, was left to the structural part of the CAP. Although when the EC started, the Guidance section of EAGGF (now part of Structural Funds) was envisaged to go hand-in-hand with price policy, it always received a very small proportion of the agricultural budget (about five per cent—compared to an envisaged figure of approximately 25 per cent). Structural Funds are not considered in this study and therefore their favourable impact, especially on the cohesion member states with the poorest farm structures (Greece and Portugal), is not considered here.

Economic and social cohesion, which has become a dominant issue since the Maastricht Treaty, was not an explicit objective of the original CAP. One of the basic aims spelled out in Article 39 of the Treaty of Rome (now Art. 33), however, was to increase productivity in order to ensure a fair standard of living for the agricultural population.

---

[1] According to OECD estimates, in 1997 the total transfers associated with agricultural policies in the EU have been 107.2 bn. ecus (54.8 bn. ecus from taxpayers and 42.4 bn. ecus from consumers). The EU agricultural Value Added in the same year was 117.5 bn. ecus and the EU budget in 1996 was 81 bn. ecus.

6.1.2. Objectives of the study

In order to assess the likely effects of the CAP on cohesion, it is essential to analyse the income redistribution generated by its main instrument, the Agricultural Price Policy, and its impact on the competitiveness of the European economy.

Income redistribution should be examined mainly from two points of view: territorial (national and regional) and social. From a territorial perspective the redistribution generated among member countries, among European large regions (NUTS I), and among different smaller regions in each member country (NUTS II) should be examined. The national and regional aspects of cohesion in the European Union deserve special consideration, given the essentially geographic nature of the ongoing process of European integration and of future EU enlargement to other European countries. Furthermore, political movements opposing European integration are mainly framed on a national or regional basis.

In an economic union involving a common market and common policy measures, price support policies involve a substantial redistribution of income at national and regional levels because of the existing differences between regions in terms of concentration and composition both of population and of agricultural output. From a social perspective the analysis should concentrate on the income redistribution generated by the price policy between social groups or sectors (consumers, producers, and taxpayers), between citizens belonging to different classes of income, and between different groups of producers differing in terms such as type or size of farm. The impact on competitiveness and economic development should be taken into consideration by analysing the effects of price support on resource allocation both among sectors of the EU economy and within the agricultural sector.

The CAP is still governed by the 1992 reform, the most radical reform since the European Community was established. Its main feature was the de-coupling of farm support from the quantity of each commodity produced by farmers in order to avoid food surpluses and reduce distortions in output markets and investments. This goal has been achieved by substituting part of the domestic price support by direct payments to producers, thus shifting part of the burden of farm support from consumers to taxpayers.

Analysis of the impact of the agricultural price policy on European cohesion is complicated by the 1992 reform, which involves some important agricultural commodities but has not yet been extended to all farm products. Given the present state of transition between a 'traditional CAP' and a fully 'reformed CAP', these social and regional aspects of EU cohesion should be analysed before and after the 1992 reform in order to identify the actual and potential effects of the reform.[2]

A further reduction in price support was proposed by the EU long-term document *Agenda 2000* (European Commission 1997), but completion of the reform is still being discussed because of the strong implications it would have both for the economy of the member states and for the future enlargement of the EU towards the Central and Eastern European countries (Tarditi, Marsh and Senior 1995).

---

[2] Various quantitative analyses of the impact of price policy in the pre-reform CAP are compared in Tarditi *et al.*, 1989.

6.1.3. Plan of work

The impact of agricultural price policy on European cohesion will be assessed for the time-period 1989–95 according to available information at regional and national levels. The analysis will concentrate on three scenarios.

The first scenario (which we label <1991>) will refer to the 'traditional' or 'pre-reform CAP'. The quantitative analysis will be based on the year 1991. In order to provide a more stable picture of the pre-reform CAP, information on some policy variables, such as the amount of government support depending to a certain extent on the level of volatile world market prices, will be based on the three-year average preceding the reform (1989–91).

The second scenario (referred to as 1995) will outline the likely effects of the 1992 reform and will be based on 1995 statistics. Implementation of the reform was planned to extend over three years (from 1993/4 to 1995/6), so the full impact of the reform is not yet evident. This second scenario will be based on the database of the first scenario, updating all available information to 1995. Unfortunately, statistical data on most recent years is not fully available, especially at a regional level, however changes in the modalities and intensity of agricultural market support due to the reform will allow us to detect the possible trends of the impact of Community price policy on European cohesion.

The third scenario (referred to as 1995f) will examine the likely effects of completing the CAP reform by extending the 1992 shift of farm support from consumers to taxpayers for all farm products and by fully de-coupling compensatory payments to farmers.

The quantitative analysis of these scenarios will include estimates of the income redistribution generated by the price support policy among EU social groups or sectors (producers, consumers, and taxpayers), among member countries (NUTS 0) among large regions (NUTS I), and among smaller regions within each member country (NUTS II).

Following the analysis on national and regional income redistribution, we will sketch the main effects of the common agricultural price policy on social cohesion between citizens of different income classes and within the agricultural sector.

After analysing the effects generated by the price support policy on income redistribution, we will examine the likely effects on EU competitiveness and economic development with reference both to the agricultural sector and to the whole economy.

6.2. The Pre-Reform CAP

6.2.1. Main features of EC traditional price policy

The traditional agricultural price policy, conceived in the early sixties when the European Community was a net importer of staple agricultural products, was based mainly on market price support for farm output. This approach to agricultural policy, being directly related to domestic supply, generated a rapid increase in the EC's agricultural self-sufficiency ratio.

Initially, border protection, in addition to increasing domestic prices and farm incomes, also provided an extra source of financial resources for the EC budget. The burden was borne almost totally by consumers, but some of the higher cost of food paid by consumers came to the budget through import levies. As almost all citizens are both consumers and taxpayers, part of the higher food cost generated by the price support indirectly benefited the same people[3] by reducing the need to raise extra taxes. Increasing the EC self-sufficiency rate in food is usually considered beneficial for a net-importing country, as it becomes less subject to the instability of agricultural prices in the world market and less dependent on foreign supply for such a basic item as food in case of famine or war.

Despite an average rate of increase in domestic supply (about 2 per cent per year) and a much lower increase in domestic demand (about 0.5 per cent per year), in the years following institution of the CAP the level of price support granted to farmers was not reduced enough to avoid imbalances on the domestic market. As a consequence of domestic price support, from the end of the sixties onwards domestic supply expanded much faster than domestic demand, creating alarming surpluses, especially of dairy products, meat, and cereals. As the EC became a net exporter of agricultural products, its budget no longer benefited from significant import levies, but had to pay export subsidies in order to dump on the world market commodities which were produced but not consumed at the administered level of domestic prices.

The non-farm population then faced the effects of the price support policy from a different position. Not only were households supporting farmers by paying higher food prices, but they also had to pay extra taxes to finance the increasing needs of the EC budget for export subsidies, as well as for storing and disposing of food surpluses.

6.2.2. *Attempts to reform EU price policy*

A number of attempts to reform the traditional CAP have been implemented in the last thirty years, from the structural reform proposed by Commissioner Sicco Mansholt in the late sixties, to co-responsibility levies and stabilizers in the eighties. In fact, if the output prices are distorted, any reform financing structural change is doomed to failure. Farmers, rightly operating as good entrepreneurs, invested extra funds provided by structural policies in more profitable activities, which largely coincided with the production of commodities with higher levels of price support. In consequence, the extra production was profitable for individual farmers who sold at domestic prices, but it was a liability for society as a whole which had to sell agricultural surpluses at much lower world market prices and pay the difference through higher taxes.

In 1984, in order to limit budgetary costs that were particularly high in the dairy sector, the EC Council of Ministers decided not to reduce price support but to impose production quotas on dairy farmers. By limiting supply, export subsidies were reduced

---

[3] At a different rate, however, because of the generally income-progressive nature of taxation and the regressive nature of income transfers related to increased food prices.

at the cost of a higher economic burden, especially in terms of the reduced mobility of agricultural resources. Farm resources excluded by administrative constraints on production were invested in other commodities, worsening their already precarious market balances. Consequently, a further step towards limiting supply was taken a few years later by introducing the land set-aside, i.e. by paying farmers for keeping agricultural land idle. By means of these policy measures directly managing supply, a substantial level of price support could be maintained without generating higher costs for export subsidies and without further depressing and destabilizing prices in the world market.

From the point of view of consumers and of society as a whole, however, the overall economic cost probably was not reduced. Savings in export subsidies were offset by reduced efficiency in the agricultural sector in terms of restricted agricultural resources and by distortions between sectors in prices and investments. This led to less mobility between and within sectors and worse allocation of resources.

6.2.3. *Quantitative analysis*

Our quantitative analysis[4] will refer only to EU price policy, including price support (the difference between domestic and border prices) and payments to farmers or levies directly related to commodities. This wedge between world market prices and the farmer's revenues per unit of output will be called 'market support'. Total support to farmers would also include subsidies from the Guidance section of the EAGGF and subsidies or levies related to national agricultural policies. These will be mentioned but not analysed in this chapter.

6.2.3.1. *Transfers to farmers*
Total support granted by the EU to farmers is indicated in Figure 6.1 as a percentage of domestic prices.[5] The difference between total and market support is relatively small, less than 10 per cent of the domestic price for all commodities. This is further evidence that most of the CAP impact on EU national and regional economies is due to the market support policy decided by the EU Council of Agricultural Ministers and implemented by the European Commission.

---

[4] The general features of the analysis are outlined in the appendix to this chapter.

[5] Based on OECD data used to calculate in PSEs and CSEs. This measure of price support does not take into consideration the impact of EU price policy on international terms of trade. In other words, in the absence of the CAP, world market prices would be slightly higher. Consequently, EU price support is overestimated. In order to introduce the impact of CAP on international terms of trade into our model a number of assumptions on price elasticities in world markets was needed. Since these parameters are difficult to estimate, we chose an analysis possibly less precise but easier to understand, less dependent on uncertain assumptions and estimated parameters. The OECD does not calculate support for fruit, vegetables, wine, and olive oil. Updated information on these supports was provided by Sarri, based on Nucifora and Sarri (1997). These four commodities are not included in the CAP reform and their market conditions are relatively more unstable. In the quantitative analysis a three-year average level of protection was assumed.

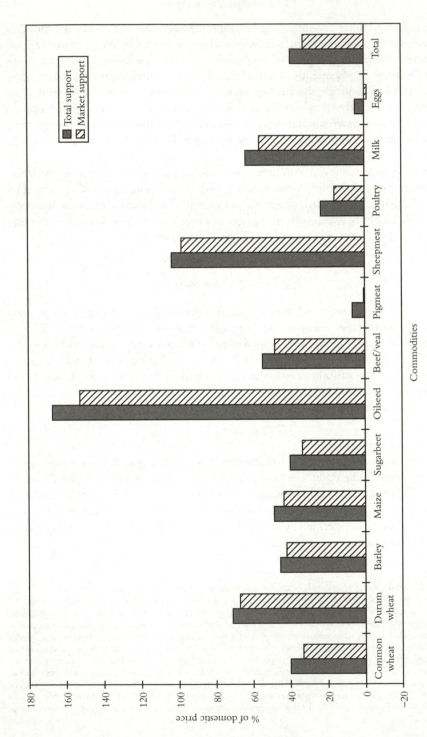

Fig. 6.1. EU: total and market support in 1991

Structural policies implemented through the Guidance section of the EAGGF and national policies are likely to play a minor role in quantitative terms, although their impact on regional income redistribution should be more evident, as they can be targeted on specific areas in need of support.

Transfers to producers in each region related to each commodity are calculated by multiplying the regional final production by the rate of EU market support for each commodity.

6.2.3.2. Transfers from consumers and taxpayers

Transfers from consumers are calculated by multiplying the availability for consumption[6] of each commodity in each country by the EU price support. Regional disaggregation is carried out assuming equal per capita consumption in each region of a single country. While per capita food expenditure presumably varies between regions, probably being greater in regions where incomes are higher, such a difference should not be substantial as far as the agricultural share of food consumption is concerned, given the substantially similar physiological per capita need for food among regions.[7]

National transfers from taxpayers are calculated by attributing a share of the agricultural EU budget to each member country equal to the share of its own contribution to the general EU budget. The disaggregation of the cost paid by taxpayers has been carried out by assuming regional shares of the agricultural national costs proportional to their share of the national GDP.[8] This is equivalent to assuming that each region contributes to the national transfers from taxpayers to agricultural producers generated by the CAP in proportion to its gross income. Subtracting the outflows paid by consumers and taxpayers for each region from the inflows to agricultural producers leads to the estimated net regional transfers generated by the EU agricultural price policy.

These net transfers tend to be positive and higher the greater the share of agriculture in the region's economy (higher inflows) and the poorer or depopulated the region (lower outflows). Conversely, net transfers tend to be increasingly negative in densely populated and richer regions, where agricultural plays a marginal role in the local economy.

---

[6] Domestic availability is calculated as final production minus net exports, taking account of the variation in stocks when data is available. Figures for some commodities are still provisional due to difficulties in finding consistent comparable data. Homogeneity between domestic and imported goods is usually assumed.

[7] In terms of evaluating the possible income redistribution generated by the CAP among regions of a single country, this assumption, if not verified, could lead to an underestimation of the burden on rich regions as compared to poorer regions. Our results in terms of a positive impact of the CAP and of its reform on EU cohesion (i.e. redistribution from rich to poor regions) will, therefore, be treated cautiously. Assuming a positive relation between regional per capita income and the per capita consumer expenditure in agricultural goods would lead to an even more consistent proof of the positive impact of the CAP and of its reform on EU cohesion.

[8] It could be argued that if taxation on the whole is income progressive, richer regions would bear a larger share of the taxpayer transfers generated by the CAP. According to this approach, our results in terms of the positive interregional redistribution of income generated by the CAP and its reform would, again, be treated cautiously and these positive effects on EU cohesion would be proved even more strongly under different assumptions.

6.3. The 1992 Reform of the CAP

6.3.1. Main features of the 1992 reform

The 1992 reform of the CAP involves some of the most important subsectors of EU agriculture, namely cereals, oilseeds, and meats.

The major aim was to reduce agricultural surpluses and the related budget expenditure (export subsidies, storage and surplus disposal costs) by de-coupling farmers' support from the quantity of commodity produced. Some of this objective was reached by substantially reducing government interference in market prices and by providing compensatory payments to farmers to offset income losses due to lower price support. These changes in the CAP price support, however, were an important move towards the long-term goals set in the agreement signed in Marrakesh in April 1994.[9]

Payments to farmers are not related to actual yields, but are calculated on records of the pre-reform years. Since these compensatory payments, however, are still related to the area cultivated year by year, although constrained by regional ceilings, the decoupling of compensatory payments from the quantity of product supplied by each farmer is not complete. This support still creates part of the pre-reform market distortions, hindering the mobility of resources within and between sectors and within regions, preventing a better allocation of economic resources in the EU among and within member states.

---

[9] In order to clarify the long-term objectives of the international community of nations, during the Uruguay Round of GATT negotiations the various instruments of agricultural policy were classified as follows.

A first group of agricultural policy instruments was qualified as 'under reduction commitment'. They include, essentially, policy measures generating market price support obtained through border protection of domestic agricultural markets (import levies and export subsidies); or in conjunction with direct control of domestic supply for specific products by means of production quotas; or, on a larger scale, by reducing the most important farm inputs by means of land set-aside. Price support for farmers is sometimes granted by direct production subsidies which are in some ways coupled with the quantity produced. A number of policy measures reducing input costs are also distorting relative prices faced by farmers and, consequently, are also considered as 'under reduction commitment' by the GATT agreement.

We may specify these policy measures as follows: (a) production subsidies (e.g. deficiency payments); (b) border protection (e.g. import levies, export subsidies, non-tariff trade barriers); (c) production quotas (in conjunction with border protection); (d) land set-aside (in conjunction with border protection); (e) input cost reduction (e.g. subsidies on fertilizers, fuel, etc.).

A second group of policy measures 'exempt from GATT reduction commitment' are described in detail in Annex 2 of the GATT agreement signed in Marrakesh on 14 April 1994. These measures cover a wide range of policy instruments which should (i) have no, or at most minimal, trade distorting effects, (ii) be financed by public funds, (iii) not involve transfers from consumers, and (iv) not provide price support for producers. They can be classified in six major groups: (a) stabilization measures (public stockholding for food security, government participation in insurance programmes, payments for relief from natural disasters, domestic food aid); (b) General services (research, training, extension services to agriculture, marketing, infrastructures); (c) Income support measures (direct payments to producers, de-coupled income support); (d) Structural adjustment assistance (investment aids, resource retirement programmes, producer retirement programmes); (e) Agri-environmental programmes (payments under environmental programmes); (f) Agri-regional programmes (payments under regional assistance, rural development programmes).

The most important changes in policy instruments implemented by the 1992 CAP reform refer to the first group of instruments, where we are going to concentrate our analysis.

Accompanying measures encourage less intensive farming, afforestation of agricultural land, and early retirement schemes for farmers. Neither these measures nor the impact of structural funds, however, will be examined in this report.

6.3.2. The second scenario, 1995

The amount of EU market price support and direct payments granted to farmers in <1991> and 1995 is reported in Figure 6.2 for the most important commodities, together with the other components of the aggregated value of EU agricultural production in the last 17 years. Our second scenario (1995) examines the income redistribution generated by the EU agricultural price policy in 1995. Where statistical data on land use, especially at regional level, is not available, the 1995 changes in price support are referred to the <1991> territorial pattern of agricultural production. In such cases the changes in land use between 1991 and 1995 are not taken into account. Given the present rigidity of agricultural structures, however, the main results of the analysis on income redistribution should not be much affected.

The impact of the reform became evident in 1995. Since data are available for that year we must refer to 1995 although international and domestic market developments could alter future effects of the reform. In addition to directly affecting income redistribution, compensatory payments generate extra costs for society in terms of administrative work needed both in raising extra taxes and in implementing the agricultural policies, some of which need extensive controls at farm level. We will not take into account these social costs in our analysis due to the uncertain information available on the subject.[10]

6.3.3. The third scenario, 1995f

In our third scenario we will assume that compensatory payments would be totally de-coupled from the quantity of agricultural production and equal to the current market support provided by the CAP to farmers in 1995. In the second scenario (1995), market support to farmers is still paid partly by taxpayers and partly by consumers. In the third scenario, all the 1995 transfers to farmers are assumed to be paid only by taxpayers as de-coupled payments, calculated over a defined transition period and paid as bonds to producers.[11]

This analysis indicates the difference in income redistribution that would be achieved by completing the CAP reform. Although in the longer term the mobility of resources among sectors and within agriculture is likely to be higher, nevertheless the intersectoral income redistribution generated by the CAP would be defined when de-coupled

---

[10] Administrative costs in implementing direct payments are likely to be proportional to the number of farms in each region, although in the 1992 CAP reform some procedures have been simplified for smallholdings. Less developed regions, especially in southern Europe, usually present a larger number of small farms, consequently average administrative costs per unit of output should be higher.

[11] Producers could cash the bonds every year during the transition period or sell them on the financial market. For a detailed description of such lump-sum compensation, see Marsh *et al.* (1991).

OECD commodities (million ecus)

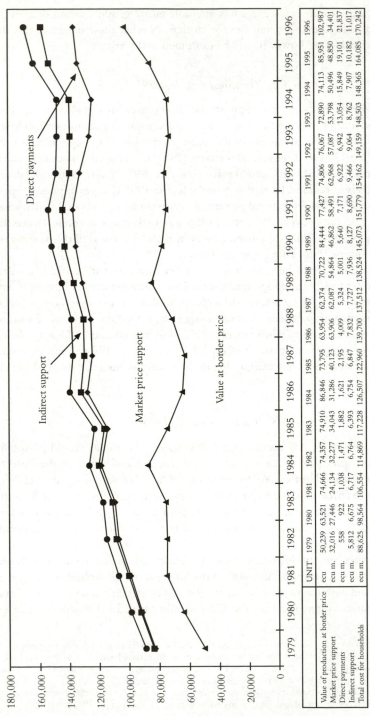

	UNIT	1979	1980	1981	1982	1983	1984	1985	1986	1987	1988	1989	1990	1991	1992	1993	1994	1995	1996
Value of production at border price	ecu	50,239	63,521	74,666	74,357	74,910	86,846	73,795	63,954	62,374	70,722	84,444	77,427	74,806	76,067	72,890	74,113	85,951	102,987
Market price support	ecu m.	32,016	27,446	24,134	32,277	34,043	31,286	40,123	63,906	62,087	54,864	46,862	58,491	62,968	57,087	53,798	50,496	48,850	34,401
Direct payments	ecu m.	558	922	1,038	1,471	1,882	1,621	2,195	4,009	5,324	5,001	5,640	7,171	6,922	6,942	13,054	15,849	19,101	21,837
Indirect support	ecu m.	5,812	6,675	6,717	6,764	6,393	6,754	6,847	7,832	7,727	7,936	8,127	8,690	9,466	9,064	8,762	7,907	10,182	11,017
Total cost for households	ecu m.	88,625	98,564	106,554	114,869	117,228	126,507	122,960	139,700	137,512	138,524	145,073	151,779	154,162	149,159	148,503	148,365	164,085	170,242

Notes: Value of production at the border: (Level of production/1,000) × (Reference price); Indirect support: (General Services + Sub National + Other production subsidy).

Commodities included: cereals, rice, oilseeds, sugarbeets, milk, beef and veal, pigmeat, poultry meat, sheep meat, wool, eggs (63% of agricultural output in 1994).

Source: OECD, Tables on Producer and Consumer Subsidy Equivlents on diskettes, 1996, Paris.

Fig. 6.2. Cost for households of agricultural production (OECD commodities)

compensation were decided and would remain the same for the transition period. If, for example, compensatory payments will be paid for 20 years, most farmers working today will receive them until their retirement age.

After the transition period, however, a consistent structural adjustment would have occurred in agriculture. The conspicuous share of the EU budget spent on compensatory payments could be used for other policies, or for reducing the burden on European taxpayers.

6.4. Effects on Cohesion among Member Countries

6.4.1. *Income transfers among member states*

Each country's financial transactions with the EU and the internal EU trade of agricultural products at prices considerably higher than world prices generate significant income transfers among member states. In addition to subsidizing their own producers, taxpayers in one country subsidize producers in other member states through EU direct payments to farmers and export refunds. Consumers also may subsidize producers in other member states by paying a higher price for internal EU imports of agricultural products.[12] The income transfers within sectors between consumers, taxpayers, and producers were calculated for each country or region and the net benefits or costs to each country or region were obtained from their algebraic sums. The results concerning national aggregates are shown in Table 6.1 and Figure 6.3.

Results are provided in tables, bar charts, and scatter diagrams so the reader may trace the effect of the price support policy, of the 1992 reform, and of a full reform of the CAP for each region. This is made easier by providing a detailed graphic presentation. Obviously, detailed comment for each chart would be tedious for readers not interested in the specific agricultural region, so only few charts are mentioned for each group of tables and charts.[13]

6.4.2. *The traditional CAP*

In an economic union, price support policies favour net exporting countries at the disadvantage of net importing countries. This major effect is clearly apparent in Table 6.1 and Figure 6.3, where Ireland and Denmark, which are large net exporters of agricultural products, benefit most from the traditional CAP. On the other hand, Belgium-Luxembourg, Germany, the UK, and Portugal, who are net importers, are the largest losers.

The net trade situation in agricultural products in each country is not the only factor in determining the net benefit or loss. The relative size and commodity mix of agricultural production is also important. Differences in per capita income, however, play a

---

[12] Consumers also bear the cost of imports into the EU at higher than world prices.
[13] All tables and charts are available in Tarditi (1997*a*).

Table 6.1. EU-12: intersectoral and international income transfers

Member country	To producers		From consumers		From taxpayers			Net transfers			GDPpc	Net transfers per capita		
NUTS 0	1991	1995	1991	1995	1991	1995	1995f	1991	1995	1995f	GDPpc	1991	1995	1995f
EU-12	71,739	73,680	57,039	48,861	25,704	36,925	85,086	-11,004	-12,105	-11,405	17,236	-31	-35	-33
B	1,998	2,111	1,676	1,445	1,112	1,587	3,656	-790	-921	-1,545	19,720	-75	-87	-147
DK	2,422	2,439	1,317	1,000	501	721	1,662	604	718	777	19,860	116	138	149
D	12,649	12,464	10,413	9,177	7,257	11,586	26,698	-5,021	-8,299	-14,234	18,924	-62	-102	-175
GR	3,376	3,615	2,900	2,410	372	558	1,285	103	647	2,330	10,885	10	62	223
E	7,470	7,852	5,700	4,898	2,095	2,478	5,711	-325	476	2,141	13,198	-8	12	55
F	17,310	17,603	12,296	10,994	5,164	6,995	16,118	-151	-386	1,485	18,486	-3	-7	26
IRL	2,131	2,310	676	578	228	443	1,021	1,227	1,289	1,289	15,578	343	360	360
I	9,869	10,445	9,548	7,756	4,065	4,493	10,353	-3,744	-1,804	93	17,827	-65	-31	2
NL	5,532	5,568	4,306	3,568	1,557	2,312	5,328	-331	-313	239	17,906	-21	-20	16
P	1,011	1,095	1,111	961	343	581	1,339	-442	-447	-244	11,876	-45	-45	-25
UK	7,972	8,178	7,097	6,073	3,009	5,170	11,914	-2,134	-3,066	-3,737	17,054	-36	-52	-64
Correlation								-0.22	-0.28	-0.35		-0.08	-0.17	-0.41

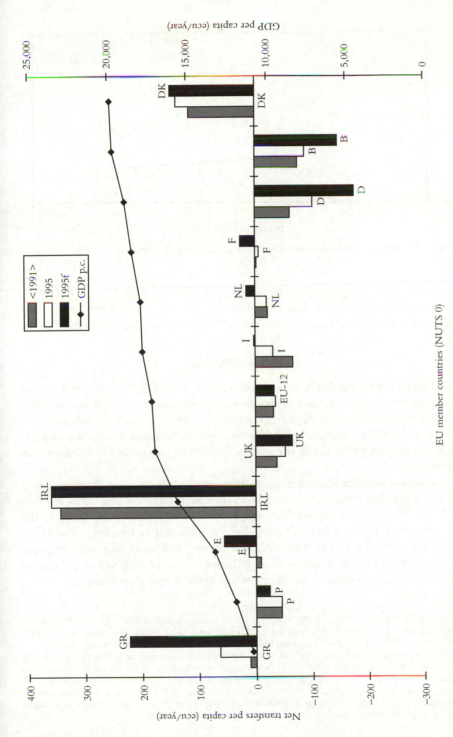

Fig. 6.3. EU-12: international transfers generated by the agricultural price policy

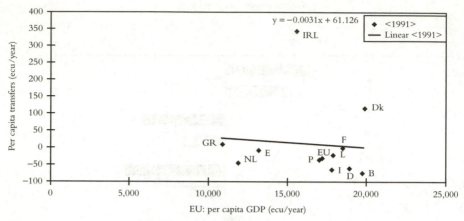

Fig. 6.4. Pre-reform income redistribution among member countries

perceivable role in mitigating the preferential trade effect. In Table 6.1 and Figure 6.3 countries are listed in order of their per capita income[14] which is indicated by the dots on the continuous line and measured on the vertical axis on the right side of the charts.

6.4.3. The 1992 reform

By shifting part of the burden from consumers to taxpayers, the 1992 reform improves the transparency of the CAP and the position of poorer countries as net beneficiaries, while increasing the burden on richer countries. Changes in each country between <1991> and 1995 are directly related to their production mix and to the changes in support of each product. On the whole, the impact on income redistribution is improving.

Correlation coefficients between national gains (or losses) and the average per capita income of member states,[15] computed both on national and on per capita transfers (Table 6.1) increase between <1991> and 1995. The regression lines shown in the scatter diagrams (Figs. 6.4 and 6.5) are helpful in indicating the positive or negative sign of the existing correlation between the vertical and horizontal axis. Negative slopes indicate that the poorer countries (on the left side of the diagram) are gaining on average, while richer countries (on the right side of the diagram) are losing.

---

[14] In terms of Purchasing Power Parity Standards (PPS). Source: European Commission (1997b). If the monetary GDP per capita were used, the ranking would be different, especially in low-income countries. PPS are assumed to be a better indicator of the differences in actual income levels among countries.

[15] These are the two variables indicated in the vertical and horizontal axes of the scatter diagrams. As is well known, correlation coefficients indicate the higher or lower correspondence between observations of two variables. If the correspondence is high, the coefficient of correlation approaches unity (if all observations are located on a straight line in the diagrams the correlation coefficient is 1). If the correspondence between the two variables is very low the coefficient approximates zero (the scatter diagram does not show any notable clustering in one direction or another).

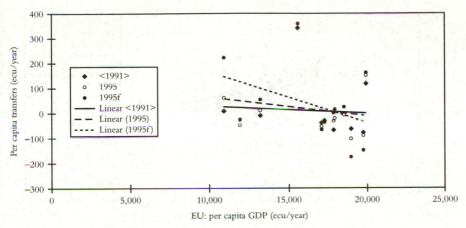

Fig. 6.5. EU–12: impact of different CAP reform options among member states

6.4.4. *Completion of the reform*

In the third scenario (1995f in Table 6.1 and Figs. 6.3–6.5) the effects of a total shift of the farm support from consumers to taxpayers are examined. In this hypothetical situation, the EU budget, in addition to the transfers indicated in scenario 1995, would also pay producers the share of their income transfers now received from consumers. All the burden of farm price support would be borne by member countries in proportion of their national GDP and the present price support, equivalent to an income regressive tax on food consumption, would disappear. Consequently income distribution among member countries and EU cohesion would improve substantially.

Moreover, by dismantling market price support, the EU budget would save almost all the cost of export restitutions and a share to the costs related to market intervention and surplus disposal.[16]

6.5. Effects on Cohesion among EU Regions

6.5.1. *Income redistribution among EU regions (NUTS I)*

In Figure 6.6, the sixty-nine large regions (NUTS I) of EU-12 are pooled together. Some of these regions account for a whole country, as in the cases of Ireland, Luxembourg, and Denmark.

Comparing the 'gaining' regions to the 'losing' regions immediately gives the impression of a substantial positive effect caused by the traditional agricultural price policy

---

[16] As a preliminary assumption, storage costs in scenario 1995f have been assumed as 33% of scenario 1995 (339 mn ECU). This residual budget expenditure is assumed to be needed by measures oriended only to stabilise agricultural prices in the domestic market.

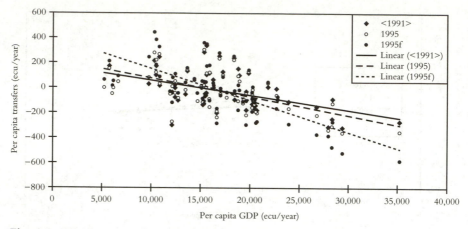

Fig. 6.6. EU-12: impact of policy reforms on interregional redistribution (NUTS I)

on EU redistribution of income between regions. This impression is supported by the negative coefficients of correlation between net gains and average regional income. On average, poorer EU regions benefit from the price support policy at the expense of richer regions.

These results can be explained as follows. Although price support operates as a regressive income tax on consumers and is biased in favour of commodities produced in richer EU regions, agriculture is proportionally more important in the less developed regions, while other economic activities are more concentrated in the urbanized areas, usually located in richer regions. As a result, income transfers to agriculture on average have a positive impact in reducing income disparities between regions. The cost paid by consumers and taxpayers as a consequence of the CAP price support in predominantly rural and poor regions tends to be smaller than the benefit accruing to farmers in the same regions. The opposite happens in richer urbanized regions. As a result, a flow of income is generated from richer to poorer regions.

This positive effect of agricultural price support on regional cohesion was increased by the 1992 reform, as indicated by the higher slope of the 1995 regression line. In fact, the burden of farm income support shifted onto taxpayers is even more concentrated in urbanized, richer regions than before, when it was paid mainly by consumers.

If we consider the income redistribution within the agricultural sector, the results are quite different. According to a study (Brown 1989) carried out in the late 1980s (using, however, data from the mid-1980s), the CAP price policy negatively affected agricultural cohesion. This is because price support was greater for certain 'northern' products (dairy, cereals) than for other products (vegetables, fruits) grown mainly in southern EU regions. In this way, the Mediterranean member states, which are on average poorer, tended to receive lower income transfers to agriculture than the northern EU member state, which are richer on average. Actually, certain Mediterranean agricultural products, such as tobacco, olive oil, and durum wheat, enjoy high levels of support. The southern farmers, however, tend to benefit less because fruit and vegetables, which constitute a significant part of their production, enjoy a relatively lower degree of support than 'northern' commodities.

That fruit and vegetables are less protected than other agricultural commodities may support the conclusion that agriculture in Mediterranean regions is less protected than agriculture in the rest of Europe. However, if we consider the whole impact of the agricultural policy on Mediterranean regions, including the impact on consumers and taxpayers, then the conclusion is the opposite. Although, on average, the common price policy is less protective of Mediterranean agriculture, it does benefit a large number of poor Mediterranean regions.[17]

6.5.2. *Analysis of cohesion countries*

If the regions belonging to the cohesion countries are analysed separately, the effect of the price support policy on income distribution between regions is also evident (Table 6.2 and Figs. 6.7 and 6.8). The regions with positive net inflows clearly outnumber the regions with negative net inflows. Some exceptions to the general rule are because some peripheral regions do not produce agricultural products and, consequently, are net losers.

The 1992 reduction in the prices of cereals and, especially, of beef/veal benefits countries which are net importers of these products. The Mediterranean cohesion member states belong to this category. The reduction in compensation payments to tobacco producers will not favour the southern members of the EU, which are also poorer on average.

Overall, the 1992 CAP reform is not a burden for the richer regions of the cohesion countries, while poorer regions earn substantial benefits. The straight lines interpolating the points representing each region after the reform are only shifted upwards. The pivoting effect, on average, does not reduce net income gains or losses even in the richest regions.

6.6. Effects on Cohesion within Member Countries

The effects of the CAP price policy within each EU member country will be analysed first for the cohesion countries. Then Italy will be analysed, because of its division between a rich 'continental' northern part of the country and a poorer southern part whose characteristics are largely similar to many regions of the cohesion countries. Finally, the northern European countries will be examined. As the cohesion countries have already been examined, only charts concerning Germany are produced here as examples of a northern and richer country with some poor regions, the former DDR regions.

---

[17] Only some charts are presented here. All tables and charts related to each country are presented in Tarditi (1997*a*).

Table 6.2. Cohesion countries: intersectoral and regional transfers

Code	Regions	to producers		from consumers		from taxpayers			Net transfers			GDPp.c.	Net transfers p.c.		
	NUTS II	1991	1994a	1991	1994a	1991	1994a	1994b	1991	1994a	1994b		<1991>	1995	1995f
gr11	Anatoliki M. Thr	358	377	159	132	19	28	65	181	217	312	10,076	316	380	546
gr12	Kentriki Makedo	731	774	484	402	60	90	207	187	282	568	10,485	107	162	326
gr13	Dytiki Makedoni	136	155	83	69	10	16	36	43	70	119	10,622	143	235	397
gr14	Thessalia	552	594	208	173	24	36	83	319	385	510	9,839	426	513	681
gr21	Ipeiros	172	175	96	80	9	14	32	66	82	143	8,285	193	237	414
gr22	Ionia Nisia	48	52	54	45	6	9	21	-12	-2	31	9,631	-64	-9	160
gr23	Dytiki Ellada	352	363	200	167	22	33	76	130	163	287	9,261	180	226	398
gr24	Sterea Ellada	327	355	164	136	25	38	88	138	180	267	13,120	233	305	452
gr25	Peloponnisos	290	305	171	142	22	33	75	96	130	230	10,788	156	210	372
gr3	Attiki	68	71	1,001	832	142	213	492	-1,075	-975	-421	12,063	-298	-270	-117
gr41	Voreio Aigaio	58	62	54	45	5	8	18	-1	9	44	8,240	-6	45	223
gr42	Notio Aigaio	60	63	72	60	9	14	32	-22	-11	31	10,808	-83	-41	121
gr43	Kriti	224	237	153	127	18	26	61	53	83	176	9,735	97	152	320
es11	Galicia	608	618	411	353	114	135	312	83	130	306	10,005	29	46	108
es12	Asturias	178	186	165	142	56	66	152	-42	-21	35	12,121	-37	-19	31
es13	Cantabria	130	135	77	66	27	32	74	26	36	61	12,582	48	69	115

es21	País Vasco	155	157	312	268	134	159	366	−292	−270	−209	15,436	−136	−126	−97
es22	Navarra	148	156	76	66	35	41	95	37	50	62	16,292	70	95	118
es23	Rioja	106	109	38	33	16	19	44	52	57	65	15,097	196	217	248
es24	Aragon	457	498	178	153	73	86	198	206	259	299	14,697	169	212	245
es3	Madrid	81	86	717	616	331	392	903	−967	−921	−817	16,602	−196	−187	−166
es41	Castilla-Leon	1,104	1,118	385	331	123	146	336	596	641	782	11,492	225	242	296
es42	Castilla-La Man	829	841	251	216	77	91	210	500	534	632	11,001	290	309	366
es43	Extremadura	481	504	166	142	40	47	109	275	315	395	8,686	242	277	347
es51	Cataluña	683	745	881	757	396	469	1,081	−595	−481	−335	16,149	−98	−79	−55
es52	Comunidad Vale	15	48	556	478	206	244	563	−747	−674	−515	13,337	−196	−176	−135
es53	Baleares	73	77	100	86	49	57	132	−75	−67	−56	17,396	−109	−97	−81
es61	Andalucia	2,105	2,182	1,017	874	288	341	786	800	966	1,395	10,181	114	138	200
es62	Murcia	199	210	151	130	52	61	141	−4	19	69	12,331	−4	18	66
es7	Canarias	148	151	218	188	77	91	210	−147	−127	−58	12,645	−98	−85	−39
ie	Ireland	2,132	2,276	676	578	228	443	1,021	1,228	1,256	1,255	15,578	343	351	351
pt11	Norte	313	325	412	356	112	190	437	−211	−221	−112	10,455	−57	−60	−30
pt12	Centro (P)	288	298	204	177	44	75	172	40	47	126	8,300	22	26	69
pt13	Lisboa E Vale Do	208	217	390	338	164	279	643	−347	−399	−426	16,239	−100	−115	−122
pt14	Alentejo	170	185	65	56	12	20	46	94	109	139	7,010	163	190	242
pt15	Algarve	34	37	40	35	11	18	41	−17	−16	−5	10,066	−46	−45	−13
	Correlation							−0.27	−0.27	−0.31		−0.32	−0.35	−0.48

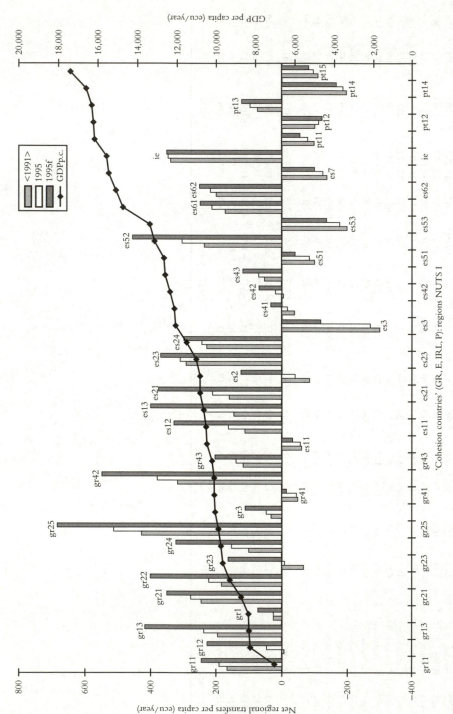

Fig. 6.7. Cohesion countries: regional net transfers due to the agricultural price policy

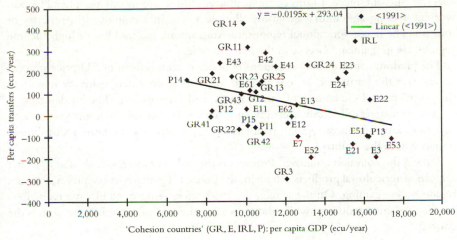

Fig. 6.8. Cohesion countries: pre-reform income redistribution among regions (NUTS I)

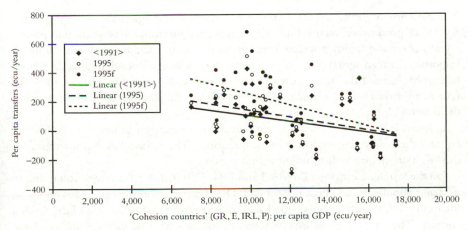

Fig. 6.9. Cohesion countries: impact of the price policy reform

6.6.1. Cohesion countries

Almost all regions of Greece benefit from the traditional agricultural price policy. Only the metropolitan area of Attiki, with its urban population and non-agricultural economy, is a net loser (Table 6.2). The total benefits of Greece from agricultural price policy are increased by its more than proportional share of structural funds.

Notwithstanding this positive effect of EU agricultural price policy throughout the entire country, the effect of agricultural price support on income redistribution among Greek regions appears relatively weak, both if we analyse data in terms of total regional or per capita transfers. This peculiar situation, unique in the EU, is due to a particular characteristic of Greece. In this country, poorer regions are mostly peripheral islands, without a stong agricultural economy. People are mainly employed in fisheries or tourism. The major agricultural regions, ranking among the middle- or high-income regions, are in mainland Greece or the Peloponnese.

The predominance of poorer regions benefiting from reform of EU price support policy over the losing, richer regions is apparent in Spain where gains are mainly in the central part of the country: Castilla, Rioja, and Estremadura. The burden falls on metropolitan areas of Madrid, Valencia, and Pais Vasco. The reform improves the cost-benefit situation in most regions, maintaining approximately the same redistributive impact within the country.

Among the cohesion countries, Portugal is the only net loser, mainly due to its net imports of agricultural products. Alentejo, the poorest region in the country, is the only region largely gaining. On the whole, the 1992 reform improved income redistribution for the entire country, while also increasing the rate of redistribution within the country.

6.6.2. *Other member countries*

Italy has some contrasts. Some rich northern regions where agriculture is concentrated and highly productive, such as Emilia Romagna, benefit from the price support policy, while poorer and highly populated regions in the south such as Campania, although important from an agricultural point of view, are net losers. Poor depopulated regions such as Molise and Basilicata show the highest per capita gains. On average, the CAP reform improved both the total gain for the country and income redistribution within the country.

Belgium is a net loser from EU agricultural price support policy, but within the country the policy helps reduce income disparities. The reform has slightly improved this effect on income redistribution within the country.

On the whole, Germany (Table 6.3 and Figs. 6.10–6.12) is the largest loser, due to its dense population and high per capita GDP. The situation in regions belonging to the former DDR, however, is remarkably different from that of the rest of the unified country. These new regions are characterised by a low average income and by a large agricultural labour force. As a consequence, these regions are generally gainers. The redistribution generated by the agricultural price support policy within the country is substantial and is further increased by the reform of the CAP.

France is the largest agricultural producer in Europe. As a consequence, the vast majority of its regions benefit substantially from the price support policy of the European union. The high concentration of population and wealth in the Île de France, however, offsets the benefits enjoyed by the rest of the regions. On the whole, the country is a net loser although the reform improved the net income flow.

Of all EU countries, the Netherlands show the neatest regional income redistribution within the country. The five regions with a lower per capita GDP are net gainers, while the seven regions with a higher per capita GDP are net losers. The 1992 reform did not substantially modify the situation.

Table 6.3. Germany: intersectoral and regional transfers

Code	Regions	to producers 1991	to producers 1994a	from consumers 1991	from consumers 1994a	from taxpayers 1991	from taxpayers 1994a	from taxpayers 1994b	Net transfers 1991	Net transfers 1994a	Net transfers 1994b	GDP p.c.	Net transfers p.c. <1991>	Net transfers p.c. 1995	Net transfers p.c. 1995f
de11	Stuttgart	462	458	481	424	473	754	1,739	−491	−720	−1,281	26,684	−130	−191	−340
de12	Karlsruhe	170	169	331	291	287	459	1,057	−448	−581	−888	23,588	−173	−224	−343
de13	Freiburg	248	251	258	228	199	318	732	−209	−294	−481	20,933	−103	−146	−238
de14	Tuebingen	390	386	213	187	171	273	628	6	−74	−242	21,805	4	−44	−145
de21	Oberbayern	714	705	496	437	517	825	1,902	−300	−558	−1,197	28,282	−77	−144	−308
de22	Niederbayern	421	414	141	124	91	145	335	189	144	79	17,565	171	131	71
de23	Oberpfalz	308	302	132	116	87	139	321	89	47	−19	17,958	86	45	−18
de24	Oberfranken	205	198	140	124	100	159	366	−35	−85	−169	19,273	−32	−77	−153
de25	Mittelfranken	266	267	209	184	178	285	656	−121	−202	−389	23,198	−74	−123	−238
de26	Unterfranken	256	231	164	145	116	185	427	−24	−100	−197	19,180	−19	−77	−153
de27	Schwaben	525	517	212	187	160	255	588	153	75	−71	20,439	92	45	−43
de3	Berlin	15	17	448	395	274	438	1,008	−707	−816	−992	16,600	−201	−232	−282
de4	Brandenburg	542	548	337	297	82	131	302	124	120	246	6,617	47	45	93
de5	Bremen	11	12	89	78	93	148	342	−171	−215	−329	28,324	−245	−308	−473
de6	Hamburg	40	41	216	190	280	446	1,029	−455	−595	−987	35,190	−269	−352	−584
de71	Darmstadt	200	195	463	408	535	853	1,967	−797	−1,066	−1,772	31,343	−220	−294	−488
de72	Giessen	134	131	131	115	90	143	330	−87	−128	−199	18,610	−85	−125	−194
de73	Kassel	248	234	158	140	117	187	430	−27	−93	−197	20,055	−22	−75	−159
de8	Mecklenburg-V.	639	612	251	221	53	84	195	335	306	417	5,715	170	156	212

Table 6.3. (cont'd)

Code	Regions	to producers		from consumers		from taxpayers			Net transfers			GDPp.c.	Net transfers p.c.		
		1991	1994a	1991	1994a	1991	1994a	1994b	1991	1994a	1994b		<1991>	1995	1995f
de91	Braunschweig	301	275	214	189	154	246	566	−67	−159	−291	19,520	−40	−95	−174
de92	Hannover	413	393	269	237	213	340	784	−70	−185	−391	21,514	−33	−88	−186
de93	Lüneburg	671	654	195	172	112	179	412	365	303	242	15,612	239	199	159
de94	Weser-Ems	987	1,007	287	253	193	309	711	507	446	296	18,304	226	199	132
dea1	Düsseldorf	333	329	682	601	566	904	2,083	−915	−1,175	−1,753	22,553	−171	−220	−329
dea2	Köln	305	288	526	463	410	655	1,510	−631	−830	−1,221	21,203	−153	−202	−297
dea3	Münster	340	364	323	285	209	333	768	−192	−254	−404	17,522	−76	−100	−160
dea4	Detmold	265	263	247	218	181	288	664	−163	−243	−401	19,811	−84	−125	−207
dea5	Arnsberg	195	192	487	429	353	563	1,297	−645	−800	−1,105	19,651	−169	−210	−290
deb1	Koblenz	175	176	183	161	119	189	436	−126	−175	−260	17,593	−88	−122	−182
deb2	Trier	146	146	63	56	38	60	139	45	29	6	16,275	90	60	13
deb3	Rheinhessen-Pfalz	252	242	245	216	184	293	676	−176	−267	−434	20,349	−92	−139	−226
dec	Saarland	46	48	140	123	101	162	372	−195	−237	−324	19,611	−178	−216	−296
ded	Sachsen	557	550	622	548	137	219	504	−203	−217	46	5,982	−42	−44	9
dee	Sachsen-Anhalt	501	471	375	331	84	135	310	42	6	161	6,105	14	2	55
def	Schleswig-Holstein	993	940	343	302	237	378	872	413	259	68	18,771	154	96	25
deg	Thüringen	412	410	341	300	65	104	240	6	5	170	5,186	2.40	1.98	63.74
Correlation									−0.49	−0.54	−0.68		−0.60	−0.68	−0.85

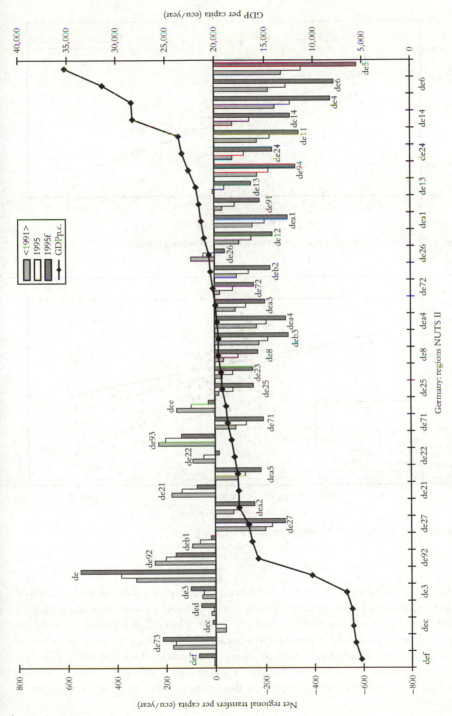

Fig. 6.10. Germany: regional net transfers of the agricultural price policy

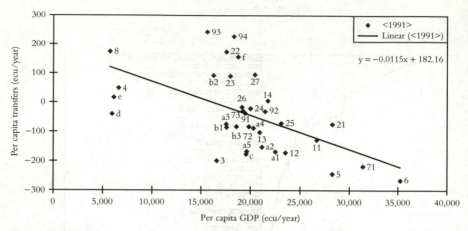

Fig. 6.11. Germany: pre-reform income redistribution among regions

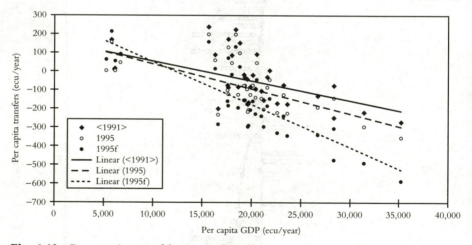

Fig. 6.12. Germany: impact of the price policy reform

In the United Kingdom the effect of the price support policy is peculiar because some richer regions have high agricultural production and in some poorer regions agriculture is not very developed. The poorest regions (Northern Ireland and Wales), however, as expected, are gainers, while the richest south-east region is a loser. The rest of the country shows a quite different pattern of income redistribution. Rich regions such as East Anglia are substantial gainers from the price support policy, while north-west is among the losers. The reform slightly improved the existing interregional redistribution of income.

6.7. Effects on Social Cohesion

In addition to the effects of the CAP and of its reform on EU regional cohesion, the effects on social cohesion will be discussed. It relates to the inter-sectoral and interpersonal redistribution of income in the society as a whole and within the agricultural sector.

6.7.1. Intersectoral and interpersonal redistribution of income

According to OECD estimates (OECD 1997), in 1995 total transfers in the EU associated with agricultural policies were 111 bn. ecus, 51 bn. from taxpayers and 60 bn. from consumers, costing 315 ecus per capita, 1,260 ecus per four-member household. On average, the transfers were 14,960 ecus per full-time farmer equivalent, or 996 ecus per hectare of agricultural land.

The traditional price support implemented by the CAP was often justified on the grounds of its social effects, as it transferred income from allegedly richer non-agricultural sectors to poorer agricultural sectors. In fact, this has been true in some countries if we consider the so-called average non-farm income and compare it to the so-called average income of people involved in farming. At present, however, agriculture is only one income source in a large share of households in rural areas, and average income in agricultural households is frequently higher than average income in non-farm households.

The statement that CAP improves income distribution within society will be overturned if we go deeper into the analysis and examine the income redistribution generated at the level of individuals. Agricultural price support operates as a regressive tax on consumers as lower income households spend a higher share of their family budget on food. On the other hand, it transfers income to farmers in proportion to their production capacity, mostly favouring more wealthy farmers. The EU Commission repeatedly pointed out that 80 per cent of transfers flowed to the 20 per cent of better-off farms. Moreover, the benefit of higher market prices goes mainly to landowners (farmers and non-farmers), whose income is often higher than the average non-farm income, while small farmers and landless hired workers benefit much less from this policy measure. The alleged positive effects of the intersectoral income redistribution brought about by the traditional price support policy should, therefore, be balanced by considerations at the level of individuals.

Nonetheless, the beneficial effects on regional redistribution previously described largely maintain their significance. This is especially so if we consider the income-multiplier effect at a regional level in poorer regions where there tend to be more unexploited resources, and the consistency of these effects with the EU regional policy aiming at a convergence of living standards over the whole European territory.

The CAP reform, which was adopted in 1992 and implemented starting from 1993/4, includes policy changes that led to a more equitable distribution of the benefits of price support. At the heart of the 1992 reform lies reform of the cereal regime, for which support prices were reduced considerably (30 per cent). Producers were compensated for their losses with compensatory amounts paid out of the budget[18]. In this way consumers benefit, especially those consumers in the poorer member states who spend a larger proportion of their income on food.

The 1992 reform reduced price supports on the domestic market especially for cereals and meat. In following years, however, thanks to the reduction of supply generated by the land set-aside measures and to the developments on world markets, the reduction in actual market prices was modest, much lower than the implemented reduction in institutional prices.

6.7.2. Cohesion within the agricultural sector

The direct link existing between price support and agricultural production has some undesirable consequences for economic and social cohesion, as price support tends to benefit the large and more efficient farmers more, rather than those in greater need. The CAP price support did not involve only spatial transfers of resources but it affected the various groups of farmers inside each member state differently. For cohesion purposes, there is an important distinction in each member state between small and large farmers.

In Table 6.4, farms were classified by size (European Size Units—ESU).[19] Calculation of the price support benefits for different farm sizes was carried out for two years, 1990 and 1994. Benefits for each class size, including benefits from border protection as well as direct payments from the budget, were converted into a per farm and per Annual Work Unit (AWU) basis.

It is clear from these results that the CAP price support benefits per AWU are positively related to farm size. The differences are so large that the benefit per AWU to the larger farms in some member states are more than ten times greater than the benefit to the smaller farms. In some cases the difference in the benefits is considerably smaller, but always greater than double.[20]

These results indicate, at least for 1990, that the CAP price support policy has not promoted cohesion among different farm sizes but has contributed to widening the gap between small and large farms. The 1992 reform did not substantially change the existing pattern of income redistribution within the agricultural sector. When compared with large producers, however, small producers are slightly favoured by the reform because they are not requested to set-aside a share of their cultivated land and the premiums for their cattle are less constrained by headage limits. Consequently, the benefits of the income transfers are slightly more oriented to small producers.

---

[18] The compensation for durum wheat in traditional producing areas is especially high, mainly for social reasons.

[19] Information on these classifications can be obtained from the Farm Accountancy Data Network (FADN-RICA) surveys. The calculations for 1994 were made under the assumption that the RICA survey in that year was the same as that in the 1990.

[20] Something of an anomaly exists for Germany and the Netherlands, where the CAP benefits per AWU for very large farms declined sharply compared to the previous size class. Careful examination of the RICA data showed that the production of these farms is dominated by 'vegetables and flowers', for which protection either has not been taken into account or does not exist. In addition, these are labour-intensive farms.

Table 6.4. Total transfer per AWU (by economic size of farms) (1990)

	Very small		Small		Lower medium		Upper medium		Large		Very large	
	F	L	F	L	F	L	F	L	F	L	F	L
Belgium	—	—	—	—	13,297.0	11,664.0	26,020	17,761.0	56,410	28,134.0	79,546	25,446.0
Denmark	—	—	3,293	9,601	7,574.8	13,336.0	23,114	22,119.0	58,610	35,201.0	111,315	28,324.0
Germany	—	—	—	—	11,272.0	9,923.1	30,111	18,854.0	52,318	25,696.0	42,168	8,000.2
Greece	2,782	1,720	4,806	2,768	7,306.5	3,841.5	10,861	4,868.5	14,083	5,829.2	—	—
Spain	2,737	2,972	5,307	4,700	9,643.3	7,003.1	18,436	11,401.0	38,281	14,152.0	97,787	13,047.0
France	—	—	—	—	10,489.0	7,886.7	23,998	15,956.0	43,197	22,257.0	60,573	16,751.0
Ireland	2,585	2,875	5,650	5,305	12,714.0	10,204.0	31,084	20,223.0	78,081	31,611.0	191,154	41,938.0
Italy	1,602	1,580	3,173	2,695	6,776.8	4,709.4	14,935	7,791.1	34,297	13,268.0	96,189	24,964.0
Luxembourg	—	—	—	—	—	—	37,727	22,605.0	70,996	36,315.0	—	—
Netherlands	—	—	—	—	—	—	23,362	16,759.0	59,929	31,278.0	68,425	13,085.0
Portugal	1,477	968	3,099	1,747	5,707.8	2,742.8	12,791	4,486.8	32,067	6,850.5	72,692	11,846.0
UK	—	—	5,202	4,876	11,628.0	9,469.2	25,793	16,141.0	60,598	25,558.0	143,913	26,019.0

F: Total benefit per farm (ecus/farm). L: Total benefit per farm and AWU = F/AWU (ecus/farm).

Sources: RICA 1990/1; 20th financial report on the EAGGF guarantee section. Commission 1991.

Table 6.5. Total transfer per farm and AWU (1994)

	Very small		Small		Lower medium		Upper medium		Large		Very large	
	F	L	F	L	F	L	F	L	F	L	F	L
Belgium	—	—	—	—	13,820.0	12,123.0	24,414	16,665.0	47,301	23,592.0	61,504	19,675
Denmark	—	—	23,730	69,187	20,630.0	36,320.0	27,279	26,104.0	61,330	36,835.0	134,948	34,338
Germany	—	—	—	—	14,182.0	12,484.0	30,098	18,846.0	55,384	27,202.0	162,155	30,763
Greece	3,538	2,188	5,942	3,422	8,786.3	4,619.5	14,037	6,291.8	61,764	25,564.0	—	—
Spain	4,180	4,538	7,217	6,392	12,795.0	9,292.0	24,684	15,265.0	77,741	28,761.0	515,507	68,780
France	—	—	—	—	13,895.0	10,447.0	25,176	16,739.0	50,289	25,922.0	112,409	31,086
Ireland	2,607	2,900	5,369	5,042	11,864.0	9,521.8	29,435	19,151.0	73,118	29,602.0	190,420	41,777
Italy	2,026	1,998	3,498	2,972	6,481.4	4,504.1	14,006	7,306.6	32,491	12,569.0	100,549	26,096
Luxembourg	—	—	—	—	—	—	36,613	21,937.0	68,706	35,143.0	—	—
Netherlands	—	—	—	—	—	—	21,405	15,355.0	53,982	28,174.0	58,102	11,111
Portugal	1,672	1,096	3,434	1,936	5,554.1	2,669.0	11,992	4,206.4	25,266	5,397.6	74,725	12,178
UK	—	—	12,150	11,388	14,291.0	11,638.0	27,931	17,478.0	61,884	26,100.0	153,242	27,706

F: Total benefit per farm (ecus/farm). L: Total benefit per farm and AWU = F/AWU (ecus/farm).

Sources: RICA 1990/1; 24th financial report on the EAGGF guarantee section. Commission 1994.

Nevertheless, comparison of the 1990 and 1994 results does not show any improvement in the distribution of benefits among different farm sizes, indicating that the price policy reform has not remedied the bias in favour of larger farms under the CAP.[21] The compensatory payments to cereal growers effectively freeze the subsidies given to all farmers and are especially beneficial to the larger farmers, as was the previous openended support at the previously higher prices. Also, it can be argued that the reduction in the prices of cereals and the compensation through direct payments based on historical yields increases the profit per hectare of cultivated land, which is more to the benefit of large farmers.

The headage quotas for which certain premiums are granted favour the smaller farmers, who receive these premiums for all or most of their livestock. Reduction in the price of cereals, however, will be more to the benefit of larger livestock producers (as well as some small intensive livestock producers), for whom the costs of feed will be reduced considerably. Reduction in the price of domestically produced cereals encourages substitution of imported for domestically produced feed.

6.8. Effects on Competitiveness and Economic Development

Mainly the structural part of the CAP is associated with changes in the competitiveness and economic development of agriculture in the various regions of the EU. The price support policy, however, also has remarkable influence on competitiveness because it changes the allocation of resources in both the short and the long term.

6.8.1. Resource allocation in the short term

Since the impact of the traditional price support on resource allocation has been widely discussed in the literature, we will not repeat what is now commonly accepted among scholars and policymakers. Perhaps it is worth noting the different interpretations of the same policy measures when considered from a short-term or a long-term point of view.

Figure 6.13 shows the inverse correlation existing in developed countries between the percentage of agricultural support and the per capita value added of agriculture relative to the economy as a whole.[22] From a short-term point of view, it looks quite plausible that in countries in which farmers earn an average income lower than non-farm people, funds are transferred to the farm sector either through direct price supports or direct payments. At first glance, these transfers seem consistent with the general aims of governments on income redistribution.

Seen from a long-term point of view, however, the same negative correlation can be interpreted quite differently. Where government support to agriculture is high, the

---

[21] Because the RICA results for 1994 are not yet available, however, it should be borne in mind that the 'land set-aside' policy introduced by the CAP reform, which is associated with the larger farms, is not taken into account in the calculations. The 1990 RICA results were used for both 1990 and 1994. Including the 'land set-aside' results in the calculations would have mitigated the bias in favour of the larger farms.

[22] A similar relationship is presented in CEC (1994), 111.

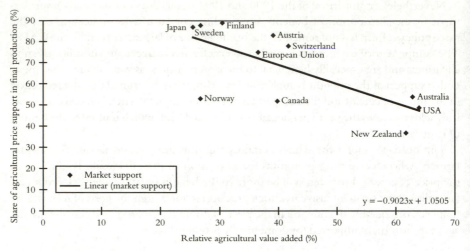

Fig. 6.13. Agricultural support vs. relative agricultural value added per capita

difference between farm incomes and non-farm incomes is high, and where government support is low the difference between farm and non-farm incomes is low as well. Price support maintains excess labour in agriculture together with its low productivity as compared to the other sectors of the economy.

   The marginal and average productivity of the labour force in agriculture, if computed in social terms—i.e. net of income transfers generated by CAP price support—is low, especially in less developed member states and regions. Transferring income to farmers by distorting market prices helps hide the real productivity in social terms of agricultural resources in general and of labour in particular. The difference between farmer earnings at domestic market prices and the lower social value of the goods produced is the origin of misunderstandings and social problems arising between farmers and governments when the EU Commission suggests reducing price support. According to GATT-WTO principles, whenever possible income redistribution should be achieved through visible budgetary transfers, without interfering with market prices.

6.8.1.1. *Impact of the 1992 CAP reform*

The short-term impact of the 1992 reform on resource allocation is mixed. On the one hand, drawing domestic market prices nearer to world market levels removes distortions in trade and production, reduces inflation, and increases economic efficiency both within and between sectors. Production surpluses are reduced and, as a result, the costs of disposing of them by dumping on the world market or by their destruction are reduced as well.

   On the other hand, direct budgetary payments involve substantial administrative costs, both for raising taxes and for distributing payments to millions of farmers. These administrative costs should be considered dead-weight losses for society to a large extent, as budgetary expenditure could be used for more socially valuable purposes.

Only part of these costs is drawn from the EU budget, while a considerable share is paid by national and local governments. These costs, however, are generated by the CAP farm support and are a burden on all EU citizens.

The drain of financial resources from the rest of the economy slows the process of macroeconomic stabilization. Given the alarming size of the public debt of various member countries, additional expenditure raises interest rates and inflation while reducing the competitiveness of national economies as a whole.

Land set-aside substantially reduces surpluses and export subsidies. The economic costs for society as a whole, however, probably have not been reduced, although these costs have been made less visible.[23] Taking land, often very fertile land, out of production is a conspicuous misallocation of resources that must be taken into account in any economic analysis. What would happen to the EU economy if in other sectors, such as manufacturing or in the service sector, it were decided to increase border protection and reduce production? It would be even more odd if such a policy were implemented to limit supply and prevent product prices in the domestic market from adjusting to lower levels. Obviously, the entire economic system would collapse. Reducing the area of land cultivated directly changes the input mix in a way not chosen by the entrepreneur and without any economic logic related to good management practices. Distortions in the allocation of resources inside farms increase.

6.8.2. Effects on economic development

The objectives of the CAP spelled out in Article 39 of the Treaty of Rome (now Art. 33)[24] on income support (letter 'b') refer to 'individual earnings' of persons engaged in agriculture, subordinated to letter 'a' explicitly aiming at the best use of labour in the economy. Therefore, increased farm incomes should be the result of a 'rational development of agricultural production', which implies a timely structural adjustment. When not used as a short-term tool for stabilizing income, income transfers generated through price supports retain labour in agriculture, hindering structural adjustment. They are, then, not the best policy and are not consistent with the Treaty of Rome.

The misallocation of human resources within sectors caused by price support is well known. Since income transfers still benefit mainly large farms, qualified human

---

[23] Policymakers sometimes do not sufficiently take into consideration the economic damage to society of a reduction in the use of available resources. Paying farmers not to use land they own is, obviously, inefficient use of land. Moreover, a substantial part of farm production comes about by using other factors such as chemical fertilizers, which are expensive, may have to be imported, and cause damage by polluting water and soil, especially in intensely cultivated rural areas.

[24] According to Article 39 of the Treaty of Rome (now Art. 33), 'the common agricultural policy shall have as its objectives:

(a) to increase agricultural productivity by developing technical progress and by ensuring the rational development of agricultural production and the optimum utilization of the factors of production, particularly labour;

(b) to ensure **thereby** a fair standard of living for the agricultural population, particularly by the increasing of the individual earnings of persons engaged in agriculture;

(c) to stabilize markets;

(d) to guarantee regular supplies; and

(e) to ensure reasonable prices in supplies to consumers.'

resources are retained in agriculture, where private incomes are high. Marginal productivity, however, if calculated in social terms, is quite low, if not negative. As a result, the competitiveness of the economic system as a whole is reduced.

The CAP price support provides an incentive to increase production and keeps marginal producers in business. The available evidence shows that the adjustment towards improving farm structures is very slow, indicating a relative failure of the price policy to promote a more competitive agricultural sector over a reasonable period of time. By considerably prolonging the engagement of marginal producers in agricultural production, the CAP price support positively affects agricultural employment. This effects non-farm employment, however, as human resources are lured away from non-farm sectors.

In this way, the policy, especially in member states with small farm sizes, does not encourage more competitive farm structures. The two weakest member states (Greece and Portugal) have the smallest farm sizes in the EU. Keeping marginal producers in business through high agricultural product prices does not help establish a more competitive agriculture in these countries, although to a certain extent it does preserve farm employment.[25] Incentives aimed at labour mobility would have a more desirable effect on incomes, overall employment, and resource allocation.

6.8.2.1. *Effects of the 1992 CAP reform*

In the long run, the effects of the 1992 reform of the CAP are quite mixed. Lower distortions in farm prices are likely to encourage both a greater mobility of the labour force within the sector and adjustment of the productive structure towards a larger number of viable farms capable of providing sufficient income to the labour force employed without a large income transfer generated by price support. Particularly in the poorer regions, the average size of farms (often less than two to three hectares) is too small for modern techniques and too small to generate enough income to the farming population.

The 1992 reform does not properly tackle the bottlenecks which prevent better mobility of human resources within and between sectors in the EU. Fully de-coupling payments from the quantity produced would increase the transparency of the CAP and the mobility of human resources in the economy, moving toward greater efficiency. Current compensatory payments granted to farmers every year according to their cultivated area prevent farmers from looking for alternative jobs which are more productive in social terms. This hinders the mobility of the labour force and other resources within and between sectors. Especially in less developed areas, excess resources are held in agriculture, favouring the continued existence of inefficient farm sizes and outmoded farming techniques.

The measures accompanying the CAP reform are expected to encourage economic and social cohesion. This encouragement derives from improvement in farm structures and, therefore, in competitiveness, which can be achieved especially in the weakest member states, most of which have poor farm structures.

---

[25] This is a rather general statement. Considerable variations exist among different regions and sectors. It must be recognized that the slow move towards larger farm sizes in the southern member states is also because of social reasons, inheritance law, etc.

In the short term, without CAP price support and without targeted regional policy measures, the depopulation of the rural areas would have been much faster, with obvious implications for the social fabric. Moreover, the income earned by farmers in relation to other professional and social groups in these rural areas would have been less. In the short term, then, the CAP price support has encouraged cohesion between farmers and non-farmers in rural areas. However, such rural development targets could be pursued more effectively with a different set of policy measures designed to make agriculture more competitive, focusing support on attaining the highest efficiency, equity, and sustainability of public intervention.

6.9. Conclusions

The impact of the agricultural price policy of the European Union on cohesion is a result of different and contrasting effects both in terms of equity (income redistribution) and efficiency (competitiveness and economic development).

Positive effects of the agricultural price policy are detectable in terms of territorial income redistribution among countries but especially within each member country at regional level (NUTSI and NUTSII). On average, the agricultural price support transfers income from richer urbanized and industrialized regions towards poorer regions where agriculture accounts for a larger share of the regional GDP. This overall redistribution favouring European cohesion has been enhanced by the 1992 reform of the CAP, which shifted the burden of price support from consumers to taxpayers for some basic commodities such as cereals and oilseeds.

In contrast, the overall effect of the agricultural price policy on interpersonal income redistribution is likely to be negative, both within society as a whole and within the agricultural sector. Higher food prices operate as a regressive tax on consumers because lower-income households spend a higher share of their family budget on food. Furthermore, the agricultural price support transfers income to farmers in proportion to their production capacity, mostly favouring better-off farmers. Income transfers to agriculture after the reform are still largely proportional to the economic size of farms. Moreover, the benefits of higher market prices in the longer run tend to be capitalized in land values and flows largely to landowners (farmers and non-farmers), whose income is often higher than the average non-farm income. Workers in small farms and landless and hired workers benefit much less from price support.

Farm price support generates large distortions in the domestic market both at intersectoral and intrasectoral level, reducing EU competitiveness and generating social costs and conspicuous budgetary expenditure for disposing of food surpluses and for setting aside arable land in order to reduce domestic supply. In the long term, price support hinders structural adjustment in rural areas, especially where farms are small and the agricultural workforce is still redundant.

The impact of the 1992 reform on resource allocation in the short term is mixed. On the one hand, approaching domestic market prices to world market levels removes existing distortions in trade and production, reduces the rate of inflation, and increases economic efficiency both within and between sectors. On the other hand, land set-aside and direct budgetary payments involve waste of economic resources and substantial administrative costs both in raising extra taxes and in distributing payments to farmers.

On the whole, the prevailing negative effects on resource allocation and competitiveness generated by the EU price policy have a detrimental effect on European cohesion. In order to improve cohesion in the EU, price support policy should be substantially dismantled, while more targeted policy measures should be implemented to reduce negative externalities and stimulate all territorial and environmentally positive externalities related to agriculture. Future targeted policy measures aiming at enhancing the cohesive effects of agricultural policy should take into account the likely impact on income redistribution among member states and regions, as well as among social groups (consumers, producers, taxpayers) and within the agricultural sector.

APPENDIX. GENERAL FEATURES OF THE QUANTITATIVE ANALYSIS

Commodities $i = 1, \ldots, 20$
Member Countries (NUTS 0) $j = 1, \ldots, 12$
Macro-regions (NUTS I) $K = 1, \ldots, 69$
Regions (NUTS II) $k = 1, \ldots, 159$
$<1991> = $ average 1990, 1991, 1992
'1995' = year 1995 (some components of the computation may refer to $<1991>$)
Underlined variables are 'per cent' (%) coefficients on Final Agricultural Production, when not specified differently

Regional (national) inflow: market transfers to producers
$\underline{MTP}_i = \underline{PSE}_i - \underline{FGE}_i - \underline{NAE}_i = \underline{MPS}_i + (\underline{DSP}_i - \underline{APL}_i);$
$MTP_{ij,k} = \underline{MTP}_i \times FAP_{ij,k}$
$MTP_{j,k} = \Sigma_i MTP_{ij,k}$

Fiscal outflow: market transfers from taxpayers
$TMT_j = TMT \times \underline{NCO}_j$
$TMT_{j,k} = TMT_j \times \underline{VAF}_{j,k}$

Invisible outflow: market transfers from consumers
$CAE_{ij} = FAP_{ij} + NT_{ij}$
$CMT_{ij} = CAE_{ij} \times \underline{MPS}_i$
$CMT_j = \Sigma_i CMT_{ij}$
$CMT_{jik} = CMT_j \times \underline{POP}_{j,k}$

Net regional transfers
$RNT_{j,k} = MTP_{j,k} - TMT_{j,k} - CMT_{j,k}$

Legend

APL = Agricultural Producer Levies
CAE = Consumer's Agricultural Expenditure
CMT = Consumers Market Transfers to producers
DSP = Direct Payments to Producers
FAP = Final Agricultural Production
FGE = EAGGF Guidance Expenditure
NT = Net trade in value
MPS = Market price support
MTP = Market Transfer to Producers
NAE = National Agricultural Expenditure
NCO_j = National share of Contributions to EU budget
$POP_{j,k}$ = Regional share of POPulation
PSE = net Producer Subsidy Equivalents
TMT = Taxpayers Market Transfers to producers
$VAF_{j,k}$ = Regional share of Value Added at Factor cost

Data sources

PSE_j; FOE_j; NAE_j; DSP_j; APL = OECD, Database on Producer Subsidy Equivalents
$FAP_{ij,k}$; $VAF_{j,k}$; $POP_{j,k}$ = EC, REGIO Database
ASS = EC, Agricultural Situation in the Community
NCO_j = Eurostat
For fruit, vegetables, wine, and olive oil, support levels are taken from A. M. Nucifora, D. Sarri (1997)

References

Brown, C. (1989). *Distribution of CAP Price Support*, Report no. 45. Danish Agricultural Economics Institute.

C.A.P. Monitor. Continuously updated information service. London: Agra Europe.

European Commission (1994). *European Economy* 4.

European Commission (various years). *The Agricultural Situation in the Community*. Brussels.

European Commission (1997). *Agenda 2000, vol. i. Communication: For a Stronger and Wider Union*. Strasbourg.

GATT-WTO (1994). *Establishing the World Trade Organisation: Agreement on Agriculture*, Marrakesh.

Goldin, I., Knudsen, O., and van der Mensbrugghe, D. (1993). *Trade Liberalisation: Global Economic Implications*. Paris: OECD.

INEA (1997). *Rapporto sulle Politicha Agricole dell Unione Europea*. Rome.

FAPRI (1997). *1997 Outlook*. Iowa State University.

Marsh, J., Green, B., Kerney, B., Tangermann, S., and Tarditi, S. (1991) *The Changing Role of the Common Agricultural Policy*. London: Belhaven Press.

Nucifora, A., and Sarri, D. (1997). *Levels of Protection for the Fruit, Vegetables, Olive Oil and Wine Sectors of the European Union*. CIPAS Paper 19. University of Siena: CIPAS.

OECD (1997). *Agricultural Policies, Markets and Trade in OECD Countries: Monitoring and Evaluation*. Paris: OECD.

OECD (1997). *Statistics on Microcomputer Diskette. PSE and CSE*. Paris: OECD.

Tarditi, S. (1997). *The Impact of the Agricultural Price Policy on EU Cohesion*, Background paper, Cohesion report. Bruges: College of Europe.

Tarditi, S., Marsh, J., and Senior, S. (1995). *Agricultural Strategies for the Enlargement of the European Union to Central and Eastern European Countries*. European Commission, Directorate Genera 1. Brussels.

Tarditi, S., Thomson, K., Pierani, P., and Croci Angelini, E. (eds.) (1989). *Agricultural Trade Liberalization and the Common Agricultural Policy*. Oxford: Clarendon Press.

World Bank (1996). *Commodities Markets and the Developing Countries*. Washington, D.C.: World Bank.

Zanias, G. (1996). *The Impact of the Price and Market Part of the CAP on EU Cohesion*. Background paper, Cohesion report. Bruges: College of Europe.

7

Transport Policy

FRANCIS MCGOWAN

7.1. Introduction

Transport policy has been a long-standing concern of the European Union: responsibilities were embodied in the treaties of Paris and Rome and the first attempts at policy
were made in the 1950s. The priorities and objectives have changed over time but the
outcomes have for the most part been relatively modest. Within that framework, cohesion has only occasionally been a priority. Yet aspects of the common transport policy
have had a significant effect upon cohesion and continue to do so.

The main objective for transport policy from a cohesion perspective ought to be the
reduction of geographical peripherality, a factor which is reflected in relatively higher
costs and poorer quality of provision. The main means of tackling this objective has
been to improve infrastructure thereby reducing costs and increasing access. European
policies—especially financial ones—have been particularly important in seeking to
alleviate the disparities of infrastructure endowment between member states as well as
between regions in the EU. European policies tackle other aspects of transport, such as
support for new technologies, control of environmental externalities, and improvements in safety. While these initiatives may have an impact on cohesion, potentially the
most important aspect of policy is one which has only become salient in the last ten
years—the completion of the internal markets.

This chapter assesses the impact of EU transport policies on cohesion, focusing on
two key areas of policy which are likely to have the most signficant effect: infrastructure
provision and market liberalization. While EU policies ought to ensure a reduction in
peripherality and an increase in convergence, the extent to which they do so is debatable. The chapter will examine the development and impact of EU policies in the light
of recent theoretical and empirical research. After a brief overview of some general
characteristics of transport policy I review the specificities of the sector, the rationale
and content of European interventions, and the impact of policies. In my assessment of
this impact I distinguish between financial and non-financial policies, with the emphasis in the former on infrastructure-related support and in the latter on liberalization. I
conclude with a consideration of the overall effectiveness of EU transport policies upon
cohesion[1].

This chapter is based on a report prepared for DG XVI. The author acknowledges the contributions of
Alasdair Young and Wolfgang Stehmann to those earlier reports. He also thanks Commission officials and
editors, particularly Ronnie Hall, for their comments and suggestions.

7.2. The Political Economy of Transport Policy

Transport forms the backbone of modern societies. While it is a modest cost input for most economic activities and constitutes a significant item of household expenditure in its own right, its importance can only really be judged by the effects of a serious disruption of provision. The absence of transport is likely to prevent the production or distribution of almost all economic activity and jeopardize a good quality of life. The transport sector is characterized by a physical infrastructure, a network of roads and tracks with particular economic properties. It consists of a set of long-term and capital-intensive assets, the investment and operation of which have required coordination and planning. The networks themselves constitute near-natural monopolies while other aspects, such as service provision, are often closely integrated with the monopolistic components or are themselves highly concentrated. As such they require some form of economic regulation. Regulation is also often needed to tackle the significant negative externalities associated with their development and operation (emissions, residues, congestion, safety, etc.).[2]

Given these characteristics, it is hardly surprising that governments have been closely involved in planning and regulating (and even owning) these activities. Moreover, governmental intervention in the transport sector has often been intended to meet broader public interest objectives such as social, industrial, and regional policies. Yet, in addressing market failures in transport, governments have themselves fallen short in their performance. Aside from poorly executed policies, many critics of the record of public policies on transport have highlighted the dominance of producer concerns and argued that policies and structures have been overly protective of incumbents and have fostered inefficiency. From this vantage point, claims about the special nature of the transport sector have been seen as largely the special pleading of vested interests. The solution, instead, has been to open the sectors to competition wherever possible and regulation only where necessary, allowing market forces to perform many of the tasks hitherto provided or controlled by the state.[3]

Whether one agrees with it or not, this critique is important because it underlies the types of reforms which have been taking place in the sector since the 1980s at both the national and the European levels. The shift from a producer to a consumer perspective is central to the prominence of market liberalization in recent transport policy initiatives (even though the shift in emphasis towards regulation is not unproblematic).[4] The emphasis on the overall gains rather than the sectoral impact of market-led transport

---

[1] For space reasons this chapter focuses on the cohesion countries rather than on regional and social cohesion. However many of the conclusions are applicable to poorer and peripheral regions and marginalized social groups.

[2] On the general characteristics of infrastructures see World Bank (1994). On the regulatory aspects see Crew and Kleindorfer (1986).

[3] For accounts of the shifting balance in policies see Veljanowski (1987), Swann (1988), and Bishop, Kay, and Mayer (1995).

[4] The classic text on regulatory capture is Stigler (1971). On EU regulation see McGowan and Seabright (1995).

policy means that it is the broader effects of such policies on the overall economy (and thereby on cohesion) which are highlighted in this chapter rather than the short-term but serious adjustments which have to made within the sector itself.

The transport sector has been undergoing radical changes in recent years. But how does this shift affect cohesion? One might expect the change to encourage productivity improvements, lowering costs and facilitating convergence. But how does market liberalization resolve the persisting market failures, particularly those associated with lagging development?

7.3. EU Transport Policy and Cohesion

7.3.1. *The EU transport endowment*

While the EU transport sector is important in its own right, accounting for about 4 per cent of GDP and employing over 5 million, for those not directly employed in the industry its importance derives from its position as either a factor of production or an item of consumer expenditure (see Table 7.1). In both respects, moreover, that significance increasingly depends on the quality of the service provided: rapid and reliable transport provision is essential for competitiveness in a range of agricultural and industrial sectors while access to safe and well-maintained transport infrastructure and services is essential for a good quality of life (Nijkamp, Reichman, and Wegener 1990).

As noted, an objective of cohesion policy has been the reduction of peripherality through improvements of the networks on which passenger and freight services depend. In terms of both infrastructure and services the endowment in the cohesion countries is generally agreed to be below that in the rest of the EU. Moreover, due to a mix of geographical and economic factors, the cohesion countries find themselves as more or less peripheral 'spokes' within these networks. While levels of investment in transport infrastructure have generally been higher in the cohesion countries in recent years, this reflects a catching-up process reflecting both the poorer position of infrastructure in those countries and the contribution of EU financial support. In this section I review the transport 'endowment' in the EU, noting overall trends in the main sectors and contrasting the situation in the cohesion states with that in the rest of the union.

The overall demand for goods and passenger transport has risen steadily over the last years but there have been important differences between sectors. Road and air transport have shown the strongest growth rates with rail and to some extent shipping being slower (see Table 7.2). As a result there have been significant shifts in the transport modal shift to the advantage of motor and air transport (see Table 7.3). This bias is particularly acute in the cohesion member states.

The road transport sector has been the most dynamic part of the transport market, in terms of growth in both traffic (passenger and freight) and infrastructure. In terms of infrastructure endowment, road networks across the Community have developed considerably with much of the growth in the motorway sector: between 1980 and 1996 the network increased by nearly 50 per cent (see Table 7.4). For cohesion countries the

Table 7.1. Transport and the economy

1995 (except [a] and [b]) % of total	GDP	Employment	Household spending
Austria	3.9	6.0	13.3
Belgium	6.8	5.0[b]	11.1
Denmark	6.9	5.3	15.5
Finland	2.7	5.0	13.5
France	3.6	4.0	14.0
Germany	3.0	3.8[a]	13.9
Greece	—	5.3	
Ireland	2.9[b]	3.3	11.4
Italy	4.8	5.4	10.7
Luxembourg	—	4.5	20.0[c]
Netherlands	4.7	5.4[a]	11.5
Portugal	4.2	3.4	14.3
Spain	3.5[a]	3.2[a]	11.4
Sweden	3.2	5.1	14.3
UK	6.0	4.0	15.2

[a] 1993
[b] 1994
[c] includes communications

Source: Eurostat: National Accounts ESA: Detailed Tables by Branch.

Table 7.2. Transport growth trends, EU–15

Passenger, m.p/kms[a]	Cars	Buses	Urban rail	Rail	Air	Total
1980	2,349	338	40	253	96	3,075
% 1980/70	4.0	2.5	0.4	1.6	8.4	3.7
1990	3,317	355	48	274	204	4,198
% 1990/80	3.5	0.5	1.8	0.8	7.8	3.2
1996	3,748	366	42	279	290	4,726
% 1996/90	2.1	0.5	−2.2	0.3	6.1	2.0

Freight, m.t/kms[b]	Road	Rail	Waterway	Pipeline	Total
1980	665	287	108	93	1,154
% 1980/70	4.4	0.2	0.2	3.4	2.6
1990	944	256	109	77	1,386
% 1990/80	3.6	−1.1	0.1	−1.9	1.9
1996	1,159	219	111	86	1,575
% 1996/90	3.5	−2.6	0.3	2.0	2.2

[a] Million passenger kilometres
[b] Million tonne kilometres
Percentages refer to annual average change.

Source: DG VII Transport in Figures, 1998.

Table 7.3. Transport modal split
(% shares)

Passenger	Cars	Buses	Urban rail	Rail	Air
1980	76.4	11.0	1.3	8.2	3.1
1990	79.0	8.5	1.1	6.5	3.1
1996	79.3	7.7	0.9	5.9	6.1
1996		Cars/bikes	Bus	Urban rail	Rail
Austria		74.6	11.5	1.7	10.7
Belgium		82.2	11.0	0.7	6.0
Denmark		79.9	13.6	—	6.4
Finland		81.5	12.8	0.6	5.1
France		86.6	5.2	1.1	7.1
Germany		84.0	7.8	1.0	7.2
Greece		92.4	5.5	0.7	1.5
Ireland		90.9	6.4	—	2.7
Italy		82.3	10.6	0.6	6.5
Luxembourg		83.8	10.2	—	6.0
Netherlands		83.3	8.1	0.8	7.8
Portugal		84.9	10.7	0.4	3.9
Spain		84.9	10.0	1.1	4.1
Sweden		84.1	8.4	1.4	6.1
UK		88.5	6.2	1.0	4.2
EU–15		84.9	8.2	0.9	6.0

Freight	Road	Rail	Waterway	Pipeline
1980	57.7	24.9	9.4	8.1
1990	68.2	18.4	7.9	5.5
1996	73.6	13.8	7.0	5.5
1996	Road	Rail	Waterway	Pipeline
Austria	42.4	34.2	5.4	18.1
Belgium	75.0	12.7	9.6	2.6
Denmark	82.9	6.2	0.0	10.9
Finland	72.7	26.6	0.7	0.0
France	67.2	21.0	2.4	9.3
Germany	66.2	15.9	14.4	3.4
Greece	98.1	1.9	0.0	0.0
Ireland	90.6	9.4	0.0	0.0
Italy	85.3	9.2	0.1	5.4
Luxembourg	71.2	18.4	10.4	0.0
Netherlands	58.2	2.9	33.2	5.6
Portugal	90.3	9.7	0.0	0.0
Spain	91.9	5.0	0.0	3.0
Sweden	62.4	37.6	0.0	0.0
UK	85.0	7.5	0.1	7.3
EU–15	73.6	13.9	7.0	5.5

Source: DG VII Transport in Figures, 1998.

Table 7.4. Motorway network
(km)

	1980	1990	1996
Austria	869	1,470	1,607
Belgium	1,192	1,666	1,674
Denmark	516	601	880
Finland	204	225	431
France	5,264	6,824	8,300
Germany	9,225	10,809	11,300
Greece	91	190	470
Ireland	0	26	80
Italy	5,900	6,185	6,439
Luxembourg	44	78	115
Netherlands	1,773	2,092	2,360
Portugal	132	318	710
Spain	1,933	4,425	7,293
Sweden	850	939	1,330
UK	2,573	3,181	3,344
EU-15	30,566	39,029	46,333
EU-4	2,156	4,959	8,553
EU-11	28,410	34,130	37,780

Source: DG VII Transport in Figures, 1998.

endowment of road infrastructure is much lower than elsewhere in the Community, a factor which adds to the costs, and detracts from the quality, of transport in these countries. In recent years, however, investment in motorways has increased. As a result, road transport is likely to remain the principal mode of freight transport in these countries.

As Table 7.3 shows, in the road passenger sector, the bulk is carried out through private car transport though there is also a significant if declining role played by public road transport for short- and long-distance traffic. While car ownership is on the increase across the Community, there are still very marked differences from country to country with the cohesion countries having the lowest car ownership rates (Spain being an exception). At the same time, however, accident levels are higher in these states than elsewhere in the EU (see Table 7.5).

Road haulage is the most important means of transporting goods within the European Union, and the trend is for it to become increasingly so: road haulage accounted for 74 per cent of inland freight transport in the EU, and over 90 per cent in the cohesion countries, in 1996 (see Table 7.3). The transport of goods by road takes place overwhelmingly over short distances: in 1995, 60 per cent of all tonnage transported travelled 50 kilometres or less. Despite the international road haulage market growing faster than the domestic market since the mid-1980s, in 1991 just 3.5 per cent of goods transported by road crossed national boundaries. Road haulage accounts for a significantly larger

Table 7.5. Car ownership and accident levels

	Cars/'000	Deaths/'000
Austria	458	150
Belgium	424	143
Denmark	329	111
Finland	379	86
France	477	145
Germany	501	116
Greece	223	195
Ireland	272	121
Italy	571	114
Luxembourg	559	166
Netherlands	370	86
Portugal	277	217
Spain	376	147
Sweden	413	65
UK	369	64
EU-15	444	119
EU-4	323	164
EU-11	475	110

Source: DG VII Transport in Figures, 1998.

share of inland transport in the cohesion countries than it does in the rest of the EU (Bayliss and Coleman 1994).

The European air transport market has enjoyed considerable growth over recent decades.[5] Air traffic operations are widely dispersed across the EU though a high proportion of operations are concentrated on a relatively small number of hub airports in both the scheduled (regular passenger services, with a high proportion of business travel) and charter (seasonal services concentrating on holiday destinations) markets. For the cohesion countries, air transport markets have been as important as elsewhere in the Community, not least because key market segments are focused on the Mediterranean states and because air transport is important for domestic travel given long distances and poor road and rail links. However, the overall robustness of the market in terms of growth levels cannot detract from the fact that cohesion countries are relatively less well connected into European networks, in part a function of geographical and economic peripherality and relatively lower population densities (see Table 7.6). Moreover, the quality of air services (as reflected in travel delays) is poorer for services involving most cohesion countries due to relatively poorer air traffic control infrastructure.

Rail transport within the European Union has undergone a significant decline over much of the postwar period as a result of its failure to overcome a vicious circle of poor

[5] In this chapter we are concentrating on passenger traffic, the largest section of the air transport market.

Table 7.6. Air traffic in the EU

	Traffic to Country (m. passengers)	Population (m.)	Ratio
Austria	6.64	8.0	0.830
Belgium	9.16	10.1	0.907
Denmark	7.82	5.3	1.475
Finland	3.74	5.1	0.733
France	23.48	58.1	0.404
Germany	41.55	81.7	0.509
Greece	15.17	10.5	1.445
Ireland	8.37	3.6	2.325
Italy	19.91	57.2	0.348
Luxembourg	0.94	0.4	2.35
Netherlands	13.67	15.5	0.882
Portugal	8.37	9.9	0.845
Spain	46.68	39.2	1.190
Sweden	8.42	8.8	0.957
UK	59.48	58.6	1.010
EU-15	273.33	373.2	0.732
EU-4	78.59	63.2	1.244
EU-11	195.74	310.0	0.630

Source: DG VII Transport in Figures, 1998.

demand and supply conditions. On the demand side, its relatively inflexible characteristics *vis-à-vis* other modes has meant it has lost out to private motor transport in freight and some passenger (short–medium haul) markets and to air transport in longer-haul passenger transport. In passenger terms the decline has been relative, as modest growth in passenger movements has been overtaken by much stronger growth in other modes: share of passenger traffic has declined from 8.2 per cent in 1980 to 5.9 per cent in 1996. In freight terms, the decline has been absolute and the loss of market share correspondingly more acute, falling from 24.9 per cent to 13.8 per cent (see Table 7.7). On the supply side, high costs of maintenance and investment have affected overall performance. Whereas road networks have expanded considerably over the period, rail networks have decreased in size as low-use lines have been closed and very few new lines have been constructed (the main exceptions are high speed routes in some member states and urban networks in a number of cities across the Union) (CEC 1995c).

   Against this general background of overall decline, the cohesion impact is mixed. For cohesion countries there are quite wide divergences in outcomes (passenger growth has been low in Portugal, modest in Greece, and high in Ireland and Spain, while freight transport has been low in all countries except Portugal). The shortcomings of the rail network in cohesion countries are most apparent when one considers infrastructure indicators. With the exception of Greece, all the cohesion countries have systems based

Table 7.7. The EU rail network

	1980 (km)	1990 (km)	1996 (km)	Electrified (%)	Gauge
Austria	5,847	5,624	5,672	60	1,435
Belgium	3,978	3,479	3,380	73	1,435
Denmark	2,015	2,344	2,349	17	1,435
Finland	6,096	5,867	5,881	35	1,524
France	34,382	34,260	31,852	45	1,435
Germany	42,765	40,981	40,826	45	1,435
Greece	2,461	2,484	2,474	0	1,435
Ireland	1,987	1,944	1,945	2	1,600
Italy	16,133	16,086	16,014	64	1,435
Luxembourg	270	271	274	95	1,435
Netherlands	2,760	2,798	2,739	73	1,435
Portugal	3,588	3,592	2,850	22	1,668
Spain	13,542	12,560	12,284	56	1,668
Sweden	11,382	10,801	10,923	68	1,435
UK	18,490	17,406	17,128	30	1,435
EU-15	165,696	160,497	156,591	47	n.a.
EU-4	21,578	20,580	19,553	39	n.a.
EU-11	144,118	139,917	137,038	48	n.a.

Source: DG VII Transport in Figures, 1998.

on non-standard gauges, which present interoperability problems. The proportion of the network served by a single track is much higher than in the rest of the union (80 per cent compared with 53 per cent average). Taken together these factors point to a poorer standard of service in cohesion countries. Moreover, one of the few promising areas of the rail system—the development of the high speed rail network is unlikely to have a major impact on the cohesion countries. Only Spain has an embryonic high speed system—the AVE between Seville and Madrid—and this has yet to be integrated into the much larger high speed network. Indeed, that network is by definition focused on the Euro-core, with only limited direct connections to cities on the periphery. As with all hub-and-spoke systems, such peripheral access is to one or two core cities only while, conversely, any one hub location can access many peripheral places (ECMT 1995).

Shipping is responsible for the bulk of the Community's external trade and a good share of its internal trade (I do not consider inland waterways transport because of its limited relevance for the cohesion countries). Maritime shipping—both short sea and longer-distance traffic—is closely linked to the levels and structure of international trade. For the most part, trade has been on the increase while, over the last decade or so, shipping costs have been generally low. Market conditions should have fostered growth and cohesion, and falling transport costs could be seen as increasing the competitiveness of imports against the industrial and agricultural sectors of cohesion countries and

Table 7.8. EU shipping industry

	Total controlled fleet (no.)	Total controlled fleet (tonnage)	% Foreign flagged (no.)	% Foreign flagged (tonnage)
Austria	45	0.6	38	79
Belgium	137	4.1	96	100
Denmark	575	12.3	33	42
Finland	149	3.1	32	64
France	217	7.6	42	45
Germany	1,388	17.2	69	65
Greece	2,821	1,150	68	60
Ireland	40	0.2	23	14
Italy	546	11.1	26	35
Luxembourg	2	0	23	14
Netherlands	508	5.2	28	39
Portugal	44	0.9	27	58
Spain	207	2.8	42	51
Sweden	343	13.9	45	85
UK	641	20.1	68	80
EU-15	7,663	214.1	57	61
EU-4	3,282	118.9	62	60
EU-11	4,381	95.23	53	63

Source: DG XVII, Transport in Figures 1998.

regions (Krugman and Venables 1990, 1995). Unlike other transport sectors, however, the bulk of this trade is carried out by non-Community operators: the sector is international in a way that other transport markets are not. Most of the fleet is flagged to non-EU countries (even though many of the shipowning companies may themselves be European). It should be stressed, however, that the flag fleet is only one part of the industry. A number of shipping services, from chartering to port operations, are based inside the Community—some estimates indicate that these account for more of the value added in the shipping sector than the carriage of goods itself—and contribute to economic growth in their own right.

The cohesion states diverge quite widely in their shipping industries (see Table 7.8). Both Ireland and Portugal have small shipping sectors which seem likely to shrink further, despite their positions on the Atlantic periphery and dependence on trade, while the Spanish fleet has also undergone substantial decline over the years. By contrast, the Greek fleet—which has always been the largest single fleet within the Community—has maintained a strong presence in world shipping (CEC 1996*d*).

The cohesion countries are at a distinct disadvantage in terms of port facilities: lower levels of efficiency (partly due to less investment) contribute to slower turnaround of cargoes and high freight charges. Moreover, the technical trends in the sector—allied with local and national government support in the core countries—are likely to reinforce the peripherality of cohesion country ports. The Community's freight transport systems—along with maritime transport and to a lesser extent air transport—are increasingly seen as part of a single multi-modal transport system for many freight markets. Containerization and other transportation innovations, such as roll-on/roll-off shipping, have provided a means of easing the transfer of freight between transport modes, providing cost, timing, and other advantages. The advantages are particularly important for trade with the rest of the world (where container shipping now accounts for much of non-bulk transport) and for trade around the Community. There is, moreover, a potential benefit for peripheral regions and countries as they provide a means of circumventing long land-based transportation (the normal length for a viable multi-modal journey is 600 kilometres compared with a Community average of 200 kilometres). However, given that handling infrastructure is critical to the success of multi-modal systems, the relatively underdeveloped facilities in most cohesion countries leave them at a disadvantage to other countries. Moreover, even as facilities are developed, it may be that the centralizing tendencies in multi-modal transport will reinforce the peripherality of cohesion country ports. Yet the incentives to develop facilities may increase given that centralization may bring serious environmental and economic disadvantages. The development of a small number of ports as multi-modal hubs (Rotterdam being the prime example) creates long road journeys through congested areas—enhancing ports elsewhere in the EU may be beneficial environmentally as well as economically (CEC 1995*d*, CEC 1997*c*).

7.3.2. *The development of EU transport policy*

Initiatives on European transport policy are as old as the Community itself—a section of the Paris Treaty explicitly dealt with the transport of coal and steel. Moreover, at least since the EEC Treaty was signed, the contribution of transport to economic development in poorer parts of the Community was recognized explicitly. Cohesion has not always been to the fore in the substance of European transport policy, however, figuring only sporadically in initiatives. Instead, it was primarily in the context of EU regional policy that a cohesion dimension to transport policy emerged. Indeed, in many respects it has been the contribution of Structural Funds which has had the most significant impact on the peripherality of cohesion countries and regions. In the wake of a renewed commitment to a single market in transport, however, the impact of such liberalization on the provision of services in poorer regions and countries has raised the question of how transport policy affects cohesion.

An analysis of treaty provisions and Commission proposals for a common transport policy (CTP) draws attention to one overarching rationale for Community involvement: the achievement of an integrated European economy requires an open transport market free of entry barriers and discriminatory practices. Given the predominance of such measures in most member states at the time of signing the treaties (and for many years after), a European policy could be justified as necessary to shift the centre of gravity of policy away from protection and support of local producers (and, as noted, it appears that national policies were historically skewed in this direction). By extension, any exceptions to the general thrust of policy (and the measures which we now associate with cohesion might be regarded as such) would of necessity have to be agreed at a European level. Given the broader objectives of the treaties (before as well as after the articulation of cohesion as an explicit treaty objective) and the specific provisions of the transport chapters, such considerations were recognized as a legitimate component of policy. As a result, the Common Transport Policy could have embraced a much wider range of measures than a purely market-oriented approach would imply (Abbati 1987, McGowan 1998*b*).

Article 74 of the Rome Treaty (now Art. 70) embedded the CTP in the broader goals of the Community while Article 75 (now Art. 71)—ostensibly concerned with liberalization and an end to discrimination in transport markets—allowed a derogation 'where the application of provisions concerning the principles of the regulatory system for transport would be liable to have a serious effect on the standard of living and on employment in certain areas and on the operation of transport facilities'. Furthermore, the provisions of Article 80.2 (now Art. 76.2) designed to curtail government support, required that the Commission also take into account 'the requirements of an appropriate regional economic policy and the needs of underdeveloped areas'. Taken together, these provisions indicate that, long before the Maastricht Treaty and even before the accession of Ireland, Greece, Portugal, and Spain to the EC, Community transport policy was expected to take account of the exigencies of what we now refer to as cohesion, albeit as exceptions to a general principle of liberalization.

Given the original focus of the Rome Treaty (and the conduct of the ECSC transport policy), European transport policy was largely concerned with intra-EC modes and with the transport of freight rather than people. The main modes covered were road haulage, rail, and inland waterway. Article 84 (now Art. 80) of the Treaty explicitly excluded air transport and maritime transport because they were based on 'international' and, in the case of air transport, 'passenger' markets. It might be argued, however, that omitting these cartelized and protected markets from the treaty suited most governments and established firms. The coverage of the CTP was, therefore, significantly circumscribed (Abbatti 1987).

In any case—and despite the prominence of the issue in the original treaties—the effects of the CTP were very limited, since it proved hard to secure the agreement of member states to Community policies or even to implement those policies which had been agreed. Proposals for policy in the 1960s and 1970s generally stressed harmonization over liberalization, yet the differences between member states and their reluctance to accept a major role for the Community prevented very much of substance being achieved (Lindberg and Scheingold 1970, McGowan 1998*b*). To the extent that European transport policy measures were agreed, they did not provide much scope for addressing cohesion-type concerns except indirectly with regard to infrastructure. The question of infrastructure finance raised important questions of cost allocation and introduced measures recognizing regional considerations (such as the Public Service Obligations in inland transport). Moreover, as subsequent regional policy initiatives emerged, they included financial support for transport infrastructure.

By the 1980s, the logjam in the CTP began to shift (not least because of a court judge-ment upholding a parliamentary complaint against the Council's lack of progress in the matter). In particular, the single market initiative, by giving considerable emphasis to the transport market, advanced the CTP's objectives of liberalization and harmoniza-tion (CEC 1985). The White Paper's provisions on service sector markets gave pro-minence to transport and included a number of initiatives (most of which had been proposed some years before but had failed to secure Council approval), allowing the freedom to provide services (in road haulage, inland waterways, maritime transport, and air transport). Along with proposals to remove other barriers to a single market (notably in the field of customs inspections), the single market initiative shifted the balance of transport policy toward liberalization.

With an accelerated drive towards a single transport market, it might have been thought that cohesion considerations would have been neglected. However, much of the legislation took account of cohesion concerns quite explicitly. The freedom to pro-vide services in airlines, maritime transport, and road haulage was limited by deroga-tions designed to support the underdeveloped regions and member states (see below), slowing the application of policies to allow for adjustment by local producers.

Overall, 1992 marked a turning point for the CTP. The progress made in legislating for the removal of barriers and an internal market enabled the Community to address other aspects of transport policy, in particular the issues of the environmental con-sequences of transport supply and use, the promotion of a truly integrated European transport system and the pursuit of social and economic cohesion. Moreover, the Treaty of European Union's refocusing of objectives for the Union changed the terms on which a CTP should be based. The Maastricht Treaty entrenched economic and social cohesion as an explicit objective of the EU, building on the earlier Single Act amend-ments which brought cohesion into the treaty. Moreover, the provisions on trans-European networks, by explicitly referring to the objective, reinforced the link between cohesion and transport in the treaty.

Yet the evolution of the CTP over the 1990s revealed a certain ambiguity towards cohesion. It was addressed in the Commission's 1992 White Paper on a Common Transport Policy, though the main emphasis in the proposals was that of 'sustainable mobility' (CEC 1992*b*). The problems of cohesion states and regions are touched upon primarily in the light of comments on infrastructure (e.g. TENs, EIB loans, Structural Funds). Moreover, issues which would normally arise in the context of social cohesion have also been addressed. Labour conditions—both in terms of health and safety and of working hours—have been tackled extensively, as have employment issues, while access for the disabled has also been given attention. However, the incorporation of cohesion into subsequent policy initiatives has been rather limited. In the Commission's programme of action to implement the Common Transport Policy, cohesion was not articulated as a focus for initiatives (and even explicit discussion is limited). Instead, the programme was designed around the goals of quality improvement, the single market, and external policy (CEC 1995*b*).

More recently, however, the Commission has sought to improve the profile of cohe-sion in transport policy. A report published in 1998 stressed the importance of transport policy in reducing disparities across the EU but recognized that more needed to be done to achieve this, giving cohesion a higher profile in EU transport policy. The report stresses the need for a more balanced approach to infrastructure funding and places greater emphasis on public transport and improving access to it. The underlying analysis also seems to imply that the principles behind infrastructure development and market liberalization may be examined more carefully for their effects on cohesion (CEC 1998*d*). More generally, recent initiatives on transport policy appear to be more mindful of the cohesion dimension (a prime example being the proposals for fair and efficient infrastructure charges). While these developments indicate that the Commission is aware of a failure to address the issue in the past, it remains to be seen whether future initiatives can be as 'cohesion-friendly' as intended, given the potential for conflicts with other transport policy objectives.

7.3.3. *The impact of EU transport policies*

In this review of EU transport policies I focus on the main financial and non-financial initiatives. The account of financial policies concentrates on those programmes which have the improvement of basic transport infrastructure as one of their objectives—taking together the relevant aspects of Structural and Cohesion Fund policies and of Trans European Networks—though I also touch upon the transport dimension of European R&D programmes. On non-financial policies, the focus is on specific initiatives towards sectors, with liberalization as the principal concern.

7.3.3.1. *Financial policies*

Infrastructure. Over much of the history of the Community, funds in the form of either grants or loans have been available from European institutions to support the construction of new, or the upgrading of existing, transport infrastructures. Loans from the European Investment Bank have fostered investments across the Community while grants from European Structural Funds have underpinned projects in less developed regions across the Community (CEC 1997*h*). Since 1994 there has been an additional Cohesion Fund, which has targeted transport infrastructure (along with environmental programmes) within the four cohesion countries (CEC 1997*a*). In addition, the Trans European Networks initiative, which has focused on transport to improve infrastructure linkages between member states, has been backed up by a modest financial package (CEC 1998*c*). Increasingly, however, this mixed package of financial support, largely based on Structural Funds, has provided significant backing for the improvement of transport networks with some programmes, explicitly targeting cohesion states while others have a regional or trans-border focus. In my analysis of this aid, I outline the incidence and the impact of support in order to establish who has received the funds in the first instance and then to consider whether these have had a positive effect, both issues being considered in the context of cohesion.

Structural Funds must dominate any assessment of the cohesion effects of Community policies. Funds for transport investment totalled 13.7 billion ecus in the period 1994–9, equivalent to 15 per cent of the total Structural Funds budget. Most of these

Table 7.9. Funds available for transport TENs
(million ecus)

	1993–94	1995	1996	1997	Total
Loans	4,028	3,310	3,021	4,943	15,302
Guarantees	76	85	303	55	519
Aids					
Structural funds	884	115	2,639	527	4,165
Cohesion funds	1,887	1,208	1,088	1,901	5,984
TENs funds	385	240	280	352	1,257

Source: Commission of the European Communities, Annual Report.

funds (70 per cent) were allocated to roads (70 per cent) with 16 per cent for railways. While these resources were distributed to those regions across the Community that meet the required criteria, they have been particularly important in supporting developments in the cohesion states. Along with the dedicated resources of the Cohesion Fund, these resources have been essential to improving motorway and secondary road networks in all the cohesion countries, though they also have been used for other major projects (urban public transport in Athens and railway improvements in all four countries, airport facilities in Ireland and Greece and port facilities in Portugal). Overall, they have constituted a major proportion of total expenditure on transport infrastructure in those countries.

Although it has become a bone of contention between and within EU institutions and member states, the financial resources provided for the TENs programme itself are much smaller than those offered by the structural and cohesion funds. These dedicated finances are intended to support feasibility studies and other preliminary activities rather than the core funding of the projects themselves. However, as noted, the TENs scheme has been conceived strategically, with the overall EU contribution to TENs consisting of support from the funds as well as loans and guarantees from Community sources. Taking this broader view, a total of just over 10 billion ecus in grants has been allocated to TENs transport projects in the period 1993–7. Of this, roughly half was allocated in the form of cohesion funds (see Table 7.9).

The cohesion states, therefore, seem to be net beneficiaries of EU initiatives (given that they are the principal recipients of structural funds and the only recipients of cohesion funds). However, we need to consider whether and how such support has improved the position of the cohesion countries—in other words, has it helped to facilitate the convergence of the cohesion economies with the rest of the EU?

Assessing the impact of infrastructure will depend upon what criteria are adopted. For example, many calculations of the effects of TENs distinguish between the financial returns of a project and the broader socioeconomic returns for the country or region overall, with the latter substantially increasing the level of returns to be expected from such schemes (CEC 1997*d*). Others, including the Commission, have drawn attention to the additional international benefits of cross-border infrastructure investments. Most nationally based assessments of project viability focus on the gains for the national economy and do not consider the wider economic impact of projects. These 'international' elements of the socioeconomic return of a project may add as much as a quarter to the return on investments (mainly for projects which are substantially international) (Roy 1994). Just as important, particularly with cohesion considerations in mind, is where those benefits are likely to be felt. Do the benefits of new infrastructure in an economically poorer member state or region accrue to that territory?

In order to illuminate this issue—and to draw attention to the various aspects of the impact of infrastructure development—it is useful to distinguish between the following effects of support for new or upgraded transport infrastructures:

> immediate impact in terms of construction and other employment at the time of the project in hand;
> reduced costs for users (fuel, labour and stock costs);
> derived demand (new business established because of improved transport linkages);
> improved journey times and expanded market access (reduced peripherality).

The first of these provides a welcome but short-lived boost to the local economy. However, while many of the benefits are derived locally or within the country, it may be that much of the value added on major capital projects (civil engineering and equipment) will be sourced elsewhere.

Other factors have been the focus of much debate in recent years, as analysis has sought to take into account the longer-term economic effects of infrastructure. Potentially, many of these benefits are enjoyed in the regions and countries where the infrastructure is located. However, the matter is one where not only the scale of the effects but the effects themselves are contested. Whose costs are reduced? Where are new businesses located? Who gains from reduced peripherality?

In this light it is worth noting recent debates on the economic effects of infrastructure. Whereas much of the older debate focused on the benefits of infrastructure for a region or urban area, the recent literature has focused more on how such investment might raise the productivity of private capital (Aschauer 1989, Munnell 1993). Although measurements of the scale of this effect varied considerably, a core estimate suggested that every dollar of public infrastructure investment increased the productivity of a dollar of private sector investment by 30 per cent (Button 1998). On the other hand, there are a range of views which dispute not only the scale of effects but also the nature of causality. There is a question over whether it is the infrastructure that generates jobs, income productivity, etc. or whether the infrastructure follows economic development (Hurst 1994, Bruinsma and Rietveld 1998). In addition, others note that infrastructure is important for growth and investments only in certain circumstances. If the infrastructure is 'national', which facilitates international relocation, then growth will focus within the country. If, on the other hand, the infrastructure is international, there is less chance of relocation. Transport infrastructure may fall into this second category. Nor is it clear where the benefits accrue. Recent work on regional infrastructures suggests that, once a certain qualitative level is established, the new investments may benefit businesses outside the region as much as they benefit businesses where the infrastructure is constructed (SACTRA 1998, Venables and Gasiorek 1996).

Bearing in mind the increasing controversy over the effects of infrastructure investment, it is surprising that the implications are not reflected in most empirical assessments of the impact of EU infrastructure policy. Even in these generally positive assessments, however, it is possible to discern some cause for concern, particularly about the relative benefits of policy.

At the time of writing, a comprehensive analysis of the effects of EU funding on transport infrastructure was not available. An attempt to gauge the overall effects of the TENs programme was published in 1997, though it provides only EU-wide data (CEC 1997*d*). Not surprisingly, it suggests that the macroeconomic effects are highly positive —a cumulative GDP gain of 560 billion ecus up to 2030 from completion of the Essen projects (the initial batch of priority projects highlighted in the TENs programme) and increases in employment (up to 230,000 permanent jobs from the Essen projects and over 1 million from the total TENs programme).[6]

Estimates of the impact upon member states are provided in analyses of the economic effects of the high speed rail network (CEC 1995*f*). According to this analysis, construction of the high speed rail network (which includes the TENs projects in cohesion countries plus a number of other routes in cohesion and non-cohesion countries) would create 5.6 million jobs across the Community over the period 1990–2010, equivalent to 0.18 per cent of employment over that period. The employment created in the cohesion countries ranged from 0.02 to 0.20 per cent of total employment. In terms of growth, the boost given by these projects would be equivalent to 2.3 per cent of Community GDP with effects in cohesion countries ranging between 0.4 per cent and 5.6 per cent. The short-term effects of these projects would be relatively modest in Greece and Ireland, reflecting the more limited scope of these projects (and the problems for those countries which are not physically connected to the Community) while the benefits for Spain and Portugal are greater. However, for this and other infrastructure projects the longer-term effects of investments should also be taken into account. The assessment points to longer-term sources of growth and employment from such projects. It has been estimated that the European high speed rail network will contribute an additional 1.5 per cent to GDP and employment equal to 0.5 per cent of the workforce by 2010 (see Table 7.10).

Accessibility is one of the most important measures of the impact of transport infrastructure. A study prepared for the Commission examined the average travel times to 194 economic centres by road, rail, and air and considered the impact of projects planned in 1992. Noting that the areas with the poorest accessibility were the south and west peripheries of Europe (effectively the cohesion countries but with some other regions), the study concluded that the biggest improvements in average travel times—

---

[6] It should be noted, however, that these figures—and the underlying methodology—have been criticized. See SACTRA (1998).

Table 7.10. Impacts from the high speed rail network 1990–2010

	Employment (m.)	% of total	Value added (% of total)
Temporary:			
Europe	5.60	0.18	2.27
Greece	0.06	0.07	2.05
Spain	0.53	0.20	2.92
Ireland	0.01	0.02	0.40
Portugal	0.14	0.13	5.62
Permanent:			
Europe	0.72	0.46	1.54
Greece	0.01	0.12	0.95
Spain	0.09	0.66	2.64
Ireland	0	0	0
Portugal	0.02	0.34	3.91

Source: European Commission, *High Speed Europe* (CEC 1995*f*).

Table 7.11. Improvements in markets due to TENs

Major cities: core (%)		Major cities: periphery (%)		Medium cities: core (%)		Medium cities: periphery (%)	
Paris	5	Madrid	20	Liege	61	Cuenca	10
Frankfurt	11	Barcelona	20	Utrecht	35	Umea	11
Brussels	28	Lisbon	16	Lille	29	Alexandropoulous	11
Amsterdam	19	Athens	26	Odense	61	Mede	5

Source: European Commission UTS study.

equivalent to an average reduction of more than 20 minutes—would be in these areas (along with pats of former East Germany and France) (BFLR 1992).

An updated assessment of accessibility examined the fourteen TENs projects and concluded that implementation of the existing TENs programme would generate a 20 per cent increase in the population accessible on a daily round trip (see Table 7.11). This average conceals considerable divergences between different types of agglomeration. The biggest gains would be cities located near new projects where links had been poor (improvements of between 80 and 800 per cent are noted here). This category included some major cities in cohesion countries. The next most important gains are for centrally located medium-sized cities (30–60 per cent increase), followed by large cities in cohesion and other countries (between 16 and 26 per cent). Cities in remote areas and some very large cities which already enjoy good infrastructure would show the smallest gains (10 per cent and under) (MCRIT/INRETS 1995).

In terms of accessibility, therefore, while cohesion capitals would see their situation improving at levels slightly greater than those in core countries, smaller cities—many are in remote areas—would see the smallest gains, particularly when compared against equivalent cities close to the 'hub' of the TENs network. Such effects can only really be countered by further investment in secondary routes in cohesion countries. However, such improvements might be judged to be insufficiently economic (even the motorway projects are likely to show substantial underutilization in the short term).

While there is a debate on the contribution of infrastructure to productivity, the broad consensus indicates a positive effect. If so, the cohesion states have been beneficiaries of these policies. Support from Structural Funds for transport infrastructure have constituted a significant proportion not only of transport infrastructure but also of infrastructure spending as a whole (10 per cent in Greece, 15 per cent in Portugal, and 20 per cent in Ireland in the period 1989–93). If the analyses of infrastructure's contribution to GDP are correct, then these increases are likely to have given a small but significant boost to the economies of the cohesion countries.

Overall, then, to the extent that Structural Funds are used to benefit intra- and inter-regional infrastructures, they contribute to regional cohesion. However, there is some evidence that, within cohesion countries, the funds are skewed toward more prosperous regions. There are concerns about the impact of TENs on regions, particularly those regions on the peripheries of national networks, unless additional resources are provided to improve linkages between the TENs and other parts of the network. Also, there must be concern about access to the TENs if they are expected to meet full costs of provision. In addition, there may be risks of skewing infrastructure investment towards TENs and related projects and away from less economically attractive but socially necessary elements in the network (Whitelegg 1992).

In the past, many of the benefits of Community financial policies were focused on larger markets (major airports, trunk routes, etc.). Such development may have created serious problems for regions on the periphery of national networks, in rural areas or other 'uneconomic' routes. The focus of current policies is mixed. In some cases there has been some refocusing of Structural Funds upon secondary routes, for example, in Portugal, where investment will shift from high capacity roads to a greater emphasis on local roads, cutting journey times by between twenty and thirty per cent.

Estimates of the economic effects of infrastructure spending suggest that conscious skewing of investment can yield important cohesion benefits (though perhaps at the expense of overall growth). Research into infrastructure improvements in Spain suggests that infrastructure helps reduce the dispersion of income. According to this analysis, Structural Funds have added two points on average to regional productivity and reduced dispersion of regional output/worker by 5 per cent (Villaverde Castro 1995). Another analysis, which points to the link between transport infrastructure and economic growth, notes the wide degree of dispersion but suggests that to favour these areas would be to pull down overall growth (de la Fuente and Vives 1995).

Research and Development. Another major area of EU funding is research and development. Transport has accounted for a modest proportion of Community research and development efforts in recent years, though the amounts are larger if programmes involving transport equipment (new designs and materials funded through BRITE/EURAM, Basic Research in Industrial Technologies for Europe/European Research in Advanced Materials) and telecommunications industries (telematics for road transportation though DRIVE/ATT, Dedicated Road Infrastructure for Vehicle Safety in Europe/Advanced Transport Telematics) are also included. The aims of Community research on transport are to foster an efficient, safe, and environmentally friendly transport sector, to facilitate interconnection and interoperability of the transport networks, to promote better design and management of infrastructures and to provide better decision-making and planning techniques. The focus for transport-specific research as been EURET (European Research on Transport) and the current work programme focuses on strategic research and the optimization of networks (CEC 1994, 1995*e*).

The impact of Community transport R&D upon cohesion is mixed, depending upon how far actual cooperation and participation in the programme or benefits from innovations are taken as the measure for success. In terms of resources received from R&D programmes, groups in cohesion countries received less than 2 million ecus out of 22 million ecus funded from the EURET programme in the period 1991–4. In terms of participation rates for EURET programmes in the 1994–8 period, groups from cohesion countries accounted for 411 out of 2,431 in responses to the first invitation to tender (see Table 7.12). Such figures, of course, give no indication of the level of participation within particular consortia. Moreover, it appears that many of these groups are academic rather than industrial groupings. Indeed, it is unlikely that industries in cohesion countries will be well placed to innovate in the highly technology-intensive areas of new transport innovations. And while many innovations will ultimately transfer to transport networks within cohesion countries, most of the value added will be derived elsewhere (though, of course, the benefits will be available to cohesion countries).

7.3.3.2. Non-financial policies

So far we have been concerned with those EU transport policies that are driven by financial resources. Yet, as is well known, expectations for such policies have to be qualified by recognition that the EU budget is limited. In contrast, the EU's regulatory significance is much greater, given the primacy of EU law and its use in supporting key EU objectives. Indeed, much of the European legislative activity—particularly with regard to transport—has been to define harmonization and liberalization measures, covering markets, technical standards, and safety and environmental issues. What, then, is the impact of such non-financial transport policies upon cohesion?

Probably the most important policies in transport over the last few years have been those designed to open up transport markets to greater competition. As noted, these initiatives are part of a shift in transport policy thinking, where the market is seen as a way of improving the productivity of both capital and labour and of promoting innovation in service delivery. Such policies promise potentially large savings in the provision of transport services, but their benefits may be skewed, as well as having short-term adverse effects upon those groups which had benefited from the status quo.

Table 7.12. EU transport research participation by country

	EURET 1991–4 ('000 ecus)	EURET 1994–8 (no. of projects)
Austria	0	69
Belgium	676	102
Denmark	4,070	60
Finland	0	76
France	7,422	287
Germany	2,193	331
Greece	900	160
Ireland	97	38
Italy	1,983	328
Luxembourg	0	0
Netherlands	1,543	185
Portugal	65	55
Spain	798	158
Sweden	0	118
UK	2,290	366
EU-15	22,037	2,443[a]
EU-4	1,860	411
EU-11	20,177	1,993

[a] Includes projects involving non EU participants.

Source: CEC DG VII.

Although liberalization has been a key feature of EU transport policy since the mid-1980s, in effect extending the principle of the internal market to the transport sector, there is nothing particularly new about the objective of a common transport market. What is new is both the emphasis on liberalization (rather than harmonization—though that is still important in some sectors) and the fact that liberalization measures are being agreed upon and implemented by the member states (Banister and Button 1991). These policies are generally regarded as being of overall benefit but at the expense (which it is hoped will be short-term) of certain groups and regions: cross subsidies to non-economic services may be cut while workforces may be reduced. Partly because of these effects, EU transport policies have also allowed—under certain conditions—derogations and exceptions designed to ease the adjustment to open transport markets. These relate to subsidies and public service obligations and cohesion considerations have figured in their design.

Given the perception that the prevailing transport industries were highly regulated and relatively inefficient, there were high expectations that liberalization would deliver significant benefits. Deregulation in the US over the 1970s and 1980s had, apparently, stimulated considerable efficiency gains in the industry as well as economic and service benefits for consumers, and it was hoped that similar effects would be achieved in the EU, since the industries were regarded as at least as protected as their American equivalents (Winston 1993). From a cohesion perspective such changes could have had a mixed outcome, with gains for consumers offset by the removal of subsidies to uneconomic routes. In practice, however, the results of liberalization have been modest at best. The persistence of other barriers to trade (linguistic and financial, in particular), coupled with the piecemeal approach to reform and the protection of publicly owned incumbents, have, with only a few exceptions, diluted the impact of the policies. Here we review developments in the different subsectors of the transport market.

Air transport—where liberalization was completed after ten years of negotiation in 1997 (though largely in place by 1993)—has seen some modest changes, mainly because drawn-out liberalization processes and substantial support to otherwise loss-making flag carriers seem to have deterred new entrants in some markets. Even so, there have been some achievements, with tangible impacts on the cohesion countries. A recent survey of the effects of liberalization (Civil Aviation Authority 1998) draws attention to an increased number of airlines offering scheduled services (up from 126 to 141 over the period 1992–7). A bigger increase has been seen in the number of independent operators able to compete with incumbent flag carriers (up from 21 to 34; see Table 7.13). This increase in operators has contributed to a significant intensification of competition on some routes; the proportion of international EU routes where more than two operators compete has increased from 4 per cent in 1992 to 7 per cent in 1997. This figure understates the impact of such changes because entry has been focused on the densest routes (where the share has increased from 12 per cent to 26 per cent). Competition has also increased on domestic routes; the proportion of services operated by two or more airlines has increased from 10 per cent to 19 per cent of routes. Price reductions have been most apparent on these more competitive routes, where incumbents have had to respond to lower prices charged by entrants, notably the 'no frills' operators.

These changes have been particularly apparent in cohesion countries. A number of new airlines have begun operations, affecting competition. In Spain approximately one-third of domestic routes are served by more than one carrier while competition on international routes has also increased in Ireland and Portugal. Flag carriers in cohesion countries have undergone significant restructuring (staff reductions have been amongst the largest in the EU—down 31 per cent at TAP, 28 per cent at Olympic, and 24 per cent at Iberia, compared with an average reduction of 9 per cent among flag carriers). Such changes have translated into lower fares for international services from Lisbon, Madrid, and Athens, among the lowest in Europe, while domestic competition has also ushered in new—and lower—fares. It could be argued, however, that the scale of changes in the cohesion countries (excluding Eire) is a function of the lack of adjustment before 1992. Whereas other states began to encourage competition in earlier phases of liberalization, it was not until the last phase that change occurred in Spain, Portugal, and Greece (see Table 7.13). Regardless of the timing, however, there have been some important benefits for air transport users in the cohesion countries.

Liberalization of road transport is more or less complete. The policy had been pursued in tandem with the harmonization of technical and operational standards (largely

Table 7.13. Development of EU air transport operators since liberalization

	No. of airlines		Independent jet operators	
	1992	1997	1992	1997
Austria	5	5	1	0
Belgium	2	5	1	0
Denmark	8	8	2	1
Finland	5	3	0	0
France	23	14	3	4
Germany	13	21	1	7
Greece	1	1	0	0
Ireland	3	4	1	2
Italy	8	13	1	4
Luxembourg	1	1	0	0
Netherlands	8	7	0	0
Portugal	4	4	0	1
Spain	5	11	1	3
Sweden	12	11	2	3
UK	20	27	6	7
EU–11	113	121	19	28
EU–4	13	20	2	6
EU–15	126	141	21	34

Source: Civil Aviation Authority.

at the request of richer member states who had feared losing market share to cohesion firms if the playing fields for working conditions and taxation were not levelled). Assessments of liberalization suggested that increased cross–border trade and competition in domestic markets (the latter only fully in operation in July 1998) would reduce costs by 4 per cent. However, this gain would be more than offset by additional costs associated with harmonization policies (CEC 1997*f*).

The effects on cohesion countries have been even more modest. The increase in competition appears to have been very limited (the very peripherality of the markets has blunted the emergence of competition). Indeed, in general neither the fears of northern hauliers of being swamped by low–wage southern hauliers, nor the concern of southern hauliers of losing out to more efficient northern hauliers, have been realized. Although southern hauliers have lower operating costs than their northern counterparts, these are not as great as the difference between wage levels would imply. The wages and subsistence costs of Spanish hauliers are, for example, about 20 per cent lower than for German hauliers, but their total operating costs are only 10 per cent lower (due to the operational and logistical advantages of northern hauliers). As in air transport, lower labour costs have not translated into significant advantages for cohesion country operators.

Rail transport is still very much in the process of being liberalized. Although the first steps to prepare the sector for competition were settled in 1991, there has been relatively little take-up of even the limited provisions agreed at that time (CEC 1996*b*). Ambitious Commission plans for extending competition (in the 1996 White Paper) have been scaled down in a proposal to amend the 1991 package. As a result, assessment of the impact is still largely speculative. We can derive a sense of the effects from the reforms in some member states (all northern)—some improvement in performance (though in the UK this is not unconnected with a doubling of the level of subsidies) but very little competition. How quickly the rest of the EU will move is debatable; outside those states which have liberalized, the performance of the industry remains very poor, not least in the cohesion states.

However, there could be grounds for concern should liberalization take effect, with poor prospects for existing rail networks after restructuring. In 1983 the British government commissioned an inquiry into railway finance in the UK which outlined a range of scenarios for the industry on the basis of different financial assumptions (specifically, the amount of government subsidy available) (Serpell 1983). The most extreme scenario was for a commercialized network (i.e. one running without the need for subsidy and meeting a modest—public sector—rate of return). This would result in a network 16 per cent the size of the then current (1982) network, carrying 44 per cent of the passengers and 25 per cent of the freight. Since the UK was—even then—by no means the poorest performer in the EU rail sector, such effects might be replicated in other states. By making the cost structures of railway operations more transparent, liberalization is unlikely to favour the sector's development in cohesion states if experience with reforms elsewhere in the Community is any guide. The privatization process in the UK—following a period of internal rationalization in the public sector—has reduced the service commitments which operators have to meet while reforms in Germany, the Netherlands, and Sweden have also brought into question the extent of operations (though in all countries reform is at a very early stage). Starting from a less advantageous position, the railway sector in cohesion countries will be subject to rationalization pressures which are at least as great as those in the rest of the EU.

In the maritime sector, EU policies have not really been driven by liberalization, since markets are either already open to competition (in bulk trades) or shielded from competition with EU agreement (liner trades). Liberalization is taking place mainly in the realm of cabotage services for freight and passengers. So far the effects on cohesion of this policy have been limited since a number of countries—including the Mediterranean cohesion countries—have enjoyed significant exemptions from legislation in this area, allowing for a phased introduction of cabotage to services. Results so far—relating to a liberalization of just over 10 per cent of the market—suggest that the effects have been limited both in terms of employment (local workforces had feared large job losses) and economy (CEC 1997*e*).

Overall, the effects of liberalization have been modest both for the EU as a whole and the cohesion countries. However, there is a widespread concern that as liberalization takes hold, there may be adverse consequences for those parts of the transport network which are less dense. An important consideration for European transport policy—

and for national transport policies—has been the maintenance of services which are (if viewed in isolation) 'uneconomic' (i.e. where the revenues derived from the provision of a service do not cover the costs of its operation). Routes of low density, particularly where infrastructure costs are large, present a policy dilemma, being financially unviable but desirable on regional or social grounds. In many countries and across most modes, this conflict is resolved primarily on the basis of equity considerations (whether on the grounds of providing an essential service or on the grounds of tackling peripherality), though in some cases the benefit which accrues to the network or the economy as a whole is also highlighted. Where such a service is supplied, there is a subsidy, explicit or implicit. In the past, an implicit public service obligation was placed upon the service provider, which required the operation of an otherwise uneconomic service on the basis of a cross-subsidy from profitable services. Increasingly, however, the public service obligation is transparent and explicit subsidies are provided by government. In both cases the service is operated in the context of an exclusive contract, whether local, regional, or national (CEC 1996c).

Although aspects of public service were included in EU policy early on (Henry 1993), it was not until the revival of attempts to liberalize transport markets that the question of subsidy and public service became more acute. The closer matching of prices to costs and greater competition implied by liberalization required that such supports be identified and justified. There may be further changes to the operation of the public service principle in transport, as noted in the Green Paper on the Citizens' Network and in the recent White Paper on the Railways (CEC 1995a, CEC 1996b). Thus, while PSOs have been used in a number of national settings, including the cohesion states, it is not clear how tenable they are in terms of EU rules or national budgetary tolerances.

7.4. Conclusion

How have European policies on transport affected cohesion? For the most part, EU policies on transport clearly have been focused on other objectives. Cohesion has not been a primary objective of the Common Transport Policy for much of the history of the Union. Yet the concerns which common policies have aimed to address have indirectly affected cohesion. Market liberalization is expected to bring about convergence in costs and prices, benefiting poorer states and regions as much as richer ones (through lower transport costs in terms of tariffs and intermediate inputs). Where there are 'market failures', the funding of infrastructure and the provision for public service obligations should help tackle deficiencies in networks and support 'uneconomic' but socially necessary services.

In the last few years, a more conscious effort has been made to look at transport policies from the perspective of cohesion. The Commission's 1998 report on transport and cohesion (in 1993 and 1998) indicates a willingness to address cohesion head-on. A final judgement on the effect of cohesion depends on how well transport policies address the two key issues of peripherality and productivity. Here the nature of the markets in the sector suggests different outcomes.

In the case of infrastructure support, it is clear that EU funds will improve the links between cohesion countries and the rest of the EU, but the consequences may vary. While new transport infrastructure will reduce costs, the effects are likely to be unpredictable. Growing scepticism over the ability of new infrastructure to generate employment (beyond a basic level) suggests that new links may help others export to cohesion countries as much as the other way round.

Liberalization is, on the surface, likely to lower costs within the cohesion countries without the more ambiguous effects associated with infrastructure development. However, two conflicting problems are apparent. The first relates to the extent of the effects of liberalization. It appears that the effect of liberalization has not been as dramatic as proponents have claimed would be the case. In part this may be due to the piecemeal way EU reform has taken place, with significant exemptions and derogations. Yet the effects of more radical liberalization—in member states and elsewhere—have skewed effects. Workforces and some groups have lost out while the benefits to the bulk of consumers have been relatively modest. Given the special conditions enjoyed by the cohesion states, it remains to be seen how liberalization will affect the cohesion countries.

References

Abbati, C. (1987). *Transport and European Integration*. Commission of the European Communities.

Aschauer, D. (1989). Is public expenditure productive. *Journal of Monetary Economics* 23: 177–200.

Banister, D. and Button, K. J. (eds.) (1991). *Transport in a Free Market Economy*. Basingstoke: Avebury.

Bayliss, B. and Coleman, R. (1994). Road Freight Transport in the Single European Market: Report of the Committee of Enquiry. Luxembourg: Office for Official Publications of the European Communities.

BFLR (1992). Accessibility and Peripherality of Community Regions: the Role of Highways, Long Distance Railway and Airport Networks. Report prepared for DG XVI.

Bishop, M., Kay, J., and Mayer, C. (eds.) (1995). *Privatisation and Economic Performance*. Oxford: Oxford University Press.

Bruinsma, F. and Rietveld, P. (1998). *Is Transport Infrastructure Effective?* Berlin: Springer.

Button, K. (1998). Infrastructure investment, endogenous growth and economic convergence. *Annals of Regional Science* 3: 145–62.

Civil Aviation Authority (1998). *The Single European Aviation Market: The First Five Years*. Cheltenham: Westwood.

Commission of the European Communities (1992b). The Future Development of the Common Transport Policy. Brussels: Commission of the European Communities.

—— (1994). European research and technological development in the field of transport. *EuroAbstracts* 32, no. 12.

—— (1995a). *Citizens Network*. Brussels: Commission of the European Communities.

—— (1995b). *The Common Transport Policy Action Programme 1995–2000*. Brussels: Commission of the European Communities.

—— (1995c). *The Development of the Community's Railways*. Brussels: Commission of the European Communities.

—— (1995d). *The Development of Short Sea Shipping in Europe*. Brussels: Commission of the European Communities.

—— (1995e). *Euret Programme Evaluation*. Brussels: Commission of the European Communities.

—— (1995f). *High Speed Europe*. Luxembourg: Office for Official Publications of the European Communities.

—— (1996b). *Revitalising Europe's Railways*. Brussels: Commission of the European Communities.

—— (1996c). *Services of General Economic Interest in Europe*. Brussels: Commission of the European Communities.

—— (1996d). *Towards a New Maritime Strategy*. Brussels: Commission of the European Communities.

—— (1997a). *Annual Report of the Cohesion Fund 1996*. Luxembourg: Office for Official Publications of the European Communities.

—— (1997c). Green Paper on *Sea Ports and Maritime Infrastructure*. Brussels: Commission of the European Communities.

—— (1997d). *The Likely Macroeconomic and Employment Impact of Investments in Trans-European Transport Networks*. Brussels: Commission of the European Communities.

—— (1997e). *Report from the Commission to the Council on the Implementation of Council Regulation 3577/92 Applying the Principle of Freedom to Provide Services to Maritime Cabotage (1995–6) and on the Economic and Social Impact of the Liberalization of Island Cabotage*. Brussels: Commission of the European Communities.

—— (1997f). *Road Haulage. Single Market Review*, Subseries 2, vol. 5. Luxembourg: Office for Official Publications of the European Communities.

—— (1997h). *The Structural Funds in 1996: Eighth Annual Report*. Luxembourg: Office for Official Publications of the European Communities.

—— (1998c). *Trans-European Transport Network: Report on Progress and Implementation of the 14 Essen Projects*. Brussels: Commission of the European Communities.

—— (1998d). *Transport and Cohesion*. Brussels: Commission of the European Communities.

Conrad, K. and Seitz, H. (1994). The Economic Benefits of Public Infrastructure. *Applied Economics* 26: 303–11.

Crew, M. and Kleindorfer, P. (1986). *Economics of Public Utility Regulation*. Basingstoke: Macmillan.

de la Fuente, A. and Vives, X. (1995). Infrastructure and education as instruments of regional policy: evidence from Spain. *Economic Policy* 20: 11–40.

European Conference of Ministers of Transport (1995). *Why Do We Need Railways? Proceedings of an International Seminar*. Paris: ECMT.

Henry, C. (1993). Public service and competition in the European Community. *Oxford Review of Economic Policy* 9: 45–66.

Hurst, C. (1994). Infrastructure and growth: a literature review. *EIB Papers* 23: 57–69.

Krugman, P. and Venables, A. (1990). *Integration and the Competitiveness of Peripheral Industry*, CEPR Discussion Paper no. 363. London: CEPR.

—— (1995). Globalisation and the inequality of nations. *Quarterly Journal of Economics* 110: 857–80.

Lindberg, L. and Scheingold, S. (1970). *Europe's Would-be Polity: Patterns of Change in the European Community*. Hemel Hempstead: Prentice-Hall.

McGowan, F. (1998). Transport policy. In A. El-Agraa (ed.), *The European Union: History, Institutions, Economics and Policies*. Hemel Hempstead: Prentice Hall.

McGowan, F. and Seabright, P. (1995). Regulation in the European Community and its impact on the UK. In M. Bishop, J. Kay and C. Mayer, eds., *The Regulatory Challenge*. Oxford: Clarendon Press.

MCRIT/INRETS (1995). *UTS Study*. Report prepared for DG VII, Brussels.

Munnell, A. (1993). An assessment of trends in and economic impacts of infrastructure investment. In B. Stevens and W. Michalski (eds.), *Infrastructure Policies for the 1990s*. Paris: OECD.

Nijkamp, P., Reichman, S. and Wegener, M. (eds.) (1990). *Euromobile: Transport, Communications and Mobility in Europe: A Cross-National Comparative Overview*. Aldershot: Avebury.

Roy, R. (1994). *Investment in Transport Infrastructure: The Recovery in Europe*. Rotterdam: ECIS.

SACTRA (1998). *Transport Investment, Transport Intensity and Economic Growth: Interim Report*. London: Sactra Secretariat.

Serpell, D. (1983). *Railway Finances*. London: HMSO.

Stigler, J. (1971). The theory of economic regulation. *Bell Journal of Economics*. 2: 3–20.

Swann, D. (1988). *The Retreat of the State*. Hemel Hempstead: Harvester.

Veljanowski, C. (1987). *Selling the State*. London: Weidenfeld.

Venables, A. and Gasiorek, M. (1996). Evaluating regional infrastructure: a computable equilibrium approach (mimeo). London: LSE.

Villaverde Castro, J. (1993). Regional disparities in Spain: recent evolution, causes and prospect. *Journal of Regional Policy* 13/3–4: 437–56.

Whitelegg, J. (1992). *Transport for a Sustainable Future: The Case for Europe*. London: Belhaven.

Winston, C. (1993). Deregulation: days of reckoning for microeconomists. *Journal of Economic Literature* 31: 1265–89.

World Bank (1994). *World Development Report 1994: Infrastructures for Development*. Oxford: Oxford University Press.

8

Telecommunications Policy[1]

DAVID YOUNG, OLIVIER LÉON, ACHILLEAS KEMOS,
PETER M. HOLMES AND MAURICE A. BASLÉ,

Telecommunications policy in the EU was left mostly to member states until 1983, when the European Commission established its task force on international telecommunications and telecoms. In 1987, the Commission produced a Green Paper which mapped out a path for the development of an EU policy over the subsequent decade.

The point of departure had perhaps more to do with competitiveness than cohesion. It had become widely accepted that technological change was threatening to erode two sets of boundaries: between monopolistic national markets on the one hand, and between different parts of the information technology and (tele-)communications business on the other, as the AT&T decision in the US indicated. The member states acknowledged a key role for EU-level policies, recognizing the need for both deregulation and 're-regulation' to ensure that asymmetries were not created by the uneven pace of liberalization. It was also clear that many of the new services linked to traditional telecoms would now have to be provided on a pan-European basis and that some common regulatory (or free market) solution would have to be accepted by all.

At the same time, it was widely acknowledged that the role of telecommunications in supporting the EU integration process in all its dimensions was central. EU institutions thus became centrally involved in ensuring that telecoms could actively play its new role in reducing the significance of geographical distance within the EU, while also ensuring that the new freer market environment did not adversely affect other aspects of social cohesion. The emphasis on the provision and regulation of traditional services (see Deacon 1995) has given way to a preoccupation with ensuring that Europe is able to fully exploit the opportunities offered by the emerging Information Society, from the point of view of both competitiveness and cohesion.

Here, we look at EU policies only in terms of their impact on cohesion. We attempt, where possible, to examine the effects on cohesion among individuals or social groups, among member states and among sub-national regions. It is impossible to give accurate quantitative estimates for several reasons. Telecommunications services are at the same time consumer goods and intermediate services for business; telecoms policy, therefore, has both direct and indirect effects. The impact of increased competition on peripheral regions, for example, is very hard to gauge until we know how each actor has finally

---

[1] This study was substantially completed in late 1997 and therefore analyses the potential cohesion impact of EU telecommunications policy on the eve of 'full liberalization', which took place on 1 January 1998. Since then, nothing has happened that would substantially alter our conclusions, although several significant developments are noted in the postscript to this chapter.

responded to the changes in prices and costs. Secondly, many other factors have affected the sector, including radical technical change and autonomous changes in national policies, which makes it very difficult to isolate the effects of EU policies. Thirdly, data limitations are a problem. Relevant indicators are not in general regionally disaggregated, while availability of cost and tariff data leaves much to be desired.

We seek to give quantitative indications of likely effects where this is feasible and to draw as many inferences as possible, but the reader is cautioned that the reasoning is necessarily tentative and often speculative as many measures have yet to bear full fruit. Our analysis of expenditure-based policies is retrospective, since many actions have been completed and their direct effects at least may be evaluated. Many key regulatory measures, however, have only recently been implemented with the full liberalization of EU telecoms on 1 January 1998, and the sector is still in transition. In many cases we must confine ourselves to analysing the broad direction of the impact of EU policies on cohesion.

The chapter is structured as follows. Section 8.1 gives a brief theoretical overview of the role of distance in economic activity and the implications for the impact of telecoms on cohesion. Section 8.2 examines the likely impact of telecoms liberalization and accompanying regulatory measures, including basic universal service. Section 8.3 looks at cohesion issues relating to trans-European telecom networks and the Information Society. Section 8.4 very briefly notes the role of Structural Fund expenditure on telecoms, and section 8.5 examines the cohesion impact of EU spending on RTD in telecoms. Section 8.6 concludes.

8.1. The Changing Role of Distance in Economic Activity

A full analysis of the role of telecommunications in the process of integration and cohesion requires some preliminary remarks on the changing role of distance in economic activity, in order to shed some light on the longer-term and indirect effects of developments such as liberalization, technical change, and the Information Society.

The theoretical model proposed by Krugman and Venables (1990) shows how complex the effects of removing barriers to trade can be. A fall in communications costs may be likened to the reduction of transport costs or the removal of other barriers to market access. It lowers production costs in both core and peripheral regions and reduces costs of communication in both directions, making it cheaper to supply the core from the periphery, but also vice versa. Consider first an initial situation, in industries where both economies of scale (intrafirm and external) and wage differences matter. Suppose there are two regions, a rich high-wage core and a poorer periphery: high barriers to market access may lead to all production being generated locally. But then a significant fall in transport costs may lead to concentration of production in the core: if the market in the periphery is much smaller, the scale or agglomeration economies available at the centre may make it worth paying the high wages there; lower wages in the periphery would not offset still non-negligible transport costs on all the sales back into the centre. But once overall barriers fall sufficiently or disappear, distance becomes irrelevant and production relocates to wherever it is cheapest. The periphery's advantage of lower wages, rents, and so on then comes into play; the centre can be easily supplied from any location.

A simple example may illustrate this: a firm establishes a freephone customer enquiry service in each city it serves, to avoid high long distance transmission costs. When long distance tariffs begin to fall, it may become economic to shut down services in peripheral regions and serve these areas from a single central location based in the city where its business is strongest. If the volume of business is much greater in the centre than in the periphery, it may be profitable to keep the service based in the centre even if wages are higher, as long as there are any significant distance-related charges. However, with a sufficient fall in long distance charges, and hence the cost of transmitting large quantities of information to and from the periphery, it will become profitable to serve the core from wherever labour costs are lowest and enquiry services will be established in low-wage areas (or areas where office rents are cheaper). Something like this does appear to be happening in telecoms.

There is not a perfect analogy between transport costs and telecoms tariffs, however. In many cases, fixed charges for access to the network will represent the barrier. Even if long distance call charges are falling, high or rising access tariffs may increase costs for some users, promoting reconcentration in core regions. While usage charges are likely to fall relative to prices in general, access charges will rise relatively, by most in peripheral areas with high infrastructure costs and low demand. Nevertheless, the comparison shows the essential ambiguity of the effects of lower communications costs and may be relevant to many service activities involving data processing. Of course, some data inputting may be relocated offshore to third world locations, bypassing the rest of the EU, but services involving actual telephone conversations are unlikely to move so far.

Liberalization is likely to lower costs everywhere, but initially the biggest effect will be where the greatest volume of activity is occurring. So, at first, core regions will gain most in terms of the cost savings for existing services and the ability to sustain new services and applications. In the medium to longer term, activity can be expected to relocate, and peripheral regions will gain in relative as well as absolute terms, provided that overall barriers (not just telecoms costs) fall enough. Thus, the effect of lowering distance-related telecoms tariffs depends in part on the height of other obstacles to market access, such as regulatory restrictions, lack of skill availability, or even transport costs.

However, since the marginal costs of telecommunication are very small, this is a sector where the final equilibrium is capable of reducing distance-related charges to practically zero. Hence, pro-cohesion effects should eventually be available, unless there are such major economies of agglomeration that services once established will not shift, or rising access charges effectively choke off provision or use of new services. The role of access charges may well reduce costs asymmetrically, until such time as they become very low for everyone. Such limited experience as there is to date indicates that for highly labour-intensive information services, a point does arrive in their product life-cycle where wage costs predominate.

Real problems arise if the network is asymmetrical: if the costs of establishing broadband or ISDN (Integrated Services Digital Network) links between areas, for example, are prohibitive. A more complex model could indeed generate complex multiple equilibria due to network externalities, which suggests it may be worthwhile building a network of connections to exceed a certain critical mass.

One further analogy with developments in transport should be noted. Distance may take new shapes, but it is still relevant. Physically remote locations can be made easily accessible by satellite links, but geographically closer locations may be bypassed by broadband links. Moreover, with developments such as just-in-time production, even very small differences in transport and travel times may take on added importance.

We should not, of course, confine our attention to the telecoms industry as such. Most of the telecoms and information services we are considering are intermediate products. Increased competitiveness of the centre due to falling telecoms costs will lower the costs of the periphery for the use of services that depend on telecoms. Given that these costs are likely to be relatively high initially, it seems likely that even as we move along the initial steps in the process described, industries in the periphery that use information services will benefit more than similar industries in the core, which may already have had access to such services.

We are, thus, left with a theoretical argument that the eventual impact of liberalization is likely to be positive, but with possible negative cohesion effects particularly in an intermediate phase when distance-related tariffs, though falling, still remain significant, when access costs in the periphery rise relative to the core, and while demand for telecoms related services in the periphery remains low. Of course, this discussion does not aim to complete the analysis of the consequences of technological change in telecoms on the significance of distance. The aim is merely to sketch out the shifting sands on which the additional impact of EU policies has to be assessed.

8.2. Liberalization

8.2.1. *EU telecoms liberalization: an overview*

Telecommunication in most EU countries has been run by national public monopolies for much of the century, and early EU liberalization was relatively cautious. Terminal equipment and value-added services[2] were liberalized first, and the Open Network Provision (ONP) framework was introduced to harmonize certain network offerings and thereby facilitate the provision of liberalized services. But the networks themselves, as well as public voice telephony (around 90 per cent of the services market at the time), remained the exclusive preserve of public monopolists unless member states chose otherwise.

Perhaps the main reason for caution was the fact that telecoms tariffs were (and remain) heavily cross-subsidized in two main senses:

---

[2] 'Terminal equipment' means telephones, fax machines, private switchboards, etc. Examples of value-added services include electronic mail or information/entertainment telephone lines.

- *Subsidized access*: network access (connection and exchange line rental) is subsidized by revenue from inflated call charges (especially long distance and international);
- *Geographical averaging*: uniform tariffs mean that low-cost, densely populated urban areas subsidize high-cost, remote rural and peripheral regions.

Full liberalization, it was thought, would allow new entrants to target the most lucrative clients who at present lose out from cross-subsidization—those who make many calls, especially in densely populated areas (e.g. large businesses in cities). This in turn would diminish the revenue available for subsidizing high-cost, low-usage customers. In other words, full liberalization would run counter to 'universal service'—or, broadly speaking, the notion that everyone should have access to telecommunication at an affordable price, regardless of geographical location.

Community policy since 1987 has been to encourage a gradual reduction in cross-subsidization (through 'tariff rebalancing'), in order to avoid a drastic realignment of tariffs when competition takes effect. It is hoped that gradual rebalancing together with a continuing reduction in overall costs and tariffs will mean that few people lose out in absolute terms (although of course, if some users gain more than others, there will still be implications for cohesion). Universal service is seen as something to be accommodated within a competitive environment, and the way in which this issue is addressed in the new regulatory framework will be an important factor in determining the impact of liberalization on cohesion.

By the end of 1994, the EU Council of Ministers had agreed on 'full' liberalization of telecoms services and infrastructure with a deadline of 1 January 1998 for most member states. A package of measures was adopted in 1996 and 1997 to update the Community regulatory framework (see Box 1). Although EU policy will only have a limited influence in member states where the industry was already liberalized (Finland, Sweden, and the UK), it has been a main driving force behind liberalization in the rest of the Union.

8.2.1.1. *Liberalization and the cohesion countries*

Telecoms networks in the four cohesion countries are on the whole less developed than in the rest of the Community. Greece, Ireland, Portugal, and Spain were thus granted the option of temporary derogations from certain liberalization measures, with a view to the 'reduction of regional disparities and the promotion of job creation in disadvantaged regions or those suffering from industrial decline' (Constantelou and Mansell 1994: 11). In the case of the 1998 deadline for full liberalization, the cohesion countries were able to request an extension of up to five years. However, only Greece requested the full term, of which the European Commission granted only three years. Full liberalization is due by 31 December 2000 in Greece, by 1 January 2000 in Ireland and Portugal, and by 30 November 1998 in Spain.

Delaying infrastructure and services liberalization in countries with less developed networks may make sense if the purpose is to allow these countries to catch up. Where telephone penetration is low, extensive cross-subsidy as a strategy for rapid network development may make more sense. Universal service goals retain an important

---

Box 1. Main legislative measures in EU telecoms liberalization and harmonization

1988 • Commission directive (88/301/EEC), opening up telecommunications **terminal equipment** markets.

1990 • Council directive (90/387/EEC). **Open Network Provision** (ONP) framework directive. Aimed at harmonizing access to public networks and services for liberalized services to run over.

   • Commission directive (90/388/EEC) introduces competition in telecoms **value-added services** (the main exception being ordinary voice telephony).

   • Council directive (90/531/EEC), opening up **public procurement** in the water, energy, transport and telecommunications sectors (followed by 92/13/EEC and 93/38/EC).

1991 • Council directive (91/263/EEC) on the **mutual recognition of conformity** of terminal equipment (amended by 93/68/EC, and supplemented by 93/97/EC for satellite earth station equipment).

1992 • Council directive (92/44/EEC), applying the ONP framework to **leased lines**.

1994 • Commission directive (94/46/EC) liberalizing **satellite** communications (amending directives 88/301/EEC and 90/388/EEC).

1995 • Parliament and Council directive (95/62/EC). The **ONP Voice** directive, applying ONP to voice telephony.

   • Commission directive (95/51/EC) on liberalization of **cable TV networks** for provision of already liberalized services.

1996 • Commission directive (96/2/EC) on liberalization of **mobile** and personal communications (amending directive 90/388/EEC).

   • Commission directive (96/19/EC). The **'full competition'** directive, which opens up voice telephony and telecoms infrastructure as well (amending directive 90/388/EEC).

1997 • Parliament and Council directive (97/13/EC) on **licensing**: a common framework for general authorizations and individual licences in telecoms services.

   • Parliament and Council ONP directive (97/33/EC). The ONP **interconnection** directive, setting out a regulatory framework for access to and interconnection of networks, also 'with regard to ensuring universal service and interoperability'.

   • Parliament and Council directive (97/51/EC), **adapting ONP** (the framework and leased lines directives) to a competitive environment.

1998 • Parliament and Council **revised ONP Voice and universal service** directive (98/10/EC).

---

economic element: installation and rental charges are kept low to stimulate line demand and network expansion, in part subsidized by monopolistic pricing of usage. Hence the cost of universal service in these countries is appreciably higher than in the rest of the EU.[3]

---

[3] One study found that for most member states, a rough estimate of the cost of universal service obligations (USOs) ranged from 0.5 per cent to 3 per cent of turnover, whereas for Spain the figure was 5 per cent, for Portugal over 7 per cent, and for Greece over 15 per cent (Analysys 1994). The figure for Ireland was 3 per cent, although network investment in Ireland is lower than in the other three countries, which suggests that USO costs may have to rise if Ireland is to catch up.

However, derogations from the timetable for liberalization only really make sense if the delay is used to extend universal service while at the same time rebalancing of tariff structures continues. Pending liberalization, there are concerns that incumbent operators will be allowed to focus their investment in areas where competition is expected to be fiercest, at the expense of less favoured regions. Of course, operators may still want to invest more heavily in core regions under liberalization, but at least then transparent schemes for the provision and funding of universal service, to which competitors may be asked to contribute, will have been set up.

8.2.2. *The effects of liberalization on cohesion*

Liberalization is expected to have highly beneficial effects on the economy at large, due to improved allocation of resources through reduction of monopoly power and tariff rebalancing, and also due to dynamic gains from the introduction of competition and rivalry. The question here is how any such gains are likely to be distributed among different groups in society and among EU countries and regions.

8.2.2.1. *The effects of liberalization so far*

Telecoms liberalization at the EU level began only in 1988 (see Box 1), with derogations for some countries, and is widely acknowledged to have been poorly implemented, especially as regards services. Hence one would expect only limited effects on cohesion to have materialized so far.

The liberalization of telecoms equipment markets and the opening up of public procurement could affect cohesion via its impact on industrial restructuring. Data at the regional level are unavailable, but in any case, the cohesion impact would be ambiguous. Regions or countries where the equipment industry is hardest hit may experience job losses in the short term, but in the longer term they may well be among the biggest gainers. Switching to more efficient equipment suppliers will generate the largest reductions in cost, and hence the largest benefits for telecoms operators and users.

One area where liberalization has had noticeable effects is mobile telecoms. Although EU-level liberalization has only recently been implemented, a strict application of the EC Treaty competition rules played an important part in opening up the sector at national level. Furthermore, EU policy on the standardization and harmonization of frequencies for mobile telecoms (notably GPS) has played a major role in mobile liberalization and has contributed greatly to the dynamism of the sector.

The effects on cohesion appear to be mixed. Reductions in tariffs and increased exploitation of scale economies have clearly brought mobile telephony to the mass market. It is affordable for many more firms and individuals in areas already served by mobile networks, and networks have been extended to cover far more of national territories. At the same time, however, mobile usage is still concentrated in core regions, and substantial benefits from tariff reductions will accrue here. Furthermore, mobile networks still do not cover the entire national territory in some countries. Benefits to peripheral regions may be concentrated in their least disadvantaged towns.

8.2.2.2. Tariff rebalancing

The main direct impact of telecoms liberalization on cohesion, certainly in the short term, will occur through tariff rebalancing. The attempt to link prices more closely to costs will lead to a rise in customer access charges,[4] at least as a proportion of the total bill, which will be unfavourable to both social and regional cohesion. Small and low-income users will lose out relatively. Less favoured regions also stand to lose out, since their per capita income is lower. Moreover, any geographical de-averaging of tariffs will raise access charges further in areas with low population density or difficult geographical conditions.

Removing cross-subsidy, however, will also lead to a substantial fall in long distance and international call charges. The marginal cost of calls is small, and the move to more cost-based tariffs will reduce the costs of communication to and from peripheral regions, which will probably be to their relative benefit. Although data on call patterns is not available, one would expect a higher proportion of calls made in a remote or less densely populated areas to be long distance than in a city (if only because the local calling area in a city is much larger). Hence, average *call charges* should fall by more in these regions. The impact on social cohesion is ambiguous. Higher-income individuals will benefit most in absolute terms since they will tend to make more long distance calls, but there is insufficient information to speculate on which groups would benefit most relative to their income.

Mark-ups on telecoms services between EU member states are particularly high and anomalous. Intra-EU calls generally cost far more than calls of comparable distance within one country, and can sometimes be as much as double the cost of an identical call in the opposite direction. From 1998, intra-EU calls will come under the same competitive rules as national calls, and tariffs stand to fall substantially, which is positive for cohesion among all EU countries.

Infrastructure liberalization is expected to substantially reduce leased line tariffs in Europe, which can cost several times the amount for a line of comparable distance in the USA. Indeed, tariffs are already falling and are especially low in member states where networks are already liberalized.[5] This will benefit mainly business users, but also customers of service providers who use leased lines, including Internet access providers. The effects on regional cohesion are mixed. A fall in leased line tariffs will initially benefit core regions more, since relatively more firms of sufficient size to use leased lines are located there. Users in all regions will gain through reduced subscription charges to on-line services. To the extent that a fall in tariffs means that local servers can be established in areas where this was previously uneconomic, there will be a positive effect on regional cohesion.[6]

---

[4] That is, a rise in the periodic line rental or subscription charges. Initial connection charges are not expected to rise, and may indeed fall, especially in areas where waiting times for connection are falling.

[5] See Tarifica (1996), exhibits 5 and 6, which show a clear fall in average EU tariffs for both voice grade and 2 Mbit/s lines.

[6] At one point, the lack of local Internet access providers in some rural and remote regions looked like a serious obstacle to the development of the Information Society. However, service providers are already establishing points of presence (or at least 'virtual' points of presence) in all local areas of a national territory (see OECD 1996: 40).

Local call charges are already low in most EU countries, in that mark-ups over cost are lower than for long distance calls. There is no reason on cost grounds why local call charges should rise with liberalization, but they may well do so in some countries, especially where they are currently very low. Competition will hit incumbents mostly in lucrative long distance markets, and they may be able to compensate in part by raising margins in the rather less enticing local market. The tendency appears to be for local call charges to rise in preparation for and in the early years of liberalization, but to fall quite sharply thereafter.[7] Large increases are certainly likely to slow down the development of information-based services.[8] At present, local call charges tend to be lower in the cohesion countries, and may be expected to rise more than elsewhere. On the other hand, the effect may be worse for densely populated urban areas where one would expect a higher proportion of calls to be made within the local area.

Tariff rebalancing thus has numerous effects on cohesion, both positive and negative. However, the net effect certainly looks likely to be negative, mainly because of the clearly negative effect of rising access charges. There are several qualifications to make, however, that suggest the impact will be softened, so that at least the worst potential effects (such as people being forced off the network by rising access charges) can be avoided.

First, the full extent and speed of tariff rebalancing is not clear. Grout (1996) provides rough estimates of efficient telephony tariffs based on a simple 'Ramsey' pricing model (Table 8.1). These should be treated with caution, as the calculation is based on several strong assumptions,[9] and should be regarded very much as an extreme scenario. As Grout (1996: 128) points out, tariffs are unlikely to reach efficient levels in practice because of 'universal service obligations combined with political and social objectives'.

Governments have prevented operators from rebalancing tariffs as quickly as they might have liked, precisely because of the political and social problems that this could entail. In France, for example, rentals *on average* would have to triple while long distance and international call halved in price; but rural depopulation is a sensitive issue and large increases in rural access charges are likely to be resisted. If rebalancing is spread over a number of years and overall tariffs continue to fall, the implications begin to look far less drastic than Table 8.1 might suggest. Nevertheless, even if low-usage and rural residential subscribers do not lose out in absolute terms, their bills stand to fall by a lot less than those of other users, which implies a negative impact on cohesion, both in terms of direct effects on income and indirect effects on job relocation.

---

[7] In the UK, local call charges rose substantially during the 1980s, but are now between 54 per cent and 74 per cent of what they were in 1984, when BT was privatized (Oftel 1997). They are also falling in Finland, and are free of charge in some liberalized countries, such as Canada and New Zealand.

[8] As in Italy, for instance, where the OECD's local call charge basket more than doubled between 1990 and 1994 (see OECD 1995a). Direct comparisons are difficult, owing to variations in the size of local calling zones and metering intervals, but recent data confirm a continued slight increase in local call charges in 1995–6 in all EU members except Finland, Ireland, and the UK (see Tarifica 1996).

[9] In this model, tariffs are equal to costs plus a mark-up set according to the elasticity of demand for each service. Both costs and demand elasticities are assumed, for linear demand functions and identical cost functions for all countries. Moreover, the model does not appear to take full account of demand interdependencies between access charges and usage, and may thus overstate the need to increase rental charges. See Grout (1996).

Table 8.1. Efficient telephone tariffs according to simple Ramsey pricing
(% of current tariffs)

	Rental charge	Local	National (300 km)	International
Finland	215	84	54	30
France	364	93	53	49
Germany	253	108	51	48
Ireland	208	99	47	47
Italy	300	100	50	52
Netherlands	209	75	60	37
United Kingdom	205	68	59	43

Source: Grout (1996).

   EU policy requires member states to allow operators to rebalance tariffs and adapt
rates that are not in line with costs. Where rebalancing could not be achieved by 1
January 1998, member states were to draw up a detailed timetable for the future
phasing-out of remaining imbalances, so that tariff structures would be in line with
'normal commercial practice' by 2000.[10] Judging by past experience, one might argue
that the 2000 deadline was unlikely to be met, but even if it is, the additional two year
period of leeway will help to soften the impact of rebalancing.
   Furthermore, some geographical averaging is likely to remain in most member states.
Community policy neither requires nor restricts de-averaging, but the ONP Voice
Telephony directive does specify that affordability must be maintained, particularly in
rural and high-cost areas, and that member states may use geographical averaging to
ensure this. Where de-averaging is permitted it will reflect cost differences and this is
bound to be to the relative benefit of urban users. However, basic infrastructure costs in
peripheral regions can be expected to fall by perhaps as much as 50 per cent with the
increasing use of fixed radio technology, which is effectively encouraged by the EU
framework.[11]
   Substantial progress on tariff rebalancing has been made in recent years. Table 8.2
shows how the balance between fixed and usage charges in the EU has changed in
recent years, and Table 8.3 gives the latest available figures. Rebalancing has generally
progressed further in countries where telecoms is already liberalized. Also notable is the
degree of progress made in Greece, Ireland, and Spain, although tariffs remain relatively
unbalanced in Greece, Spain, and Portugal. The ratios reported conceal large variations

   [10] The Full Competition directive allows provisionally for 'access deficit contributions' to be added to the
charges competitors will pay to interconnect with the incumbent's network, in order to share the costs of
'imbalances in voice telephony tariffs'. However, the Commission regards this as a temporary exception to
the Treaty competition rules, and has specified that access deficit schemes should be implemented until
1 January 2000 at the latest, and then only where rebalancing is subject to regulatory restrictions. Although
this is specified in the Commission's (1996a) guidelines on universal service costing and funding, access
deficit schemes should not be confused with universal service contributions.
   [11] To the extent that it establishes a liberal ('any to any') interconnection regime. Also, fixed voice telephony for universal service purposes (in the ONP Voice Telephony directive) is defined in terms of fixed user
locations, not terrestrial networks, and thus includes fixed radio access.

Table 8.2. Series index of the ratio of fixed and usage tariffs for residential users

	1990	1991	1992	1993	1994
Belgium	100	108.71	95.06	108.72	105.7
Denmark	100	90.64	95.47	95.47	95.47
Germany	100	89.24	89.13	89.13	89.13
Greece	100	46.73	48.71	34.21	49.76
Spain	100	66.2	66.19	66.17	66.07
France	100	87.14	87.13	87.12	70.55
Ireland	100	100.04	79.85	80.01	63.95
Italy	100	103.83	95.49	103.7	103.7
Luxembourg	n.a.	n.a.	n.a.	n.a.	n.a.
Netherlands	100	102.02	93.68	93.68	94.93
Austria	100	111.08	104.34	104.22	104.22
Portugal	100	96.82	96.74	101.59	93.21
Finland	100	74.94	49.39	48.02	49.56
Sweden	100	106.34	85.2	85.2	85.2
UK	100	87.55	82.79	79.31	71.6
EU-15	100	89.75	85.71	86.36	82.26

Note: The ratio is the OECD's usage tariff basket (comprising calls of various distances and length) divided by the fixed tariff basket. A fall in the index implies tariff rebalancing: rising access charges and/or falling call charges.

Source: OECD (1995*b*).

Table 8.3. Ratio between fixed and usage charges, January 1996

	Business	Residential
Belgium	3.97	1.21
Denmark	2.16	0.67
Germany	5.89	1.68
Greece	6.18	2.18
Spain	6.88	2.03
France	8.84	2.77
Ireland	4.21	1.20
Italy	7.00	2.52
Luxembourg	n.a.	n.a.
Netherlands	2.28	0.71
Austria	7.37	2.47
Portugal	7.71	2.20
Finland	1.50	0.52
Sweden	1.33	0.70
UK	2.42	1.02

Note: The ratio is the OECD's usage tariff basket divided by the fixed tariff basket. A high value implies unbalanced tariffs: relatively low fixed charges and high call charges.

Source: OECD (1997).

in overall costs, and tariff structures are unlikely to approach those of Finland and Sweden in the near future. In some cases, tariffs are unbalanced but access charges are already high, which will limit the scope for further rebalancing, especially if high operating costs are faced by competitors, or can be passed on to them via interconnection charges. Nonetheless, the difference between liberalized and non-liberalized countries shows the direction that tariff structures in the latter will have to follow.

Thus, tariff rebalancing is expected to have a negative impact on both regional and social cohesion, but the impact will be milder than a static economic analysis might suggest, for the reasons outlined. Assuming that overall bills continue to fall, a negative absolute impact can be ruled out for the vast majority of individuals and regions. For the cohesion countries, drastic rebalancing could be more risky, since it would reduce funds available for network development. It is therefore important that targeted tariff schemes are put into place as general cross-subsidy is gradually withdrawn, and that full use is made of alternative funds for network development, including the Structural Funds. The role of universal service policy will also be crucial in softening the impact of tariff rebalancing, as discussed in the next section.

8.2.2.3. Basic universal service

Universal service policy has traditionally been aimed at ensuring that everybody has access to basic voice telephony at an 'affordable' price, regardless of geographical location. The traditional means to this end (to the extent that it has been achieved) has been the type of extensive cross-subsidy described above. With liberalization, a key issue is how progress towards basic universal service is to be maintained and funded, given that extensive cross-subsidy is no longer viable.

The prominence of this issue reflects a recognition of the risks of untempered liberalization for those geographical and social groups which are particularly vulnerable to changes in tariff structures. The EU Council took the view that a liberalized market would be able to deliver universal service by itself in many cases.[12] Where operators were required to provide basic voice telephony at a loss, however, mechanisms might be put in place to ensure its provision and share the cost equitably among competing operators. The Council also recognized that account should be taken of the specific circumstances of peripheral regions with less developed networks and the role of the Structural Funds in this respect.

The cost of universal service obligations can be defined as the net loss incurred on basic services which operators are obliged to provide, but which they would not provide under normal commercial conditions. This gives a good indication of how much funding will be required to maintain current standards of universal service via targeted subsidy schemes. Recent studies have shown that the cost appears to be rather low for most EU countries.[13]

---

[12] Council Resolution of 7 February 1994 on universal service principles in the telecommunications sector, *OJ* C48.

[13] Analysis (1994) estimated that USO costs in 1992 ranged from 0.5 per cent to 3 per cent of turnover in most EU member states, and other studies have arrived at similarly low estimates (e.g. BTCE 1989, Oftel 1995a). However, estimates of USO costs for Greece, Portugal, and Spain are higher (see n. 3).

Targeted tariff schemes aim assistance at those who actually need it—that is, at those individuals, groups and regions who stand to lose out significantly from changes in tariff structures, and for whom the basic telephone service may otherwise become unaffordable. They may also attract new users, for whom the telephone service was previously unaffordable. Examples include rebates on line rental charges for those who make few calls, or direct subsidies for the purchase of a telephone to particular social groups (e.g. those receiving a state pension).

It is envisaged that new competing operators will contribute to universal service by providing USOs themselves and/or by contributing to USO costs incurred by incumbents. The precise details of how such schemes will work are not yet clear, and will differ among member states. If appropriate schemes are properly implemented and adequately funded, then it should be possible to maintain and even improve current standards of universal service. This will serve to dampen further any negative effects of tariff rebalancing on cohesion. Moreover, there is clear potential to improve social and regional cohesion by ensuring that current rates of progress towards truly universal service are maintained, and by ensuring continued convergence among member states. This applies particularly to the cohesion countries, where telephone penetration is significantly below the EU average.

The EU framework sets out a definition of universal service and guidelines on costing and funding. Universal service means 'a defined minimum set of services of specified quality which is available to all users independent of their geographical location and, in the light of specific national conditions, at an affordable price'. The responsibility for establishing mechanisms to provide and fund universal service lies primarily with national governments and regulatory authorities (NRAs), who will also decide what is 'affordable'. However, they are encouraged to employ measures such as geographical averaging, targeted tariffs, and price caps in order to maintain affordability, in particular for users in rural or high-cost areas and for vulnerable groups (such as elderly or disabled people).

Some might argue that affordability should be determined at EU level, but differing national circumstances would make this highly prone to the subsidiarity argument. Since affordability has never been explicitly required in most member states (see Garnham 1991), it can be argued that its inclusion in the definition of universal service constitutes a significant improvement. As long as the interpretation of affordability made by member states is reasonable, the introduction of an EU policy on *basic* universal service looks certain to have a positive effect on both social and regional cohesion.

Another obvious way to influence universal service is through the content of the defined minimum set of services. The key point here is that the regulatory framework does not allow services beyond the defined minimum to be financed via universal service funds or levies. At present, the defined minimum is essentially the basic telephone service—voice telephony capable of supporting fax and basic data, plus emergency calls, operator and directory services, public telephones, and special facilities or terms for customers with special needs. The issue of possible extensions to the scope of universal service is considered in section 8.3.2.

8.2.2.4. The impact of liberalization on employment

There have been widespread fears that telecoms liberalization will lead to a large number of job losses, which would clearly be negative in terms of social cohesion and also in terms of regional cohesion if unemployment is distributed unevenly. Liberalization will undoubtedly coincide with job losses in incumbent operators, as has been the case in countries where the sector is already liberalized. Some of the reduction in employment will in a sense be due to liberalization, to the extent that the introduction of competition sharpens incentives to increase productivity and efficiency, and that shedding jobs is one way to do this.

However, the available evidence suggests that the main fundamental reason for job losses in telecoms is technological change. Digitalization in particular has made telecoms networks far less labour-intensive to run and maintain. According to figures presented at a BT Employment Seminar, BT shed 102,827 jobs over the period 1985–95. From 1992 to 1995, there were 61,872 voluntary redundancies, three-quarters of which concerned engineers and network operators. Most of these job losses can be put down to technical change, although it is impossible to say exactly how many.

While figures on job losses with incumbents are readily available, it is far more difficult to gauge the extent of job creation elsewhere in the industry and the economy. Many new entrants in telecoms are small firms or established firms in other industries, and not all their employees are necessarily classified as telecoms workers. Nonetheless, it is clear that liberalization does have some positive direct effects on employment, through job creation by new operators, service providers, equipment manufacturers, and retailers. If, as expected, liberalization leads to falls in overall tariffs and improvements in quality and flexibility, the sector can be expected to grow further, thus creating more jobs. Finally, falling telecoms costs and improved services will stimulate economic activity as a whole, especially in industries where telecoms is an important input, which is expected to have a highly positive impact on employment.[14]

The effects of telecoms liberalization on employment are thus complex and sometimes subtle. While this makes it difficult to draw firm conclusions, the analysis does show that the more extreme claims, based mainly on job losses with incumbent operators, are unjustified. On the other hand, the effects of liberalization on job creation are very uncertain, and the more optimistic claims here should also be treated with caution.

In addition, we still have to consider whether old jobs with incumbent operators are actually being replaced by new jobs elsewhere in the industry. There are likely to be skill mismatch problems, whereby those who lose their jobs have difficulty in finding similar employment elsewhere, and newly created jobs require different skills. This is relevant to social cohesion because of the differential impact it has on lower- and higher-skilled employees. Operators and maintenance engineers are likely to find it

---

[14] A recent study found that, under the most optimistic scenario of rapid liberalization and rapid diffusion of technologies, 93 million jobs could be created in the telecoms sector, even allowing for job losses with incumbent operators and, in the rest of the economy 1.2 million jobs could be created by 2005. Under the pessimistic scenario of gradual liberalization and slow diffusion of technologies, there could be 216 million fewer jobs in telecoms, but 444 million extra jobs in the rest of the economy (BIPE Conseil *et al.* 1997).

harder to find comparable employment, while technical change and liberalization are likely to lead to growth in higher-skilled occupations within or related to the industry, as well as a demand for young, highly flexible, and customer service-oriented employees. One study of the effects of telecoms liberalization on employment in Finland found clearly that the number of white-collar and highly educated employees is set to grow substantially as a proportion of the total workforce (Price Waterhouse, 1995: 65–6).

In summary, technical change is the main reason behind changes in telecoms-related employment. Liberalization will play its part, but will have both positive and negative effects. Without further evidence, it is difficult to draw firm conclusions on the net effects of liberalization on social cohesion. Any net job creation will be positive, but the skill mismatch problems described mean that unskilled workers will lose out relative to skilled workers, which is negative in cohesion terms.

As far as intercountry cohesion is concerned, incumbent operators in all member states will have to shed jobs sooner or later, which suggests a fairly neutral impact. The regional distribution of employment may be affected by industrial restructuring as a result of integrating previously segmented markets. This is more relevant to telecoms equipment than services, and areas in which weak equipment manufacturers are located are likely to lose out in employment terms. In telecoms services, even if industrial restructuring does take place, most employment is likely to remain in the country where the services in question are provided. This may be to the relative benefit of the cohesion countries in the medium term, since there is plenty of scope for continued network growth and modernization. Technical change and liberalization are likely to lead to some restructuring of employment on an interregional basis through, for instance, reduced maintenance requirements and increased centralization of network management; however, more evidence is needed to estimate the nature of these effects.

8.3. Trans-European Networks and the Information Society

8.3.1. Introduction

Rapid technical change has been a dominant feature of the telecoms industry in recent years, based mainly on digitalization and the consequent 'convergence' of telecoms, information technology, and media. The cohesion objective (and other societal aspects of telecommunications) had been somewhat neglected by EU telecoms policy. But it is increasingly recognized that the 'digital revolution' has and will continue to have effects on society at large. More recently, the European Commission has actively encouraged use of the term 'Information Society'. This 'reflects European concerns with the broader social and organizational changes which will flow from the information and communications revolution' (ISPO 1995) and is preferred to the term 'information superhighway', which is technology-oriented.

The role of the Commission in trans-European telecoms networks and the launching of the Information Society is important, but characterized by a relatively low level

Box 2. Key measures on TENs and the Information Society

The European Commission's (1993) White Paper on Growth, Competitiveness and Employment recognized the importance of convergence of information and communication technologies (ICT) and the creation of a **common information area**:

- the information itself, converted and collated in digital form;
- hardware and software available to the user to process this information;
- basic telecoms services required, especially electronic mail, file transfer, interactive access to databases, and interactive digital image transmission;
- applications, providing the user with the services they need;
- users, trained in the use of applications and aware of the potential of ICTs and of the conditions required for optimum use.

The objective of **trans-European networks** (TENs), is 'to enable citizens, economic operators and regional and local communities to derive full benefit from the setting-up of an area without internal frontiers and to link the peripheral regions with the centre' (ibid.: 89). The Commission's role is to identify strategic trans-European projects in collaboration with all the various parties engaged. Three areas are of special interest: advanced physical infrastructure, generic services such as e-mail or interactive digital video, and telematic applications such as teleworking or telemedicine. The financial role of the public authorities is to be marginal and catalytic. Commission expenditure amounts to 280 million ecus for 1995–9, for projects of common interest whose potential economic benefits are established but whose financial profitability is uncertain or inadequate. It may take the form of joint financing of feasibility studies and other technical measures, interest subsidies and loan guarantees (1996 Work Programme on TEN).

The May 1994 **Bangemann Report** stressed the importance of market forces and private funding together with universal service obligations as core principles. A EURO-ISDN (Integrated Services Digital Network) as a trans-European network is seen as a first step towards the Information Society and a list of telematic applications with demonstrative value is proposed. This was followed in June 1994 by an **action plan** entitled 'Europe's way to the Information Society'.

Infrastructure liberalization is seen as critical to the development of the Information Society, so that alternative infrastructures such as cable TV (with higher bandwidth than ordinary telephone networks) can be used to carry telecoms and new multimedia services.

The social aspects of the emerging Information Society have been taken into account by the Commission by means of a **High Level Expert Group**, which published its interim report in April 1997, entitled *Building the Information Society for Us All*.

of planned expenditures. If infrastructure and services are to be financed mainly by private investors, the major task of the authorities is to adapt the regulatory environment in order to facilitate the creation of new markets and to allow market forces to operate. But if it is really to be an 'Information Society', they will also need to address the issue of ensuring a minimum level of access for every European citizen, possibly through the definition of more advanced universal service obligations.

8.3.2. The Information Society and Cohesion

8.3.2.1. The potential effects on cohesion

The Information Society will reduce the significance of geographical barriers and seems, therefore, to have the potential to improve the relative position of peripheral regions. Advanced services may enable the relocation of activities of core regions towards the periphery (or indeed outside the EU). But this will only happen if reliable infrastructure and advanced services are available at an affordable price in the periphery. Moreover, if relocation is similar to that experienced in other traditional relocating sectors, there is a risk of excessive concentration on low value–added activities in the cohesion regions.

The link between this type of relocation and the endogenous economic development of cohesion regions is relevant. Regional development is more and more conceived of as an endogenous phenomenon based on local actors. In the absence of other significant location advantages (such as lower labour costs or better skills), the potential of telecommunications may never be realized (Sociomics and Arklenson Trust 1993). Good telecommunications are a necessary condition for economic growth, but alone they may be insufficient. The relative success of Ireland in attracting tele-services is not just due to its telecoms network. Moreover, such relocation, and teleworking in general, will not always result in a net creation of jobs. But for the cohesion regions, it may help to avoid the emigration of manpower, especially young people, towards core regions.

Advanced telecoms services enable firms in both peripheral and core regions to lower their costs. Thus the impact on relative competitiveness is uncertain. The position is further complicated by the fact that a substantial lowering of the costs of provision of data services from the centre to less favoured regions would improve the relative position of the latter. Previously many such services were only available to producers in core regions. So while there is something to be gained from the relocation of labour-intensive data–inputting type jobs towards less favoured regions, users there will also gain if, for example, new financial services can now be provided more cheaply over long distances.

Relationships between firms are increasingly based on organizational networks, often at local level, which can enhance cooperation between suppliers and providers and facilitate access to information, and can be of vital importance in the process of innovation. The acquisition of human capital and upgrading of administrative facilities are also key areas where improved networking could help cohesion regions to catch up. Network efficiency can be improved with the development of advanced telecoms services, but cohesion regions seem to characterized by a relatively low level of development of this more or less informal kind of organization. Moreover, tariff rebalancing, due to liberalization, will lead to a rise in access charges and possibly local call tariffs, and so may hinder local networks.

The Information Society may also have multiple impacts on social cohesion, both positive and negative. It offers 'new opportunities for social integration, through building up communities at a local level' (HLEG 1996). But at the same time, as new avenues for interaction are opened up, the relative disadvantage of those excluded will grow (for instance, if increased use of phone and home banking leads to branch closures). Public access to advanced telecommunications (through libraries, for example) may therefore have an essential role to play. Furthermore, while developments such as teleworking may allow much greater freedom for individuals, it could become harder to exercise social rights as a result. These dimensions of cohesion need to be borne in mind. Despite the potential positive effects of the Information Society on social cohesion, we still risk the development of a two-tier society of info-rich and info-poor.

Information Society services have the potential to enhance the competitiveness of firms and regions and to increase social cohesion, but this is by no means automatic. Safeguards will need to be put in place to be sure of exploiting the benefits, especially in the case of less favoured regions and disadvantaged social groups.

8.3.2.2. The future of universal service
A market-driven Information Society raises the question of whether advanced telecoms services will be automatically available to all at a reasonable price. If not, there may be a role for public policy to enable the participation of every EU citizen by enlarging the scope of universal service obligations.

Certain problems, such as a lack of technical literacy, may require specific public policies to avoid hindering the integration of some social groups or regions. There are also some uneconomic customers and areas for which the cost of providing network access is too high to expect a positive financial return. Although there is little evidence that competitive markets have failed to maintain levels of basic universal service as long as appropriate safeguards have been put in place (OECD 1995a), their capacity to deliver universal service unchecked may be doubted, and this will apply all the more in the case of advanced telecoms services, particularly those that require new infrastructure.

There are both efficiency and equity arguments for a policy aimed at providing minimum access to the Information Society through universal service. Telecommunications are characterized by network externalities: the value of being connected to the network increases with the total number of subscribers. Potential new subscribers will not consider the benefits they may create for existing subscribers, hence the case for (partially) subsidizing those who otherwise would be unwilling or unable to pay. The normative concept of universal or public service, traditionally applied in many European countries to telecoms and public utilities, is based largely on equity grounds. With respect to the Information Society, Nexus et al. (1996: 64) argue that 'growth and change must be accompanied by equity, or cohesion is weakened and thus ultimately the basis of social consensus on which our society rests is threatened'.

An appropriate definition of universal service in this rapidly changing field will have to be accepted by all EU countries while at the same time taking account of new technological possibilities; the problem is to define a level of access which is adequate and has some long-term validity, but which is also operational at a reasonable cost (HLEG 1996). Optical fibre to every home is not feasible and, in fact, not necessary for basic Information Society services such as e-mail. Different levels of USOs may be defined, each conceived to meet the needs of specific user groups. The services and technical conditions necessary to integrate SMEs, for instance, are not the same as those required for domestic users.

The concept of universal community service has been endorsed by the High Level Experts Group, among others. This would extend universal service provision 'to incorporate a basic level of access to new information services, but limited in its universality obligation to educational, cultural, medical, social or economic institutions of local communities' (HLEG 1996). The European Commission (1996*b*) has recognized the importance of public or community access as 'an important means of bringing the Information Society to every citizen', and although it does not figure in the present framework, public access will be an important issue for the review of universal service due by the start of 1998.

Nexus *et al.* (1996) have identified and costed a hierarchy of USO priorities and they distinguish, for each of four user groups, levels of universal service to enable integration into the Information Society. Table 8.4 offers a comparison with basic universal service, and also with what Nexus *et al.* regard as optimal for cohesion.

Thus Nexus *et al.* suggest that all customers should be able to request a basic connection offering data transmission at a reasonable rate (14,400 bits per second), which would enable Internet access among other things. All new infrastructure already supports this rate, and the additional cost over and above operators' investment plans appears to be negligible. The current definition of basic universal service, however, specifies data transmission at only 2,400 bit/s, and 14,400 is already looking obsolete in new infrastructure. The next priority is universal access to digital switching, which allows for more effective e-mail and networking services as well as intelligent network functions. The EU framework requires national authorities to ensure the provision of several of these features, but only subject to technical and economic feasibility.

Whatever definition of universal service is chosen, it should allow for changes in demand patterns and technology, as the Commission (1996*b*) recognizes: any extension 'must combine a market-based analysis of demand for and availability of the service with a political assessment of its social and economic desirability'. For the time being, the scope of universal service in the EU framework remains very basic.

8.3.3. *Barriers to the Information Society in cohesion regions*

There is a risk that under full liberalization, telecoms operators will have inadequate incentives to invest in cohesion regions, which are characterized by relatively low levels of telecoms expenditure and relatively high investment costs. They offer low financial returns compared to the larger, higher-income and more densely populated economies (Preston 1995). Thus, a vicious circle could emerge, whereby low usage and higher costs lead to lower investment, less accessibility, and continued low usage; while in core regions, the opposite is happening.

8.3.3.1. *Network characteristics and use of services*
There is still a gap between core regions and peripheral regions in terms of the level of penetration and quality of telecoms infrastructure, although the gap has closed

Table 8.4. Expanding the scope of universal service?

	Voice telephony	Integration into the Information Society	Optimal economic and social cohesion
Universal access			
Use of services	Voice telephony for social needs	Basic integration with IS for social and other needs, in the home	Use of IS for economic activity, from and to the home
Network	2.4 kbit/s	14.4 kbit/s	14.4 kbit/s rising to ISDN
SME access			
Use of services	Voice telephony for business needs	Basic business interaction with IS, such as e-mail, call forwarding and call transfer	Full integration with advanced IS; new network business services
Network	2.4 kbit/s	14.4 kbit/s; digital switching in local loop	Basic rate ISDN
Community access: institutional			
Use of services		Access to health centres, educational institutions to benefit public	Advanced use of health and educational services
Network		Leased lines; ISDN	Bandwidth on demand
Community access: direct to the public			
Use of services	Public telephones	Basic interaction with IS for social and other needs in libraries, resource centres etc.	Advanced use of IS in public centres
Network	2.4 kbit/s	14.4 kbit/s; digital switching in local loop	Basic rate ISDN

Source: Nexus *et al.* (1996).

somewhat over time, as the Tables 8.5 and 8.6 show. The cohesion countries have made great progress in extending and modernizing their networks, and also in reducing waiting times for connection and in improving the quality and reliability of networks.

There are stronger disparities in the spread of higher-capacity networks that are important for the development of the Information Society. The cohesion countries have low penetration rates for ISDN and, with the exception of Ireland, cable TV networks (Tables 8.7 and 8.8).

Table 8.5. Evolution of penetration rate, 1985–95
(mainlines per 100 inhabitants)

	1985	1990	1993	1994	1995
Greece	31.4	39.1	45.7	47.7	49.4
Spain	24.3	32.4	36.6	37.5	38.5
Ireland	19.9	28.1	32.8	34.7	36.7
Portugal	14.0	24.1	33.0	34.8	36.1
EU-15	36.3	43.8	46.4	47.7	49.0

Source: OECD (1997).

Table 8.6. Digitalization, 1990–5
(no. of mainlines connected to a digital exchange, % of total mainlines)

	1990	1993	1994	1995
Greece	0.5	22.0	31.0	35.3
Spain	28.0	41.0	47.0	56.0
Ireland	n.a.	71.0	75.0	79.0
Portugal	30.0	59.0	62.0	70.0
EU-15	38.6	61.1	67	76

Source: OECD (1997) and Eurostat/ITU/OECD (1995) for 1990 figures.

Table 8.7. Number of ISDN subscribers, 1993–5

	1993	1994	1995
Belgium	1,163	9,039	26,286
Denmark	2,354	5,885	14,082
Germany	300,000	536,800	961,610
Greece	0	0	0
Spain	640	5,392	28,012
France	103,000	171,000	n.a.
Ireland	0	0	2,267
Italy	3,989	15,225	49,061
Luxembourg	0	306	1,656
Netherlands	1,175	6,000	23,700
Austria	904	3,949	16,813
Portugal	0	1,827	7,891
Finland	545	2,560	6,416
Sweden	n.a.	n.a.	19,700
UK	50,000	93,000	260,000

Source: OECD (1997).

Table 8.8. Cable television subscribers and household penetration, 1990–5

	1990 ('000)	1993 ('000)	1994 ('000)	1993 households (%)	1995 households (%)
Belgium	3,370	3,549	3,594	85	90.5
Denmark	452	626	663	54	71.0
Germany	8,059	12,580	14,600	37	—
Greece	—	—	—	0	—
Spain	110	130	310	8	—
France	515	1,320	1,626	6	—
Ireland	—	430	—	38	—
Italy	—	—	—	0	—
Luxembourg	—	110	—	86	95.4
Netherlands	4,363	5,287	5,770	85	93.0
Austria	460	619	1,030	n.a.	33.8
Portugal	—	—	—	0	9.0
Finland	671	780	—	n.a.	49.0
Sweden	1,482	1,825	1,910	n.a.	—
UK	149	610	916	n.a.	30.0
EU–15	19,631	27,867	30,419	n.a.	—

Source: Eurostat/ITU/OECD (1995); IDATE (1994) for 1993 household penetration; OECD (1997) for 1995 penetration.

8.3.3.2. *Affordability barriers*

Table 8.8 compares the affordability of key telecoms services in the cohesion countries with the EU average. There are no simple generalizations to make here and, in any case, the tariff structures reported are subject to further rebalancing (see sect. 8.2.2.2). Thus, while residential subscription charges are below the EU average in Greece, Portugal, and Spain, they can be expected to rise, as perhaps can local call charges. Installation charges are higher except in Portugal, although these may be expected to fall as waiting times for connection are reduced. Leased lines are expensive in all the cohesion countries except Greece. On the whole, key telecoms services appear expensive in the cohesion countries, especially in relation to their relatively low levels of GDP.

Expanding the scope of universal service would require some additional investment to enhance existing networks. Digitalization of the network is complete or nearing completion in some member states and is proceeding rapidly elsewhere. However, the costs of digitalizing the last 10 per cent of the network in Greece, Ireland, Italy, Portugal, and Spain has been estimated at 4 to 5 billion ecus.[15] Once digitalization is complete, though, universal access to ISDN on request can be achieved at reasonable cost (estimated at 500 million ecus for the same five countries).

[15] See Nexus *et al.* (1996: 81). This is over and above the cost of achieving 90 per cent digitalization, a target that was established by NERA (1994) as realistic for the year 2000 in Objective 1 regions.

Table 8.9. Affordability of main telecommunications services (1 January 1996) (ecus including VAT)

Service cost	Greece	Ireland	Portugal	Spain	EC Average
PSTN Costs[a]					
Residential installation	189.0	177.4	76.66	154.6	119.15
Residential subs (monthly)	6.2	14.8	9.3	9.0	10.3
Local call (3 mins., peak rate)	0.04	0.14	0.06	0.08	0.13
Leased lines tariffs[b]					
Connection	1,192	18,328	5,164	6,899	7,359
Monthly rental 50 km.	3,323	5,247	5,598	5,033	3,853
Monthly rental 250 km.	5,989	6,897	9,723	10,184	8,585

[a] PSTN: Public Switched Telecommunication Network.
[b] All leased line data refers to 2 Mbit/s leased lines.
Source: Tarifica (1996).

Table 8.10. Estimated costs of achieving 100 per cent penetration of cable TV networks and optical fibre to the home, EC–12

	Cable television		Fibre to the home	
	million ecu	% GDP (1993)	million ecu	% GDP (1993)
Belgium	200	0.11	5,800	3.16
Denmark	900	0.75	6,400	5.33
Germany	8,700	0.57	57,000	3.73
Greece	1,800	2.75	5,800	8.85
Spain	12,500	2.95	32,100	7.57
France	18,000	1.62	61,100	5.49
Ireland	400	0.98	2,800	6.88
Italy	16,000	1.79	41,600	4.66
Luxembourg	200	2.18	400	4.36
Netherlands	300	0.11	8,000	2.91
Portugal	1,200	1.81	4,200	6.34
UK	9,200	1.11	26,500	3.21
EC–12	69,400	1.39	251,700	5.21

Source: KPMG (1995).

Large investments would be required to establish universal broadband infrastructure, allowing exploitation of the full potential of advanced multimedia services. One option would be to extend and upgrade cable TV networks to offer interactive services. Better still would be optical fibre to the home. Table 8.9 reports estimates of the cost of reaching 100 per cent of households in both cases.

The costs per inhabitant and as a proportion of GDP are appreciably higher in the cohesion countries (with the exception of cable TV in Ireland, where penetration is already fairly high). Furthermore, less favoured regions have already invested a great deal in recent years in upgrading and expanding their telecoms infrastructure, and 'it will be a major challenge to raise sufficient funds to install even a single advanced broadband communications infrastructure . . . not to mention the idea of replicating these investments' (Preston 1995).

8.3.3.3. Other barriers

Availability and affordability are necessary conditions for all regions to fully exploit the benefits of the Information Society, but other requirements need to be met as well. Effective use of advanced telecoms services often requires a minimum level of computer literacy (not to mention access to a PC), both for domestic and professional use. Flexible, well-educated workers will also be needed. Nexus *et al.* note the high number of people in cohesion regions who have received little or no secondary education, as well as the relatively small proportion of 18–19-year-olds entering higher education and the lower numbers of people engaged in life-long learning. Cohesion regions also tend to lack managerial and technical skills and the local resources and expertise required for successful innovation. While none of these factors has very much to do with telecommunications as such, they may in effect act as further barriers to the participation of less favoured regions and social groups in the Information Society, thus limiting the potential benefits for cohesion.

8.4. Structural Fund Initiatives in Telecommunications

It is outside the scope of this chapter to evaluate the role of Community initiatives in telecoms financed by the Structural Funds, but for completeness we should draw attention to the relative scale of this and other spending.

The main initiatives have been STAR (Special Telecommunications Action for Regions) and Telematique. STAR ran from 1987 to 1991 and involved 761.4 million ecus of Community expenditure. It was replaced by Telematique, on which 236.9 million ecus were spent in 1992–3.

The basic objective of STAR was to ensure improved access for less favoured regions to the benefit of advanced services and networks, and to contribute to their economic development by improving access to advanced telecommunications services. When STAR was launched, telecoms infrastructure in less favoured regions was highly inferior to that in core regions. Since then, considerable progress has been made in reducing these disparities, as a result of a very high level of investment by the member states. Between 1987 and 1991, member states invested approximately 28 billion ecus in the Objective 1 regions. STAR infrastructure development funding (611 million ecus) thus amounted to only 2.2 per cent of total telecommunications investment in these regions.

The principal effect of these infrastructure development measures was to bring forward the investment plans of operators. The STAR programme promoted some

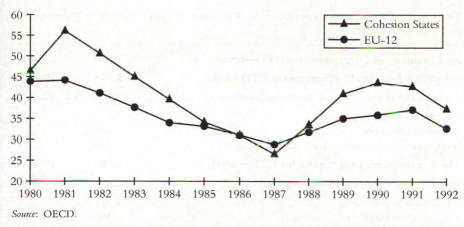

Source: OECD.

Fig. 8.1. Investments as a percentage of telecommunications revenue, 1980–92

projects which had been planned but not implemented and occasionally led to entirely new projects. In a few cases, STAR actions helped change the course of network development. Notable examples include bringing forward network digitalization in Greece and establishing cellular mobile radio in Portugal. Because the programme had a finite duration, operators were committed to a firmer investment timetable than would have otherwise been the case. Figure 8.1 shows a clear rise and fall in telecoms investment in the cohesion countries which, although not due entirely to the STAR programme, coincides with its period of implementation.

While STAR sought to develop both telecommunications infrastructure and modern services, the Telematique initiative emphasized almost exclusively new services whose viability might be ensured by reaching a 'critical mass' of users. Telematique thus stressed the stimulation of demand for services and the efficient use of infrastructure rather than the expansion and modernization of infrastructure.

8.5. Research and Technical Development Policies

8.5.1. Presentation of R&D projects in telecommunications

The main action in research and technical development in telecommunications was the RACE programme (R&D in Advanced Communications Technologies in Europe), which ran from 1987 until 1994, when it was replaced by ACTS (Advanced Communications Technologies and Services). There is also the Telematique programme, which brought together various initiatives in the field.[16]

This section examines the contribution of RACE to economic and social cohesion. It should be noted that the evaluation of RACE has been carried out mainly in terms of

[16] Notably DELTA (Development of European Learning through Technological Advance). DRIVE (Dedicated Road Infrastructure for Vehicle Safety in Europe), and AIM (Advanced Informatics in Medicine).

Table 8.11. Communications and telematics RTD funding within Framework Programmes (million ecus)

First Framework Programme for RTD—total	**3,750**	**1984–8**
Second Framework Programme for RTD—total	**5,396**	**1987–91**
Towards a large market and an information and communication society	*2,275*	*42.2%*
Information technologies	1,600	
Telecommunications	550	
New services of common interest (include transport)	125	
Third Framework Programme for RTD—total	**6,600**	**1990–4**
Information and communications technologies	*2,491*	*37.7%*
Information technologies	1,517	
Telecommunications	548	
Development of telematic systems of general interest	426	
Fourth Framework Programme for RTD—total	**12,300**	**1994–8**
Information and communications technologies	*3,405*	*27.7%*
Telematics	843	
Communication technologies	630	
Information technologies	1,932	

Source: European Report on Science and Technology Indicators 1994.

the technical objectives of the programme. Nevertheless, the 1993 strategic audit of RACE clearly indicated that the links between advanced communications, economic development and social cohesion should be reinforced.

8.5.2. Evaluation of RACE

Phase I of RACE accelerated the harmonization of European telecoms infrastructure, and the elaboration of common functional specifications has established a 'blueprint' for Integrated Broadband Communications (IBC). This has favoured close cooperation between central and peripheral regions. The mid-term and final reports on Phase I stated that the programme has paved the way for implementation of broadband trans-European networks by studying and elaborating strategies for the introduction of IBC in all European regions, especially the less favoured ones. The necessity of connecting the insular, isolate, and peripheral regions to the Community's central regions was stressed. The REVOLVE project (see Box 3) is an excellent example of research in advanced communications focused on the needs of less-favoured regions. Accompanying measures, such as workshops, seminars and summer courses, have made the results of the research accessible to researchers and engineers throughout the EU, with an emphasis on seminars in the less-favoured regions.

In Phase II of RACE, eighty-two projects (70 per cent) had participants from less favoured regions, which has contributed to the transfer of certain technologies and

---

Box 3. REVOLVE—Regional Evolution Planning for IBC

REVOLVE was a RACE-I project designed to study the introduction of IBC networks in rural areas. The project identified strategic issues relevant to the harmonized and planned evolution of telecommunications networks in less favoured regions, and then analysed the requirements and constraints affecting rural areas in the context of plans for IBC in Europe. The analysis was carried out from an economic and social as well as technical perspective, and enabled the elaboration of technical strategies for the introduction of IBC in less favoured regions, taking account of other relevant Community programmes such as STAR.

The main impact of REVOLVE was the development of a comprehensive set of tools for the strategic planning of telecoms development in rural areas. The project is also expected to influence specifications of telecoms equipment for sparsely populated regions to make implementation of IBC technically feasible. It may also provide justification for national and EU investment in extending IBC networks to less favoured regions.

The REVOLVE consortium proposed that national and regional authorities should be given the freedom and flexibility to develop telecommunications strategies appropriate to the characteristics of their regions, including the possibility of cross-subsidization to develop services regarded as key for regional development. They also recommended that universal service should be extended to include wider cohesion issues. A major investment in networks in peripheral regions, sufficient to make realistic inroads into the huge disparities in telecoms network provision within the EU, could be financed by a 1 per cent levy on telecommunications usage.

---

competencies to these regions. Nearly 20 per cent of projects had participants from the cohesion countries. The increase in the absolute number and percentage of projects having participants from the less favoured regions is a good intermediate indicator of a trend towards greater participation from these regions. However, this does not necessarily signify that a greater proportion of RTD is carried out in these regions. Every RACE project involves participants from several countries and statistical information such as man/month participation or funding per region or per country has, unfortunately, not been made available.

The first two phases of RACE focused on integrated broadband networks and associated services. Establishing common standards was a key theme. According to the 1993 strategic audit, it is now essential to stimulate innovative use, as users insist that networks meet their requirements instead of accepting what network operators find most convenient to offer. For future EU requirements, what is needed is a shift away from technology development towards a broader policy that stimulates use. Community-led RTD is still warranted in selected areas since there remain many problems that are too big for any one actor to solve alone. New applications may need to be stimulated by the Community, to be given a 'kick-start'. Experience shows that innovative use develops best when driven by consortia of interested users together with manufacturers and network providers, given the availability of service-oriented networks and open access for service providers. The Commission has made major efforts to facilitate the deployment of modern networks and applications, as demonstrated by the Telework 1995 projects (see Box 4).

Box 4. Telework 1995 projects for the less favoured regions of the EU

Teleworking has become a hot issue in the EU, especially since the Bangemann Report identified it as one of the key applications to serve as building blocks for the Information Society. Telework covers a range of new ways of working, using communications as a tool to work, for at least part of the time, outside a traditional office environment. The Commission has taken special care to ensure the full participation of less favoured regions under Telework 1995. The objective is to foster research and the establishment of supporting facilities in less favoured regions, in order to enable greater participation by organization, especially SMEs, in future European RTD in advanced communications and telematics.

Examples of Telework 1995 projects

• BINET (Broadband Interconnection Network) covers the development of an advanced broadband network, linking four telecoms RTD centres in Spain and Portugal and a high-tech industrial park in Portugal.
• SUNRISE (Satellite Used in Networking to Support Regional R&D) has installed a VSAT (very small aperture terminal) satellite system for research collaboration between SMEs and universities in less-favoured regions of the cohesion countries.
• EPRI-NET (European Parliament Research Initiative Networks) established facilities in Spain and Eastern Germany to promote RTD in advanced communications and telematics, including a VSAT network which can be extended to Central and Eastern Europe.

8.6. Conclusions

Telecommunications policies have great potential for improving economic and social cohesion in the EU. Liberalization, RTD in telecoms, and the development of the Information Society could all serve to narrow regional and social disparities, not least by reducing the significance of geographical distance in economic activity. However, there are also risks involved. EU telecoms policies will have both positive and negative effects on cohesion. The long-run impact is expected to be positive, but while safe-guards are being put in place to limit the negative effects, these may be insufficient to avoid a net negative impact in the short to medium term.

The evidence on liberalization suggests a complex and mixed impact on both regional and social cohesion. The net direct impact is expected to be negative, largely because the removal of cross-subsidies will lead to a rise in access charges relative to usage charges. The rise in access charges may be partly or wholly compensated for by lower overall costs, improved quality of service, and access to a wider range of services, but peripheral regions and small users will derive fewer benefits than core regions and high-usage customers, at least initially. Rebalancing of tariffs, however, is likely to remain a gradual process, and this will soften its impact. The clear commitment to a basic level of universal service in the EU will also limit the negative effects on cohesion.

The development of the European Information Society could have favourable effects on peripheral regions and disadvantaged individuals, but only if these regions are well provided with the essential elements of advanced telecommunications infrastructure and services, and are thus able to attain the volume of business necessary for both the use and provision of scale-intensive telecoms services. Strong commitments to an enhanced universal service may be necessary. The definition of different levels of universal service would be one solution, in order to give different user groups basic access to the Information Society while controlling costs. Ensuring a minimum level of access for every EU citizen would also help to avoid some of the potential negative effects of the Information Society on social cohesion.

In the longer run, the impact of liberalization and the Information Society on cohesion is more likely to be favourable. The development of advanced services and the fall in distance-related charges represent a lowering of barriers to market access, which should allow peripheral regions to exploit competitive advantages such as lower wages and less congestion. It is likely that, in the short run, core regions may be the main beneficiaries of these developments, for the simple reason that the lowering of service costs will initially have the greatest impact in areas where services are most heavily consumed and produced. In the longer term, as patterns of usage and location adjust to relative price changes, there is a better chance of a positive impact in peripheral regions.

The precise effects of these changes on employment are hard to predict. There will be a reduction in core jobs offered by incumbent operators, but also a growth of new service activities and equipment manufacture, while falling telecoms costs and the development of advanced services is expected to stimulate employment in the economy as a whole. However, there is likely to be a major change in the type of jobs offered, as relatively low-skilled employees are made redundant while newly created jobs generally require higher and different skills, although some new jobs perhaps initially in peripheral areas may involve low-skill data-inputting activities.

Research and technical development policies have targeted the overall competitiveness of the Union rather than cohesion. But there is now an increasing effort to take cohesion objectives into account in the design of RTD projects, and to favour participation from less favoured regions. Benefits for less favoured regions are likely to be some way downstream, in terms of the results of RTD projects, and in the form of enhanced capabilities for later generations of projects acquired through the experience of participating in RTD programmes. User-based diffusion-oriented RTD projects are more likely to have a direct impact on less favoured regions, and this is more likely to be achievable in telecoms than in other activities since advanced telecoms services can be made accessible via network systems.

A detailed evaluation of structural funding was beyond the scope of this chapter. Nonetheless, it is worth noting that structural funding, even if small compared with total telecoms infrastructure investment in peripheral regions, has played a role in accelerating the modernization and development of networks in cohesion regions.

It should be emphasized that much of our analysis is necessarily speculative, for unavoidable reasons. The number of other factors that have influenced the EU telecoms sector is so large that any assessment which tries to go beyond directions to magnitudes is fraught with difficulty. EU policies have been limited so far; indeed, key developments such as full liberalization and Information Society initiatives have only just begun.

With this in mind, the overall provisional conclusion is that while EU telecoms policy may have a positive impact on the economic development of less favoured regions in absolute terms, it is much harder to predict a favourable impact on cohesion in terms of the relative benefits for poorer regions and social groups. Core regions and richer individuals will probably benefit more initially, although in the longer term it is much more likely that telecoms policy will have a positive impact on cohesion. Policy has been refocused to take account of the risks posed by liberalization and the Information Society. But in our judgement, more could be done to avoid negative effects in the short to medium term, and to guarantee that the potential of telecommunications to improve cohesion in the EU is realized.

8.7. Postscript

Full liberalization came into force on 1 January 1998 in ten member states (and in Luxembourg in July) as planned. In February, the Commission (1998) adopted its first monitoring report on universal service. This and the data it provides will prove extremely useful to readers wishing to compare with or extend the analysis of sect. 8.2. The report notes the ongoing gradual improvement in levels of service, a narrowing in the gap in telephone penetration levels between member states, and a fall in prices in real terms for most users. At this early stage, the Commission saw no need to redefine the legislation underpinning universal service.

At the time of writing (August 1998), we may draw upon the limited experience thus far of the liberalized market in operation. As expected, competition is developing at different speeds in different countries, depending mainly on how national regulators have interpreted their roles and on the zeal with which they are implementing the new regulations. Judging by press reports, tariff rebalancing is proceeding as expected. While new entrants in public networks and voice telephony have generally been subject to licence obligations to cover a certain proportion of national or regional territory, a number of new entrants providing advanced services and infrastructures (Worldcom, for instance) have explicitly concentrated their investments in large cities within core regions.

The provisions on basic universal service do not yet appear to have had the impact one might have expected. Only two countries (France and Italy) activated national USO schemes immediately. Others, including the cohesion countries yet to liberalize, plan to establish or activate schemes in the near future, or are at least keeping that option open. Four countries (Denmark, Finland, Sweden, and the UK) do not currently plan to establish schemes at all, since USOs are not considered to impose any significant net cost on operators. As noted, there have been no moves as yet to expand the scope of universal service beyond basic voice telephony, although the Commission is consulting on this issue, which will arise again in the general review of EU telecoms legislation scheduled by the end of 1999.

Of course, the sector remains deep in transition (if not turmoil), so it remains difficult to draw firm conclusions. However, we feel the limited experience so far tends to reinforce the tentative conclusions advanced in this chapter. EU telecoms policy seems to have worked to the benefit of the majority of individuals and regions. However, even if almost everybody gains in absolute terms, it seems clear that better-off individuals and core regions are by far the greatest beneficiaries at the present time.

References

Analysys (1994). *Provision of Quantitative Data as Background Material for the Bangemann Report.* Final Report Athens.

Bangemann *et al.* (1994). *Europe and the Global Information Society: Recommendations to the European Council.* Brussels.

BIPE Conseil *et al.* (1997). *Effects on Employment of the Liberalization of the Telecommunications Sector.* Study carried out for the European Commission, DGs V and XIII. Luxembourg: Office for the Official Publications of the European Communities.

BTCE (1989). *The Cost of Telecoms Community Service Obligations.* Bureau of Transport and Communication Economics, Report no. 64. Canberra: BTCE.

Constantelou, N. and Mansell, R. (1994). *On the Road to Competition in Telecommunication: 'Catching-up' in the European Union Less Favoured Regions.* European Network for Communication and Information Perspectives.

Deacon, D. (1995). Discussion. In P. Buigues, A. Jacquemin and A. Sapir (eds.). *European Policies on Competition, Trade and Industry,* 322–8. Aldershot: Elgar.

European Commission (1987). *Towards a Dynamic European Economy: Green Paper on the Development of the Common Market for Telecommunications Services and Equipment.* Communication from the Commission, COM (87) 290 final. Brussels.

—— (1993). White Paper on *Growth, Competitiveness, Employment: The Challenges and Ways Forward into the 21st Century. Bulletin of the European Communities,* Supplement 6/93. Brussels.

—— (1996a). *Assessment Criteria for National Schemes for the Costing and Financing of Universal Service in Telecommunications and Guidelines for the Member States on Operation of such Schemes.* Communication from the Commission, COM (96) 608 final. Brussels.

—— (1996b). *Universal Service in the Perspective of a Fully Liberalised Environment: An Essential Element of the Information Society.* Communication from the Commission, COM (96) 73. Brussels.

—— (1998). *First Monitoring Report on Universal Service in Telecommunications in the European Union.* Communication from the Commission, COM (1998) 101 final. Brussels.

European Report on Science and Technology Indicators (1994).

Eurostat/ITU/OECD (1995). *Communication Indicators for Major Economies 1995.* Luxembourg: Office for Official Publications of the European Communities.

Garnham, N. (1991). Universal service in European telecommunications. In N. Garnham and R. Mansell (eds), *Universal Service and Rate Restructuring in Telecommunications.* Paris: OECD.

Grout, P. A. (1996). Promoting the superhighway: telecommunications regulation in Europe. *Economic Policy* 22: 111–54.

High Level Experts Group (HLEG) (1996). *Building the Information Society for Us All.* Interim Report.

—— (1997). *Building the Information Society for Us All.* Final Report.

IDATE (1994). *Fourniture de données quantitatives pour l'élaboration du livre vert sur les infrastructures de télécommunications et les réseaux câblés.* Final Report for the European Commission, DG XIII. Brussels.

ISPO (1995). *Introduction to the Information Society: The European Way.* Information Society Project Office. Brussels.

KPMG (1995). *Investing in Infrastructures for the European Information Society.* Final Report. Brussels.

Krugman, P. and Venables, A. (1990). Integration and the competitiveness of peripheral industry. In C. Bliss and J. Braga de Macedo (eds.). *Unity with Diversity in the European Economy.* Cambridge: Cambridge University Press.

NERA (1994). *Study of Targets for Telecommunications Services in Objective 1 Regions.* Report for the European Commission, DG XIII. Brussels.

Nexus *et al.* (1996). *An Assessment of the Social and Economic Cohesion Aspects of the Development of the Information Society in Europe.* Final Report for the European Commission, DG XIII. Brussels.

OECD (1995a). *The Benefits of Infrastructure Competition.* ICCP Series no. 35. Paris: OECD.

—— (1995b). *Communications Outlook 1995.* Paris: OECD.

—— (1996). *Information Infrastructure Convergence and Pricing: The Internet.* GD (96) 73.

—— (1997). *Communications Outlook 1997,* vol. i. Paris: OECD.

Oftel (1995a). *The Costs, Benefits and Funding of Universal Service in the UK.* London: Oftel.

—— (1995b). *Universal Telecommunications Services: Consultative Document on Universal Service in the UK from 1997.* London: Oftel.

—— (1997). *Towards Better Telecoms for Customers: A Review of Progress in the UK.* London: Oftel.

Preston, P. (1995). Competition in the telecommunications infrastructure: implications for the peripheral regions and small countries in Europe. *Telecommunications Policy* 19: 253–71.

Price Waterhouse (1995). *The Effects of Competition on Employment in the Telecommunications Industry: Case Finland.* Helsinki.

Sociomics Ltd and Arklenson Trust (Research) Ltd (1993). *Exploratory Investigation of Employment Trends in Rural Areas Related to ECS.* Report to European Commission, DG XIII/B.

Tarifica (1996). *Tariff Data 01.01.96.* Report to the European Commission, DG XIII. Brussels.

9

Social and Employment Policy

NIKOS KOUTSIARAS

Social policy consists of social insurance, health services, public assistance, education, housing policy, and labour market policies (CEC 1993*a*, Kleinman and Pianchaud 1993). Thus, it defines a wide range of collective actions seeking to protect individuals against unanticipated income losses owing to social contingencies, to ensure the attainment of a reasonable and socially acceptable standard of living for all citizens, and to ensure the active participation of all in economic and social life.

The objectives of social policy are conventionally conceptualized by the terms 'efficiency', 'equity', and 'social integration'. Accordingly, government intervention is economically justified through reference to market failures, especially asymmetric information (Barr 1992), it is morally demanded because even efficient markets are very likely to deliver unacceptably unequal income distributions (Sen 1987), and it is politically required in order to preserve social stability and maintain political order.

It is widely held that the European social model is based on a widespread appreciation of a mutually reinforcing relationship between economic and moral objectives, efficiency and equity, growth and redistribution. Reference is often made to the social and political consensus underlying post-war construction of the welfare state in Europe (Helm 1989, Wilensky 1975). Of course, this was true under exceptionally favourable economic circumstances (Eichengreen 1996).

Yet, as a result of differences in industrial structures, economic performance, and historically developed social norms and institutions, social policies across Europe exhibit wide diversities. These have to do with differences in institutional and financial arrangements, the role of the state versus the role of the social partners, the use made of different forms of government intervention—regulation, price subsidisation, public production, and income transfers—and, consequently, the scale of income redistribution entailed (Esping-Andersen and Korpi 1984, Titmuss 1974).

Being largely concerned with the regulatory framework, European-level social policy complements national social policies and is closely associated with, and may even encompass labour market policies (Molle 1990). It is an integral part of a Community range of actions aiming at the promotion of several tasks, including a high level of employment and social protection, an improvement in standards of living and the quality of life, economic and social cohesion, and solidarity between the member states (Articles 2 and 3 of the Treaty on European Union).

The following analysis attempts to assess the actual impact of EU social and employment policies on cohesion. It is divided into four sections. Section 9.1 considers the scope for EU intervention in the area of social policy, providing a framework for the understanding of its development over time and, particularly, its inevitable change of emphasis. Section 9.2 assesses the cohesion effects of EU social measures, primarily social legislation. Section 9.3 is devoted to an analysis of EU employment policies, particularly an assessment of the potential contribution of European employment strategy to employment and cohesion. In section 9.4 the main findings are summarized.

9.1. What Role for EU Social Policy?

According to the principle of subsidiarity, policy responsibility should be assigned to the lowest level of government that can effectively carry the responsibility. Therefore, a transfer of powers to the central EU level is warranted if the effectiveness of national policies is undermined by decisions made by other governments, i.e. in the presence of policy externalities between individual economies. Thus, although the diversity of social arrangements between the member states seems to provide a compelling argument in favour of decentralization, the question is whether, in the process of economic integration, these diversities become unsustainable; whether, in other words, a downward race among national social regimes is inevitable, eventually driving social protection below the levels that fulfil the preferences of EU citizens as a whole.

However imprecise, though appealing in political discourse, the term 'social dumping' has been coined to describe a pessimistic scenario of national economic adjustment to increased competition, following the establishment of the internal market and eventually EMU. Specifically, it is argued that increased consumer responsiveness to relative product prices, associated with the abandonment of the exchange-rate instrument, raises the importance of labour costs in determining trade patterns and location of investment. Thus, it is suggested, countries with lower-cost regimes are likely to gain some leverage over trade and, particularly, investment patterns, forcing in turn those countries with comprehensive social protection systems to follow suit. Furthermore, it is said, governments and firms may be tempted to manipulate labour costs in order to obtain competitive advantages, especially in strategic sectors, thus reinforcing the process of unfair competition and social devaluation.

If this was the case, EU level coordination of social policies, allowing for an upward harmonization of social provisions in the form of common minimum standards, would both remove the external pressures on social regimes and ensure that the same rules of competition apply to all. In short, a common social policy would insure against the risk of social dumping.

Nevertheless, the relevance of the social dumping thesis is doubtful. Firstly, differences in social costs between individual economies are not arbitrary. It is theoretically established and empirically maintained that these differences are largely accounted for by differences in direct wages being smaller than they would be in the absence of social protection, as well as differences in productivity levels (for a theoretical exposition, Ermisch 1991, CEPR 1993). Also, the fact that most of the elements of social costs apply across the economy renders their strategic manipulation virtually impossible; strategic labour cost policies, in general, are hardly feasible in the context of European labour markets (van Rompuy, Abraham, and Heremans 1991). Secondly, location of capital is only partly based on labour cost considerations. Quality of infrastructure and availability of skills, not to mention government subsidies and favourable tax treatment, seem to represent the most important factors in location/relocation decisions. The size of the internal market as well as market proximity is also of strategic economic importance. Nevertheless, in traditional labour-intensive sectors, labour costs may dominate the decision about location.

It has been suggested, though, that, as a result of closer economic integration, northern high labour cost economies will benefit in human-capital and technology-intensive sectors, while southern low labour cost economies will benefit in labour-intensive industries. This pattern of intra-Community specialization, albeit being increasingly challenged by international competition, implies that direct competition between high and low labour cost economies is less immediate (Adnett 1995). Of course, as it is specified by trade theory, a downward pressure will be exercised on the wages of unskilled labour in northern high labour cost economies, although the wages of skilled labour will increase, thus allowing for the implementation of compensatory policies. Besides, the wages of unskilled workers in the southern economies will also tend to rise.

It follows that an upward movement in labour costs, brought about by an upward harmonization of social provisions, would erode the comparative advantages of southern economies, especially in view of the increased competition being felt by low-wage economies in Asia and Central and Eastern Europe. Furthermore, in the context of European monetary unification, any move to reduce labour market policy autonomy would deprive national economies of the only means of adjustment to asymmetric economic disturbances, namely wage and labour cost in general. Of course, it is not advocated here that specialization of the less developed EU economies in labour-intensive sectors is advisable, or even sustainable in the long run. All that is said is that it is hard to see how a common social policy may assist their transformation into high-productivity, high-wage economies, without harming their short-run growth prospects.

Nonetheless, some analysts adopt the opposite view. They argue that the existence of low-cost regimes associated with the pattern of intra-Community specialization discussed above, may prevent the convergence of national economic performances. They also suggest that the diversity of labour market policies and institutions may create a source of instability within EMU. Furthermore, in stating their case for harmonization, they draw comfort from the fact that the costs of social protection are passed on to wages, so that unit labour costs and comparative advantages need not be negatively affected. On the contrary, they claim a positive effect, in so far as an increase in social protection may increase workers' motivation, thus leading to productivity increases (for example, Adnett 1995).

However, this is an over-optimistic view of harmonization, not least because it is founded on a weak analysis of European labour markets. It may be true that in the long term the incidence of social protection falls on direct wages, but in the short term much of this effect depends upon the degree of wage adjustment. In principle, though, slower wage adjustment entails a loss of competitiveness and an increase in unemployment, causing in turn the resettlement of wage cum social costs to their competitive level. Yet, the experience of persistently high rates of unemployment in Europe suggests that this is hardly the case with European labour markets. The recent literature has proposed several explanations for the irresponsiveness of wages and labour costs to unemployment pressures. Regardless of their origin, most of these explanations put the blame on social protection excesses, such as high unemployment benefits, high minimum wages, and extensive employment protection legislation (e.g. Lindbeck 1994). Thus, it is questionable whether an upward harmonization of social provisions would bring any of the benefits anticipated by the aforementioned analysts. Instead, an increase in the level of social protection in low-wage economies may lead to an increase in total labour costs, while its likely positive effect on productivity may be neutralized, in the sense that productivity increases may well be appropriated by (even stronger) trade unions in the form of higher wages. Moreover, the likelihood of adverse effects—i.e. increased unemployment—from harmonization may be higher in southern EU economies, the labour markets of which are riddled with rigidities (OECD 1994), than in the UK which has a flexible labour market. Obviously, this may be so in respect to certain measures falling within the broad area of social security.

As a matter of fact, it is precisely the problem of unemployment that has drawn attention to the issue of social costs in the northern EU economies. However, convergence to their model would hardly be a recipe for real convergence, which is necessary for a stable EMU. Furthermore, the source of potential instability does not lie with the diversity of social and labour market policies. Rather it has to do with the lack of labour market adjustment to competitive pressures, caused by extensive government intervention.

Social policy is often concerned with redistribution. Admittedly, the feasible extent of redistribution within EU countries has been curtailed by an increase in the mobility of capital at the expense of immobile factors, primarily unskilled labour. As a consequence, the redistributive power of social policy has been reduced, too. Arguably, fears that social policy may be in jeopardy are hardly justified; social policy also serves as an efficiency device, addressing market failures, and as a form of commitment mechanism, allowing for productivity increases. On the other hand, realization of equity objectives, in particular reduction of inequality, has led to some redistributive measures being implemented with an efficiency loss, which is only aggravated under conditions of greater economic openness. While in principle preserving a fair level of earnings for unskilled workers is a legitimate goal, its achievement at the expense of employment, through various labour market regulatory measures acting like taxes, is both economically and socially questionable. Protection of unskilled workers and improvement of their employment and income opportunities could well be accomplished through more flexible labour markets, a better targeting of social benefits, and forward-looking education and vocational training policies, rather than merely relying on costly passive and inherently short-term schemes. Social and employment policies are thus in need of wholesale reforms which will enable them to improve their effectiveness and increase their relevance to the present circumstances. Besides, pressures for reform are felt more heavily as a result of social, demographic and structural changes challenging European welfare states (Rhodes 1997). What then are the implications for EU social policy?

Firstly, it is important to recognize the interaction of harmonization of social stand-ards at the European level and the fact that differences are a legitimate source of com-parative advantage, insofar as they reflect societies' preferences and their ability to afford improvements in the quality of life. The appeal of harmonization is likely to be greater for governments engaged in more redistributive social policies and for social groups whose position is at risk, less skilled workers as well as some owners of firms in import-competing industries in northern Europe. However, unless it confers an efficiency gain to their economies, harmonization is likely to be opposed by governments with relat-ively weaker preferences for equity due to cultural, historical, and ideological reasons, or simply—and understandably—because of their countries' lower level of economic development. Hence, coordinated action at the EU level is likely to result in 'lowest common denominator' types of arrangement.

Secondly, there is a special role for Community institutions in view of the similar problems facing national welfare states and the impact, beneficent as it may turn to be, that economic integration exercises upon them. This role is concerned with the encouragement of policy cooperation amongst governments, including consultation with the social partners and the exchange of information about national policies. It is hoped that, as a result, diffusion of best practices is promoted and prospects for coherent and comprehensive national policy choices—and reform measures—are improved. Accordingly, the Community's role is that of a policy—and reform—catalyst, or, to put it differently, it resembles the role of an epistemic community developing shared ideas which are likely to influence policy outcomes (Wallace 1996).

This analysis enables one to put into perspective the experience from the develop-ment of EU social policy. Hence, one may explain why, in spite of substantial Treaty revisions, the member states have fervently preserved their sovereignty in core areas of social and labour market policy. Also, one may thus appreciate that the increase in Community social regulation, politically inspired by the Social Charter and legally based on the SEA, especially Article 118A (now Art. 138), was associated with the aban-donment of earlier harmonization principles in favour of an attempt to create a floor of basic social rights (Rhodes 1992).

It may accordingly be realized that the various dilemmas created by the Maastricht Social Protocol were practically resolved by a radical change of emphasis in EU social and employment policy, coupled with the formal endorsement of the principle of sub-sidiarity. It was actually recognized that additional labour market rigidities should not be introduced and fruitful experimentation should not be prevented (Ross 1995). High unemployment across Europe made the shift in policy inevitable. Indeed, in a series of policy documents it was made clear that social legislation might no longer be conceived as the backbone of European social policy and the priority of employment was under-lined (CEC 1993*a*, 1994*b*, 1995*d*). In the area of employment policy the Community should not have more than a coordinating role to play, through encouraging coopera-tion between the member states and supporting their action in regard to labour market reforms. The competencies of the member states should be fully respected.

From this point of view, finally, the results of the intergovernmental conference on the revision of the EU Treaty may cause little surprise. The new UK government was eager to end the notorious social opt-out, being confident that there would be little risk for its flexible labour market. After all, an important fraction of UK employers had already expressed their preference for a policy that both enables access to the positive features of the continental social model and ensures that their views are taken into consideration in the context of EU social decision-making. On the other hand, the employment chapter, which was inserted in the Amsterdam Treaty, reinforces the commitment to the development of a coordinated strategy for employment and provides the basis for improving employability, thereby ensuring a flexible labour market (EPC 1997).

9.2. The Impact of Social Policy on Cohesion

This section attempts to assess the contribution to cohesion of the introduction of minimum social standards in the context of the action programme for the implementation of the Social Charter and the medium-term social action programme, 1995–7. Emphasis is placed upon social legislation. A 'value-added' approach is followed that reveals the impact of Community legislation on national regulatory schemes. The cohesion effects of social policy are examined at two levels, the interpersonal (individual/social group) level and the country level, in order to answer two questions: first, whether there has been an improvement in social and economic opportunities facing certain social groups across the EU, and second, whether there has been a relative raising of social protection and opportunities between these groups in richer countries and their counterparts in countries perceived as 'social laggards' (the four cohesion countries and the UK). In so doing, the economic implications of social legislation are addressed, especially with respect to its differing impact among countries. The relevant question is whether the introduction of minimum standards in the less advanced economies entails an undue increase in labour costs, leading to an erosion of their competitiveness and thus raising doubts about the long-term cohesion effects of social policy.

However, the evaluation exercise faces several difficulties. Some of the Community social directives have only been adopted very recently, while others provide for gestation periods that have only been completed recently or have yet to do so. Furthermore, there are also problems of transposition and/or implementation of Community directives. On top of this, quantitative estimates of labour costs effects are difficult to obtain, since in most cases costs are of an indirect character. In consequence, conclusions will refer to the nominal rather than the real effects of social legislation, while reference will also be made to expected economic implications, meaning that the latter will be grounded on theoretical reasoning rather than empirical analysis.

9.2.1. *Policy measures and cohesion effects*

Implementation of the 1989 action programme has not been an easy task for the Community, although the adoption of the Social Protocol of the Maastricht Treaty has created conditions for further progress to be made in the fourteen member states concerned. Legal and economic controversies surrounded many of the programme's provisions (Addison and Siebert 1991).

The Community's Social Charter has generally been criticized for its neglect of other means of improving social standards, namely public provision. As a practical matter, public provision has largely remained beyond the Community's reach because of its fiscal implications (Danson 1995). Instead, a programme of mandated benefits has been put forward, the cost of which should primarily be borne by employers, especially in less advanced countries. Against a background of increasing unemployment, social improvement should not be expected without consent. In this respect, social dialogue, despite its important legal and politico-economic limitations, may probably be the best albeit long route towards social cohesion. As a matter of fact, this new decision-making procedure—i.e. formulation of EU policy through collective bargaining (Rhodes 1995)—introduced via the social agreement in the context of the Maastricht Social Protocol, has increasingly been gaining in importance (CEC 1994*d*).

9.2.1.1. *Health and safety in the workplace*

Some of the provisions of the action programme, namely those related to health and safety in the workplace, have met with notable success. While this may be attributed to ethical and political concerns, economic considerations have been of no less importance.

Economic analysis lends support to government intervention in the area of health and safety protection, as information failures severely constrain the ability of markets to deliver efficient outcomes, i.e. adequate protection against risks, or compensating wage differentials of the correct magnitude. In the absence of regulation, high incidence of work accidents and occupational diseases results in (a) increased labour costs passed on to consumers through higher prices, (b) higher social security expenditures, and (c) demoralization of the workforce and lower productivity. Thus, governments of all persuasions in all member states have introduced legislation providing for safer working conditions. Differences between national legislation have mainly been important with regard to their institutional requirements, while being much less significant with respect to their substantive provisions (risks and groups of employees covered). This in part reflects the impact of EC legislation prior to the SEA.

The impact of Community legislation enacted within the framework of the action programme has been noteworthy. This is largely due to the approach followed by the Commission, i.e. the pursuit of an innovative strategy broadening the scope of national provisions and extending the use of new policy instruments. The adoption of the Framework Directive (89/391/EEC) provides for a firm and broad-ranging base on which a series of directives have also been adopted to cover particular sectors of employment and various occupational risks. All types of work, workers, and workplaces are included, with the exception of the self-employed and domestic servants. As a result, health and safety protection of all groups of employees is expected to strengthen in virtually all member states, while disparities among them are expected to be dramatically reduced. Will this apparently cohesive effect be achieved at an economic cost, to be unevenly borne by the less advanced economies?

As a consequence of the provisions contained in health and safety directives, all member states have to modify or extend their legislation regarding the duties of employers and the rights and responsibilities of employees. However, Greece, Spain, and Ireland have to implement broader changes, especially in the area of workplace organization, i.e. the introduction of consultation and participation procedures on all issues relating to health and safety protection. While this entails an increase in fixed labour costs—and even more important, a change in industrial relations cultures—it may be argued that this increase will be compensated by labour cost savings and productivity increases, owing to better handling of occupational risks and higher workforce enthusiasm. Obviously, the crucial assumption is that of a strong correlation between institutions and effective health and safety protection.

On the other hand, since EC health and safety directives have legally been based on Article 118A (now Art. 138), small and medium-sized firms are protected against costly and rigid methods of implementation. (This was further reinforced by the Social Protocol.) In this respect, EC legislation should not be expected to undermine employment opportunities in SMEs.

Two further points should also be stressed. First, as a result of EC legislation, emphasis has now been shifted from national laws to the implementation of Community law. The resulting simplification in regulation and its beneficial effects on operational efficiency and innovation are indirectly acknowledged by UNICE. According to a recent survey of employers, almost 40 per cent of the respondents admitted that health and safety legislation has had no impact on their companies' competitiveness, while 30 per cent recognize positive effects (UNICE 1995). Second, what is most urgent in the field of health and safety legislation is the proper transposition of Community directives into national laws and their fair implementation, a conclusion stressed by the White Paper on social policy and the medium-term social action programme in view of poor compliance records in most member states (CEC 1994*b*).

The overall impression of the impact of the Community health and safety legislation is that, subject to its proper transposition and enforcement, it will improve working conditions for all employees, reduce respective disparities among member states, and possibly contribute to an improvement of productivity and competitiveness without endangering job losses.

9.2.1.2. Equal opportunities for women and men
It is well known that equal opportunities have been a long-standing policy within the EC, and for some time were the single most effective part of European social policy (Meehan 1990). This has mainly been the result of legislation and interpretations by the European Court of Justice. Furthermore, as a result of ECJ rulings, the impact of Community legislation on equal opportunities has extended far beyond the area of gender equality towards other social and employment issues. But, precisely because gender equality might become the Trojan horse in national social policies, governments are increasing their resistance to further Community involvement (Saraceno 1994). Thus, it is not a mere coincidence that the Council of Ministers approved the fourth programme on equal opportunities only after its funding package was cut by half.

Table 9.1. Wage differentials of gross monthly earnings of non-manual workers and gross hourly earnings of manual workers, 1991 (women/men in %)

	B	DK	D	GR	E	F	IRL	I	L	NL	P	UK
Manufacturing												
manual workers	−26.2	−15.5	−26.5	−20.8	−22.6	−21.4	−30.2	−:	−39.0	−24.4	−29.5	−32.0
non-manual workers	−35.5	:	−32.6	−31.5	−36.2	−32.6	:	:	−44.1	−34.2	−30.8	−41.3
Retail trade												
non-manual workers	−26.8	:	−30.0	−19.8	−36.2	−31.7	:	:	−38.0	−32.5	−19.7	−36.2

Source: Eurostat (1993), Rapid Reports: Populations and social conditions, no. 10.

Table 9.2. Ratio of unemployment rates for women to unemployment rates for men, 1991

EU-12	B	DK	D	GR	E	F	IRL	I	L	NL	P	UK
1.5	2.3	1.2	1.5	2.7	1.9	1.6	1.1	2.3	1.9	1.8	2.2	0.8

Source: Eurostat (1993), Rapid Reports: Populations and social conditions, no. 10.

However, in spite of the Community's long-term commitment to the principle of equal treatment, the position of women in the labour market has remained weak. Although their integration into the labour market has increased, there is no indication that the gender earnings gap is set to disappear (Table 9.1), nor is there evidence that occupational segregation is set to decline. Women are likely to be overrepresented among those groups of workers who are negatively affected by international competition and industrial restructuring. As a matter of fact, at the Community level and in every member state apart from the UK, female unemployment is higher than male (Table 9.2), while women are more likely to be employed on a non-full-time basis, mainly in part-time employment (Table 9.3).

Labour market segregation is primarily the product of deep-rooted cultural and social norms and values regarding gender relationships. Indeed, in most countries many social policies still assume that women are economically dependent on a husband as well as the main providers of care for children, the handicapped, and the elderly. Examples include social security measures which do not grant individual rights (as in some pension systems), fiscal systems which discourage women from working on pay, and restrictive policies in the area of social services offering care. These all contribute to strengthening a gender division of labour unfavourable to women (Pillinger 1993).

So far as legislation is concerned, a directive on the protection of pregnant women has been adopted in the context of the 1989 social action programme. It includes provisions related to the health and safety protection of pregnant women, as well as provisions dealing with maternity benefits consisting of both pecuniary and non-pecuniary elements. These refer to pregnant women's protection against dismissal,[1] and to maternity leave and maternity pay.

[1] Protection of pregnant women against dismissal has been reinforced, following a recent ECJ ruling.

Table 9.3. Percentage of male/female part-time employment over male/female total employment, 1989 and 1994

	1989	1994	1989	1994
	Males		Females	
EU–12	3.8	4.7	27.9	30.7
B	1.7	2.5	24.9	28.3
DK	9.4	10.0	40.1	34.4
D	2.3	3.2	30.7	33.1
GR	2.4	3.1	8.0	8.0
E	1.6	2.6	11.9	15.2
F	3.5	4.6	23.6	27.8
IRL	3.1	4.8	16.7	21.3
I	3.1	2.8	10.9	12.4
L	2.0	1.3	17.0	19.5
NL	15.0	16.1	59.9	66.0
P	3.1	4.7	10.0	12.1
UK	4.9	7.1	42.9	44.3

Sources: Eurostat (1989), Labour Force Survey; Eurostat (1995), Labour Force Survey: Principal results

All member states have recognized the beneficial effects of maternity coverage on women's participation in the labour force and have accordingly introduced legislation, which does not display substantial differences among member states (for national provisions, CEC 1992). However, mere reliance on maternity benefits is by no means sufficient to ensure higher participation rates. The latter may also be attributed to wage differentials, educational attainments, other social entitlements, and above all cultural factors (Meulders, Plachman, and Vander Stricht 1993).

On the other hand, economic theory suggests that an expansion of group benefits may have efficiency consequences which depend upon financial arrangements—general taxation or social security (Gruber 1994). In social security systems, prevalent in Europe, and in the absence of relative wage adjustment due to equal pay legislation, not to mention other rigidities, increased maternity benefits would lead to labour cost increases through higher employer contributions and thus result in group-specific disemployment effects. Hence, an upward harmonization of national provisions regarding maternity benefits would probably work against the interests of those who were at first glance supposed to gain, namely women in less advanced countries.

In fact, the directive provides for some minimum requirements which hardly differ from the national standards which existed prior to its approval: it foresees an entitlement to fourteen weeks' maternity leave and requires a minimum allowance equivalent to sickness benefit. Finally, eligibility is conditional on national legislation. Thus, when compared to the *status quo ex ante*, its 'cohesion effects' are expected to be insignificant.

Social dialogue proceedings have allowed for a decisive breakthrough in sex equality legislation. The social partners bargained successfully over the issue of parental leave and the Social Affairs Council enacted the terms of their agreement into Community law by adopting a directive (a proposal for such a directive had been blocked since 1983). Besides being a turning point in European collective bargaining, the agreement has also been significant with regard to the expected effects from the implementation of the directive—the latter will also be transposed into UK legislation following the country's decision to end its social opt-out. Following the provisions of the directive, three member states where the right of parental leave does not yet exist, namely Ireland, Belgium, and Luxembourg, should have to introduce legislation. Several member states should also have to introduce changes in their legislation in order to distinguish and disassociate parental leave from maternity leave and/or to allow for the possibility of exercising the right to parental leave in a flexible way (for details on national provisions, CEC 1992 and 1993*c*). The directive's expected effects should be considered important, not only with respect to women's employment opportunities, but also with regard to potential linkages with other employment measures, e.g. replacement of those on parental leave, for the duration of their leave, by unemployed people in search of training.

Negotiation between the social partners did not proceed on the subject of the burden of proof in sex discrimination cases. Nevertheless, the Social Affairs Council managed to adopt a common position on a directive. Importantly, the UK took part in the debate, following a political agreement regarding its participation in deliberations falling under the scope of the Social Protocol during the transitional period between now and ratification of the new Treaty. The directive gives a clear definition of indirect discrimination and provides for an adjustment to the burden of proof rather than complete reversal of the latter in that 'it is up to the plaintiff to provide the proof of likely discrimination and up to the defendant to prove that there was no infringement of the principle of equal opportunities between men and women' (Agence Europe, 18 July 1997). However, some areas, such as social security, are excluded from the scope of the directive, which will enter into force in 2001. Undoubtedly, the ECJ's caseload will grow rapidly. It is debatable, though, whether implementation of the directive will improve the position of women in the labour market or merely result in an improvement in the position of those women having access to well-paid jobs.

Obviously, there are serious obstacles to further legislative action in the field of equal opportunities. Economic, socio-cultural and institutional diversities constrain efforts to adjust the existing legislation to changing labour market trends. Furthermore, they preclude legislation going beyond issues related to paid employment towards broader issues which determine gender relationships. For some commentators, EU sexual equality policy has already reached its limits (Ostner and Lewis 1995).

Partly owing to the recognition of limitations concerning legislation, and partly owing to the realization that equal opportunities are not guaranteed simply by equality in law, the Community has gradually instituted a host of measures designed to promote *de facto* equality (CEC 1995*e*). The Third Action Programme on Equal Opportunities, approved along with the 1989 social action programme, resulted in the adoption and implementation of a series of projects, measures, and initiatives aiming to promote affirmative action. The most important development probably has been the integration of equal opportunities into relevant Community policies, as well as its inclusion among the new objectives of the Structural Funds. This is the course of action also proposed in the context of the Fourth Action Programme under the principle of mainstreaming. In addition, the latter calls for increased interaction and partnership at all levels of governance, including a greater role for women's organizations. While it is important to be cautious about the real impact of these measures on the status of women in the labour market and in society at large, and even to be aware of the likelihood of dead-weight losses, one should not disregard their longer-term impact, at least on women's own efforts to influence the decision-making process at both national and EU level (Pillinger 1993).

9.2.1.3. *Labour law/minimum labour standards*

EC legislation in the field of traditional industrial relations/labour market regulation issues has historically been controversial and remained so with the 1989 social action programme on the introduction of EC-wide minimum labour standards. Indeed, this is an area where efficiency considerations clash with equity concerns and national policies differ widely with regard both to outcomes (regulation) and processes (legislation, collective agreement). Besides, labour market institutions have evolved in the framework of complex welfare systems, so that piecemeal Community interventions, subject to the principle of subsidiarity, are a priori questionable as to their operational relevance. In the context of the action programme for the implementation of the Social Charter, legislative action has focused on some aspects of the employment relationship, albeit with little success when judged on the basis of original intentions.

Nevertheless, a directive on the written form of contract has been a success, in that it introduces an improvement in existing national regulatory systems, particularly in the less advanced countries. While it may serve as an effective instrument of employee protection against violation of terms of the employment contract, it does not work against internal labour market flexibility. On the contrary, it gives employers an incentive to plan long-term changes in work organization, including the use of training, and contributes to the promotion of fairness in the workplace. As the right to a written form of contract is also preserved for part-time and temporary workers, it may be said that the directive upholds the principle of equal treatment of workers, while also serving as a means of enforcing existing national legislation towards this end. On the other hand, the (administrative) cost to employers is rather trivial, thus no adverse effects on either competitiveness or employment should be expected. However, cohesion effects, whether in terms of improving working conditions or via potential productivity gains, should not be overstated. Such effects are dependent upon the interaction of this directive with national labour market regulations, e.g. on individual dismissals.

Despite legal and economic controversies, the directive on the organization of working time was finally adopted, but only after the UK was granted a number of concessions. For example, it is stipulated that the 48-hour maximum limit for the working week could be exceeded if employees so desired, that is voluntarily (!). Moreover, several sectors including fishing, transport, and security industries, as well as continuous process work, are exempted from this limit. The directive also contains provisions on paid holidays (four weeks), rest periods, night work, shift work, etc., which hardly constitute an improvement on existing national provisions (for national provisions, CEC 1992), as they are broadly set on a lowest common denominator basis. It follows that its 'cohesion effects' should be expected to be virtually insignificant.

On the other hand, despite Anglo–German reservations (Anglo–German Deregulation Group 1995), working time standards set in the context of the directive do not prevent the introduction of flexible working arrangements and the exploitation of associated gains in terms of productivity and employment. Put more precisely, they prevent it no more than national provisions do. However, a working time organization which would imply a certain amount of flexibility and would also abide by the demands of workers themselves cannot be derived from legislative provisions, but only from negotiations at the industry, company, or even plant level, as current experience shows. The working time directive may soon be an anachronism; however, the Commission has decided to bring forward proposals to complete the directive in respect to some of those sectors that have been excluded from its provisions.

Against a background of divergent national positions, a compromise was finally reached regarding the issue of workers' secondment (posting) in the context of the free provision of services. With the UK and Portugal being outvoted, the Council agreed on a formula which lays down that local work and employment conditions must apply from the first day (i.e. zero threshold). Work and employment conditions include minimum wages, annual paid holiday, maximum periods of work and minimum rest periods, health and safety at the workplace, protective measures concerning pregnant women, children, and young people, and equal treatment for women and men. However, certain exemptions are allowed, the most notable being the possibility that local minimum wage provisions will not be applied in the case of work which is not of great magnitude ('small jobs'). The latter is meant to indicate short periods of posting, i.e. less than a month, although its exact definition has been left up to the member states. An exemption is also provided in the case of the posting of workers for the accomplishment of assembly work and/or the installation of a project, if the posting is part of the supply contract. Finally, the directive will not apply to companies setting up subsidiaries in other member states, individuals going abroad, self-employed workers, and employees in certain sectors such as the merchant navy and the media.

Among the member states, only Belgium, Luxembourg, France, Austria, and Germany have laws requiring that companies posting workers respect local wage levels and employment conditions. Thus, it appears that the directive will entail a change in most national legislations. Member states will have three years in which to transpose the directive.

This subject is not free of controversies. In principle, when transnational problems arise, some central action must be taken so that externalities are internalized, otherwise economic and social pressures will eventually emerge. Indeed, posting of workers could fall under this general principle, as in the absence of some minimum provisions it might result in substantial undercutting of wages and social provisions in certain sectors in host countries or, alternatively, it might lead to increased unemployment among local workers (BMT Consultants 1995). The construction industry, where 80 per cent of posted workers are employed, is referred to as the most relevant case. However, local unemployment could well be the outcome of high minimum wages and excessive labour costs. If this were so, then application of local wages and social provisions would perpetuate local unemployment, while impeding the employment of workers from other member states. To the extent that the majority of these workers came from regions of high unemployment, this would also work against the narrowing of regional disparities in unemployment and, thus, against regional cohesion. Furthermore, competition in the provision of services would also be unduly depressed.

The implication is that the real impact of the directive will mainly depend on national conditions, measures, and practices with respect to wage-setting and labour market norms, although some reservations should also be held regarding the provisions of the directive. Obviously, the smaller the gap between the minimum wage and the market wage rate, with the latter being determined by the imported workers' low reservation wages, the higher the risk of unemployment for local workers. Conversely, if minimum wages were set at a high level, the access of foreign workers to local labour markets would be restricted.

So far as the provisions of the directive are concerned, how will the 'small job' concept be applied? Will the application of the provision relating to short-term posting lead to the imposition of constraints on competition in the provision of services and the erection of barriers to labour mobility? Or is a very flexible application of the concept (e.g. a 30-day period defined across the range of economic sectors) likely to result in a minimization of the directive's expected effects on the protection of workers?

Commission proposals for directives on atypical work have been the most controversial, the exception being a directive on health and safety of fixed-term and part-time workers. Initially, two directives were proposed granting temporary, fixed-term, and part-time workers the same rights, pro-rated, as full-time workers, in respect to training, representation in company management structures, occupational pensions, holidays, and dismissal procedures. Following legal objections expressed by the UK (Swann 1992), the Commission merged the two directives into a new text on non-standard employment, but the Council never adopted it. In fact, there are wide variations between EU countries as to the relative importance of atypical forms of employment (see Table 9.3), which may largely be attributed to their divergent regulatory regimes (Emerson 1988, CEC 1992).

Nevertheless, the importance of flexible forms of employment has been growing rapidly and their potential contribution to the improvement of the employment situation and to equality of opportunity for women and men has come to be increasingly recognized. Against this background, the Commission decided to launch consultations with the social partners, who subsequently announced their intention to negotiate. A framework agreement has been reached, albeit concerning only part-time employment,[2] and the Social Affairs Council has finally approved a Commission proposal for a directive.

---

[2] The social partners have recently agreed to negotiate over fixed-term contracts as well.

According to the provisions of the directive, part-time employees will enjoy the same rights, pro-rated, with comparable full-time employees. However, the modalities of the application of this principle will be defined by the member states. Furthermore, an allowance is made for differential treatment, provided that the latter is justified on objective, albeit non-specified, grounds. Thus, application of earnings and time thresholds will be an option left open to the member states, although their room for manoeuvre has been substantially reduced, owing to the (indirect) implications of EU sex equality legislation—this has actually been witnessed in the UK. Nevertheless, the impact from the eventual adoption and implementation of this directive *per se* on existing national legislation and practice is not likely to be significant.

It could—and should—not be otherwise. A reduction in eligibility thresholds in some countries—as originally envisaged by the Commission—might remove the incentives governing the development of certain forms of part-time work, since it would imply an increase in employers' non-wage costs and a reduction in part-timers' net earnings. In fact, in countries where eligibility thresholds are kept relatively low, governments provide offsetting financial incentives to both employers and part-time workers, e.g. by exempting their social security contributions (France, Germany). However, this is not a course of action that all member states could afford.

Finally, the only measure adopted so far in the field of industrial democracy, the first under the Social Protocol, has been the European works councils directive, renamed the directive on European information and consultation, which applies to Community-scale undertakings. A notable feature of the directive is that it has given management and employees of multinational firms operating in Western Europe sufficient room for flexibility in allowing them to choose their own consultation procedures, although this has also been perceived as a cause for worker concern. Partly owing to this, no multinational company, UK or other, has excluded its British workers from its procedures for informing and consulting. Prior to its formal repeal, the UK social opt-out has in this case been practically invalidated.

As a matter of fact, it is increasingly recognized that consultation procedures contribute to fairness in the workplace and, thus, have beneficial effects on worker commitment to their firm and on productivity, while the impact on labour costs is minimal, so that competitiveness does not suffer. Commission services estimate wage costs per worker to be 10 ecus per year at a maximum, based on a number of assumptions (CEC 1994*d*). Furthermore, it is suggested that information and consultation procedures, or the European Committees, may be a useful means for employees to achieve some reassurance in the face of global competition, enabling them to protect their jobs by negotiating the introduction of flexible working patterns. If not cohesion *per se*, the conditions for cohesion are thus being improved.

9.2.1.4. *Social policies, social protection*

A number of Community initiatives and policy measures might be included under this heading, the majority being relatively uncontroversial. First, reference should be made to measures relating to labour mobility, an area in which the Commission has been particularly active. In addition to technical amendments of regulations 1408/71/EEC and 574/72, the Commission considers bringing forward proposals concerning the coordination of pre-retirement benefits and the revision of provisions covering unemployment benefits; it has already presented a proposal on the portability of occupational pensions within the EU. In any case, in spite of the Commission's efforts, labour mobility in the EU remains at low levels. Only a small increase in the mobility of qualified labour is foreseen (Marsden 1994), which should not be expected to achieve much regional adjustment. As a matter of fact, to the extent that skilled labour is a complement to unskilled labour, a worsening of regional unemployment disparities might well be the outcome of this process, given also the continuing fall in the demand for unskilled labour (Begg 1995).

On the other hand, there has recently been an upsurge in immigration from outside the EC, which tends to exacerbate labour market imbalances by increasing labour supply, while also contributing to a widening of regional disparities in unemployment (CEC 1994c). Furthermore, in the southern member states the influx of immigrants has been associated with a substantial increase in illegal forms of employment, a factor that has to some extent contributed to the deterioration in public finances. Economic anxieties have given rise to hostile social attitudes, which in turn have been exploited by populist politicians and racist political movements. Against this background, the Commission has proposed a range of action to combat racism and xenophobia and to improve the economic and social position of migrant workers, while the social partners have adopted a joint opinion on the issue.

Turning now to the broader issues of social policy and social protection, it has to be admitted that there is no easy way to evaluate Community actions and initiatives in terms of some concrete results. Bearing in mind the principle of subsidiarity, the overall aims of these actions are to stimulate debate and action in member states related to the challenges arising from contemporary social problems such as the ageing of societies, the rise of new forms of poverty and social exclusion, the growth in single parenthood, the position of disabled persons in economic and social life, etc.

The Green Paper on social policy and various Commission communications and independent evaluation reports describe a range of actions undertaken by the Community in order to increase the awareness of government and the public at large and to stimulate national policy responses, something which has been achieved to a certain extent (e.g. Community actions for older people: Jamieson *et al.* 1994). The White Paper goes on to propose further action relating to older people and the disabled as well as to the fight against social exclusion. However, despite the relatively successful implementation of the three poverty programmes (CEC 1993b), the Council of Ministers has not yet approved the Medium Term Action Programme to Combat Exclusion and Promote Solidarity, arguing that it contradicts the principle of subsidiarity—a symbolic refusal?[3]

---

[3] Following a recent ECJ ruling, authorization by the member states is legally required for expenditure on projects relating to these issues. The case was brought to the court by the UK government; actually, the Conservative government launched the case and the new Labour government decided to proceed with it.

Within this range of actions, the most important development relates to social protection. Against a background of common pressures on social protection systems, with unemployment being the most acute one, and despite considerable national diversities, the Community has embarked on a strategy of joint reflection and exchange of experience between the member states, including concertation with the social partners, in order to improve policymakers' insight into problems and, ultimately, lead them to effective solutions. Preservation of the European social model necessitates adaptation to the ever-changing social and economic environment and, therefore, implementation of radical reforms, and to this end the Community might act as a reform catalyst.

In this respect, in 1991 the Commission proposed a convergence strategy for social protection, which led the Council to adopt two Recommendations, one on the convergence of social protection objectives and policies and the other on common criteria concerning sufficient resources and social assistance in social protection systems. Meanwhile, following the White Paper on Growth, Competitiveness and Employment, subsequent European Councils have defined a range of measures to improve the employment situation. These measures have largely been related to the social protection systems. A step towards further Community involvement in this area has also been taken in the form of a Commission proposal for a framework for debate on the future of social protection (CEC 1995*c*), which has recently been endorsed by the Social Affairs Council. Although the Community's value added on national policies is not identifiable, at least in the short term, expectations should, in principle, be positive.

9.3. European Employment Strategy: A Blueprint for Labour Market Reforms?

Unemployment in the EU reached a peak of 11.3 per cent in 1994 (CEC 1995*b* and 1997). In fact, when the Commission presented its White Paper on Growth, Competitiveness and Employment the Community was going through a deep recession, losing within two years one-half of the 9.3 million jobs created during the economic boom of the second half of the 1980s. Building on the approach of the White Paper, the European Council approved an employment action plan in December 1993; one year later a European employment strategy (EES) was adopted at the European Council meeting at Essen.

In the context of the EES a call is made for the coordinated implementation of macroeconomic and structural labour market policies, both at national and Community level. Five key areas for structural policy action are defined and the member states are urged to transpose their individual policies into multi-annual programmes, incorporating a range of recommended measures. A surveillance procedure is also introduced and the Commission, ECOFIN, and the Social Affairs Council are asked to monitor trends and national employment policies in order to ensure a cooperative approach.

Discussions on the role of the Community in the area of employment were intensive in the context of the intergovernmental conference on the revision of TEU and during the Amsterdam European Council. They materialized in a new employment chapter inserted in the revised treaty and were also reflected in the Presidency conclusions and in the Resolution on Growth and Employment annexed to the conclusions. In addition, the revised treaty reinforces the Community commitment to a high level of employment and social protection (EPC 1997). The employment chapter provides for the institutionalization of the surveillance procedure, whilst a consultative role is also prescribed for a new Employment Committee. However, it is stressed that the competencies of the member states must be respected and the Community may only support and complement, if necessary, their action. So far as the general orientation of the coordinated employment strategy is concerned, the documents of the Amsterdam summit make reference to the same broad structural policy guidelines proposed at Essen, though sometimes with a different wording.[4] Finally, at the request of France and in partial exchange for the German-inspired stability pact, the Amstedam European Council decided to convene a special jobs summit.

9.3.1. *Prerequisites for structural reform: macroeconomic policy and beyond*

The primary aim of the EES has been to increase awareness on the part of governments concerning the need for structural reforms, and to stimulate action towards this end. This is justified. European labour markets sluggishly adjust to changes in macroeconomic policy and poorly respond to pressures arising from international competition and technical progress. Thus, since the early 1970s unemployment in the Community has tended to be persistent, in most countries ratcheting up with each recession. EFTA economies, which had previously been successful in stabilizing unemployment, experienced a sharp rise in their unemployment rates during the 1990s. Furthermore, unemployment has been especially pronounced among youths, women, and unskilled workers; and a significant share of the unemployed—in some countries reaching levels well above 40 per cent—have been unemployed for more than a year (CEC 1994*a*, CEPR 1995, OECD 1994, 1995). Although economic growth in the EU has started to gather strength since 1996, unemployment is expected to decrease only slightly (CEC 1997). Meanwhile, in the US accelerated output growth has brought unemployment in 1997 to a twenty-four-year low, at 4.5 per cent, prompting facile talk of a 'new economy'.

It seems that there has been an increase in the structural or equilibrium rate of unemployment in Europe. However, there is enough evidence to suggest that the fundamental determinants of equilibrium unemployment have little changed since the early 1970s (OECD 1994). Mainstream economists have shown that the apparent increase in structural unemployment should be thought of as the outcome of past shocks having long-lived effects; it should, in other words, be attributed to hysteresis (e.g. Blanchard and Summers 1986).

---

[4] This chapter refers to the Essen formulation because the purpose of the whole volume is to provide an *ex post* evaluation of the impact of Community policies on cohesion up until now.

Various sources of hysteresis have been discussed in the literature, some operating on the demand side and some on the supply side of the labour market; although two-sided effects may also be identified. A variety of factors leading to a *de facto* erection of barriers between labour market insiders and outsiders have been proposed (e.g. Lindbeck and Snower 1988; Blanchard and Jimeno 1995), all pointing to a degree of real wage adjustment lower than would be required to make the unemployed workers employable. It is suggested that the generosity of the unemployment benefit system tends to reduce the incentives for the unemployed to undertake intensive job search and to reduce their willingness to accept job offers. It is demonstrated that strict job protection legislation, by increasing firms' labour turnover costs, enables those in employment to secure unwarranted wage increases; it also prevents firms from making new hirings and thus reducing the pool of unemployed, even if business conditions improve. Moreover, it is specified that prolonged unemployment weakens the unemployed workers' skills and motivation and makes them less attractive to employers. As a result, the long-term unemployed workers exercise little, if any, impact on wage setting.

In the presence of hysteresis factors, which tend to transform short-term cyclical effects into long-lasting ones, care should be taken to avoid big rises in unemployment, as these may not easily be reversed. Obviously, this is mostly relevant in the case of supply shocks, which tend to move prices and output in opposite directions. At the same time, structural policies should be introduced to tackle the underlying causes of hysteresis. In this respect, the view that macroeconomic policy has very little role to play in reducing unemployment and that it should primarily aim at price stability is ill-conceived, particularly when a short-term frame of reference is implied. Alas, this view has overtly influenced European economic policymaking.

The important issue is how the introduction of structural policies should shape macroeconomic policy objectives; an issue that has largely been left untouched by the EES, which has mainly—and not surprisingly—looked at it the other way round. From an economic point of view, if supply-side measures aiming at an improvement of real wage flexibility are introduced, an expansion in demand and an increase in inflation may accelerate real wage reduction and the associated increase in labour demand, thus leading to sharper employment growth. Nevertheless, this increase in inflation may not be permanent but only short-lived, as the reduction in real wages will also have been precipitated by structural measures rather than being merely the outcome of an unanticipated rise in inflation, which is, eventually, built into future wage demands. A reduction in the equilibrium rate of unemployment will obviously have been brought about (for an excellent analysis, CEPR 1995).

From a political economy perspective, it may be reckoned that structural policies attempting to shorten the distance between insiders and outsiders, unless introduced in a favourable macroeconomic environment, are very likely to be opposed by both groups of workers. In general, the short-term incidence of the unfavourable effects of reform on insiders' job and income security may not be compensated by increased employment opportunities for outsiders within the same time period. For example, the removal of excessive job protection legislation may provide some firms with an opportunity to shed unwanted labour, but it is doubtful whether other firms may readily proceed to new hirings. Anticipation of the lower cost of firing is but one element in the decision to hire; strong demand prospects are probably the most important factor. Therefore, the majority of outsiders would have little incentive to support this measure; those still employable might even join forces with insiders (different degrees of insiderness and outsiderness imply different responses on the part of the workers concerned: Lindbeck 1992). On the other hand, an increase in spending on active labour market policies financed by a reduction in expenditures on income maintenance schemes would muster the political support of neither the outsiders nor the insiders. The former would clearly not be willing to exchange a certain amount of income support for a lower amount plus uncertain employment opportunities. Insiders would also resist measures that increased competition for jobs, especially when employment prospects remain weak. Further-more, if they feel uncertain about their own job prospects, insiders may not accept the weakening of schemes on which they may need to rely.

Yet, it is maintained, the interests of insiders carry more political weight. Also, in times of better conditions the need for reforms becomes less evident, whereas in adverse conditions, when there is a higher risk of a good share of workers becoming unem-ployed, the chances for reform are increased. Thus, it is argued, when unemployment is increasing, the introduction of flexible employment contracts is a politically viable option, as it provides insiders with a 'job safety net' without affecting their own con-tracts; and empirical evidence bears this out (Saint-Paul 1996 and 1997). However, partial reform is likely to reinforce the position of a hard core of insiders, as Spanish experience has amply made clear (Bentolila and Dolado 1994).

In short, an enduring reduction in unemployment presupposes an attack on its fun-damental structural causes. It is, therefore, conditional on the introduction of reforms aiming at increasing competition in the labour market and improving wage responsive-ness. Indeed, this is a painful cure so long as its costs are felt almost immediately, while its consequential employment gains may take time to materialize. It carries a political cost too, as those who are about to lose are more numerous than the unemployed who are expected to gain. Being in any case costly, reforms may not be introduced unless supported by a macroeconomic policy allowing for a realization of employment gains sooner rather than later. This is not just a matter of pure political calculus. As a matter of fact, labour market policy reforms may often hold a prominent place in a govern-ment's policy agenda. However, in view of bitter opposition they may be partially implemented and/or inappropriately revised. The credibility of reform is then circum-scribed and the effects on employment may be virtually minimal (Bertola and Ichino 1995).

The above framework helps one to put the European unemployment experience into perspective. Thus, notwithstanding divergences in national experience, disinfla-tion in the 1980s was bought at the price of a big rise in unemployment, whereas it would have been better to reduce inflation by small amounts of excess unemployment over a longer time period. Besides, some governments' institutional commitment to price stability, via currency participation in the ERM, was not sufficient to ease wage pressures and lower the so-called sacrifice ratio. Real wage rigidities tended to frustrate wage responsiveness, thus necessitating a higher level of unemployment in order to keep inflation at a desired level; furthermore, this increased unemployment was becoming structurally embedded.

The political decision about the movement to EMU compelled European governments to ignore that, in the absence of sufficiently flexible labour markets, accommodation of the German demand shock—induced by unification—would require a realignment of parities within the ERM. Instead, they followed excessively tight monetary policies, albeit not credible in view of their implied output and employment losses. The sustainability of the ERM was jeopardized and certain currencies were forced to devalue and leave the system. There was also a widening of fluctuation margins for the rest. However, some governments, most notably the French, wishing to preserve their parities with the D-mark, continued to follow tight macroeconomic policies, which led to heavy employment losses. With the benefit of hindsight, it may be argued that increased unemployment in the 1990s also reflected the failure of governments to introduce reforms during the later 1980s, when economic conditions were very favourable. It certainly was not easier to do so during the first half of the 1990s, when conditions severely deteriorated.

As a matter of fact, labour market reforms are much needed in the context of EMU, particularly in view of its institutional provisions and policy arrangements, as well as its underlying structural and economic imbalances (for a review of empirical studies inspired by the OCA theory, Bayoumi and Eichengreen 1996). Nevertheless, it is precisely the mix of institutions and policy arrangements that raises doubt whether substantial progress towards labour market flexibility is likely to be made and causes concern about the impact of EMU on employment and real convergence. Thus, it is unlikely that an excessively tight monetary policy—followed by the European Central Bank at least during the early phases of a broad EMU in order to ensure anti-inflationary credibility—associated with heavily restricted national fiscal policies—as implied by the stability and growth (?) pact—will provide for a macroeconomic policy stance conducive to reform, let alone sufficient stabilization against common (especially supply) and asymmetric shocks. If this is the case, pressures may arise for a stronger EU fiscal role in terms of stabilization and redistribution (Tsoukalis 1997: 186), albeit with unforeseen financial implications (for a pessimistic view, see von Hagen and Eichengreen 1996).

Here lies the main issue in regard to an effective EU-level response to the unemployment crisis and not in the cooperation among national governments in the context of the surveillance procedure provided for by the EES and the employment chapter. However important, as institutional integration analysts would maintain, the surveillance procedure is not likely to deliver major results in the area of labour market policy reform. This will be made evident in the following paragraphs. As an appetizer, it may be noted that divergent labour market traditions, policies, and institutions imply different reform priorities. Besides, similar measures may dramatically differ in their impact, depending on the structural and economic background of the individual member states. Finally, policy effects may be very different from those initially anticipated and even minor changes may exert their impact in the long term; this being it so, annual policy appraisals may be of limited real value.

9.3.2. The relevance of the Community structural policy recommendations

Community structural policy recommendations could only signify a general policy stance, taking into consideration the various national concerns but not specifying the actual policy means. The following five priorities for structural policy action were defined at Essen (CEC 1995*b*):

1. Investment in vocational training;
2. Making growth more employment intensive;
3. Reducing non-wage labour costs;
4. Improving the effectiveness of labour market policy;
5. Improving measures for groups particularly hard hit by unemployment.

What follows is an attempt to assess these recommendations, with emphasis being placed on mutual interactions between policy measures.

9.3.2.1. Investment in vocational training

The need for more and better training seems to be one of the most uncontroversial ideas about economic policy, underpinned by the fact that unskilled and unqualified workers face the possibility of a continuing decline in their earnings relative to the skilled labour force.

Privately provided training is bound to be inadequate. A market failure case may be established, owing to employers' reluctance to equip workers with improved skills when there is a high risk that these workers will be poached by competing firms (Booth and Snower 1996). Hence, there is a strong argument in favour of government provision, although this may not meet firms' needs.

On the other hand, public spending on labour market training is mainly concentrated on training for the unemployed and those at risk of becoming redundant. However, there is now enough evidence to suggest that training schemes may well deliver poor results when measured in terms of post-scheme employment rates for participants. Deadweight costs as well as substitution effects are very likely to occur (OECD 1994). It is found that training programmes are more likely to be effective when targeted on groups for which it is possible to attribute identifiable training needs that can be met. At the same time it is deemed essential that training for the unemployed is associated with improved counseling, thus being an integral part of active labour market policies; but then consideration should also be given to the likely interactions between the unemployment insurance systems and training provisions. Negative effects on search behaviour or prolonged dependency on state support may well appear.

On the other hand, given that on-the-job training caters effectively for firms' demands, while being conducive to employment by definition, it is appropriate that policy action should also aim at improving incentives for private provision. In this respect, minimum wages that set too high a wage floor and high tax wedges may work against private arrangements. Firms would not be willing to incur higher labour costs, nor would workers accept lower net earnings. Policy reforms to encourage private provision may be indispensable in times of 'fiscal prudence'.

9.3.2.2. *Making growth more employment-intensive*

According to the Essen conclusions, an increase in the employment intensity of growth may be achieved by:

- a more flexible organization of work;
- a wage policy which encourages job-creating investments and which in the present situation requires moderate wage agreements below increases in productivity;
- finally, the promotion of initiatives, particularly at regional and local level, which create jobs that take account of new social requirements.

So far as the first issue is concerned, flexibility in working time arrangements has been associated with a reduction in working time. It is suggested that the latter may be brought about by a reduction of standard full-time hours, short-term work, replacement of full-time by part-time jobs, limits to permissible overtime working, and the introduction of career breaks and other special forms of leave.

Discussion has currently focused on the question whether governments should impose a generalized reduction in working hours in order to increase employment and reduce unemployment. However, empirical evidence suggests that if wages are not reduced and/or the operating time of productive capacities is not increased, a generalized reduction in working time will result in increased wage costs and inflation, thus minimizing if not worsening employment prospects (for a survey of empirical evidence, OECD 1994). Yet, despite the opposition of employers' organizations, the French and the Italian governments have recently decided to introduce a 35-hour week by 2000 and 2001 respectively, albeit with substantial qualifications and special exemptions—not to mention deliberate ambiguities.

On the other hand, while working time arrangements are more often than not a matter of collective bargaining, labour market regulations and employment protection legislation can either promote or hinder flexibility in the organization of working time. This applies to all sorts of measures previously mentioned. Labour market regulations which may influence working time arrangements include statutory limitations to normal working hours and overtime, flexible distribution of working hours, including annualized work hours, shift work, and regulation of part-time employment. Furthermore, employment protection legislation seems to play a quite important role in the evolution of flexible work patterns, since it is linked with employer attitudes towards overtime working.

Turning to the issue of wage policies, the relevant question is whether government policies and labour market institutions allow for a degree of wage flexibility conducive to employment growth, especially with regard to monetary unification and increased international competition. There are two aspects to this: the first relates to minimum wage policies and the second to wage bargaining institutions.

So far as minimum wages are concerned, many Community countries impose a minimum wage which is either statutory—France, Luxembourg, Netherlands, Portugal, Spain—or is established via collective bargaining at national—Greece, Belgium, Sweden—or sectoral level—Germany, Italy, Denmark—(on national provisions, Bazen and

Benhayoun, 1992; CEPR 1995). Economic analysis has made it evident that minimum wages have adverse employment effects. By compressing wage differentials at the lower end of the pay scale, they prevent an expansion of low-skilled jobs and exclude the unskilled, particularly young workers, from the labour market. Although recent research has suggested that imposition of minimum wages may increase both wages and employment (Card and Krueger 1994; but see Deere, Murphy, and Finis 1995), this has not been intended to imply that a high level of minimum wages may also have positive employment effects.

Nevertheless, minimum wages are not meant as an efficiency/job-creation device. They aim at a better distribution of income. Therefore, a very low minimum wage level may have very poor distributional implications. However, the minimum wage is not an appropriate means to achieve equity, given its unpleasant employment effects. On the other hand, a mere reduction in minimum wages would have the effect of raising reservation wages, thus increasing the risk of the unemployed being caught in an unemployment trap. Therefore, a reduction in minimum wages should be associated with changes in the structure of social benefits, towards an expansion of in-work benefits. But this may not be the happy end of a reform scenario. Higher in-work benefits tend to be associated with high implicit marginal tax rates. If targeted on the lowest paid, the amount of in-work benefits actually received declines as wage rises, and real take-home pay does not follow wage increases. This being so, a work disincentive emerges, eventually leading to the creation of a poverty trap. (UK experience is particularly pertinent to this problem.) This discussion suggests that, unless major reforms are introduced in social protection and taxation systems, abolition of minimum wages may hardly be considered as a feasible policy measure.

On the other hand, labour market organization and, in particular, wage bargaining institutions are thought to bear significantly on wage flexibility and employment (e.g. Newell and Symons 1987; Calmfors and Driffil 1988). However, in the light of recent experience in Sweden and Germany, the anything but conventional argument that both centralized/coordinated and decentralized wage bargaining may be consistent with low unemployment should be re-examined. As a matter of fact, centralized wage bargaining has always been one pillar of a wider social contract, the other pillars being industrial policy, macroeconomic coordination, and the welfare state. Leaving aside the other aspects, wage moderation has been exchanged for higher welfare provisions, including job security and income protection. However, the burden of the subsequently higher taxes—broadly conceived—on economic activity may hardly be sustained for much longer. Economic integration and international competition make it even harder. Also, Summers (1987) has pointed out that strong central-level labour unions are very likely to succeed in their demands for stricter employment protection legislation, the adverse effects of which may eventually offset the favourable effects of wage moderation. On the other hand, centralized wage bargaining, while allowing for wage moderation, has tended to constrain relative wage flexibility so that wage structures have only partially reflected sectoral and regional productivity differences, not to mention differences among specialized types of labour, the importance of which has been growing rapidly. Therefore, the economic feasibility of centralized wage bargaining may be questioned.

The above discussion does not necessarily imply that European economies, most of which are placed at the intermediate level of the wage bargaining scale, should unconditionally opt for the decentralized model. In the presence of strong lower-level trade unions, this may well lead to undesirable effects (Soskice 1990). Nevertheless, the debate on wage bargaining systems has largely been misplaced, if anything because of its inherent neglect of factors other than wages with significant effects on employment (e.g. employment protection legislation, social protection systems). In this respect, policy action should primarily be directed towards these areas. Meanwhile, a flexible approach to wage bargaining might be helpful, e.g. by allowing for multi-level agreements in order to ensure both a degree of wage coordination and relative wage flexibility. However, this is an area of national experimentation, for which the outcome will be determined by economic as well as political factors; no doubt, labour market institutions are hardly exportable (Freeman 1988; Heylen and van Poeck 1995).

The issue of local employment, as well as other employment initiatives, has received considerable attention from the Community. A programme called LEDA was introduced in 1993 to stimulate research and action in this area. Seventeen areas of activity were identified, which might potentially expand to meet new needs in the areas of personal, communal, and social services and environmental protection. However, the extent of this potential as well as its realization are dependent on both demand and supply factors. Given a high elasticity of income demand, total demand for these services and their employment share will obviously depend upon income developments. Nevertheless, social and demographic factors may also play a role, e.g. the greater the proportion of older people, the higher the demand for home-care services.

However, demand and employment may remain subdued because of the relatively high cost of labour. This has been made evident by the spread of illegal labour in domestic and home-care services. On the other hand, high reservation wages, owing to generous unemployment benefits and/or relaxed eligibility criteria, combined with the low esteem of these jobs, may also hinder employment (the supply side).

9.3.2.3. *Reducing non-wage labour costs*
Non-wage costs constitute a significant proportion of total labour costs in many Community economies. Thus, it has been suggested that a reduction in non-wage costs, in particular social contributions by employers, would allow for an increase in labour demand. There are two issues to be considered. The first is whether a reduction in non-wage costs would bring a reduction in total labour costs, and the second is how the reduction in social security contributions would be financed.

As far as the first issue is concerned, the relevant question is whether a change in non-wage costs would affect wage determination, thus bringing a change in total labour costs and consequently in labour demand. If labour and product markets were perfectly competitive, wages would fully respond to unemployment and the labour market would clear. An increase in social contributions by employers would, initially, result in increased total labour costs, but the consequential rise in unemployment would push wages down. In other words, an increase in social contributions by employers would be compensated by a wage reduction.

Table 9.4. Elasticity of labour costs with respect to employer social security contributions

Germany	1.0
Canada	0.8
Japan	0.5
Finland	0.5
Australia	0.5
France	0.4
Italy	0.4
Sweden	0.0[a]
United States	0.0[b]
UK	0.25

[a] The estimated zero elasticity is obviously questionable; yet, in the same study, the elasticity of labour costs with respect to income taxes and employer social contributions is estimated to be 1.0.

[b] This is again questionable. The explanation offered is that for both USA and Sweden the data may simply reflect the period covered.

Source: OECD (1994: 246).

However, markets are not perfectly competitive. Thus, an increase in social contributions by employers may not be compensated by a wage cut if employees are able to resist it successfully. Thus, the result may be a rise in unemployment. Besides union bargaining power, such an effect also depends upon the degree of competition in product markets. Employers may yield to employee wage demands if social contributions are likely to be shifted into product prices. This may then lead to a reduction in the demand for products and labour.

Nevertheless, while in general an increase in social contributions by employers may increase total labour costs and reduce labour demand in the short term, the size of this effect, as well as its longevity and, therefore, its potential to increase unemployment, are dependent upon the degree of wage rigidity. Conceivably, the incidence of an increase in social contributions by employers differs among countries and is largely determined by structural and institutional labour market factors. In principle, one should expect that in countries characterized by flexible labour markets, an increase in social contributions by employers might be shifted to wages sooner rather than later, so that total labour costs are not affected and unemployment is not increased.

The balance of evidence from empirical studies, reported in the OECD *Jobs Study* (1994), supports the view that in countries with inflexible labour markets, an increase in social contributions by employers is not absorbed by a lower wage increase and thus affects total labour costs and employment. This is certainly found to occur in the short term, and it may occur to a smaller extent in the longer term. Below are presented estimates of the elasticity of labour cost with respect to employer social security contributions for various countries (Table 9.4). These estimates, again reported in the OECD *Jobs Study*, corroborate the aforementioned theoretical suggestions.

In policy terms, the case for a permanent reduction in employer social contributions in order to secure a permanent reduction of unemployment seems to be weak. As a matter of fact, on the basis of the estimates contained in Table 9.4, as well as empirical evidence reported in the OECD *Jobs Study*, the case appears stronger for Germany, Spain and Austria.[5] However, there is some scope for temporary reductions, e.g. in the aftermath of a recession for a certain period of time. Furthermore, reductions in employer social contributions, targeted at certain segments of the workforce such as the long-term unemployed and the young, may well increase employment opportunities for these people. Indeed, a reduction in employer social contributions will cause a permanent reduction in labour costs, which could not otherwise be brought about, owing to the operation of wage floors. However, it is clear that reform priorities should extend over a far wider area than that of pecuniary non-wage costs.

A further issue is raised in the White Paper on Growth, Competitiveness and Employment. Given the fact that in most European economies (except Belgium, Portugal, and the UK) the rates of employer social contributions are regressively related to wage levels, a change in formula towards progressivity or proportionality would reduce the relative cost of labour for the lower-paid unskilled workers and would allow for an increase in demand for unskilled labour. However, unless changes were also introduced in the formulae for benefits, a change in the formula for contributions would have distributional implications likely to be resisted by higher-paid skilled workers.

With regard to the question of how a targeted reduction in employer social contributions may be financed, the issue raised above could also be argued as an option. Furthermore, a number of additional options have been proposed, ranging from taxes on consumption and investment income to charges on scarce national resources and energy. Besides the different economic and distributional implications as well as the political feasibility of each option, there is the vital issue of whether the compensatory sums raised by each measure would or actually should be spent again on social security. It goes beyond the purposes of the present paper to comment on this issue, which, admittedly, has come to the centre of European politics.

9.3.2.4. *Improving the effectiveness of labour market policy*

The high increase in European unemployment, which has been concentrated among particular groups and which has been associated with a rise in long-term unemployment, has brought to the surface the issue of the effectiveness of labour market policy towards the unemployed. Economic research has produced much evidence to support the view that labour market policy has been counterproductive. This has, in turn, been attributed to policy preoccupation with passive measures, especially income support for the unemployed, at the expense of measures designed to promote re-employment of those workers (active policies). As a matter of fact, this practice has been followed in most of the Community member states (CEC 1994*a*). Furthermore, income support policies have tended to distort incentives, primarily in relation to the unemployed but also to employed workers, and thus reinforce their negative implications.

---

[5] The evidence for Germany and Austria also suggests problems pertaining to centralized wage bargaining; cf. earlier discussion.

Table 9.5. The value and duration of unemployment benefits[a]

	1st period (% of earnings)	Duration (months)	2nd period (% of earnings)	Duration (months)
Belgium	79	12	55	Indefinite
Denmark	73	30	63	Indefinite
Germany	63	12	56	Indefinite
Greece	28	12	0	n.a
Spain	80	6	70	18
France	80	12	67–33[b]	Indefinite
Ireland	41	12	32–35[c]	Indefinite
Italy	26	6	0	n.a
Luxembourg	85	12	46	Indefinite
Netherlands	74	24	49	Indefinite
Portugal	81	21	44	21
UK	23	12	23	Indefinite
EC average	61	14	42	

[a] 40-year-old with 20 years of employment, earning the average wage.
[b] August 1992: 67 per cent for 4 months, then 46 per cent, 38 per cent for another 4 months and 33 per cent thereafter.
[c] 32 per cent for 3 months, then 35 per cent.

Source: European Economy (1994), 56: 190.

The level of unemployment benefits and hence the replacement ratios to which they give rise, their duration and their administration, have rendered unemployment compensation systems in most Community countries susceptible to massive problems of moral hazard. Although a high replacement ratio *per se* is found to have little direct effect (Atkinson and Micklewright 1991), its association with lengthy periods of coverage may generate substantial negative externalities. Reference is made in particular to the impact of unemployment compensation systems on wage determination. There are several channels through which this impact may be felt. Unemployment compensation systems may weaken the job-search intensity of the unemployed to such an extent that they put only little downward pressure on the wage level. For obvious reasons, the longer-term unemployed may have virtually zero influence on the wage level. On the other hand, a generous unemployment compensation system may allow unions to push their wage claims, since it implies that those who may become unemployed will still maintain an income comparable to their previous earnings. Finally, unemployment compensation systems may cause higher wage floors, which hinder wage adjustments at the lower end of the pay scale. However, this is dependent upon the character of the unemployment compensation system (earnings-related or flat-rate benefits), while such an effect may be more frequent in the case of open-ended unemployment assistance.

An indication of how Community unemployment compensation systems are structured is provided in Table 9.5. Only in Spain and Italy is the duration of the initial benefit less than one year, while in seven member states unemployment benefits during the first (insurance) period exceed two-thirds of earnings in previous employment. On the other hand, during the second (assistance) period, the benefit is reduced in virtually all member states. However, eight member states have unemployment assistance of indefinite duration. This may more than offset the effects that lower second-period benefits are expected to have on wage determination. Longer spells of unemployment render the unemployed less competitive (for an almost precise calculation of replacement ratios, see CEC 1995*f*).

However, unemployment compensation systems may in principle help a better allocation of labour, by encouraging job search and allowing for a better matching of skills. Thus, shortening the duration of unemployment benefits may force people to opt for lower quality jobs with the consequence of human capital losses. Indeed, unemployment compensation systems allow some individuals to wait for the right offer, while pushing others into permanent unemployment. Economies should thus strike a balance between these positive and negative aspects in order to establish an optimal level of unemployment insurance benefits.

On the other hand, in his 1942 report, Lord Beveridge proposed that 'unemployment benefits will continue at the same rate without means test so long as unemployment lasts, but will normally be subject to a condition of attendance at a work or training centre after a certain period. . . . The normal period of unconditional benefit will be six months'. After all, 'complete idleness even on an income demoralizes' (adopted from Layard, Nickell, and Jackman 1991: 62). However, this simple truth has been side-stepped. Neither has the test-work received attention, nor have sufficient activation measures been introduced.

Active labour market policies aim at enhancing labour market mobility and adjustment, facilitating the re-employment of workers and enabling them to take advantage of opportunities. Recently, it has been argued that active labour market policies, co-ordinated with the unemployment benefit system, may make union wage behaviour more aggressive, owing to anticipation of government help in case of job loss (Calmfors 1993). In addition, it is claimed that active labour market policies may involve substantial deadweight losses and substitution effects, which make their real impact doubtful. Much of this criticism has been fuelled by the Swedish failure. However, it seems that this failure was caused mainly by a central element of the Swedish model, namely that of the state being an employer of last resort. One may even think that this element has caused an overestimation of the country's past employment records. But it has, in any case, caused a significant rise in taxes and probably has further contributed to the reported excessive public provision of household services (Rosen 1996) at the expense of privately produced material goods. On the other hand, if administered with caution and subject to certain conditions, active policy measures may be less exposed to risks of deadweight losses and substitution effects.

Furthermore, animation of public employment services may be important. A range of measures, including frequent monitoring of job-search efforts, improved counselling for unemployment benefit claimants, and rapid training courses, may improve the employability of the unemployed, reduce the risk of demotivation, and curtail moral hazard.

Table 9.6. Number of unemployed per staff number in employment offices and related services, 1992

	Employment offices only	Plus network and programme management	Plus unemployment benefit administration (when separate)
Belgium	118	76	44
Denmark (1988)	134	102	
Germany	70	60	39
Greece	994	497	172
Spain	350	191	191
France (1988)	276	124	79
Ireland	788		100
Netherlands	103	80	32
Austria	70	49	34
Portugal	169	51	51
Finland	136	105	
Sweden	38	28	27
UK	82	72	72

Source: OECD (1994: 104).

The activities of public employment services are more often than not labour-intensive, so that their effectiveness seems to be dependent upon the availability of human resources. Table 9.6 shows pronounced differences among Community countries with respect to the expected effectiveness of public employment services in performing their tasks. However, recent unemployment experience suggests that effective public employment services and active labour market policies in general may not be the most important determinants of labour market performance.

Making the unemployed more competitive may not by itself lead to a reduction in unemployment. Besides policies aiming at bringing the 'outsiders' closer to the labour market, policies are also required in order to make the 'insiders' less insulated from labour market developments. Reduction of unemployment presupposes a reduction in wage pressure, and, in this respect, action should be directed towards tackling all those factors that make wages unresponsive to unemployment.

9.3.2.5. Improving measures for groups particularly hard hit by unemployment
The long-term unemployed, young people, older workers, and women are included among those groups that have been hard hit by unemployment. So far as policies targeted at the long-term unemployed are concerned, attention should be paid to the fact that these workers are much less employable than the short-term unemployed, so that they can exert virtually no influence on wage determination and, thus, may be unable to help contain inflationary pressures. In addition, long-term unemployment may often lead to the marginalization of these people. Their exit from the labour market also weakens their political voice.

On economic grounds, when active policies are contemplated, it should be acknowledged that the benefit to the taxpayer is greater when a long-term unemployed person is removed from unemployment than when a short-term unemployed person is removed from unemployment (Layard, Nickell, and Jackman 1991). Nevertheless, the cost may be higher because of the substantial amount of human capital investment involved in placing one of the long-term unemployed. Employment subsidies may be the most important policy instrument, also implying relatively unimportant deadweight and substitution-related costs in comparison with other active policy measures against long-term unemployment.

Measures targeted at young people often take the form of training programmes. However, attention should be paid to the operation of education systems and their interaction with the labour market. The German experience of apprenticeships suggests how effective interaction may be achieved. On the other hand, the employment effects of income protection policies operating via labour market channels should not be overlooked. Restriction of early retirement and promotion of equal opportunities may be beneficial for older workers and women.

It is clear from the above discussion that labour market reform requires decisive action. More importantly, an effective structural policy requires a coordinated rather than fragmented approach towards reforming labour markets. Given strong policy interactions, if reform measures were implemented in isolation, their effects would probably be minimized, while in some cases their impact would even be detrimental. Community policy recommendations seem generally to reflect the need for reforms to improve flexibility in European labour markets, but they conspicuously lack any reference to distortionary employment protection legislation. (For a comprehensive review of employment protection legislation as well as an assessment of its strictness, see OECD 1994; for a survey of European employers' attitudes, see *European Economy* 1991 and 1995).

Undoubtedly, there are efficiency limits to flexibility. Nevertheless, how labour markets function is greatly affected by equity concerns—labour markets do not resemble markets for fish, as Solow (1990) puts it. If labour market flexibility is important for employment—and, indeed, it is—a change in social policy arrangements is urgently needed and hence a wholesale reform in social protection systems may not be sidestepped. As a matter of fact, European societies are now confronted with an equity–unemployment trade-off; searching for easy solutions to the problem of unemployment would be a futile exercise. Ideology, though, may continue to influence policy choices (Saint-Paul 1996).

Considering the evidence from the member states, it seems that policy action has seldom been coordinated, let alone comprehensive. It may be true that, besides the UK, some other member states have actually made progress, e.g. Spain, the Netherlands and to a lesser extent Denmark and Sweden, although even in these member states there is much left to be decided, as well as uncertainties to be clarified (for a detailed reference to recent national experience, see CEC 1995*a* and 1995*b*; for an assessment of the 1998 national action plans, see CEC 1998). All things considered, the effective role of the

Community may not exceed that of a reform catalyst. Its coordinating role may, in principle, be positive, but this is easy to claim and hard to assess.

Would further Community involvement in the area of employment policy, by setting quantified policy guidelines, and especially employment targets, be necessary? Certain sides, most notably the Commission, suggested that the jobs summit, decided at the Amsterdam European Council, should opt for such an approach to labour market policy coordination, thus copying the Maastricht method for economic convergence. However, numerical EU-wide employment targets might well be arbitrary, if not largely irrelevant. It is worth bearing in mind that the White Paper on Growth, Competitiveness and Employment set a target of cutting unemployment in half by the year 2000, which was reiterated in the context of the EES (CEC 1995*b*), but does not appear to have achieved any concrete results. Furthermore, quantified policy guidelines might not be appropriate as a commitment for everyone.

In fact, the outcome of the special jobs summit, which was held in Luxembourg on 20 and 21 November 1997, has fallen short of the aspirations of the Commission. Despite the Commission's efforts, numerical job creation targets have not been endorsed by the European Council, nor have employment rate increases been defined. Nevertheless, a range of structural policy guidelines has been adopted and the surveillance procedure has been given further impetus. With two exceptions, the Luxembourg guidelines differ little in substance from those analysed above, i.e. the Essen recommendations. The first exception is that within a period of five years member states will ensure that young persons and unemployed adults are offered a new start, in the form of a job, training, work practice, etc., before being out of work for six and twelve months respectively. However, it has also been acknowledged that those countries with a higher than the EU average unemployment rate may implement this measure within a longer period of time. The second exception is that member states will gradually raise the percentage of the unemployed benefiting from training to at least 20 per cent from the EU average of 10 per cent (for the full text of the Presidency conclusions, see Agence Europe 26/11/1997).

In addition to what has been argued so far in regard to EU-level employment policy coordination, a further comment may also be made concerning the aforementioned definite active policy objectives. The latter may be attainable if governments embrace a decisive labour market reform agenda—arguably a more inclusive one than that portrayed by the Luxembourg guidelines—thus allowing for the realization of employment gains from policy interactions and, consequently, creating sufficient room for fiscal support. Yet, should governments fail to tackle labour market rigidities, and for this purpose reform the welfare state,[6] pressure to meet these objectives might cause an increase in taxation, particularly labour taxation, which might, in turn, result in increased unemployment, mainly owing to substitution of capital for

---

[6] On the occasion of the jobs summit, and in view of the political unfeasibility of comprehensive welfare state reform, seven CEPR economists argued in favour of a conditioned relaxation of the stability pact. Governments would be allowed to borrow temporarily in excess of the 3 per cent limit, on the condition—strictly enforced—that they implement labour market reforms, including introduction of active policies (Andersen *et al.* 1997). Their line of argument is, apparently, similar to the one followed in this chapter.

labour.[7] Thankfully, this need not be the case; unlike the Maastricht monetary stability criteria, quantified employment guidelines are not legally binding. Meanwhile, unemployed workers have little reason to share the enthusiasm of the jobs summit participants, who have complacently praised its results.

9.4. Conclusions

The conclusions drawn from the above discussion are not encouraging about the direct impact of EU social policy on cohesion. Specifically with reference to legislation which became the core of EU social policy, especially following the endorsement of the Social Charter and the adoption of the action programme for its implementation, with the exception of health and safety protection in the workplace and equal opportunities, the effect of Community legislation on social policy at the national level has ranged from minimal to insignificant. In other words, Community social legislation has neither helped increase national social provisions nor helped decrease international differences in levels of social provision.

It could—and should—not be otherwise, since levelling-up of social provisions would entail a significant cost for the less advanced economies in terms of competitiveness and employment. Besides, measures designed to benefit specific social groups would probably harm them, causing a decline in their real wages or disemployment effects, this being dependent upon the peculiarities of national labour markets. Nevertheless, it may be argued that the promotion of social dialogue could improve the conditions for social cohesion, primarily due to its consensual character. Also, policy cooperation among the member states, in the face of similar internal and common external pressures, might eventually lead to more effective social policies. To those prophesying a 'social dumping' scenario, the above arguments would seem to confirm the failure of EU social policy. However, their fears are not justified; national diversities in social arrangements are both sustainable and desirable. EU social policy has not failed. It simply should—and could—not have been so ambitious.

Partly owing to this but mainly because of the acute crisis in unemployment and the dangers it entails for European societies, emphasis has steadily shifted to the employment and labour market policy front. Recognition of the need for labour market reforms has underpinned a series of Community initiatives and has furnished the basis for the adoption of a coordinated (European) employment strategy. Furthermore, the Amsterdam Treaty has provided for a Community coordinating role, which mainly refers to the encouragement of cooperation between member states, and has accordingly established—in fact completed and formalized—the institutional machinery.

However, coordinated employment policies may accomplish little. Different labour market traditions involve different reform priorities and, given strong policy interactions,

[7] It may cause no surprise that, in all their readiness to submit their action plans for employment in accordance with the process agreed at the Luxembourg jobs summit, national governments have not set fiscal targets, esp. regarding the reduction of labour taxation, nor have they translated their policy commitments into budgetary commitments (CEC 1998).

similar measures may dramatically differ in their effect, depending on the underlying structural and economic conditions of each member state. Moreover, labour market reforms involve painful trade-offs and are often determined by ideological considerations. Hence, the Community may only support the member states and stimulate structural policy action via policy recommendations providing for genuine labour market flexibility. Nevertheless, the gains from labour market reforms may take time to materialize, while their costs are felt almost immediately. This being so, the need for a supportive macroeconomic policy stance may not be neglected. However, it is doubtful whether the EMU macroeconomic policy framework will be conducive to reform and there are fears that EMU will even tend to aggravate regional unemployment disparities. In this case, would the Community be able to move along a fiscal federalist path?[8]

References

Addison, J. and Siebert, W. S. (1991). The social charter of the European Community: evolution and controversies. *Industrial and Labour Relations Reviews* 44: 597–625.

Adnett, N. (1995). Social dumping and European economic integration. *Journal of European Social Policy* 5: 1–12.

Andersen, T., Begg, D., De Grauwe, P., Dolado, J., Giavazzi, F., Wyplosz, C., and Zimmerman, K. (1997). Make room for outsiders. *Financial Times*, 20 November.

Anglo-German Deregulation Group (1995). *Deregulation-Now.* Group Report. London and Bonn.

Atkinson, A. and Micklewright, J. (1991). Unemployment compensation and labour market transitions: a critical review. *Journal of Economic Literature* 29: 1679–1727.

Barr, N. (1992). Economic theory and the welfare state: a survey and interpretation. *Journal of Economic Literature* 30: 741–803.

Bayoumi, T. and Eichengreen, B. (1996). Operationalising the theory of OCA. CEPR Discussion Paper no. 1484.

Bazen, S. and Benhayoun, G. (1992). Low pay and wage regulation in the European Community. *British Journal of Industrial Relations* 30: 623–38.

Begg, I. (1995). Factor mobility and regional disparities in the European Union. *Oxford Review of Economic Policy* 11: 96–112.

Bentolila, S. and Dolado, J. J. (1994). Labour flexibility and wages: lessons from Spain. *Economic Policy* 18: 53–99.

---

[8] Since early 1998, when this chapter was finalized, the European economy has been enjoying a strong recovery associated with a satisfactory employment performance and a substantial reduction in unemployment rates. Besides, cooperation among the member states in the area of employment policy has been enhanced; and a new term has been coined to describe enhanced cooperation, namely open coordination (method). Following the decisions of the Lisbon European Council the open coordination method will also apply to the area of social protection, particularly in regard to policies against poverty and social exclusion. However, little, if any, progress has been achieved in the area of social legislation and new initiatives have almost exclusively focused on the issue of discrimination. In any case, we think that these developments do not ask for any major amendment to the analysis pursued in this chapter; nor do they challenge the conclusions reached.

Bertola, G. and Ichino, A. (1995). Crossing the river: a comparative perspective on Italian employment dynamics. *Economic Policy* 21: 359–420.

Blanchard, O. and Jimeno, J. (1995). Structural unemployment: Spain versus Portugal. *American Economic Review* 85: 212–18.

—— and Summers, L. (1986). Hysteresis and the European unemployment problem. *NBER Macroeconomic Annual* 1: 15–78.

BMT Consultants (1995). Temporary employment across borders: posting in accordance with Regulation 1408/71 in practice. Unpublished paper, Utrecht.

Booth, A. and Snower, D. (eds.) (1996). *Acquiring Skills: Market Failures, their Symptoms and Policy Responses.* Cambridge: Cambridge University Press.

Calmfors, L. (1993). Lessons from the macroeconomic experience of Sweden. *European Journal of Political Economy* 9: 25–72.

—— and Driffil, J. (1988). Centralisation of Wage Bargaining and Macroeconomic Performance. *Economic Policy* 6: 13–61.

Card, D. and Krueger, A. (1994). Minimum wages and employment: a case study of the fast-food industry in New Jersey and Pensylvania. *American Economic Review* 84: 772–93.

Centre for Economic Policy Research (CEPR) (1993). *Making Sense of Subsidiarity: How Much Centralisation for Europe?* Monitoring European Integration 4. London: CEPR.

—— (1995). *Unemployment: Choices for Europe.* Monitoring European Integration 5. London: CEPR.

Commission of the European Community (CEC) (1992). The regulation of working conditions in the Member States of the European Community. *Social Europe* 1, supplement 4.

—— (1993*a*). Green Paper on *European Social Policy.* COM (93) 551. Brussels.

—— (1993*b*). *Medium-Term Action Programme to Combat Exclusion and Promote Solidarity and Report on the Implementation of the Community Programme for the Social and Economic Integration of the Least-Privileged Groups (1989–1994).* COM (93) 435. Brussels.

—— (1993*c*). *Social Protection in Europe, 1993.* COM (93) 531. Brussels.

—— (1994*a*). Annual Economic Report for 1994. *European Economy* 56.

—— (1994*b*). White Paper on *European Social Policy: A Way Forward for the Union.* COM (94) 333. Brussels.

—— (1994*c*). *Competitiveness and Cohesion: Fifth Periodic Report on the Social and Economic Situation and Development of the Regions in the Community.* Luxembourg: Office for the Official Publications of the European Communities.

—— (1994*d*). *Proposal for a Council Directive on the Establishment of European Committees of Procedures in Community-scale Undertakings and Community-scale Groups of Undertakings for the Purposes of Informing and Consulting Employees.*

—— (1995*a*). *Employment in Europe.* COM (95) 381. Brussels.

—— (1995*b*). *The European Employment Strategy: Recent Progress and Prospects for the Future.* Communication from the Commission on trends and developments in employment systems in the European Union. Brussels.

—— (1995*c*). *The Future of Social Protection: A Framework for a European Debate.* COM (95) 466. Brussels.

—— (1995*d*). *Medium-Term Social Action Programme, 1995–1997.* COM (95) 134. Brussels.

—— (1995*e*). *Proposal for a Council Decision on the Fourth Medium-Term Community Action Programme on Equal Opportunities for Women and Men (1996–2000).* COM (95) 381. Brussels.

—— (1995*f*). *Social Protection in Europe, 1995.* COM (95) 457. Brussels.

—— (1997). Annual Economic Report: Growth, Employment and Convergence on the Road to EMU. COM (97) 27. Brussels.

—— (1998). *From Guidelines to Action: The National Action Plans for Employment*. COM (98) 316. Brussels.

Danson, M. (1995). The spatial impact of the Social Chapter. In S. Hardy, M. Hart, L. Albrechts, and A. Katos, (eds.), *An Enlarged Europe: Regions in Competition?* Regional Policy and Development 6, Regional Studies Association. London: Jessica Kingsley.

Deere, D., Murphy, K. M., and Finis, W. (1995). Employment and the 1990–1991 minimum-wage hike. *American Economic Review* 85: 232–7.

Eichengreen, B. (1996). Institutions and economic growth: Europe after World War II. In N. Crafts and G. Toniolo (eds.), *Economic Growth in Europe since 1945*. Cambridge: Cambridge University Press for CEPR.

Emerson, M. (1988). Regulation or deregulation of the labour market: policy regimes for the recruitment and dismissal of employees in the industrialised countries. *European Economic Review* 32: 775–817.

Ermisch, J. (1991). European integration and external constraints on social policy: is a social charter necessary? *National Institute Economic Review* 136: 93–108.

Esping-Andersen, C. and Korpi, W. (1984). Social policy as class politics in post-war capitalism: Scandinavia, Austria, and Germany. In J. Goldhorpe (ed.), *Order and Conflict in Contemporary Capitalism*. Oxford: Oxford University Press.

European Policy Centre (EPC) (1997). *Making Sense of Amsterdam*. Brussels.

Freeman, R. B. (1988). Labour market institutions and economic performance. *Economic Policy* 6: 64–80.

Gruber, J. (1994). The Incidence of Mandated Maternity Benefits. *American Economic Review* 84: 622–41.

Helm, D. (1989). The economic borders of the state. In D. Helm (ed.), *The Economic Borders of the State*. Oxford: Oxford University Press.

Heylen, F. and van Poeck, A. (1995). National labour market institutions and the European economic and monetary integration process. *Journal of Common Market Studies* 33: 573–95.

Jamieson, A., Grube, M., Malpas, N., and Baetsen, M. J. (1994). Evaluation report: Community actions for older people 1991–1993 including the European Year of Older People and Solidarity between Generation. Unpublished.

Kleinman, M. and Pianchaud, D. (1993). European social policy: conceptions and choices. *Journal of European Social Policy* 3: 1–19.

Layard, R., Nickell, S., and Jackman, R. (1991). *Unemployment: Macroeconomic Performance and the Labour Market*. Oxford: Oxford University Press.

Lindbeck, A. (1992). Macroeconomic theory and the labour market. *European Economic Review* 36: 209–35.

—— (1994). The welfare state and the employment problem. *American Economic Review* 84: 71–5.

—— and Snower, D. (1988). *The Insider-Outsider Theory of Employment and Unemployment*. Cambridge, Mass.: MIT Press.

Marsden, D. (1994). The integration of European labour markets. *Social Europe* 1: Supplement, 1–38.

Meehan, E. (1990). Sex equality policies in the European Community. *Journal of European Integration* 13: 185–96.

Meulders, D., Plachman, R., and Vander Stricht, V. (1993). *Position of women on the labour market in the European Community*. Aldershot: Dartmouth.

Molle, W. (1990). *The Economics of European Integration*. Aldershot: Dartmouth.

Newell, A. and Symons, J. S. V. (1987). Corporatism, laissez-faire and the rise in unemployment. *European Economic Review* 31: 567–601.

OECD (1994). *The Jobs Study.* Paris: OECD.

—— (1995). *Economic Outlook.* Paris: OECD.

Ostner, I. and Lewis, J. (1995). Gender and the Evolution of European Social Policies. In S. Leibfried and P. Pierson (eds.), *European Social Policy: Between Fragmentation and Integration.* Washington, D.C.: Brookings Institution.

Pillinger, J. (1993). *Feminising the Market: Women's Pay and Employment in the European Community.* London: Macmillan.

Rhodes, M. (1992). The future of the 'social dimension': labour market regulation in post-1992 Europe. *Journal of Common Market Studies* 30: 23–51.

—— (1995). A Regulatory Conundrum: Industrial Relations and the Social Dimension. In S. Leibfried and P. Pierson (eds.), *European Social Policy: Between Fragmentation and Integration.* Washington, D.C.: Brookings Institution.

—— (1997). The welfare state: internal challenges, external constraints. In M. Rhodes, P. Heywood and V. Wright (eds.), *Developments in West European Politics.* London: Macmillan.

Rosen, S. (1996). Public Employment and the Welfare State in Sweden. *Journal of Economic Literature* 34: 729–40.

Ross, G. (1995). Assessing the Delors era and social policy. In S. Leibfried and P. Pierson (eds.), *European Social Policy: Between Fragmentation and Integration.* Washington, D.C.: Brookings Institution.

Saint-Paul, G. (1996). Exploring the political economy of labour market institutions. *Economic Policy* 10: 265–315.

—— (1997). The rise and persistence of rigidities. *American Economic Review* 87: 290–4.

Saraceno, C. (1994). Review of *Feminizing the Market: Women's Pay and Employment in the European Community,* by Jane Pillinger. *Journal of European Social Policy* 4: 308–10.

Sen, A. (1987). *On Ethics and Economics.* Oxford: Blackwell.

Solow, R. M. (1990). *The Labour Market as a Social Institution.* Cambridge, Mass.: Blackwell.

Soskice, D. (1990). Wage Determination: The Changing Role of Institutions in Advanced Industrialised Countries. *Oxford Review of Economic Policy* 6: 36–61.

Summers, L. (1987). Comments: Corporatism, laissez-faire, and the rise in unemployment by A. Newell and S. S. V. Symons. *European Economic Review* 31: 606–14.

Swann, D. (1992). The Social Charter and other issues. In D. Swann (ed.), *The Single European Market and Beyond.* London: Routledge.

Titmuss, R. M. (1974). *Social Policy.* London: George Allen & Unwin.

Tsoukalis, L. (1997). *The New European Economy Revisited.* Oxford: Oxford University Press.

UNICE (1995). Releasing Europe's potential through targeted regulatory reform. *The Unice Regulatory Study: An Interim Report.* Brussels.

van Rompuy, P., Abraham, F., and Heremans, D. (1991). Economic federalism and the EMU. *European Economy* special edn., 1: 109–35.

von Hagen, J. and Eichengreen, B. (1996). Federalism, fiscal restraints, and European monetary union. *American Economic Review* 86: 134–8.

Wallace, H. (1996). Politics and policy in the EU: the challenge of governance. In H. Wallace and W. Wallace (eds.), *Policy-Making in the European Union,* 3rd edn. Oxford: Oxford University Press.

Wilensky, H. (1975). *The Welfare State and Equality: The Roots of Public Expenditures.* Berkeley, Calif.: University of California Press.

10

Structural Policies

ANDREA MAIRATE AND RONALD HALL

Community structural policies are the main instrument promoting cohesion, i.e. reducing socioeconomic disparities between regions and social groups not only between, but also within, the member states of the European Union. In financial terms, they represent more than one-third of the EU budget, or an average of 30 billion ecus a year. Their importance is likely to increase in the future as a result of the further enlargement towards Central and Eastern European countries.

The pursuit of cohesion as a political objective *at the supranational level* is linked to the perceived need to correct geographical and social imbalances arising in the context of the implementation of the European single market programme—removing national barriers to the movement of capital and labour, goods and services—and, from 1999, the introduction of the single currency. As integration measures giving rise to an increasingly competitive environment, the risk is one of widening socioeconomic disparities across the Union unless compensatory policies are pursued with appropriate vigour.

Cohesion policy was given considerable impetus in the context of the Maastricht Treaty negotiated by member states in 1991, which elevated the pursuit of economic and social cohesion to one of the three main priorities of the Union, alongside completion of the single market and monetary union. It paved the way for a subsequent decision to significantly increase resources for cohesion policies financed from the EU's Structural Funds. In addition, it led to the creation of a new 'Cohesion Fund' to help weaker countries prepare for monetary union by alleviating some of the burden on their public finances of undertaking major infrastructure investments.

Since their creation in the early 1970s and their reform in 1988, the aims of EU structural policies have shifted in character from simple redistribution to a genuine development policy. In the previous system, assistance was guaranteed to each member state according to predefined quotas, without any clear relationship to a development strategy.

The delivery system for cohesion policies is substantially that which was put in place with the 1998 reform, although it was modified and refined in 1993. Its basis is the notion of an integrated approach to development delivered through programmes based on a strategic vision for the assisted regions and social groups. As discussed below, it also recognizes the role of institutions in economic development, seeking to involve all the relevant actors in the implementation of European policies.

The opinions expressed in this paper do not necessarily represent the views of the European Commission. We are grateful to Carole Garnier from DG II for her valuable comments.

After a decade of experience, evaluation is a central issue, not only for assessing the impact of the interventions but increasingly for *accountability* reasons, i.e. *vis-à-vis* the European and national institutions and the European taxpayer. The current regulations governing the Structural Funds emphasize the role of evaluation by making EU assistance conditional on an economic appraisal in order to verify that the expected benefits are commensurate with the resources deployed. In particular, the regulations require that the attainment of the general objective of economic and social cohesion must be assessed by comparing outcomes against targets, these being specified in sectoral and macroeconomic terms (CEC 1996b). Substantial effort has, therefore, gone into raising the importance of evaluation, notably with regard to the improvement of methods and tools and to ensure their widespread use throughout the Union (MEANS 1999, Bachtler and Michie 1995).[1]

This chapter looks at the record of achievement of EU cohesion policies through a multi-layer evaluation of the impact of EU structural policies. After this introduction, it is divided into seven sections. Section 10.1 considers equity and efficiency arguments underpinning EU cohesion policy as it affects geographical imbalances. Section 10.2 examines the scale of transfers and the redistributive effects of Structural Funds and the Cohesion Fund. Section 10.3 discusses key macroeconomic impacts resulting from the interventions on the main recipients. Section 10.4 focuses on the *allocative* function of Structural Funds, i.e. how they contribute to capital accumulation in less developed areas in the Union, as well as on cost–effectiveness considerations. Section 10.5 deals with institutional impacts arising from the delivery system for Structural Funds. Section 10.6 addresses some key policy developments in the pipeline affecting the future of the Structural Funds. Finally, section 10.7 contains concluding remarks.

10.1. Need for EU Structural Policies

Traditionally, cohesion policies to reduce interregional disparities are justified on the basis of two major arguments: efficiency and equity. A discussion of the first argument is prevalent in mainstream economic theory and is at the heart of evaluation. An important feature of the second is that it can be achieved either by interpersonal transfers or by targeted measures to equalise supply-side conditions.

10.1.1. *Efficiency vs. equity*

Efficiency arguments for and against regional policy pervade both the traditional and modern economic literature. Traditional neo-classical economics suggest that regional disparities cannot exist, because the market mechanism tends to ensure a full utilization

---

[1] In 1994, the Means programme was launched to assist the European Commission with co-ordinating and providing guidance on evaluation methods and practices in the member states. This three year programme has produced a series of handbooks and guides for programme managers and policy makers (see Means 1993, 1999).

of resources within each region. Where such disparities are observed, they can be attributed to regional differences in endowments of factors of production and to certain imperfections or rigidities in the economic system. But the success (or failure) of the market mechanism in eliminating regional differences depends, on the one hand, upon the existence of price competition and negligible transport costs and, on the other, on full mobility of labour and capital.

The problem is that such conditions do not exist in practice, and, consequently, the self-adjustment mechanism tends not to work, or at best to work only very slowly. Assuming economies of scale and economies of agglomeration in a wider context (for example, in the European single market), the regions that have an initial competitive advantage will find it reinforced as their output increases and other regions find it more difficult to catch up. If a strong region attracts capital and well-qualified labour from weaker regions this will further enhance its economic potential and, because of economies of scale and agglomeration, strengthen its competitive advantage. The result is a process of 'cumulative causation' (Myrdal 1957), in which trade and factor movements cause relative competitive advantages in the central regions and relative disadvantages in the peripheral regions. In this view, economic disparities, and the underutilization of some national resources, far from being self-adjusting as in the mainstream theory, tend to be self-reinforcing. However, the peripheral regions can benefit from a high degree of integration as the advantages in terms of costs would offset agglomeration effects in the central regions and, thus, a dispersion of industry would take place (Krugman 1991).

The concept of *equity*, as indicated above, is more complex. Within an EU policy framework, its interpretation relates to concerns to ensure that equal conditions for growth exist throughout the Union. Here, much of the theoretical inspiration for policy intervention is derived from growth theories. Recent developments in growth theory (Romer 1990; Barro and Sala-I-Martin 1995, Mankiw *et al.* 1992) have opened new directions of research, overcoming the neo-classical hypothesis of constant returns to scale and exogenous technical progress. This new analytical framework focuses on externalities arising from the increase in inputs of human capital, R&D expenditure, and physical investment.

It is supported by a number of empirical works (Barro and Sala-I-Martin 1991, 1995, Neven and Gouyette 1994) suggesting that there is no automatic income convergence between regions. Rather, regions can attain steady states at different income levels. Each country or region tends to converge towards its own steady state (Canova and Marcet 1995) determined according to the strength of its economic fundamentals, e.g. technological advancement.

The possible persistence of inequality increases the need for an active structural policy. However, such a policy can only be effective if it can influence the determinants of long-run relative income levels. The main implication of modern growth theories is that they stress that there are other factors, beyond physical capital, that are important, underlining, in particular, the role of human capital (Lucas 1988).

One result of these insights is that conventional regional policy—essentially providing investment grants in support of the movement of capital to designated areas—has come under increasing criticism. This has led to a refocusing of regional policy emphasizing two aspects. The first recognizes the importance of indigenous enterprise and resources rather than the attraction of mobile investment projects from outside (see also Armstrong and Taylor 1985). The second focuses on the need to increase the innovation potential of weaker regions (see Amin and Goddard 1986, Landabaso 1995).

Both of these aspects are present in EU regional policy. In the EU, it has also been recognized that cohesion is not merely a regional problem and cannot be tackled only by a policy addressing the situation within weaker regions. This explains why wider policy priorities that are not directly linked to regional policy, such as those in the fields of employment, the environment, and equal opportunities, have been introduced recently in an effort to extend the scope of economic and social cohesion policy (CEC 1996a).

10.1.2. The logic of Structural Funds

Structural Fund expenditure is *selective* in its application. This means that financial assistance does not flow automatically if relevant circumstances apply, as in the case of the EU's Common Agricultural Policy. The essential difference lies in the fact that cohesion is a shared responsibility between the Union and the member states, where EU policies seek to complement and reinforce policies at national level. The division of responsibilities is a matter of political judgement set within a broad legal framework.

Resources are allocated only for *investment* purposes rather than consumption, in the form of grants, subsidies, or loans. They are generally made available to the member states or regions in the context of agreed programmes providing assistance to three main production factors: economic infrastructure, aid to the private sector, and human capital. As indicated above, this essentially supply-side focus reflects the view that differences in per capita income levels across countries or regions are mainly attributable to different endowments in key supply-side factors, and that correcting the disparities in these areas would, therefore, translate into a reduction of the existing income imbalances. It should be noted in this context, however, that differences in factor accumulation rates are not the only source of long-term income disparities. Other elements, such as the degree of openness of a given economy or a stable macroeconomic framework, also contribute to regional performance and competitiveness.

The shares of each of the three factors in EU expenditures has been similar up to the present, although there has been some shift away from supporting infrastructure towards productive and human capital investment (CEC 1996b). On average, expenditure during the programming period 1994–9 is divided into 30 per cent for infrastructure investment, 30 per cent for human resources development and 40 per cent for aid to the productive sector.

Structural Funds do not operate on their own, but require *matching funds* provided by the recipient member state (Fig. 10.1). They also involve specific channels of delivery that seek to influence the institutional context in which they operate. Their impact in terms of factor accumulation is, thus, related in important respects to the way funds are delivered and managed (see below, sect. 10.6).

Box 1. EU structural policies: main features

The Union has six major financial instruments with which to implement its structural policies: the Regional Development Fund, the Social Fund, the EAGGF–Guidance Fund, the Financial Instrument for Fisheries Guidance, the Cohesion Fund, and loans from the European Investment Bank (EIB). The Cohesion Fund and the EIB are based on a project financing approach and are governed by their own specific rules. The Structural Funds operate within an integrated programming framework according to a set of principles contained in implementing regulations.

The interventions of the Structural Funds address regional problems through four Objectives:

- Objective 1, for regions where development is lagging behind (accounting for almost 70 per cent of total resources);
- Objective 2, for restructuring in regions affected by industrial decline (11 per cent);
- Objective 5b, for structural development in rural areas (4 per cent);
- Objective 6, for structural development in sparsely populated areas (0.5 per cent).

In the period, 1994–9, the population in regions covered by the regional Objectives was 51 per cent of the EU total. Some 55 per cent of the total resources goes to the 16 per cent of EU population in four countries—Greece, Spain, Ireland, and Portugal—mostly delivered through Objective 1 programmes.

Three other Objectives are problem centred and do not follow a regional methodology:

- Objective 3 focuses on long-term and youth unemployment;
- Objective 4 assists the adaptation of workers to industrial change;
- Objective 5a promotes adjustment in the agricultural and fisheries sectors.

Separate Community Initiative programmes exist in pursuit of transnational, cross–border and interregional actions organized under thirteen different themes. In addition, a small proportion of total resources, some 1 per cent, is reserved for technical assistance, pilot projects, and innovative measures.

10.2. Scale of Transfers and Redistributive Effects

The main redistributive mechanism within the Union is in the hands of the member states and results from the geographical effects of national systems for the interpersonal transfer of income, mainly through taxation and social security systems (see the MacDougall Report—CEC 1977). Regions contribute tax to the centre broadly in proportion to their income while they receive transfers in the form of income and services broadly in proportion to their population. As a result, the distribution of personal disposable income (PDI) differs significantly from the distribution of income before tax and social transfers. Some recent estimates (EPRC 1996) suggest that regional disparities, taking account of these transfers, are between 20 and 40 per cent lower than the per capita income disparities. In net terms, interregional transfers account, on average, for 4 per cent of the GDP of the donor regions or 8 per cent of the recipient regions.

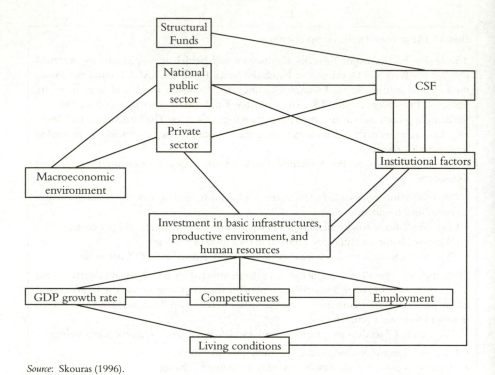

Source: Skouras (1996).

Fig. 10.1. Rationale of Structural Funds

At the EU level, the logic of the Structural Funds as described above also means a positive *redistributive* effect, i.e. resources tend to flow in net terms from the richer regions to the poorer ones. But their specificity also means that the redistributive role is related to their allocative role (Reichenbach 1992). Both aspects are discussed below.

10.2.1. *Scale*

The scale of transfers organized at the EU level is a matter of political judgement, taking account of factors such as the importance of regional and labour market imbalances, an appreciation of the overall costs and benefits of European integration, and the economic effectiveness of transfers. In the context of the 1988 reform of the Structural Funds, the volume of funds was decided on a political basis (based on the European Commission's proposals in the Delors I package) and taking account of social costs arising from the completion of the single market. Further growth in the Structural Funds (based on the Delors II package), together with the concentration of resources in favour of the poorest 'Objective 1' regions, was decided by EU governments at the Edinburgh Council of 1992, with a view to achieving an increased macroeconomic impact of Community

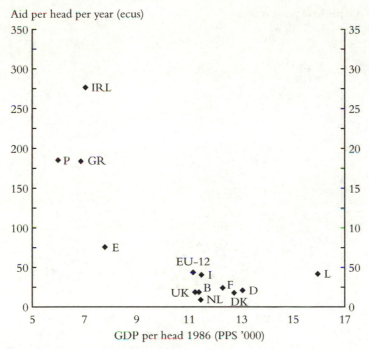

Fig. 10.2. Structural aid and GDP in member states, 1989–93

assistance, in particular in Mediterranean regions and Ireland. Under this financial package, the in-year expenditures under the EU structural policies reach their peak of 0.46 per cent of Community GNP in 1999.

A comparison is sometimes made with the assistance granted under the Marshall Plan, the aid programme for the reconstruction of post-war Europe. During the period 1948–51, the USA granted the equivalent of around 1 per cent of GNP every year (representing some 2 per cent of the recipient countries' annual GNP) or 4 per cent over the full period (Eichengreen and Uzan 1992). The Community's efforts over the decade 1989–99 under the Structural Funds and the Cohesion Fund amounts to some 6.5 per cent of Union GNP.

For each of the major recipients of EU aid—Greece, Spain, Portugal, and Ireland—the position is quite different. The three smaller member states (Greece, Portugal, and Ireland) receive the larger annual transfers (as percentage of their national GDP in 1994, respectively, 2.8 per cent, 3.7 per cent, and 4 per cent for the 1994–9 programmes), while the amount of funds for Spain is more modest in relative terms although it is the largest absolute recipient (about 1.7 per cent of GDP each year). As a whole, the four countries, generally referred to as the 'cohesion countries', receive more than half of the transfers from the EU under structural policies, and the scale of aid per capita is much larger than for the rest of the Union (see Figs. 10.2 and 10.3).

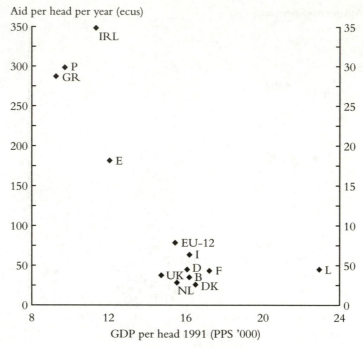

Fig. 10.3. Structural aid and GDP in member states, 1994–9

10.2.2. *Redistributive effects of funds*

The key question is to assess whether the distribution of EU transfers is progressive, i.e. do the poorer regions, those with the lowest GDP per head, receive more funds? A recent analysis (CEC 1996*b*) based on expenditure data of structural interventions (including the Cohesion Fund),[2] confirms the positive redistributive effect in favour of the weaker regions during the period 1989–93, which means that resources were concentrated on the economies with the lowest per capita income levels. The degree of concentration of transfers was somewhat less in the period 1994–9, despite the reinforcement of structural policies via the creation of the Cohesion Fund (Fig. 10.4). This is mainly explained by the wider coverage of areas eligible under Objective 1 in the more prosperous member states (including the whole of the new German Länder) and a comparatively generous extension of the policy to three new member states (Austria, Finland, and Sweden).

As regards the group of Objective 1 regions, the Lorenz curve shows a progressive incidence of the distribution of funds, which is more marked during the current period

---

[2] The analysis is based on a coherent set of regional data for all structural interventions. Actual expenditure data were used for the period 1989–93 while planned figures were used for the subsequent period 1994–9.

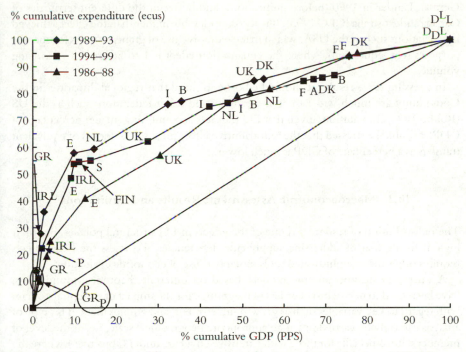

Fig. 10.4. Concentration of Community structural assistance by member state, 1986–88, 1989–93, and 1994–99

than in the period 1989–93, partly because of a partial integration of the new Länder, which received interim assistance during this period.

These results are supported by various studies (Franzmeyer *et al.* 1991; Gordon 1991, Roger Tym 1996). It has been argued, however, that regions with the same level of GDP per head are treated differently by the EU, depending on the country to which they belong (Gordon 1991). Such criticism fails to take account of the fact that cohesion is a shared responsibility between the Union and the member states. In effect, the degree of Community support has been adjusted according to the economic strength (and, by implication, the national budgetary capacity) of the country in which the assisted region is situated. As a result, regions with equivalent levels of GDP per head have tended to receive different EU aid intensities according to the level of national GNP.

A revealing comparison is with the flow of funds through explicit interregional transfer mechanisms in existing federations, such as Germany (Costello 1993). EU structural transfers amount to some 16.7 billion ecus in 1992, equivalent to approximately 0.3 per cent of Community GDP, and achieve an income equalization effect in terms of GDP per head of 3 per cent, i.e. a reduction in interregional disparities (Gini coefficient) in income per capita. For the Delors II package, for 0.46 per cent of Community GDP the equalization effect is estimated at 5 per cent. This equalization effect is more or less on the same order of magnitude as estimates for the interregional transfers between the

German Länder in 1990 (before unification)[3] and between the different territories of Canada and Australia (CEC 1993). It is also considerably higher than the effect achieved in federations such as the USA, which make extensive use of grants to states for specific purposes (e.g. education), where the equalization effect is 1 to 5 times the financing volume.

In assessing these results, it should be borne in mind that regional disparities in the Community are much wider than in Germany and other federations such as the US (Boltho 1994). In addition, given that EU transfers account for a smaller percentage of GDP, it should be stressed that the redistributive effect (in absolute terms) of equivalent transfers as a percentage of GDP is much lower.

10.3. Macroeconomic Assessment: Results and Limitations

The redistribution of resources is one of the effects of EU structural policies, but their logic is firmly that of addressing supply-side deficiencies. To assess the latter effects requires other more sophisticated tools, notably those of economic evaluation.

A variety of macroeconomic models, based on different theoretical foundations, have been used to derive broad orders of magnitude for the impact of structural policies with regard to key variables such as growth, investment, and employment. This type of analysis can only be carried out at an appropriate geographical scale, i.e. at the level of member state, especially for those with extensive coverage under Objective 1 where the interventions of the Union have a macroeconomic dimension: Greece, Spain, Portugal, and Ireland. There is no standard model to evaluate this impact, but important insights can be gained by comparing and contrasting results obtained by different models.

Basically, the economic impact can be examined from two different perspectives. First, Structural Fund transfers tend to boost domestic demand in the recipient regions, producing a *Keynesian* impact on output and employment. Secondly, they raise efficiency on the supply side by improving production structures. This latter kind of impact is often less evident in macroeconomic evaluations, mainly for practical reasons because some programmes or projects have long lead times before they effect the economy.

In view of these different impacts, different models have been used to measure outcomes: a demand-side model based on input-output techniques ('Beutel'); a pure supply-side approach ('Pereira'); and a category of models based on both demand and supply-side effects ('Hermin' and other related models). All three modelling approaches incorporate a counterfactual scenario, drawing on observed empirical data, providing simulations to measure the impact of EU transfers relative to the counterfactual.

The following summarizes the main features of these models and critically assesses the results.

---

[3] The redistributive effect for the largest net recipient regions are between 0.8 per cent and 2.9 per cent of their GDP in 1990, whereas the figures for the Community range between 1.7 per cent for Spain and 4 per cent for Portugal on an annual average basis for 1994–9 (Costello 1993).

10.3.1. Demand-side models

Beutel (1993, 1995) has developed an input-output model that has been used over a number of years. This model focuses on short-term demand impact and captures the effects triggered by EU transfers for given input-output coefficients. These effects relate to aggregate variables such as economic growth, structural change, foreign trade, and employment. The model seeks answers to the following questions: how much of the actual or expected economic growth can be attributed to the EU co-funded programmes (known as Community Support Frameworks or CSFs) in general and to EU grants? How do the CSFs influence the economic aggregates and structure of the recipient economies, and, in particular, what part of EU grants will be transformed into domestic demand and output? How many jobs depend on structural interventions? What is the extent of leakage effects through imports into other parts of the EU?

Beutel (1993, 1995) provides an assessment of the impact of transfers for both programming periods 1989–93 and 1994–9. The model draws on a set of harmonized input-output tables for 1990 and 1991 for twelve member states, projected for the period 1994–9 on the basis of Eurostat national accounts and the latest official economic forecasts of the Commission. These tables include twenty-five branches and separate import matrices for trade with EU and non-EU countries. This allows them to capture the sectoral impact and inter-industry activities. Final demand is divided into private and public consumption, investment (as measured by gross fixed capital formation), and exports to EU and non-EU countries. Input coefficients are updated on the basis of relevant sectoral information and macroeconomic forecasts.

The counterfactual is determined through growth projections in the absence of Structural Funds determined through the input-output system of the economy. This leads to a prediction of the effects on production, employment, final demand, and imports.[4]

In an updated version of his model, Beutel (1996) has attempted to capture long-run supply and demand effects, especially on capital, labour, and productivity. With this extended model, he has evaluated the effects of all structural interventions for the periods 1989–93 (*ex post*) and 1994–9 (*ex ante*). Since this model allows for some supply-side effects, the growth effects predicted for 1989–93 are lower than Beutel (1993) and those for 1994–9 stronger than in Beutel (1995).

On average, the simulations predict that EU transfers from 1989–93 (*1994–9*) will have an additional impact on annual average economic growth of 0.8 (*1.0*) percentage points for Greece, 0.9 (*1.1*) for Portugal, 0.9 (*0.6*) percentage points for Ireland and 0.3 (*0.5*) for Spain. This compares to annual transfers on average over 1994–9 of 3.2 per cent of GDP for Portugal, 3.4 per cent for Greece, 2.1 per cent for Ireland and 2.2 per cent for the Spanish Objective 1 regions. When setting the additional output growth achieved against the level of the annual transfer, the performance emerges as slightly

---

[4] In his model, Beutel (1995) also estimates the additional effects on growth and employment of the full CSF. In this case, the counterfactual would be a situation without the CSF, implying a greater contribution of EU structural policies to economic development in the recipient countries.

better for Ireland and Spain. The poorer performance of Greece and Portugal can be explained by the fact that, because of a narrow industrial base, they tend to import a higher share of capital goods. In addition, the impact would be lower in relative terms compared to the previous period because of the improved growth conditions in the four countries.

This impact on economic growth is largely due to the contribution of gross fixed capital formation. On average, the proportion of the total investment effort depending on current structural interventions (national plus EU grants) is near a quarter of total investment of the country, and in the smallest countries this amounts to more than 30 per cent in Ireland and Portugal and more than 40 per cent in Greece. But, without EU funding, this ratio would have been, on average, almost 14 points lower in the four countries. As a result, an increasing part of their capital stock (from 2 per cent to 3 per cent) will be attributable only to Community transfers.

In contrast to the contribution to the rate of investment, the impact on employment appears to be relatively limited. One major reason for this is that capital grants or subsidies to the private sector will be used to replace the capital stock and to increase productivity of labour. Estimates suggest that by 1999, around 800,000 jobs or the equivalent of 3.6 per cent of total employment in the cohesion four will depend upon implementation of Community interventions. However, this figure is derived from a restrictive assumption based on a one-to-one relationship between output and employment. Whatever the order of magnitude for job creation, there is, of course, no guarantee of a commensurate effect in terms of the reduction of unemployment in the regions in view of the other factors involved.

Structural Fund expenditures tend to generate high leakage effects, through trade, to other EU and non-EU countries. Beutel (1996) estimates that more than a quarter of the amount of EU transfers to the four countries return to the other member states in the form of imports. Through the multiplier, a considerable part of the additional demand concerns investment in construction and buildings with a high local content, while there is a partial leakage in the form of imports of capital goods.

The results of the model appear consistently favourable for the four cohesion countries in the medium term. Substantial convergence towards the EU average income levels might, under the assumptions of the model, be attributed to structural interventions. However, the model does not provide clear indications on the nature of these changes; for example, whether Structural Funds contribute to increased demand in non-tradable sectors (building and construction) or protected sectors, or whether their impact produces more changes in the direction of self-sustaining development.

10.3.2. Supply-side models

Pereira (1994) has developed an intertemporal, optimal growth model which reflects some key features of the cohesion countries. The model is in sharp contrast to the demand-oriented approaches and concentrates exclusively on supply-side effects. An *ex ante* simulation of the impact of Structural Funds has been carried out for Greece, Portugal, and Ireland.

Its central mechanism involves the adaptation of the economy under the constraint of an aggregate production function with three inputs: private capital (productive sector), public capital (infrastructure), and human capital. Government in the recipient country, acting as a social planner, has an intertemporal social welfare function which includes both private and public consumption. The social planner maximizes the social welfare function under production conditions, the accumulation of private, public, and human capital (taking into account investment adjustment costs and capital depreciation), goods market equilibrium, balance of payments constraint, public and private sector budget constraint, and full respect for EU rules on additionality and co-financing obligations. The two consumption variables and the three investment variables constitute the control variables for the optimizing social planner.

Against the counterfactual based on the calibration of parameter values, the impact of Structural Funds is estimated for different scenarios. We only present the main results of the scenario held to represent most closely real circumstances. From the programming period 1989–93, Pereira derives a yearly transfer ratio in terms of GDP and assumes a doubling of the transfers for the following programming period. The allocation of the transfers on human, public, and private capital are assumed to be the same as in 1989–93.

Assuming continuous Structural Fund transfers, Pereira estimates that the annual additional GDP growth effect of the EU transfers is 0.4 to 0.6 percentage points for Greece and Ireland, and from 0.6 to 0.9 percentage points for Portugal. The main cause of the positive effect on economic growth is the triggering of additional investment for all three forms of capital. The main explanation for better results for Portugal relates to higher fund receipts and additional investment. However, the positive income shock and the need to comply with the additionality principle will affect the fiscal deficit and the current account balance.

As a consequence of the growth stimulus of EU transfers, values of GDP per capita will rise for the three countries relative to the baseline situation. But this will not be sufficient for convergence relative to the rest of the EU (which is assumed to continue to grow at the same rate GDP per capita as in the period 1980–8). For Greece, GDP per capita falls from 54.4 per cent of the EU average in 1988 to 50.5 per cent, while for Ireland and Portugal, it rises from 64.6 per cent to 69.3 per cent and from 53.8 per cent to 62.1 per cent, respectively. In the case of Greece, given the significantly lower growth rates in the 1980s, probably the most that can be said is that the Structural Funds are preventing disparities from getting worse.

Against the background of the results obtained by the various models, it is also revealing to examine the experience of the four cohesion countries, as derived from the statistical time series, and to compare these with the expectations generated *ex ante* by the model. The statistical data show that there have been considerable differences in economic performance between countries, exemplified by the cases of Greece and Ireland. In Greece, GDP per head increased from 60.0 to 64.4 per cent of the EU average and, Ireland, from 67.6 to 82.2 per cent.

In both cases, the observed values for GDP per head have risen more rapidly than predicted by the model. Since the direct effects on growth are similar for both countries, transfers cannot explain this outcome. This would allow for at least two quite different conclusions to be drawn. The first is that other factors have had a more important impact than the Structural Funds in generating results. Notable among these is the maroeconomic context, which has been remarkably more stable in Ireland than in Greece. The second conclusion is that the Structural Funds may have produced behavioural changes not captured by models based on past relationships. In particular, the promotion of institutional innovation and change as result of the partnership arrangements that form a key part of the delivery system may have played a key role (see sect. 10.5, below). The question is that why this may have been favourable in Ireland and not in Greece.

10.3.3. Combined demand- and supply-side models

HERMIN is a neo–Keynesian macroeconometric framework that covers both demand- and supply-side aspects.[5] It consists of about 100 to 150 equations describing economic interactions in an open economy. Within a common base, it allows for country specific variations, with parameter values derived from past national data, but the basic structure is the same for all countries.

The model distinguishes the tradable sector (industry), the non-tradable sector (services, utilities, construction), the public sector (administration, education, health), and agriculture. Production of tradables depends on world demand and local competitiveness. Production of non-tradables depends on domestic demand. Wages, unemployment, investment, and consumption are determined endogenously. Fiscal policy is exogenously given on the basis of past national trends, deficits and debt being the endogenous outcome. Exchange and interest rates are assumed to be fixed. Expectations are static, i.e. extrapolated from past trends.

In their simulation scenarios, the model assumes that the cohesion countries continue to receive Structural Funds after 1999, but the amount in real terms is frozen at the level of 1999 (so that it declines in terms of GDP). This scenario is run until 2020.

The demand effect is measured in a different way to Beutel, as there are price effect and feedback mechanisms in the labour market. The supply-side effects are considered through externalities associated with the CSF expenditure on infrastructure, human capital, and aid to the private sector. These externalities may arise through increased total or factor-specific productivity or through increased (price) competitiveness of domestic production (e.g. through exports).

The results provide several interesting insights. The initial impact comes only from the Keynesian demand effects since the supply-side effects take time to materialize. The demand effects are only a temporary effect on the process of real convergence. Over time, the externalities induced by the Structural Funds contribute significantly to increasing total factor productivity. This supply-side reaction means that there

---

[5] The HERMIN project is a reduced version of the HERMES model, supported by the European Commission. A detailed presentation of the methodology is provided in the journal *Economic Modelling* (see in particular, Bradley, Modesto, and Sosvilla-Rivero 1995).

are lasting effects on the economy. In 2020, GDP for Ireland is about twelve percentage points higher than in the counterfactual situation (i.e. in the no–CSF situation). For Portugal, the supply-side effects are considerably lower than for the other countries.

Annual growth effects—which are more or less similar to those of the Pereira model (Pereira 1994)—are higher at the beginning (because of the demand effect) and lower later on (because of the labour market reactions). These imply that supply-side effects tend to diminish over time. In the case of Greece, the additional GDP growth rate amounts, on average, to 0.55 percentage point per annum; in 2010, the additional effect will have fallen to 0.26 percentage point (Christodoulakis and Kalyvitis 1995). In Spain, the relatively large GDP means that the CSF shock is smaller than the equivalent ratios for the other three countries, amounting to 4.3 percentage points by 1999.

In the long run, the model shows clearly that employment effects are stronger in the presence of externalities. In the short run, the contrary is the case since the increase in factor productivity is used for structural adjustment in the tradable sector. As a result, employment will decline in manufacturing, but this is more than offset by increased employment in the service sector. This drives up the wage levels and also induces higher inflation. However, wage pressures are contained by the large stock of unemployment and increases in productivity. The trade balance worsens and so does the fiscal deficit because of the CSF co-financing requirements. In the long run, the public sector balance improves considerably because of the growth-induced higher tax revenues.

In interpreting these results it should be noted, however, that in the Hermin model, the elasticities associated with externalities are set *ex ante* in an 'arbitrary way' without any differentiation between countries and have little microeconomic foundation.

Further work has been undertaken in a recent study on the single market impact (ESRI 1996), which adopted a more cautious approach on the empirical magnitudes of the output elasticities associated with the externality mechanisms, leading to smaller supply-side impacts of the CSFs.

Other related models have been used in the context of Structural Funds. Bourguignon, Lolos, and Zonzilos (1995) provide a general equilibrium modelling framework for assessing the impact of Structural Funds for the period 1989–93 in Greece. The model exhibits both classical and Keynesian features. In contrast to Beutel and Pereira, it takes into account a financial sector, foreign exchange, and capital movements. The Greek economy is divided into nine sectors.

The most revealing insight given by the model is that it compares the effect of transfers in a hypothetical full-employment situation with flexible markets with the real situation of sectors with underemployment (like energy) due to insufficient demand. Unsurprisingly, the demand effects of transfers occur only in the underemployment situation and the initial impact of transfers is stronger in the initial case. Nevertheless, the macroeconomic effects of transfers are much stronger in the full-employment situation. For the period 1988–95, it is predicted that the cumulative effect of transfers on GDP would have been three percentage points higher if the Greek economy had been supply-constrained.

In a situation of constrained supply, durable supply-side effects in the form of pro-ductivity increases induce an extension of production possibilities. In a situation of underemployment, an increase in production capacities through transfers has only weak effects on output because of an insufficient demand. The difference between these two scenarios can be seen as a quantification of the aggregate efficiency loss in the use of transfers resulting from economic distortions that lead to a non-optimal use of resources.

The QUEST II model seeks to estimate the combined effects of supply-side improvements and short-term demand effects taking into account the influence of monetary variables (interest rate, inflation).[6] Compared to Hermin, this model exhibits three main differences: first, private economic agents are forward-looking, including in their consumption-investment decisions, which imply quicker responses to policy changes; second, interest rates and exchange rates are endogenously determined, which means that Structural transfers, by contributing to an expansive fiscal policy, will lead to an increase in interest rates and a real appreciation of the currency, including a (partial) crowding out of private investment; third, the model does not distinguish between the output elasticities of the different types of investment.

Since there are no differences in the externalities for public and private capital and the demand effects of transfers lead to crowding-out effects, it is not surprising that Quest II is, of all models surveyed, the one which predicts the lowest impact of EU transfers on economic growth. The yearly additional effect on GDP for the program-ming period 1989–93 (*1994–9*) is only 0.3 (*0.1*) percentage points for Greece, 0.25 (*0.29*) for Ireland, 0.3 (*0.15*) for Portugal, and 0.1 (*0.1*) for Spain. Ireland is the only country where the doubling of Structural Funds has brought additional (minor) growth effects, but this does not take account of supply-side effects which may materialize later on.

In summary, the models reviewed have helped in our understanding of the way EU structural policies impact on the poorest member states, providing a common frame-work for measuring and comparing their effect (Table 10.1). It should be clear, how-ever, that the differences in the nature of these models and the assumptions on which they are based are so great as to severely limit comparisons across models. However, some approaches may be of greater relevance, for example the Hermin model, which is specifically adapted to the special characteristics of the CSFs.

As regards the results, too much importance should not be attached to the precise magnitude for the outputs, although the fact that these widely differing models point in the same direction is encouraging. The general conclusion appears to be one of an important cohesion impact, in terms of the reduction in income disparities, and this is supported by a variety of theoretical approaches. This, in turn, suggests that the broad approach adopted by EU structural polices is on the right track, even if, as discussed in section 10.6 below, there remains scope for improvement.

---

[6] The QUEST II macroeconomic model is the official model used for all macroeconomic projections of the European Commission. For a presentation, see Roeger (1996).

Table 10.1. Impact of Structural Funds: comparison of simulation results obtained from macroeconomic models (growth effects in % differential from baseline)

Country	Pereira 1994–99 yearly average		long-run	Beutel 1989–93 yearly average	1994–99 yearly average	Hermin[a] 1994 total effects (of which demand effects)	1999 total effects (of which demand effects)	2020 total effects (of which demand effects)	Quest 1989–93 yearly average	1994–99 yearly average
Greece	0.4	to	0.6	0.8	1.0	1.23 (1.09)	9.41 (4.77)	9.53[b] (1.53)	0.3	0.1
Ireland	0.4	to	0.6	0.9	0.6	6.23 (6.23)	9.33 (5.94)	12.40 (4.03)	0.25	0.29
Portugal	0.6	to	0.9	0.9	1.1	7.03 (1.90)	9.17 (2.92)	8.94 (7.64)	0.3	0.15
Spain	—			0.3	0.5	1.90 (1.90)	4.33 (2.92)	8.65 (1.93)	0.1	0.1
Average EU–4				0.5	0.7					

[a] For the whole CSF.
[b] 2010.

Source: Pereira (1994), Beutel (1996), Bradley *et al.* (1995), Christodoulakis and Kalyvitis (1995), Cordero (1996), Roeger (1996).

10.4. Microeconomic Impacts

Microeconomic assessments consider the extent to which the specific goals defined under the structural interventions have been attained. Since Structural Funds are focused on efficiency improvements, it is important to examine their effect on structural factors such as infrastructure or human resources endowment in the recipient countries or regions.

This type of analysis is, however, constrained by the lack of systematic information on structural achievements in the recipient regions or member states. The collection of microeconomic data is essential for a solid assessment of the efficiency of the Community's structural policies. The Commission has developed a set of indicators to measure the effects of structural policies. These range from physical (output) indicators (infrastructure endowment, training provision, etc.) to intermediate effects (or results) and socioeconomic (impact) indicators described in terms of evolution of production structures and employment.

Despite strong limitations in the measurement of these indicators, there is some empirical evidence on how Structural Funds contribute, through a balanced package of measures, to creating long-term growth conditions in the less favoured regions. The factors for enhancing the economic potential are determined by the three main types of investment: public infrastructure, aid to the productive sector, and human resources development.

10.4.1. *Infrastructure provision*

The link between the provision of economic infrastructure and competitiveness of the regions finds clear evidence in a number of studies (Biehl 1986, Gillespie 1996). However, the question of whether the realization of infrastructure programmes for regional policy reasons represents an efficient use of cohesion resources is complex. In the short term, many analyses, in particular cost-benefit analyses (Florio 1995), show that motorways and other facilities are often constructed ahead of demand potential and operate at less than full capacity for some years. But in the medium and long term, the provision of infrastructure facilities in line with the national or, possibly, the Community average is a necessary, if not sufficient, condition for the successful economic development of the less favoured regions of the Union.

Objective 1 regions have the lowest levels of infrastructure endowment (CEC 1994). In particular, the cohesion countries suffer from problems of distance and relative inaccessibility. In 1988, the provision of motorways was only a third of the Union average, with Greece having no motorways at all. The density of the remainder of the road network as also relatively low, with relatively poor quality standards. The provision of rail lines was generally below average, with many being single track and with low levels of electrification (except in Spain) as well as an underutilization of this infrastructure. The telephone density was also scarce, particularly in Portugal, with low levels of digitalization as well as negative performance in terms of call failure rates and waiting times for new connections. These infrastructure deficiencies have had a number of

Table 10.2. Disparities in transport infrastructure in the EU (1996)

Indicators	Cohesion countries (average)	Other member states (average)	EU-15 (average)	Cohesion gap (%)
Motorways (km/1,000 km²)	11.7	16.3	15.2	−40
Railways (km/1,000 km²)	24.5	56.0	48.2	−128
Railways (km/million inhab.)	309.4	441.3	418.8	−42
High Speed Rail Network (km/km²)	590.5	749.9	744.5	−35

Source: European Commission based on Eurostat (1997).

economic consequences: high transport costs, constraints for local industry, fragmentation of markets, high levels of accidents.

Structural expenditure on infrastructure amounts to some 82 billion ecus, of which some 68 billion from Structural Funds (28 billion during CSF 1 and 40 billion during CSF 2) and 14.5 billion from the Cohesion Fund. In addition, a large part of loans from the European Investment Bank (more than 28 billion ecus since 1993) are devoted to the development of major infrastructure networks. This effort has largely been focused on transport infrastructure, which accounts for nearly 60 per cent of such investment, and is particularly concentrated in the cohesion countries. For the current period (1994–9), ERDF investment in transport infrastructure amounts to some 12 billion ecus in the cohesion countries, which receive additional funding (7 billion ecus) from the Cohesion Fund.

Notable advances are being made in addressing key disparities between the cohesion countries and the rest of the Union, although these remain considerable, in particular for railways infrastructure (Table 10.2). Major achievements concern the development of strategic road networks, for example, through the improvement of the four key corridors in Ireland and the completion of the Corinth–Tripoli–Kalamata motorway in Greece. The length of the major roads scheduled to be constructed or improved under the two programming periods together amounts to 900 km. in Greece, 400 km. in Ireland, 1,960 km. in Portugal, and 14,000 km. in Spain.

Despite these achievements, the rate at which disparities are being reduced is relatively modest. It is estimated, for example, that in Spain at current rates of progress, the density of the motorway network will not match the Union average until the middle of next century (QUASAR 1996). This, however, understates the strategic significance of the projects underway. In Greece, 60 per cent of the projects relating to the completion of the trans–European network are scheduled to be completed by 1999. In Portugal, interregional journey times have been reduced by around 30 per cent, on average. In Spain qualitative improvements are suggested by a standardized index of accident victims, which was halved between 1988 and 1994.

From a cost-effectiveness view, a distinction should be made between two different situations. First, early attempts at improving the standard of infrastructure provision in a less developed region, from very low levels of existing provision, are likely to bring disappointing results. Businesses, whose operating efficiency is dependent, *inter alia*, on infrastructure facilities, will not respond to marginal improvements until all the relevant facilities are brought up to a threshold standard similar to that in more prosperous regions. Second, some low-income regions—especially those located in more prosperous member states—will have a standard of infrastructure provision which is close to or even exceeding that of other Community regions. It would not be appropriate or economically efficient to take it to an even higher level or to devote Structural Funds to make further improvements.

In general, positive long-run effects on the economic development of the regions might be expected from such investments. A study on the Cohesion Fund impact (LSE 1996) shows that potential benefits on the supply side will occur, since a reduction in transport costs changes the structure of industry in different regions, creating forward and backward linkages and agglomeration effects. In the case of the Madrid ring road, the real income effects, measured as a ratio of the total direct effect, had multipliers exceeding 1.50 in the medium and long run, indicating significant gains from induced changes in activity and industrial location. However, the success of the infrastructure improvements made under the Structural Funds will depend on complementary efforts on the stimulation of economic activity in the regions.

10.4.2. *Aid to the private sector*

Aid to the private sector is generally given in the form of subsidies or grants designed to encourage the private sector to undertake certain investments considered highly desirable or of strategic importance. Such aid can take the form of incentives to expand or develop new industries: incentives for investment in tourism or agriculture, and incentives and subsidies to increase the international competitiveness of firms and to encourage the greater use of research and development capabilities.

The impact of assistance to the private sector should be examined in two different ways. In the short term, it has an impact on investment behaviour of firms, i.e. the leverage effect on financial resources deployed. This reduces the cost of capital for firms, which results in more capital-intensive production techniques. However, the initial impact of the increase in investment could be unfavourable to the economy as a whole, since investment in machinery and equipment has a high component of imported capital goods. In the medium and long term, aid to firms will produce stronger supply-side effects, as once the new capital stock is in place and becomes more productive it will result in an increase in production and factor productivity and, thus, in employment.

In the cohesion countries, progress in eliminating disparities in productivity and in adapting their industrial structures towards higher value-added activities has been achieved to different degrees. Changes in GDP per head are linked to their different rates of productivity growth. This was particularly evident in Ireland in the large foreign-owned sector, which generates over half of the manufacturing value added. In

Spain some regions (e.g. Valencia) experienced productivity growth, while in regions where employment grew more rapidly, average productivity actually declined. In Portugal, where promoting industrial restructuring has been a priority under a co-ordinated programme (PEDIP), more than 7,000 projects were funded, involving investments for 3.8 billion ecus. Assisted firms under this programme benefited on annual average of productivity increases of about 5 per cent and employment growth of 2.4 per cent. In Greece, however, investment on an equivalent scale has not been forthcoming, perhaps because of macroeconomic instability—high inflation and public sector deficits.

The performance assessment of the great variety of measures deployed in different regions is still at an early stage. The experience to date shows that the demand for some schemes has been sufficiently great to absorb further increases of funding, regardless of any clear *market failure* justification for use of public funds. This is clearly the case of poorly targeted schemes or subsidies whose primary effect is redistributive. In this regard, microeconomic analysis of public spending, used, for example, in the context of the Irish CSF mid-term evaluation, provides a powerful tool for improving efficiency and reducing undesirable effects (Honohan *et al.* 1997).

10.4.3. *Human resources*

Education and training policies have as a major objective the improvement of the stock of human capital in an economy, through enlarging the pool of skilled labour. It aims also to increase the labour market participation of certain disadvantaged groups, such as the long-term unemployed, young people, and the disabled. The wider dynamic effects in terms of increased efficiency and productivity are described in Bradley *et al.* (1995), but the measurement of rates of return to investment in human capital is still problematic due to limited empirical evidence.

The main objective of Structural Fund intervention is to improve the social integration of disadvantaged groups. Beyond the immediate benefits of a more efficient labour market and employment policies, these interventions seek to promote social cohesion by combating social exclusion. Given the complex nature of this phenomenon, more targeted actions were implemented to increase the *employability* of target groups (young people, long-term unemployed, disabled, etc.).

A common indicator to measure the output of these actions is to consider the 'coverage rates', measured by the number of beneficiaries as a proportion of potential target groups. For the 1989–93 period, the estimated rates varied from 21 per cent in Spain to 60 per cent in Belgium for young people and from 9 per cent in Denmark to 32 per cent in Portugal for long-term unemployed. These figures reflect differences in the type of actions funded as well as the quality of monitoring systems in place.

Concerning the impact of training and education programmes, placement rates (i.e. the percentage of trainees placed into jobs) were estimated on the basis of surveys among beneficiaries. At EU level, results were quite disparate, with mainstream target groups being placed at an average of 50 per cent, and net effects being much lower, around 10 per cent.[7] This considerable difference (40 percentage points) result from the distinction between gross and net effects, which means that a significant proportion of beneficiaries would have found a job even in the absence of Structural Fund intervention (the deadweight effect).

These results are not surprising, compared to the efficiency of active labour market measures. However, available data suggest that displacement and deadweight effects are much lower for the most disadvantaged groups (unskilled labour force, long-term unemployed, migrant workers, etc.). In the Netherlands, for example, the overall net placement rate is of 7 per cent, whereas this proportion rises up to 15 per cent and 28 per cent respectively for unskilled people and long-term unemployed. As a general conclusion, net placement rates do not compare favourably with national averages because EU-supported interventions appear not to have been successful in reaching the most vulnerable groups in the labour market. Nevertheless, the need for increasing the focus on these groups appears to be a major item of the agenda, together with the reform of labour market policies along the lines addressed in the Luxembourg Summit of the European Council in November 1997.

10.5. Process Effects

This section considers the theory and practice with regard to an additional factor that is increasingly recognized as important for determining the outcomes achieved by programmes for regional development: the process effects resulting from the nature of the policy delivery system itself.

In particular, the institutional processes through which policy is pursued is increasingly recognized as having an important bearing on economic growth. Institutions are generally considered to include the formal public and private agencies and entities at national, regional, and local level, usually defined by their specific legal status. But it is important not to overlook the informal networks and coalitions that come together in joint pursuit of economic goals at regional level 'that facilitate learning, innovation, the sharing of knowledge and the creation of specific types of knowledge that are central to competitiveness' (Dunford and Hudson 1996).

There is a growing body of literature on all of these aspects, which has highlighted the contribution of institutions—in both the formal and informal sense of the term—in at least three key domains: promoting the accumulation and dissemination of knowledge and information, reducing uncertainty, and establishing relations of trust. These features can have real economic impact by reducing the cost of doing business as well as by establishing conditions favourable to the introduction of change and innovation.

[7] According to an evaluation of structural policies in the UK (Cambridge Policy Consultants 1996), Structural Fund expenditure devoted to human resources interventions—which represent almost half of total expenditure—is estimated to benefit over 3.5 million people during the 1989–99 period. Using data on activity rates and employment, it was also estimated that these interventions will have contributed to 1.2 million placements and the placement into jobs of 440,000 targeted disadvantaged people. In net terms, such results would probably be lower, considering labour market substitution as well as the quality of human resource improvement and its duration.

The transaction-cost theory of Coase (1937) and Williamson (1985) abandoned neo-classical notions that tended to minimize the influence of institutional structures and relations on behaviour and decisions. For neo-classical economists, where such factors do exert influence they are seen as unwelcome impediments to perfect competition. A feature of transaction-cost theories, on the other hand, has been to highlight the role of information in economic behaviour. Some information can be best obtained on the market, but firms also need to internalize certain kinds of information in order to guarantee access to it and minimize costs, by creating appropriate hierarchical and functional structures (with, for example, divisions devoted to R&D, market research, etc.). In addition, and as a possible alternative, firms may establish cooperative relations with other firms to reduce the cost of access to certain kinds of information (Richardson 1972).

The information aspect of transaction-cost theories is especially relevant to understanding the economic role performed by institutions. In a world increasingly dominated by knowledge-based activities, information is essential for economic success. A key role of institutions is to access and manage information at minimum cost.

Other research has focused on the contribution of the institutions established by Western nation states, especially since the Second World War, in promoting wealth creation—sectoral development agencies, research facilities, and so on. Such institutions have been shown to perform an essential task in overcoming market failure—quite apart from the resources they bring to bear—by helping to promote a long-term perspective with regard to R&D, the training of highly qualified labour, and the organization of the dissemination of knowledge and information (Lundvall 1992). At the regional level, Dunford and Hudson (1996) stress the importance of institutions such as local development agencies in regenerating regional economies.

The research has also identified the role of institutions in reducing uncertainty (North 1990) and underpinning mutual trust among economic actors (Putnam 1993). For North, institutions reduce uncertainty by structuring expectations with regard to the behaviour of the different participants: 'Institutions are the rules of the game in a society, or, more formally, are the humanly devised constraints that shape human interaction. In consequence, they structure incentives in human exchange, whether political, social or economic' (North 1990: 3). Putnam takes the discussion beyond the formal institutions, identifying the role of 'social capital' in successful economics defined as 'features of social organization, such as trust, norms and networks, that can improve the efficiency of society by facilitating co-ordinated actions' (Putman, 1993: 167). By establishing relationships of trust, the cost of doing business is reduced while cooperation provides favourable circumstances for innovation.

10.5.1. *The delivery system for EU structural policies: the creation of partnerships*

The importance of social capital as described by Putnam has been explicitly recognized in the operation of EU structural policies right from their reform in 1988. The principle of 'partnership' has been a central element of the delivery system of EU structural policies where the Union has promoted the establishment of coalitions representing different sectoral and geographical interests in pursuit of medium-term economic development programmes.

The original regulations of 1988 that specified the content of the delivery system set out a vision for EU structural policies based on 'close consultations between the European Commission, the member state concerned and the competent authorities designated by the latter at national, regional, local or other level, with each party acting as a partner in pursuit of a common goal'.[8] This was extended in the 1993 revision of the Structural Funds regulations to include 'the competent authorities and bodies— including, within the framework of each member state's national rules and current practices, the economic and social partner, designated by the member state at national, regional, local or other level'.[9]

The importance attached to partnership by the European Union is justified on two principal grounds. The first is closely related to the insights developed by the literature whereby partnerships are seen as a way of improving the final outcomes obtained from regional development programmes. The partnerships created under EU structural policies are there to see that public resources are properly used and to raise the effectiveness of measures undertaken, for example, by improving the conditions necessary for innovation and the management of change. The second aspect is, inevitably, less emphasized in the economic literature, whereby partnerships are seen as a way of increasing involvement in European policy. They are concerned with increasing the visibility of European policy on the ground, establishing a consensus around European priorities and contributing to democratization in a European Union often subject to public criticism for its alleged deficit in this regard.

This second aspect is not the principal concern of the present analysis, although in many parts of the Union it is an acclaimed part of structural policies. In fact, many would claim that the political virtues of partnerships reflect the fact that they are not so much a means to an end but an end in themselves (CEC 1997c. See also Keating and Hooghe n.d.).

Initial evaluation work has focused on those aspects relating more directly to the effects of partnerships on economic development. A general conclusion has been that partnerships have been a force for 'the acquisition of new development expertise as well as the creation of new institutional arrangements' (Stern 1997).

There have, however, been wide variations between and within member states (Stern 1997, Bachtler and Turok 1997). To a large extent, this can be attributed to the degree of adaptability to the partnership principle on the part of the administrative and other structures already present. These structures reflect the different economic, social, and political traditions that can facilitate or impede the introduction of the collaborative structures characteristic of the partnerships. Thus, in some member states (for example, Greece and the UK) the involvement of actors at the regional level has been impeded by the fact that regional government has not had a strong role in economic development matters, whereas in others (such as Sweden), the regional authorities have often played a key role.

---

[8] Council regulation (EEC) no. 2052/88, Article 4.
[9] Council regulation (EEC) no. 2081/93, Article 4.

In many member states, there have been difficulties in integrating the 'horizontal' partners (including business and trade unions, statutory bodies, the voluntary organizations, and other interests) into the delivery system. In part, this derives from the tensions between, on the one hand, the public authorities ('vertical partners') who contribute, and are accountable for, part of the financing of the programmes and, on the other hand, the horizontal partners that often do not contribute in this way and do not carry the same responsibilities. In part, it reflects the lack of resources and experience of many horizontal partners.

While there have been differences in experiences, and these, in turn, undoubtedly explain some of the variation between, and within, member states in terms of the concrete achievements of EU co-funded programmes, at the same time it has been found that, in most cases, 'Structural Fund arrangements, by highlighting inconsistencies and capacity problems do act as a spur towards institutional innovation and capacity building' (Stern 1997). It seems, in other words, that the Structural Funds have contributed to the accumulation of the kind of social capital that should have positive effects for their development prospects.

The initial evaluation work also provides certain indications for the future development of the partnerships that could be summarized as follows:

- the more generalized development of the skills necessary for economic development and the accumulation of social capital tend to take considerably longer than the five- and six-year programme cycles associated with the Structural Funds up to the present;
- at least for some countries, the development of partnerships has been impeded by the perception that they represent a vehicle for supranational 'interference' in their affairs through the involvement of the European Commission, generally at the expense of the influence of the national authorities;
- the different roles and responsibilities have not been sufficiently clarified and this has produced a climate of suspicion and misunderstanding between partners.

While the general conclusion seems to be one where the partnerships are viewed positively, even though their full effects will only emerge over the long term, there seems little scope for complacency on the part of EU policymakers in view of the imperfections identified. On the basis of past experience, certain adaptations will be required to the working of the partnerships, as well as to other aspects of the delivery system, in order to overcome perceptions that persist that administrative provisions for the Structural Funds represent a system where 'money flows from national exchequers to Brussels, is subject to a bureaucratic charge, then returns with conditions' (Begg 1997).

10.6. Outlook

The results discussed in previous sections suggest that EU structural policies have succeeded in improving economic conditions even in the medium term, although the infrastructure and other investments that have taken place are only likely to yield their full benefits over the longer term. At the same time, the results have been patchy across the member states and regions, as is exemplified by the widely different economic performances of Ireland, on the one hand, and Greece, on the other, even though the level of transfers has been equivalent in per capita terms in each case. More remains to be done to close the gaps between the regions and to improve the prospects for disadvantaged groups in the labour market.

The persistence of significant 'cohesion gaps' was a basic point of reference for the Commission's reflections on the next generation of cohesion policies due for introduction in the year 2000. These were presented in the publication *Agenda 2000* in July 1997 (CEC 1997*a*) and followed up in March 1998 by concrete proposals in the form of draft regulations for the Structural Funds and Cohesion Fund (CEC 1998*b*).

In presenting the proposals, the Commission has also had to take account of two other important factors. First, public expenditure throughout the EU is under restraint, influenced in part by the need for member states to respect the Maastricht criteria for monetary union that constrain levels of public debt and indebtedness (the same criteria are taken up in the Stability and Growth Pact agreed by the member states setting out the rules governing macroeconomic policy for countries participating in the single currency). This has militated against another major expansion of the financial resources, as happened in 1988 and again in 1992.

Second, an important feature of the next period will be the progressive extension of cohesion policies to Cyprus and Central and Eastern European Countries (CEECs) beginning with a 'pre-accession' package in the year 2000.

10.6.1. *The future of EU policies: consolidation*

In view of these factors, the Commission's proposals for the future focus on consolidation, both in financial terms and in terms of addressing the shortcomings identified in the delivery system in order to enhance value for money in the use of the limited resources.

With regard to finance, the Commission proposes to stabilize the resources for EU cohesion policies at a level equivalent to 0.46 per cent of Community GNP, the level to which it will rise by the final year of the current budgetary period, 1993–9.

In absolute terms, and compared to the current period as a whole, this amounts to an increase of over 30 per cent, from 208 billion ecus (in 1999 prices) for the period 1993–9 to 279 billion ecus for 2000–6, partly because it maintains as constant the marginal level reached only at the end of the current period and partly because of the effects of expected GNP growth (Table 10.3). Of this amount, some 39.6 billion ecus, 14 per cent of the total, are set aside for the new members. Each new member state would see the maximum aid transfer from the EU capped at 4 per cent of GDP in an effort to ensure consistency with their absorptive capacity. In the preparatory phase before enlargement, a new instrument, modelled on the existing Cohesion Fund, has been proposed with resources of 1 billion ecus per year to help to promote investment in prospective member countries in transport and environmental infrastructures. Finally, some 20 billion ecus of the total would be earmarked for the Cohesion Fund.

Table 10.3. EU Structural policies, 1988–2006: financial allocations (millions, 1999 prices)

	Planning period 1		Planning period 2		Planning period 3[a]	
	Total	Average per year	Total	Average per year	Total	Average per year
Structural actions	77,900	15,580	190,500	27,200	218,400	31,200
Cohesion Fund	—	—	17,500	2,500	21,000	3,000
Total	77,900	15,580	208,000	29,700	239,400	34,200
% EU budget	22%	—	34%	—	33%	—

New Member states	39,600
Total enlarged Europe	279,000
% EU budget	35%

[a] European Commission proposal.

Source: CEC (1998), CEC (1997). Calculations by the authors.

These amounts mean that the Structural Funds would, therefore, not be in a position to assume any major new role in the fields of economic stabilization or income redistribution, but would retain their existing function of structural support for weaker parts of the Union.

In particular, it would not be the role of the Structural Funds to compensate for the effects of asymmetric shocks arising in the context of the single currency. Under these circumstances, devaluation would no longer be an option open to the national authorities in seeking to compensate for a sudden loss of competitiveness. Adjustment would have to come about through the labour market supported by national fiscal policies. This means that the member states would have to retain sufficient flexibility within their budgetary policies to have the margins necessary to respond to pressures arising from unexpected events. In this regard, the Stability and Growth Pact foresees balanced budgets over the economic cycle, well within the limit value for public expenditure of 3 per cent of GDP that would trigger sanctions, including fines.

With regard to the delivery system, the Commission's proposed reforms seek to strengthen the achievements of the Structural Funds in both their *strategic* and the *process* functions.

In *strategic* terms, the Commission proposes:

- the maintenance of Objective 1 as the top priority of the Structural Funds;
- a new Objective 2 to address the problems of other areas undergoing restructuring, adding a new emphasis to the problems of the urban areas;
- a redesigned Objective 3, which would act in support of the European Employment Strategy agreed by the member states in December 1997;
- a reduction in the number of the special programmes or 'Community initiatives';

- a greater emphasis in the regional development programmes on the promotion of innovation, durable job creation, sustainable development, and equality between men and women;
- a more limited geographical coverage of eligible areas and an overlap with those covered by derogations necessary for the payment of state aid to large enterprises under competition policy rules.

The priority accorded to the Objective 1 regions is reflected in the Commission's proposal to concentrate two-thirds of the available resources on these areas, around the same proportion as at present. As the Cohesion Report demonstrated, the infrastructure and other gaps between the Union's least developed regions and the rest remain significant and there is considerable catching up still required. Meanwhile, the new Objective 2 would bring together support for the old industrial areas and the rural areas previously orgaized separately under Objectives 2 and Objectives 5b, respectively.[10] In recognition that some of Europe's most serious problems are in its cities, and that not all of these can be traced to the decline of industrial sectors, a new emphasis on urban crisis areas is proposed, while help could also be granted to areas, probably limited in number, where the problems relate to dependence on services.

In order to achieve greater critical mass with the limited resources available, the Commission proposes that coverage under EU regional policies should be reduced by one-fifth, from 51 per cent of EU population at present to a maximum of 40 per cent. There would be phasing out arrangements for the regions currently eligible but not supported after the year 2000 under Objectives 1 or 2.

The new Objective 3 of the Structural Funds is 'problem-' rather than 'region-centred', potentially offering support for human resources development across the whole territory of the Union under national programmes. To avoid a duplication of activities, it would not intervene in the regions eligible under Objectives 1 and 2. The antecedents of the policy are those of the present Objectives 3 and 4, which have sought to combat unemployment and exclusion and prepare workers for the effects of economic change. The proposals for the future seek to insert the actions supported into the developing framework for tackling unemployment in Europe that member states have been negotiating since 1994 and that led to the inclusion of an employment chapter in the Amsterdam Treaty drafted in 1997.

For the regional development programmes supported under both Objectives 1 and 2, the emphasis will remain that of seeking to promote self-sustaining growth in assisted regions. As indicated above, the Funds have never been seen as a permanent transfer, but as a way of improving supply-side conditions to allow regions to compete in the single market on a more equal footing and on a self-sustaining basis. It is for this reason that the Commission wishes to see greater emphasis in the future on actions affecting regional dynamics, especially through a closing of the 'knowledge gap' between the regions, via innovation and improvements to the quality of human resources. The Commission also wishes future programmes to emphasize development that is sustainable in

---

[10] In parallel, *Agenda 2000* includes a proposal for a significant reform of the Common Agricultural Policy that, outside the realm of the Structural Funds, would offer support for rural development programmes proposed by member states.

environmental terms and open up the opportunities created by Union support to men and women on a more equal basis. A thread running across the new programmes would be that of maximizing job creation, which should act as a point of reference underlying strategic choices made.

Community initiatives provide additional scope for structural policies with a specific European dimension. They have been in existence as a complement to the mainstream regional development programmes since the reforms of 1988, and for the areas that have been assisted they have provided 'a vehicle for political expression and debate about the nature of policies towards these localities' (Dabinett 1997).

At the same time, Community initiatives have been used to support a vast range of development themes, resulting in a fragmentation of the effort in both management and financial terms. At present, nearly half of the one thousand programmes supported by the Structural Funds relate to Community initiatives, while only 9 per cent of financial resources are allocated to them. In certain cases, the Community initiatives cover the same or similar areas as the mainstream regional development programmes.

The Commission, therefore, proposes a major reduction in the number of Community initiatives from thirteen at present to just three, focusing on those with a specific European added value:

- transnational, cross–border, and interregional cooperation to stimulate economic development and encourage balanced spatial planning at European level;
- rural development, especially to explore bottom–up approaches to the creation of opportunities in rural areas as a complement to top–down market policies of the CAP;
- transnational cooperation to develop new ways to fight all types of discrimination in the labour market.

The share of Community initiatives in total Structural Funds appropriations would be reduced from 9 per cent to 5 per cent, with those currently undertaken, but discontinued, being integrated as appropriate into mainstream programmes.

A further goal of the Commission is to bring state aid policies and Community regional policies into line by seeking to ensure that the national and Community resources involved are focused as far as possible on the same areas (CEC 1997*a*). Under EU competition rules, state aid in support of larger enterprises can be given for regional development purposes in predefined eligible areas formally approved by the Commission. The Commission takes the view that EU regional policy areas should be the largely the same, the main difference being that certain additional areas may be eligible for state aid (national priority areas) even if they are not supported by the Structural Funds.

Such policy coherence has not been universally accepted by the member states, many of whom contend that overlapping maps are unjustified because the two policies are different. As such, they seem to making a case for state aid support that has more do with supporting industrial sectors in the first instance than helping to promote regional development, an interpretation that is difficult to sustain in terms of the legal framework provided by the relevant treaty. This is, however, a discussion that is likely to continue over the coming years until greater clarity is brought to bear on the respective roles of the Community policies involved.

With regard to the *process* aspects of the Structural Funds, the Commission proposes a reform of the delivery system in an effort to raise efficiency and accountability:

- greater decentralization of EU structural policies, with

  a more widely drawn multi-level partnership more actively involved in all aspects of the regional programming process;
  a clearer division of responsibilities between the Commission and the national and regional authorities;

- new incentives to improve programme performance.

The proposals with regard to decentralization are intended to achieve three main objectives. First, they are intended to contribute to the establishment of consensus around the programme objectives and in that way to reinforce the commitment of the relevant actors. To that end, they should involve a multi-level partnership of, first, the regional and local authorities, second, business and other social partners, and, third, other bodies including non-governmental organizations. Their involvement should extend through all stages of the process beginning with the conception of the regional strategy itself.

Second, in an effort to remove the tensions and suspicions between the partnerships, the Commission's proposals attempt to clarify the respective roles. The Commission itself would assume less responsibility for day-to-day management, focusing instead on strategic aspects. This would include decisions on eligible areas, financial allocations, and the issuing of guidelines establishing Community priorities to help member states prepare regional plans.

Inside the member state, a single authority would be designated to manage each programme, in collaboration with a monitoring committee appointed by it, involving all aspects relating to detailed programming, reprogramming, and the selection of projects. The Commission would be represented on the monitoring committee—which would have the same role as at present in ensuring the successful implementation of the programmes—but only in an advisory capacity. Only those partners on the Committee contributing to financing would have voting rights.

Third, in order to help to strengthen capacities in terms of the acquisition of social capital, the partners would be able to draw on outside expertise funded under a technical assistance budget equivalent to up to 0.3 per cent of the annual resources available.

A thread running through the proposals is that of improving accountability in the use of European taxpayers' funds. A corollary to decentralization is that the partners inside the member states would have to assume greater responsibility with regard to financial control. The Commission would retain the role of undertaking checks and systems audits to ensure that appropriate systems are in place.

The proposals to provide incentives for improving the efficiency of the delivery system derive from a concern that the current system, which gives member states predictable financial allocations from the outset for the entire planning period, is indifferent to the quality of the regional programmes that subsequently emerge. For the future, the Commission proposes that an 'efficiency reserve' should be withheld from the initial financial allocations for the programmes, with the equivalent of 10 per cent of total resources, which would be only allocated at the mid-term according to programme performance. Performance would be assessed according to transparent criteria agreed with the member states at the beginning, including the realization of predetermined objectives, the quality of the management, and the rate of absorption of financial resources. Programmes performing below expectations according to the mid-term assessment would not receive the allocations held in reserve.

In this way, the Commission hopes to achieve a new balance between the need for guaranteed financing over the programming period and incentives for better perform-ance. Moreover, the mid-term review would perform an additional role by creating an opportunity to reorganize programme priorities according to new needs that may arise during the course of the relatively long, seven-year programming period.

10.7. Concluding Remarks

There seems little doubt that the period since the reform of the Structural Funds in 1988 has been a new era for regional policy inside the European Union. The previous sec-tions have shown that the Funds appear to have made a difference, both in terms of the economic impact on investment and growth and in terms of important behavioural changes, notably by bringing together new strategic coalitions in pursuit of regional development objectives. They have also had an important impact in terms of bringing the European Union closer to its citizens and are one of the major ways in which regional and local authorities and the various interest groups and organizations come into direct contact with EU institutions.

At the same time, it is clear that there is scope for improvement. The European Commission's proposals for the future are based on consolidation against a background of fiscal austerity throughout the member states of the Union.

In presenting proposals based on the notion of consolidation, there is the risk, how-ever, that the Commission's ideas are likely to come under attack from different inter-ests, albeit for entirely divergent reasons. They will be regarded as insufficient, on the one hand, by a constituency that includes many regional authorities and local interests and a large section of the European Parliament, who seek a more active and more highly resourced cohesion policy at EU level, especially in the context of the introduction of the single currency. On the other hand, they will be regarded as insufficient by some national governments because of a failure to go far enough in terms of delegating responsibilities to the member states in accordance with the principle of subsidiarity. For some national governments, the ambition would be to limit as much as possible the role of the Union (in other words, the European Commission) in fields such as the decisions on eligible areas under Objectives 1 and 2, the content of the development programmes, and the reporting requirements in terms of monitoring, evaluation, and financial control.

This clash of mutually opposing interests is possibly a main reason why the Com-mission's proposals are likely to succeed as a suitable compromise. At the same time, by opting for consolidation at this stage, the Union is possibly leaving certain important issues open for the future. Two questions seem particularly relevant in this context. First, can monetary union, with a single monetary policy for all, survive without the EU assuming more responsibility for interregional transfers? Should the EU have more powers to tax and spend, for example, analogous to those of the federal level in the US? Second, are the sums set aside for enlargement realistic in view of both the potential demands from poorer member states in the existing EU for compensation for its effects in terms of increased competition and the considerable needs in the new countries themselves? In the latter context, a subsidiary question concerns the political acceptability to the newly entrant member states of the recommended 4 per cent cap on EU transfers.

References

Amin, A. and Goddard, J. B. (eds.) (1986). *Technological Change, Industrial Restructuring and Regional Development*. London: Allen & Unwin.

Armstrong, H. and Taylor, J. (1985). *Regional Economics and Policy*. London: Macmillan.

Aschauer, D. (1997). *Dynamic Output and Employment Effects of Public Capital*. Jerome Levy Economics Institute Working Paper no. 191.

Bachtler, J. and Michie, R. (1995). A new era in regional policy evaluation? The appraisal of the Structural Funds. *Regional Studies* 29/8: 745–51.

—— and Turok, I. (1997). *The Coherence of EU Regional Policy: Contrasting Perspectives on the Structural Funds*. Regional Studies Associates.

Barro, R. and Sala-I-Martin, X. (1991), *Convergence Across States and Regions*. Brookings Papers on Economic Activity no. 1. Washington, D.C.: Brookings Institute.

—— (1995). *Economic Growth*. McGraw-Hill.

Begg, I. (1997). The Structural Funds beyond 1999. Paper presented at the 37th European Congress of the Regional Science Association, Rome.

Beutel, J. (1993). *The Economic Impacts of the Community Support Frameworks for Objective 1 Regions 1989–93*. Report for the European Commission. Brussels.

—— (1995). *The Economic Impacts of the Community Support Frameworks for the Objective 1 Regions 1994–99*. Report for the European Commission. Brussels.

—— (1996). Dynamic input-output model to evaluate the economic impacts of the Structural Funds. Paper presented at the European Conference on Evaluation Models for Structural Fund Interventions, Berlin, 2–3 December 1996.

Biehl, D. (1986). *The Contribution of Infrastructure to Regional Development*. Luxembourg: Commission of the European Communities.

Boltho, A. (1994). *A comparison of regional differentials in the European Community and the United States*. In J. Mortensen (ed.), *Improving Economic and Social Cohesion in the European Community*. New York: St Martin's Press.

Bourguignon, F., Lolos, S., and Zonzilos, N. (1995). Evaluating the CSF with an extended computable general equilibrium model: the case of Greece (1988–1995). *Journal of Policy Modelling* 17: 177–97.

Bradley, J., Modesto, L., and Sosvilla-Rivero, S. (1995). Hermin: a macroeconometric modelling framework for the EU periphery. *Economic Modelling* 12: 221–47.

—— (1995). *Regional Aid and Convergence*. Perspectives on Europe. Avebury.

Cambridge Policy Consultants (1996). *The Impact of Structural Interventions on Economic and Social Cohesion in the UK*. Report for the European Commission, DG XVI. Brussels.

Canova, F. and Marcet, A. (1995). *The Poor Stay Poor: Non-Convergence across Countries and Regions*. CEPR Discussion Paper no. 1265. London.

CEC (1977). *Report of the Study Group on the Role of Public Finance in European Integration* (MacDougall Report). Collection studies, Economic and Financial Series no. 13. Brussels.

—— (1993). *The Economics of Community Public Finance*. European Economy Reports and Studies no. 5. Brussels.

—— (1994). *Competitiveness and Cohesion: Trends in the regions*. Fifth Periodic Report on the Social and Economic Situation and Development of the Regions. Brussels.

—— (1996a). *First Report on Economic and Social Cohesion*. Luxembourg: Office for Official Publications of the European Communities.

—— (1996b). *Structural Funds and Cohesion Fund Regulations and Commentary*. Brussels.

—— (1997a). *Agenda 2000: For a Stronger and Wider Union*, COM (97) 2000. Brussels.

—— (1997b). *Communication from the Commission to the Member States on the Links between Regional and Competition Policy*, COM (97) 673. Brussels.

—— (1997c). *European Forum on Cohesion: Speeches and Summaries of Debates, 28–30 April 1997*. Luxembourg.

—— (1997d). *Vade-Mecum budgétaire*, SEC (97) 1200. Brussels.

—— (1998a). *Communication from the Commission to the Council and the European Parliament on the Establishment of a New Financial Perspective for the Period 2000–2006*, COM (98) 164. Brussels.

—— (1998b). *Proposal for a Council Regulation Laying Down General Provisions on the Structural Funds*, COM (98) 131, Brussels.

Christodoulakis, N. and Kalvitys, S. (1995). *Likely Effects of the CSF, 1994–99, on the Greek Economy*. Centre of Economic Planning and Research Working Paper no. 46. University of Athens.

Coase, R. (1937). The nature of the firm. *Economica* 4: 386–405.

Costello, D. (1993). The redistributive effects of interregional transfers: a comparison of the European Community and Germany. In European Commission, Directorate General for Economic and Financial Affairs, *European Economy: The Economics of Public Finance*, no. 5.

Dabinett, G. (1997). The EU Community initiatives and the management of industrial charge in the UK. In Bachtler and Turok (1997).

Dunford, M. and Hudson, R. (1996). *Successful European Regions: Northern Ireland Learning from Others*. Northern Ireland Economic Council Research Monograph no. 3. Belfast.

Eichengreen, B. and Uzan, A. (1992). *The Marshall Plan: Economic Effects and Implications for Eastern Europe and the Former USSR*. CEPR Discussion Paper no. 638. London.

EPRC (1996). *The Impact of Member States Policies on Economic and Social Cohesion*. University of Strathclyde, Glasgow, Report for the European Commission, DG XVI. Brussels.

—— (1997). *Study of the Business Aid Systems in the Three New Member States*. Report for the European Commission. Brussels.

ESRI (1996). *Trade Liberalisation and Structural Change in Small-Open Economy Macromodels: The Internal Market and EU Periphery*. Report for the European Commission, DG II. Brussels.

Eurostat (1997). *EU Transports in Figures*, 2nd issue. Luxembourg.

Florio, M. (1995). Survey of 200 major projects of the first generation of reformed Structural Funds, 1989–93. Unpublished report. Brussels.

Franzmeyer, F. (1991). *The Regional Impact of Community Policies*. Report to the European Parliament, Regional Policy and Transport Series no. 17.

Gillespie (1996). Infrastructure and regional development. Paper for the European Forum on Cohesion. Brussels.

Gordon (1991). *Structural Funds and the 1992 Program in the European Community*. IMF working paper 65/91.

Honohan, P. (ed.) (1997). *EU Structural Funds in Ireland: A Mid-Term Evaluation of the CSF 1994–99*. ESRI Policy Research Series, paper no. 31. Dublin.

Keating, M. and Hooghe, L. (n.d). By-passing the nation state? Regions and the EU policy process (mimeo).

Krugman, P. (1991). *Geography and Trade*. Cambridge, Mass.: MIT Press.

Landabaso, M. (1995). The promotion of innovation in Regional Community policy: lessons and proposal for a Regional Innovation Strategy. Paper presented at the RESTPOR '95 meeting, Brussels.

LSE (1996). *The Socio-Economic Impact of Projects Financed by the Cohesion Fund*. Report for the European Commission. Brussels.

Lucas, R. (1988). On the mechanics of economic development. *Journal of Monetary Economics* 22.

Lundvall, B. (1992). *National Systems of Innovation: Towards a Theory of Innovation and Interactive Learning*. London: Pinter.

Mankiw, G., Romer, P. and Weil, D. (1992). A contribution to the empirics of economic growth. *Quarterly Journal of Economics* 107: 407–37.

MEANS (1999). *Evaluating Socio-economic Programmes*. 6 vols. Luxembourg.

Myrdal, G. (1957). *Economic Theory and Underdeveloped Regions*. London: Duckworth.

Neven, D. and Gouyette, C. (1994). *Regional Convergence in the European Community*. CEPR Discussion Paper no. 914. London.

North, D. C. (1990). *Institutions, Institutional Change and Economic Performance*. Cambridge: Cambridge University Press.

Pereira, A. (1994). *Structural Policies in the European Community: An International Comparison*. Report for the European Commission, DG XVI. Brussels.

Putnam, R. D. (1993). *Making Democracy Work: Civic Traditions in Modern Italy*. Princeton: Princeton University Press.

QUASAR. (1996). *The Impact of Structural Interventions on Economic and Social Cohesion in Spain*. Report for the European Commission, DG XVI. Brussels.

Reichenbach, H. (1992). *The implications of cohesion policy for the Community budget*. In J. Mortensen (ed.), *Improving Economic and Social Cohesion in the European Community*. London: St Martin's Press.

Richardson, G. B. (1972). The organisation of industry. *Economic Journal* 82: 883–96.

Roeger, W. (1996). Macroeconomic evaluation of the effects of Community Structural Funds with Quest II. Paper presented at the European Conference on Evaluation Models for Structural Fund Interventions, Berlin, 2–3 December 1996.

Roger Tym and Partners (1996). *The Regional Impact of Community Policies*. Report for the European Parliament, Regional Policy series W-16. Luxembourg.

Romer, P. (1990). Endogenous technological change. *Journal of Political Economy* 98: 70–102.

Skouras, T. (1996). *The Impact of Structural Interventions on Economic and Social Cohesion in Greece*. Report for the European Commission, DG XVI. Brussels.

Stern, E. (1997). *The 'Partnership Principle' in European Structural Funds*. Draft synthesis report prepared for the European Commission by the Tavistock Institute, London.

Williamson, O. E. (1985). *The Economic Institutions of Capitalism*. New York: Free Press.

11

Conclusions

RONALD HALL, ALASDAIR SMITH, AND LOUKAS TSOUKALIS

The purpose of this book has been to show the many different ways in which European Union policies impinge on its territory and society. More specifically, the various contributions consider the effect of key European policies on the Union's internal economic and social cohesion. This remains a matter of the utmost political importance for a Union which recognizes that improvements in cohesion are necessary to secure its further integration.

As discussed in the introduction, cohesion is a complex issue in methodological terms, especially for economists, and distilling its essence into measurable indicators has presented a particular challenge. In broad terms, cohesion has been given a geographical point of reference—reducing income inequalities between countries and regions —and a social one—improving the relative position of disadvantaged social groups across the Union as a whole. This book has concentrated more on intercountry and interregional cohesion rather than its social dimension (interpersonal disparities), mainly because of reasons of data availability. This relative concentration is, however, also consistent with European political reality based on an implicit division of labour between EU and national institutions: EU policies address mostly intercountry and interregional disparities, while social cohesion is still the main responsibility of the nation-state.

In the course of the different analyses, two major themes are recurrent. First, it is clear that there is great complexity in the cause and effect relationships that exist between EU policy interventions and their final impact on the ground in different countries, regions as well as on social groups. Of particular interest is the way that this complexity relates to the manner in which European policy is delivered through shared responsibilities between national administrations and the European Commission. This, in turn, reflects the stage of integration reached by the EU, which is the determining factor in the distribution of powers between the European and national level.

Secondly, the various contributions highlight the classical conflict that often exists between competitiveness and cohesion (in the language of welfare economics, the potential conflict between efficiency and equity), and the limits that exist in seeking to achieve cohesion with policies whose primary purpose is to promote competitiveness. These issues are considered below; and this analysis will be used, in turn, as a basis for an examination of possible next steps for the Union, and the prospects for the further development of the cohesion agenda at European level.

11.1. Complex Cause and Effect Relationships

A key feature of the Union is that it has not been able to pursue its objectives in the most direct manner through a reallocation of resources using powerful systems of taxation and expenditure/transfer at the European level. These systems remain in national hands. National public expenditure is equivalent to between 40 per cent and 60 per cent of GNP across the different member states whereas at the EU level, expenditures are limited to a maximum of 1.27 per cent of total EU GNP. The impact of EU policies considered in this volume, therefore, largely concerns the effects of common frameworks that have been agreed and which govern actions mostly financed and implemented by national governments.

Two major exceptions exist to this general rule. These concern, first, the Common Agricultural Policy (CAP) and, secondly, structural policies financed by the EU's Structural and Cohesion Funds. Together, these policies account for over 80 per cent of the EU budget. Among the other policies, only those to promote research and technological development could be said to lead to significant expenditures at EU level, although the major effort in the field is overwhelmingly in national (public and private) hands.

Agricultural policy under the CAP is the only field where responsibility for managing the sector can be said to have passed comprehensively to the European level. Markets for the major sectors are organized at European level, creating a genuine single market for agricultural products that has existed for almost four decades. The result of market interventions under the CAP is an extensive set of first-round redistributive effects. But the geographical impact of even these market interventions remains notoriously difficult to measure. As Tarditi and Zanias point out (Chapter 6), the net effect lies concealed beneath the surface of the superficial financial flows of the public accounts and emerges only through detailed analysis of the complex production, trading, and consumption patterns in the member states and regions.

Structural polices, acting in support of regional development and employment, are the other major expenditure item at European level (Chapter 10). Their macroeconomic dimension means that it is possible to assess their impact using economic models as well as more detailed evaluation at the microeconomic level. A complicating factor is that structural policies are different from the CAP in that they are a *shared* responsibility with the member states. As a result, many of the key decisions on resource allocation are devolved to the national and regional level.

This sharing of responsibilities is, itself, a major issue. It has resulted in an ongoing, and unresolved, debate about where the lines should be drawn between the decisions best taken by national governments and those that should be the responsibility of Union institutions, notably the European Commission. This is a political reality that reflects the persistence of an EU caught between 'intergovernmental' and more integrated, federal-style political arrangements. For the Commission, this has meant that part of the added value sought from structural policies has resided in efforts to change the aims and associated decision-making paths and patterns within the national administrations in order to improve their quality as a delivery mechanism for economic development policy.

In relation to the impact of structural policies, a key issue is the interrelationship between EU regional policies financed by the Structural Funds and EU policies under competition rules that create the framework under which member states can subsidize productive investment from national funds (Chapter 4). The potential for mutual contradiction between these policies is considerable, a matter taken up below.

As already indicated, another policy which carries significant expenditure at European level (4 per cent of the budget) is in the field of research and technological development (RTD), where up to the present a series of four framework programmes setting RTD priorities at European level have been established, while a fifth is in the final stages of preparation. These policies give rise to a geographical pattern of expenditure resulting from the allocation of research contracts. However, as Sharp and Santos Perreira point out (Chapter 5), imputing the cohesion effects is again complex matter. First, the contracts themselves generally support transnational networks of researchers and the final beneficiaries of research policy are more widely dispersed than the principal contractors. Secondly, the cohesion impact depends on the nature of the research being developed and its suitability to different regional economic circumstances. In other words, it relates back to the original selection of priorities. In their contribution, Sharp and Santos Perreira focused on the notion of developing research capacities in the weaker member states and regions as the principal measurable cohesion effort. This implies an approach that places less emphasis on measuring the overall level of effort by the Union in the member states and regions, and more on, first, its size relative to the pre-existing effort and, secondly, its qualitative suitability to the economies of weaker member states and regions.

The other chapters in this volume consider the impact of European policy frameworks. The most important of these concerns the single market, which has had an influence in virtually every other policy area and which has sought to remove the legal and institutional barriers to the free movement of capital and labour, goods and services throughout the member states of the Union. Bohan and Muylle (Chapter 2) draw on a variety of techniques to indicate how these freedoms have impinged on trade and investment flows throughout the Union: trend analysis and impact assessments conducted respectively at macroeconomic and sectoral level. As they point out, however, a major difficulty is the classical one of disentangling the impact of the single market from the other factors, notably the rapid economic growth during the world upturn at the end of the 1980s and the effects of the Structural Funds in the assisted regions. Hine and Padoan, in their chapter on the cohesion effects of trade policy, adopt similar methodological frameworks, using sectoral impact assessment to estimate employment effects and patterns of trade specialization to assess geographical effects at national and regional level (Chapter 3). Regional-level analysis is impeded by an absence of data and requires simplifying assumptions about the relationship between output and employment. Hine and Padoan also consider the politically sensitive issue of the cohesion impact of future enlargement inside the Fifteen, which, as discussed below, is a conditioning factor in the Union's discussions about its future.

For EU policies to promote the creation of networks in transport and telecommunications, there is limited direct expenditure. However, as McGowan (Chapter 7) and

Mairate and Hall (Chapter 10) point out, the EU contribution to total investment has been highly significant in the least developed regions, containing around 25 per cent of total population, eligible under Objective 1 of the Structural Funds where the development of the networks has absorbed a significant proportion of the resources. There are, in other words, transport and telecommunications elements implicit in the global macroeconomic assessment of the impact of the Structural Funds in these regions.

The cohesion effects of communications networks are particularly difficult to predict. Krugman and Venables have demonstrated that new communications networks can have either positive or negative effects on weaker regions. Much depends on their impact on transaction costs: if these are relatively small, then they are unlikely to counteract the attractions of the central regions in terms of economies of scale; if they are relatively large, then profitable opportunities for locations in lower-cost regions are likely to increase. These theoretical propositions are, however, extremely difficult to operationalize (Chapter 8).

11.2. Competitiveness and Cohesion: A Review of the Results

What, then, does the record show with regard to the cohesion effects of the major policy areas? An obvious starting point is *structural policies* where the reduction of economic and social disparities is the specific objective. Here, Hall and Mairate paint a broadly positive image of the impact of EU polices in reducing intercountry and interregional income disparities, especially with regard to average levels of income per head in the four poorest member states—the major beneficiaries of EU structural aid—compared to the rest of the Union. By helping to change national public expenditure priorities in favour of strategic investment, EU policies appear to have helped to accelerate growth in these member states and their regions. The emphasis placed on fostering the development of 'social capital'—improving the institutional capacities of actors and agencies in the regions—appears to have been a contributory factor and to have merited the emphasis placed on it by the European Commission. The priority given to investment has, at the same time, had the effect of accelerating productivity growth. This has meant that the contribution of EU structural policies to reducing sometimes acute levels of unemployment has been much more limited.

The authors draw on a range of evaluation results based on different macroeconomic models. One noteworthy result is the quite different outcomes that the different models produce, which means that the results have to be treated as illustrative and provisional at this stage. In addition, the models are unable to produce a convincing explanation as to why there have been important differences in performance between major recipients of assistance under EU structural policies, such as Greece, on the one hand, where growth was relatively weak during most of the period under consideration, and Ireland, on the other hand, where growth has been remarkably strong.

Regional policies across the EU are not delivered exclusively through the Structural Funds, although they are of predominant importance for the poorest member states. In addition, under EU competition rules—which seek to control the payment of state aid to enterprises to avoid distortions to competition—there are specific derogations that allow investment aid to be delivered by the national authorities to enterprises in weaker regions. As Dunford, Louri, and Rosenstock point out in Chapter 4 on *competition, competitiveness, and enterprise policies*, this has produced results that are in contradiction with those under EU structural policies. In particular, it has permitted a situation to arise where levels of expenditure on state aid for regional purposes follow a pattern that is determined by member states' budgetary capacity at national level and not by the relative needs of the regions on an EU-wide basis. As a result, some 85 per cent of regional aid is granted to two of the most prosperous member states, Germany and Italy, while aid per capita in the four traditionally poorest member states varies between 5 per cent and 34 per cent of German levels, even after receipts from the Structural Funds.

Turning to the *CAP*, the EU's major policy area in expenditure terms, the dominant responsibility here is exerted at the supranational level. As Tarditi and Zanias point out, cohesion has not been a central aim of the CAP. However, cohesion issues have been close to the surface, since among the explicit aims of the CAP are those relating to both the achievement of 'a fair standard of living for the agricultural community' and 'the optimum utilisation of the factors of production, in particular labour'. Because of the particular geographical concentration of agricultural activity in rural areas, in general, and in the poorest regions of the Union, in particular, policies affecting the sector inevitably have a geographical impact.

Tarditi and Zanias have analysed these distributional aspects, focusing on the period since the 1992 reform of the CAP. As the authors demonstrate, this has significantly altered the arrangements for agricultural support. Prior to the reform, these arrangements were characterized by a concentration of support on maintaining high prices, especially for so-called 'northern' products (dairy products and cereals) and less on other products typically of more importance for the south of the EU (fruits, horticultural products). The 1992 reforms, seeking to address the problems of mounting agricultural surpluses, redirected support from markets and prices towards direct compensation payments.

The overall assessment of the cohesion effects of these policies has produced mixed results. The net position of countries with major agrarian regions such as Greece and Spain has improved and is now positive, while Ireland has remained in large surplus. Portugal, as a traditional importer of basic agricultural products, still comes out as a net loser, although the size of the deficit halved between 1991 and 1995. On the other hand, big farmers gain much more than small ones, and this situation has not changed dramatically since the 1992 reform.

The reform of the CAP exposes the fundamental dilemmas in the CAP between competitiveness and cohesion. The results of public support under the CAP are seen in the concentration of excess resources in the agricultural sector with the persistence of inefficient farm sizes and farming techniques. While this has undoubtedly helped to mitigate the exodus from the sector, the authors suggest that more targeted measures in favour of occupational mobility could be more efficient. They, therefore, support the broader notion of a rural development policy that seeks to create alternatives to traditional agriculture in rural areas.

The third area carrying significant expenditure implications at European level is that relating to *research and technological development*. This is a policy area where the pursuit of excellence at the European level is accepted as the prime objective in order to ensure that the EU economy is present in the forefront of technological development and the associated spin-offs in terms of product and process innovation. At the same time, there are potential benefits for the EU as a whole and for individual regions by seeking to maximize the use of all the Union's resources—human and other—in the field. Although most EU expenditure on RTD goes to the technologically more developed (and richer) countries, Sharp and Santos Perreira in Chapter 5 conclude that EU policies have helped to close the knowledge gaps, when measured in terms of the investment in RTD and the growth in RTD personnel in the poorest member states and regions. A mechanism for this change has been the increasing involvement of RTD centres in poorer member states in the networks of research sponsored by EU RTD Framework Programmes. Less positively, they note that involvement in EU RTD pro-grammes is disproportionately a matter of relatively large public institutions in the poorer member states and regions with less private involvement. The association of the SME sector with EU initiatives also emerges as a particular difficulty.

As already indicated, the remaining EU policies examined in this volume are con-cerned with creating common frameworks in the different fields. This does not mean that they are less important and that their eventual impact is any less than the three 'expenditure' areas just considered. It does, however, mean that cohesion impacts are considerably more difficult to quantify.

The extensive deregulation under the *single market programme* (SMP) with regard to the free movement of capital, goods, and services is argued to have contributed to eco-nomic growth. But Bohan and Muylle conclude that it has fallen short of the expecta-tions generated by the *ex ante* evaluations that had predicted a step increase in GDP of 4.5–7 per cent over the long term, creating 1.8 to 5 million net additional jobs. *Ex post* macroeconomic assessments put the figure at 1.5 per cent in terms of GDP and 900,000 new jobs. The SMP increased competition across the Union, with effects characterized by the expectation that those member states and regions previously the most sheltered by different forms of protection would have the most to lose from business restructur-ing, but also the most to gain from the accompanying spur to greater efficiency. In other words, the effects of the single market would also impinge on regional distribution.

Bohan and Muylle suggest that the SMP has not been to the disadvantage of the weakest member states of the Union in any systematic way, and all appear to have seen improvements in terms of productivity, GDP, investment including FDI, private con-sumption, and employment. This has been attributed to small open economy effects, characteristic of Greece, Ireland, and Portugal in particular, where the transmission of the effects of the SMP tends to work more quickly and more extensively than in larger and more closed economies.

Bohan and Muylle indicate that the effects of the SMP have been constrained by failure to address satisfactorily the question of labour mobility. In this area, the SMP was limited to removing impediments to geographical mobility; extensive national regula-tions in the labour market were untouched by Community legislation even though there was a substantial body of evidence that they were a major factor in persistently high European unemployment levels.

Koutsiaras takes this important and politically sensitive theme up in Chapter 9. He points out that there has been a particular reluctance on the part of national governments to surrender responsibility to the EU level in the field of *social policy* in general and social protection in particular. The only areas where an EU added value is identified relate to health and safety at work and equal opportunities. Koutsiaras concludes that this is a policy area where it is extremely difficult for future development in the absence of further progress towards real economic convergence. Attempting to prefigure such convergence through a levelling–up of social provisions risks damaging fatally the economies of weaker member states. Their present advantages are sometimes misconstrued as social dumping, but Koutsiaras points out that these advantages are legitimate, given the stage of development of the economies concerned and the persistence of large differences in productivity levels.

The basic mechanism for the transmission of SMP effects is in the process of trade between member states. But the EU is also a major trading partner in the global context and the effects of the policies adopted in this field are the focal point of the analysis by Hine and Padoan in their overall assessment of EU *external trade policy* and cohesion. They indicate that, even after a variety of agreements, much of it to liberalize trade with the Third World, import penetration from low–wage countries remains limited. The major exceptions are clothing from Asia, the Mediterranean, and Central and Eastern European countries, as well as electrical/electronic goods from the emerging economies in Asia. The clothing sector is particularly important for many of the poorest regions of the Union, and the maintenance of its position has depended on extensive bilateral quota restrictions. Hine and Padoan also show that EU trade policies have also had more important effects on more prosperous regions, citing the use of anti-dumping legislation in sectors where these regions predominate. Much in the field of trade is now subject to change following the conclusion of the Uruguay Round and the signing of Europe Agreements with Central and Eastern European countries. Hine and Padoan conclude that the effects are likely to be limited overall, but some regions, such as those dependent on textiles, could experience more significant negative impacts.

With regard to policies in the fields of *transport and telecommunications*, there has been increasing involvement of the EU since the mid-1980s. Traditionally, transport and telecommunications services have been provided by the public sector in European countries, reflecting a general acceptance of public good and public service arguments. As McGowan (transport, Chapter 7) and Young *et al.* (telecommunications, Chapter 8) point out, this situation has changed towards one of greater emphasis on liberalization and privatization driven by new European policy frameworks. This has created new distributional issues at the geographical and social level and, as a result, has generated new demands for the protection of the general interest through public service and universal service contracts.

Telecommunications services have been the field where EU intervention has been the most extensive, with the full liberalization of markets for services and infrastructure. As Young *et al.* point out, this is accompanied by the elimination of cross-subsidization that has traditionally helped to reduce costs in the less densely populated, remoter regions both in terms of access to the networks and tariff structures. Liberalization is, therefore, likely to have negative effects in these regions especially with regard to the costs of network access, and some countries have moved only slowly in this direction as a result.

Recognizing the risks, the EU has sought to accompany liberalization with a set of 'general interest' requirements—'universal service obligations' (USOs)—in an effort to make sure that everyone has access to services at affordable prices. The problem in the rapidly evolving telecommunications sector is that USOs are difficult to define. Increasingly, regions require sophisticated telecommunications services, and the definition of USOs needs to take this into account if the less densely populated and remote regions are to compete.

Similar conclusions apply to the transport sector, where air and rail transport have been subject to extensive deregulation. EU policy includes provision for public service obligations, with the insistence that these should be transparent and clearly defined in accounting terms. One important suggestion emerging is that since transport (and telecommunications) represents a relatively small component of total production costs —with some notable exceptions—the provision of new links to the less developed regions is unlikely to make much difference on its own. Rather, they are more likely to exert an influence where they form part of an integrated regional development strategy.

11.3. Cohesion in the New Phase of Integration

Cohesion occupies a prominent place on the EU agenda. This is entirely consistent with the importance attached to equity and solidarity in European political culture. The contributions in this volume go to the heart of the debate on European construction. They examine the impact of EU policies in terms of economic and social cohesion, and in so doing they also point to the conflict which sometimes exists between the objective of cohesion and that of competitiveness. This conflict arises in different forms in different policy domains and, to assess how well it is dealt with, one needs to understand both the assignment of policy objectives to policy domains and the assignment of policy responsibility to different levels of governance.

There is often the temptation to argue, especially in official documents, that different policy objectives are not in conflict with each other, that a more equitable distribution of income is beneficial to long-run efficiency, and that boosting the efficiency of production is the best protection for the economically vulnerable. Such complementarities may, indeed, be important but they are not universal, and a clear-minded assessment of policy requires recognition of conflicts as well as complementarities.

The EU enters a new phase of integration, trying to reconcile once again the further deepening of integration with the accession of new members. It has been faced with this task before, although this time it will be much more difficult. Monetary union, as the most important manifestation of deepening, is qualitatively very different from anything that has happened until now in the context of European integration, being, arguably, the most important development since the signing of the Treaty of Rome in 1957. On the other hand, both the number and the nature of the applicant countries will make this new round of enlargement a totally different affair from any previous one.

EMU is bound to raise the issues of stabilization and redistribution, which, in turn, will have a direct impact on the budget. The fact that EMU comes to life in times of budgetary consolidation will certainly not make things easier. EMU will have a direct impact on a wide range of EU policies, including social and taxation policies, and there will also be a cohesion dimension to it. The literature on EMU has not produced a clear and consensual view concerning the impact of monetary union in terms of cohesion. Are the less developed countries more likely to suffer from asymmetric shocks and the loss of the exchange rate instrument? Those that have been more inflation–prone will at least benefit from imported stability and also from lower interest rates.

All candidate countries have lower levels of economic development than even the poorest member of the EU. Further enlargement will, therefore, lead to a considerable increase in economic disparities inside the Union. The challenge of cohesion will become even more difficult in the context of a wider EU. Preparing for enlargement, the Union will need to reconcile the interests of those inside and the others waiting to join.

The EU will also face a different kind of challenge. There has been all along an implicit division of labour between EU policies and institutions concentrating on inter-country and interregional cohesion on the one hand, and the welfare state on the other, dealing with social cohesion inside national boundaries. As income inequalities grow in several member countries and those who lose from rapid economic change tend to rally behind nationalist flags, this division of labour may no longer prove sustainable.

Cohesion and competitiveness will remain at the very centre of the European debate, even though the economic and political context will be changing fast in the next few years.

INDEX